Fodor's First Edition

W9-CIN-018

Berlin

The complete guide, thoroughly up-to-date

Packed with details that will make your trip

The must-see sights, off and on the beaten path

What to see, what to skip

Mix-and-match vacation itineraries

City strolls, countryside adventures

Smart lodging and dining options

Essential local do's and taboos

Transportation tips, distances and directions

Key contacts, savvy travel tips

When to go, what to pack

Clear, accurate, easy-to-use maps

Background essays

Fodor's Travel Publications • New York, Toronto, London, Sydney, Auckland
www.fodors.com

Fodor's Berlin

EDITOR: Christina Knight

Editorial Contributors: Daniel Adler, Jody K. Biehl, Jen Makin, Alan Posener, Tim Reid, Jürgen Scheunemann, Nicola Varns

Editorial Production: Tom Holton

Maps: David Lindroth, Mapping Specialists, *cartographers;* Rebecca Baer and Robert P. Blake, *map editors*

Design: Fabrizio La Rocca, *creative director;* Guido Caroti, *art director;* Jolie Novak, *senior picture editor;* Melanie Marin, *photo editor*

Cover Design: Pentagram

Production/Manufacturing: Robert B. Shields

Cover Photograph: Blaine Harrington III

Copyright

Copyright © 2002 by Fodors LLC

Fodor's is a registered trademark of Random House, Inc.

All rights reserved under International and Pan-American Copyright Conventions. Published in the United States by Fodor's Travel Publications, a unit of Fodors LLC, a subsidiary of Random House, Inc., and simultaneously in Canada by Random House of Canada Limited, Toronto. Distributed by Random House, Inc., New York.

No *maps, illustrations, or other portions of this book may be reproduced in any form without written permission from the publisher.*

First Edition

ISBN 0-676-90144-1

ISSN 1069–4593

Important Tip

Although all prices, opening times, and other details in this book are based on information supplied to us at press time, changes occur all the time in the travel world, and Fodor's cannot accept responsibility for facts that become outdated or for inadvertent errors or omissions. So **always confirm information when it matters,** especially if you're making a detour to visit a specific place.

Special Sales

Fodor's Travel Publications are available at special discounts for bulk purchases for sales promotions or premiums. Special editions, including personalized covers, excerpts of existing guides, and corporate imprints, can be created in large quantities for special needs. For more information, contact your local bookseller or write to Special Markets, Fodor's Travel Publications, 280 Park Avenue, New York, NY 10017. Inquiries from Canada should be directed to your local Canadian bookseller or sent to Random House of Canada, Ltd., Marketing Department, 2775 Matheson Boulevard East, Mississauga, Ontario L4W 4P7. Inquiries from the United Kingdom should be sent to Fodor's Travel Publications, 20 Vauxhall Bridge Road, London SW1V 2SA, England.

PRINTED IN THE UNITED STATES OF AMERICA

10 9 8 7 6 5 4 3 2 1

CONTENTS

Maps

ON THE ROAD WITH FODOR'S

The more you know before you go, the better your trip will be. Berlin's most unusual museum (or its liveliest beer garden) could be just around the corner from your hotel, but if you don't know it's there, it might as well be on the other side of the globe. That's where this book comes in. It's a great step toward making sure your trip lives up to your expectations. As you plan, check out the Web as well. Guidebooks have been helping smart travelers find the special places for years; the Web is one more tool. Here at Fodor's, and at our on-line arm, Fodors.com, our focus is on providing you with information that's not only useful but accurate and on target. Every day Fodor's editors put enormous effort into getting things right, beginning with the search for the right contributors—people who have objective judgment, broad travel experience, and the writing ability to put their insights into words. There's no substitute for advice from a like-minded friend who has just come back from where you're going, but our writers, having seen all corners of Berlin, are the next best thing.

Australian world-travelers **Daniel Adler** and **Jen Makin** made their mark in Berlin at the on-line guide berlinfo.com, as managing editor and contributor, respectively. With degrees in law and German between them, who better to advise you on local etiquette, claiming your VAT tax back, and ways to save money in town?

Jody K. Biehl is an avowed cultural junkie who simply adores Berlin. Much of her insider knowledge comes from working at *Zitty,* Berlin's savvy nightlife and entertainment guide. She holds masters degrees in art history and journalism and freelances for *The San Francisco Chronicle, The Boston Globe, Newsweek,* and *USA Today.*

Alan Posener is an editor with *Die Welt,* one of Germany's premier newspapers. His father was a German-Jewish emigre who returned with his family to his native city Berlin in 1961. Alan taught school in Berlin and authored several books before taking up journalism. Alan is married and has one daughter.

After completing a statistics degree at the University of Glasgow **Tim Reid** headed straight to Berlin, dusted off the certificate of merit he earned in a 1993 Perth Young Wordsmiths competition, and began posting his observations of Berlin on berlinfo.com. An avid sports fan, he has also tested the waters for you in every body of water Berlin offers, be it lake, fountain, or steam bath.

A Berlin resident for over 15 years, **Jürgen Scheunemann** fell in love with the city after moving here from Hamburg. An award-winning journalist and former writer for Berlin's leading daily, *Der Tagesspiegel,* Jürgen has written and translated many travel, photo, and history books on Berlin, Germany, and the United States.

Nicola Varns has been an astute shopper since receiving her first candy allowance. She moved to Berlin from Britain in 1997, and embarked on a career as a writer, translator, and self-confessed shopaholic. She contributes to the online guide berlinfo.com, and has written about Central Europe and the former Soviet Union. She lives off the Ku'damm for maximized shopping proximity.

Special thanks to Berlin Tourism Marketing and Lufthansa, who provided invaluable help in making this book possible.

Don't Forget to Write

Your experiences—positive and negative—matter to us. If we have missed or misstated something, we want to hear about it. We follow up on all suggestions. Contact the Berlin editor at editors@fodors.com or c/o Fodor's, 280 Park Avenue, New York, New York 10017. And have a fabulous trip!

Karen Cure
Editorial Director

ESSENTIAL INFORMATION

ADDRESSES

Reunification meant a major overhaul of German addresses, zip codes, and phone numbers. Street names that reflected East Germany's ideology were often changed to their pre–Communist era ones. The process is now complete, so make sure you have an up-to-date map. If you plan to tour Berlin extensively, buy a map plan by Falk once in Berlin.

In this book the word for street (*Strasse*) is abbreviated as str. within italicized service information. Friedrichstrasse will appear as Friedrichstr., for example. Street numbering can be confusing as there are two systems in operation. Although some streets have odd numbers on one side and evens on the other, numbers can also run consecutively up one side of the street and back down the other. A good map will show some numbers on longer streets, and corner street signs will indicate what numbers are on the block.

Note that floor numbering in Europe is different than in the United States. What Americans refer to as the second floor is Europe's first (since it is the first floor above the ground floor).

AIR TRAVEL

TO AND FROM BERLIN

Flights to Berlin from outside Europe almost always require a connecting flight.

BOOKING

When you book, **look for nonstop flights** and **remember that "direct" flights stop at least once.** Try to avoid connecting flights, which require a change of plane. For more booking tips and to check prices and make on-line flight reservations, log on to www.fodors.com.

CARRIERS

Lufthansa is Germany's national carrier and the only airline to have nonstop service from Washington, D.C., to Berlin. Northwest shares the route with its partner, KLM. From Britain, British Airways and its German branch, Deutsche BA, are the major carriers. The only budget airline serving Berlin is Buzz, which flies from London's Stansted Airport and uses the Internet for all its bookings. Many European carriers serve Berlin from North America.

➤ MAJOR AIRLINES: **Air Canada** (☏ 888/247-2262; 030/882–5879 in Berlin, WEB www.aircanada.ca). **American Airlines** (☏ 800/433–7300; 0180/324–2324 in Germany, WEB www.aa.com). **Delta** (☏ 800/241–4141; 0180/333–7880 in Germany, WEB www.delta.com). **Lufthansa** (☏ 800/645–3880, 0180/388–7588 in Germany, WEB www.lufthansa.com). **Northwest/KLM** (☏ 800/447-4747; 0180/521–4201 in Germany, WEB www.nwa.com).

➤ FROM THE U.K.: **British Airways** (☏ 0345/222–111; 0180/334–0340 in Germany, WEB www.british-airways.com). **Buzz** (www.buzzaway.com). **Lufthansa** (☏ 020/8750–3300 or 0345/737–747; 0180/388–7588 in Germany, WEB www.lufthansa.com).

➤ SMALLER AIRLINES: **Deutsche BA** (☏ 0180/535-9322 in Germany). **Eurowings** (☏ 084/5773–7747 in the U.K., 0180/387–6946 in Germany, WEB www.eurowings.de).

CHECK-IN & BOARDING

Assuming that not everyone with a ticket will show up, airlines routinely overbook planes. When everyone does, airlines ask for volunteers to give up their seats. In return, these volunteers usually get a certificate for a free flight and are rebooked on the next flight out. If there are not enough volunteers, the airline must choose who will be denied boarding. The first to get bumped are passengers who checked in late and those flying on discounted tickets, so **get to the gate and check in as early as possible,** especially during peak periods.

Always **bring a government-issued photo I.D. to the airport;** even when it's not required, a passport is best.

CUTTING COSTS

The least expensive airfares to Berlin must usually be purchased in advance and are nonrefundable.

It's smart to **call a number of airlines,** and when you are quoted a good price, **book it on the spot**—the same fare may not be available the next day. Always **check different routings** and look into using different airports. Travel agents, especially low-fare specialists(☞ Discounts & Deals, *below*), are helpful.

Consolidators are another good source. They buy tickets for scheduled international flights at reduced rates from the airlines, then sell them at prices that beat the best fare available directly from the airlines, usually without restrictions. Sometimes you can even get your money back if you need to return the ticket. Carefully read the fine print detailing penalties for changes and cancellations, and **confirm your consolidator reservation with the airline.**

When you **fly as a courier,** you trade your checked-luggage space for a ticket deeply subsidized by a courier service. There are restrictions on when you can book and how long you can stay.

➤ CONSOLIDATORS: **Cheap Tickets** (☎ 800/377–1000). **Discount Airline Ticket Service** (☎ 800/576–1600). **Unitravel** (☎ 800/325–2222). **Up & Away Travel** (☎ 212/889–2345). **World Travel Network** (☎ 800/409–6753).

ENJOYING THE FLIGHT

For more legroom, **request an emergency-aisle seat.** Don't sit in the row in front of the emergency aisle or in front of a bulkhead, where seats may not recline. If you have dietary concerns, **ask for special meals when booking.** These can be vegetarian, low-cholesterol, or kosher, for example. On long flights, try to maintain a normal routine, to help fight jet lag. At night, **get some sleep.** By day, **eat light meals, drink water** (not alcohol), and **move around the cabin** to stretch your legs. For additional jet-lag tips consult *Fodor's FYI: Travel Fit & Healthy* (available at bookstores everywhere).

FLYING TIMES

Most flights to Berlin from the United States and Canada are not direct. Travel time will depend on where your connection is made and how long the layover is. Berlin is roughly a one hour and 45 minute flight from either London or Paris and a one-hour flight from Frankfurt.

HOW TO COMPLAIN

If your baggage goes astray or your flight goes awry, complain right away. Most carriers require that you **file a claim immediately.**

➤ AIRLINE COMPLAINTS: U.S. Department of Transportation **Aviation Consumer Protection Division** (✉ C-75, Room 4107, Washington, DC 20590, ☎ 202/366–2220, WEB www. dot.gov/airconsumer). **Federal Aviation Administration Consumer Hotline** (☎ 800/322–7873).

RECONFIRMING

Most airlines ask that you confirm your outbound flight 72 hours in advance.

AIRPORTS & TRANSFERS

Berlin has three airports, all of which are relatively small for a major capital city. Most international airlines serve Tegel Airport (TXL), northwest of central Berlin, after a first stop at a major European hub. Because of increased air traffic, the former military airfield at Tempelhof (THF) is used as an alternate airport for commuter flights to western Germany. Schönefeld Airport (SXF) is about 24 km (15 mi) east of the downtown area. It is used principally for flights to and from European holiday destinations.

➤ AIRPORT INFORMATION: **Central service phone** (☎ 0180/500–0186).

AIRPORT TRANSFERS

Tegel Airport is approximately 6 km (4 mi) from central Berlin. The Nos. 109 and X9 (express) airport buses run at 10-minute intervals between Tegel and Zoo station, the center of former West Berlin. From here you can connect to buses, trains, and subway lines. The trip takes 30 minutes; the fare is €2.10. If your destination lies along the U–6 or U–7 subway lines, you can take Bus 128 to Kurt-Schumacher-Platz or Bus 109 to Jakob-Kaiser-Platz and change to the subway, where your bus ticket is also valid. Expect to pay about €20 for the same trip by taxi. If you rent a car at the airport, follow the signs for the Stadtautobahn into Berlin. The Halensee exit leads to Kurfürstendamm.

Unless you have extremely heavy luggage, **don't bother taking the shuttle bus from Schönefeld to the nearby S-Bahn station**—it's only a five-minute walk. If you need it, it's free and leaves every 10–15 minutes. The airport express train leaves from the station every 30 minutes, stopping at Ostbahnhof, Friedrichstrasse station, and Zoo station. The journey takes 20–30 minutes. Bus 171 also leaves every 10 or 15 minutes for the Rudow subway station in southeast Berlin. A taxi ride from Schönefeld Airport takes about 40 minutes and will cost around €35. By car follow the signs for Stadtzentrum Berlin.

Tempelhof is linked directly to the city center by the U–6 subway line.

DUTY-FREE SHOPPING

Buying goods at special duty-free stores is not guaranteed to save you money. You can generally buy alcohol more cheaply in supermarkets and specialized drink stores, and you can claim back the value-added tax you pay on other major purchases when you leave the country (☞ Taxes, *below*).

BIKE TRAVEL

Cycling has many advantages in a city like Berlin. The land is relatively flat, the side streets are quiet, and an adequate bike lane system in the major streets offers moderate protection from the Berlin motorist. Bikes should be in good working order, have both front and rear lights, and be ridden by someone whose alcohol level is under the legal limit. Don't even think about running a red light, even if the coast is clear. If there are no signposts or lines at an intersection, you must always give way to the vehicle on the right. It is inevitable that you will see fellow cyclists breaking these rules everywhere you go. However, on a quiet day the police will not hesitate to give you a ticket and a relatively large fine if they see a contravention of any traffic laws. Sometimes police roadblocks are even set up to trap offenders. You can take your bike onto the S-Bahn, but the bike will need a ticket just as a person would. This is also possible on the U-Bahn but not at the designated rush hours (6–9 and 2–5).

BUS TRAVEL
TO AND FROM BERLIN

Buses are generally cheaper than trains and are surprisingly comfortable. Eurolines (Deutsche Touring) and Gullivers Reisen operate coach services to most major European cities. Berlinien Bus has services to more than 300 destinations, mostly in Germany, but also to cities in neighboring countries. The Zentrale Omnibusbahnhof is the main bus depot for intercity services and is in the western part of the city. Some services also depart from the Zoo station, but there's no official bus depot there, only Gullivers Reisen's office. You can reserve tickets through the bus companies, commercial travel agencies, or through the travel service at the bus depot itself.

➤ BUS STATIONS: **Zentrale Omnibusbahnhof** (⊠ Masurenallee 4–6 at Messedamm, Charlottenburg, ☎ 030/302–5361 between 5:30 AM and 10 PM for information or 030/301–0380 for reservations). **Zoo station** (Hardenbergpl., at eastern end of a large parking area.

➤ BUS COMPANIES: **Eurolines (Deutsche Touring)** (⊠ Am Römerhof 17, Frankfurt am Main, ☎ 069/790–

350). **Gullivers Reisen** (✉ Hardenbergpl. 14, Berlin, ☎ 030/3110–2110). **Berlinien Bus** (Mannheimerstr. 33–34, Berlin, ☎ 030/861–9331).

PAYING

Bus companies accept major credit cards, but not traveler's checks.

RESERVATIONS

In peak travel seasons **book your seat in advance,** but in general you'll get a seat even if you purchase a ticket just before boarding.

BUSINESS HOURS

BANKS & OFFICES

Standard office hours are weekdays 9 to 5. Banks are generally open weekdays from 8:30 or 9 to 3 or 4 (5 or 6 on Thursday), sometimes with an hour lunch break at smaller branches. Banks at airports and main train stations open as early as 6:30 AM and close as late as 10:30 PM. Government offices tend to have restricted opening hours, often only being open from 8:30 to noon on selected days of the week—always **call ahead** to check.

GAS STATIONS

Gas stations and their small convenience shops are often open late, if not around the clock.

MUSEUMS & SIGHTS

Most museums are open daily (except Monday) 9–5 or 10–6. A few stay open as late as 10 PM on Thursday.

PHARMACIES

Most pharmacies are open 9–6 weekdays and 9–1 on Saturday. Those in more prominent locations often open an hour earlier or close an hour later. A list of pharmacies in the vicinity that are open late or on Sunday is posted on a pharmacy's door.

SHOPS

Department stores and larger stores are generally open from 9 or 9:15 to 8 on weekdays and until 4 on Saturday. Smaller shops open later and close earlier. Supermarkets and other stores at major stations (Ostbahnhof, Friedrichstrasse, Zoo) can stay open until 9 and are also open on Sunday.

CAMERAS & PHOTOGRAPHY

Berliners generally won't mind an appearance in your snapshots, but German law protects the right of individuals not to be photographed against their will. With the exception of people in the public eye, all citizens may insist that you do not photograph them, even in a public place. This only applies to photographs in which individuals are recognizable, not to landscapes or photographs of groups of people.

Generally, you can take photos in most public buildings, museums, churches, and the like, but the use of a flash or tripod will be restricted.

The *Kodak Guide to Shooting Great Travel Pictures* (available at bookstores everywhere) is loaded with tips.

➤ PHOTO HELP: **Kodak Information Center** (☎ 800/242–2424).

EQUIPMENT PRECAUTIONS

Don't pack film and equipment in checked luggage, where it is much more susceptible to damage. X-ray machines used to view checked luggage are becoming much more powerful and therefore are much more likely to ruin your film. Always **keep film and tape out of the sun.** Carry an extra supply of batteries, and **be prepared to turn on your camera or camcorder** to prove to security personnel that the device is real. Always **ask for hand inspection of film,** which becomes clouded after repeated exposure to airport X-ray machines, and **keep videotapes away from metal detectors.**

FILM & DEVELOPING

Film is available at drugstores, supermarkets, and specialty photo shops. A 36-exposure 400 ASA roll of film will run about €3. The cost of having your photos developed increases if you want them back quickly. You can **save at least 50% on developing costs by avoiding one-hour services and going for an overnight deal at a drugstore such as Schlecker or Drospa.** The cost for film developing is calculated per print plus a flat rate for developing the negatives.

VIDEOS

The German standard for video is VHS–PAL, which is not compatible with the U.S. VHS–NTSC standard.

CAR RENTAL

Rates with the major car-rental companies begin at about $45 per day and $220 per week for an economy car with a manual transmission and unlimited mileage. Volkswagen, Opel, and Mercedes are some standard brands of rentals; most rentals have a manual transmission, so if you want an automatic, be sure to **request one in advance.** Rather unhelpful is the fact that some rental locations only have a general Germany map to give out, and not one of Berlin.

➤ MAJOR AGENCIES: **Alamo** (☎ 800/ 522–9696; 020/8759–6200 in the U.K., WEB www.alamo.com). **Avis** (☎ 800/331–1084; 800/879–2847 in Canada; 02/9353–9000 in Australia; 09/525–1982 in New Zealand; 0870/ 606–0100 in the U.K., WEB www.avis. com). **Budget** (☎ 800/527–0700; 0870/156–5656 in the U.K., WEB www.budget.com). **Dollar** (☎ 800/ 800–6000; 0124/622–0111 in the U.K., where it's affiliated with Sixt; 02/9223–1444 in Australia, WEB www. dollar.com). **Hertz** (☎ 800/654–3001; 800/263–0600 in Canada; 020/8897– 2072 in the U.K.; 02/9669–2444 in Australia; 09/256–8690 in New Zealand, WEB www.hertz.com). **National Car Rental** (☎ 800/227–7368; 020/8680–4800 in the U.K., WEB www.nationalcar.com).

➤ IN BERLIN: **Avis** (✉ Schönefeld Airport, ☎ 030/6091–5710; ✉ Tegel Airport, ☎ 030/4101–3148; ✉ Budapester Str. 43, at Europa Center, ☎ 030/230–9370; ✉ Holzmarktstr. 15–18, ☎ 030/240–7940). **Europcar** (✉ Schönefeld Airport, ☎ 030/6349– 1644; ✉ Tegel Airport, ☎ 030/417– 8520; ✉ Kurfürstenstr. 101-104, ☎ 030/235–0640). **Hertz** (✉ Schönefeld Airport, ☎ 030/6091–5730; ✉ Tegel Airport, ☎ 030/4101–3315; ✉ Tempelhof Airport, ☎ 030/6951– 3818; ✉ Budapester Str. 39, ☎ 030/ 261–1053). **Sixt** (✉ Schönefeld Airport, ☎ 030/6091–5690; ✉ Tegel Airport, ☎ 030/4101–2886; ✉ Tempelhof Airport, ☎ 030/6951– 3816; ✉ Nürnberger Str. 65, ☎ 030/

212–9880; ✉ Spandauer Str., at SAS Radisson Hotel, ☎ 030/243–9050).

CUTTING COSTS

To get the best deal, **book through a travel agent who will shop around.** Even by making the calls yourself, you'll nearly always get a better deal by booking a rental before you leave on your trip, rather then renting once you arrive.

Do **look into wholesalers,** companies that do not own fleets but rent in bulk from those that do and often offer better rates than traditional car-rental operations. Payment must be made before you leave home.

➤ WHOLESALERS: **Auto Europe** (☎ 207/842–2000 or 800/223–5555, FAX 207/842–2222, WEB www. autoeurope.com). **Europe by Car** (☎ 212/581–3040 or 800/223–1516, FAX 212/246–1458, WEB www. europebycar.com). **DER Travel Services** (✉ 9501 W. Devon Ave., Rosemont, IL 60018, ☎ 800/782–2424, FAX 800/282–7474 for information; 800/860–9944 for brochures, WEB www.dertravel.com). **Kemwel Holiday Autos** (☎ 800/678–0678, FAX 914/825–3160, WEB www.kemwel. com).

INSURANCE

Third-party insurance is compulsory in Germany, so the cost of this is generally included in the quoted rental price. This insurance doesn't cover any damage to or loss of the rental vehicle. Before you rent, see what coverage your personal auto-insurance policy and credit cards already provide. Collision policies that car-rental companies sell for European rentals often do not include stolen-vehicle coverage. Before you buy extra insurance coverage, check your existing home and travel policies—you may already be insured.

REQUIREMENTS & RESTRICTIONS

In Germany you must be 21 to rent a car, and rates may be higher if you're under 25. Children under 12 years of age and under 5 ft must use an approved child's seat. Specify your child's weight when renting so that you receive the proper seat.

SURCHARGES

Before you pick up a car in one city and leave it in another, **ask about drop-off charges or one-way service fees,** which can be substantial. Note, too, that some rental agencies charge extra if you return the car before the time specified in your contract. To avoid a hefty refueling fee, **fill the tank just before you turn in the car.**

CAR TRAVEL

Although Berlin doesn't suffer the traffic chaos of cities like London or Rome, exploring by car can still be frustrating for out-of-towners. The city has many one-way streets and large intersections that make navigation difficult. Parking is scarce in most inner-city districts and traffic moves slowly during business hours, so **avoid driving and take public transport.**

EMERGENCY SERVICES

The German auto clubs ADAC and AvD operate tow trucks on all autobahns; they also have emergency telephones every 2 km (1 mi). On minor roads **go to the nearest call box and dial 01802/222–222** (if you have a mobile phone, just dial 222–222) Ask, in English, for road-service assistance. Help is free (with the exception of materials) if the work is carried out by the ADAC. If the ADAC has to use a subcontractor for the work, charges are made for time, mileage, and materials.

GASOLINE

Gasoline (petrol) costs are between €.90 and €1.05 per liter. Most German cars run on lead-free fuel. Some models use diesel fuel, so if you are renting a car, **find out which fuel the car takes.** Some older vehicles cannot take unleaded fuel. German filling stations are highly competitive, and bargains are often available if you shop around but *not* at autobahn filling stations. Self-service, or *SB-Tanken,* stations are cheapest. Pumps marked *bleifrei* contain unleaded gas.

PARKING

Parking in Berlin can be very difficult, particularly in Mitte and around the Ku'damm. Parking on side streets is generally free, though watch out for zones that are for residents (*Anwohner*) only. All German cars should be equipped with a parking clock (*Parkuhr*). As a driver you must place one of these on the dashboard when parking in a time-restricted spot (such as for two-hour parking). Set the rotating disk to show what time the car was parked. Parking police will fine you if you overstay the time limit or fail to display a parking clock. Larger parking lots have parking meters (*Parkautomaten*). After depositing enough change in one of the meters, you will be issued a ticket to display on your dashboard. Parking fines are high, and there is no shortage of officious inspectors.

In German garages you must **pay immediately on returning to retrieve your car,** not when driving out. Put the ticket you got on arrival into the machine and pay the amount displayed. Retrieve the ticket, go to your car, and on exiting, insert the ticket in a slot to raise the barrier.

ROAD CONDITIONS

Road conditions in Berlin are improving as the reconstruction of the city progresses, but building sites still cause havoc in some districts. **Ask your hotel concierge or receptionist which areas to avoid.**

RULES OF THE ROAD

Germans **drive on the right,** and road signs give distances in kilometers. Contrary to popular belief, autobahns do have a speed limit. On some parts of the autobahn speed restrictions of 130 kph (80 mph) or less have been introduced. Even on stretches where there is no speed limit, drivers are advised to keep below 130 kph (80 mph). Speed limits on country roads vary from 80 to 100 kph (from 50 to 60 mph). The blood-alcohol limit on drivers is very low—.05%. Note that **seat belts must be worn at all times by front- and backseat passengers.** Passing is permitted on the left side only, and likewise, only use the left lane for passing. Headlights, not parking lights, are required during inclement weather.

Don't enter streets with signposts bearing a red circle with a white horizontal stripe—they are one-way streets. The blue sign *EINBAHNSTRASSE* (one-way) indicates you have the right of way.

CHILDREN IN BERLIN

Although Berliners have a reputation for lavishing more attention on dogs than children, the city still has a lot to offer kids, so **make Berlin Tourismus Marketing your first stop.** It has brochures on sights and events suitable for children, and also a map with all the many playgrounds and other outdoor activity locations marked. The weekly listings magazines *Tip* and *Zitty* have children's sections, albeit in German. There is also a hot line, which provides information on activities for children and adolescents.

Summer events are fun for visitors both old and young, including the Carnival of Cultures, open-air concerts, and the Christopher Street Day parade, with its flamboyant costumes and dancing. (Stay away from the parade if you're concerned about scantily clad revelers.) Seasonal activities range from ice-skating and tobogganing in winter to swimming in the lakes in summer. Children's theater and school holiday activities are available, but the language barrier makes them less entertaining for English-speaking children.

If you are renting a car, don't forget to **arrange for a car seat** when you reserve. For general advice about traveling with children, consult *Fodor's FYI: Travel with Your Baby* (available in bookstores everywhere).

➤ LOCAL INFORMATION: **Activities Infoline** (Kinder- und Jugendinfofon; ☎ 030/2949–2121, weekdays noon–8).

BABY-SITTING

Berlin's universities have agencies that can arrange for an English-speaking student baby-sitter. Both the TUSMA and Heinzelmännchen organizations cost around €10 per hour (minimum three hours). While you enjoy the city alone, your kids will be truly entertained by Kinderinsel, whose international staff lead activities from museum visits to archaeological digs to behind-the-scenes theater tours. They'll pick the children up and drop them off again at your hotel. Prices range from €12 to €18 per child per hour, depending on the activities (sibling discounts are available).

➤ AGENCIES: **Heinzelmännchen** (☎ 030/831–6071). **Kinderinsel** (☎ 030/4171–6928, FAX 030/4171–6948. WEB www.kinderinsel.de). **TUSMA** (☎ 030/315–9340).

FLYING

When booking, **confirm carry-on allowances** if you're traveling with infants. In general, for babies charged 10% of the adult fare you are allowed one carry-on bag and a collapsible stroller; if the flight is full, the stroller may have to be checked or you may be limited to less.

Experts agree that it's a good idea to use safety seats aloft for children weighing less than 40 pounds. Airlines set their own policies: U.S. carriers usually require that the child be ticketed, even if he or she is young enough to ride free, since the seats must be strapped into regular seats. Do **check your airline's policy about using safety seats during takeoff and landing.** And since safety seats are not allowed everywhere in the plane, get your seat assignments early.

When reserving, **request children's meals or a freestanding bassinet** if you need them. But note that bulkhead seats, where you must sit to use the bassinet, may lack an overhead bin or storage space on the floor.

FOOD

Younger children are generally not welcome in Berlin's finer restaurants, so stick to less formal, larger establishments. In summer, garden and courtyard tables make for more relaxed dining. Many restaurants have children's menus, usually variations on spaghetti bolognese or schnitzel with fries. The local steakhouse chains such as Blockhaus are family-friendly and affordable. Charlöttchen, in Charlottenburg, has a separate playroom; there are theater performances for the kids on Sunday at 11:30 AM. The restaurants near the lakes on the outskirts of Berlin are ideal in summer—there is usually a playground nearby and plenty of room to run around. Homesick kids may feel better at the sight of a Mc-

Donald's or Burger King, which aren't hard to come across.

➤ RESTAURANTS: **Charlöttchen** (✉ Droysenstr 1, ☎ 030/324–4717).

LODGING

Most hotels in Berlin allow children under a certain age to stay in their parents' room at no extra charge, but others charge for them as extra adults; be sure to **find out the cutoff age for children's discounts.** Cots and cribs are generally free of charge, but to avoid any surprises, ask when you reserve.

The Econtel in Charlottenburg has multibed rooms, baby-sitting services, and helpful accoutrements free for the asking. In Spandau, the church-run Hotel Christopherus-Haus is in a countrified setting and offers baby-sitting, plus an indoor pool, bicycles, and other young guests with which yours can mingle. For something completely different, the wildly creative and bohemian Propeller Island City Lodge has a special "Gnome Room" only available to children traveling with their parents. The ceiling is under 5 ft. Parents may also choose from themed rooms.

➤ BEST CHOICES: **Econtel** (✉ Sömmeringstr. 24–26, D–10589, ☎ 030/346–810, FAX 030/3468–1163, WEB www.econtel.de). **Hotel Christopherus-Haus** (✉ Evangelisches Johannisstift Berlin, Schönwalder Allee 26, D–13587, ☎ 030/336–060, FAX 030/3360–6114, WEB www.vch.de/christopherus.berlin). **Propeller Island City Lodge** (✉ Paulsbornerstr. 10, D–10709, ☎ 030/893–2533, FAX 030/891–8720. WEB www.propeller-island.net4.com).

SIGHTS & ATTRACTIONS

The interactive exhibits at Labyrinth-Kindermuseum, in Mitte, are a kid's delight. Attractions fun for all ages include the trains, planes and automobiles at the Deutsches Technikmuseum Berlin; the critters and beasts at either of the two zoos; and the medieval crafts demonstrations at the Museumsdorf Düppel in Zehlendorf.

The largest dinosaur skeleton in the world, at the Natural History Museum (Museum für Naturkunde), has peren-nial appeal, and kids under 12 will enjoy the free tour through the Musical Instrument Museum (Musikinstrumentenmuseum), which culminates in a Wurlitzer organ demonstration. A trip on one of the city's canal boats can be fun in summer.

Places that are especially appealing to children are indicated by a rubber-duckie icon (🦆) in the margin of this guide.

SUPPLIES & EQUIPMENT

Supermarkets and drugstores (not pharmacies) such as Drospa and Schlecker have a good range of disposable diapers (*Windeln*) in all sizes from newborn to junior. They also stock several brands of baby formula, which is available in powder form and comes in two types: *Anfangsmilch/nahrung* is labeled with a big number 1, and is suitable for infants age 0–4 months; *Folgemilch/nahrung* is labeled with a big number 2 and is suitable for infants from 4 months. *Dauermilch/nahrung* is for all ages. Coloring books (*Malbücher*) and crayons (*Buntstifte*) are widely available, as is modeling clay (*Knetmasse*).

TRANSPORTATION

Children under six travel free on Berlin's public transport system; children age 6–14 travel at a reduced rate (*Ermässigungstarif*).

COMPUTERS ON THE ROAD

If you use a major Internet provider, getting on-line in Berlin should be easy. Contact your Internet provider to get the local access number for Berlin and to find out the surcharge. Larger hotels have Internet centers from which, for a fee, you can access a Web site or send e-mail. There are also plenty of cybercafés at which you can go on-line, either with their equipment or your own laptop. You may, however, need to buy an appropriate adapter for your laptop's phone jack. If you're traveling with a laptop, carry a spare battery and adapter. Never plug your computer into any socket without asking about surge protection. IBM sells a pen-size modem tester that plugs into a telephone jack to check if the line is safe to use.

➤ ACCESS NUMBERS IN BERLIN: **AOL** (01914; 0171–41914 or 0172–22144 for cell access). **Compuserve** (01088–0191919; 0172–22188 for cell access).

➤ INTERNET CAFÉS: **Alpha Internet Café** (⊠ Dunckerstr. 72, Prenzlauer Berg, ☎ 030/447–9067. **Hai-Täck** (⊠ Brünnhildestr. 8, Schöneberg, ☎ 8596–1413). **surf-inn at Galerie Kaufhof** (⊠ Alexanderpl. 9, Mitte, ☎ 030/247–430).**Website** (⊠ Joachimstalerstr. 41, Charlottenburg, ☎ 030/8867–9630. **Webtimes** (⊠ Chausseestr. 8, Mitte, ☎ 030/2804–9890).

CONCIERGES

Concierges, found in many hotels, can help you with theater tickets and dinner reservations: a good one with connections may be able to get you seats for a hot show or prime-time dinner reservations at the restaurant of the moment. You can also turn to your hotel's concierge for help with travel arrangements, sightseeing plans, services ranging from aromatherapy to zipper repair, and emergencies. Always, **always tip** a concierge who has been of great assistance(☞ Tipping, *below*).

CONSUMER PROTECTION

Whenever shopping or buying travel services in Berlin, **pay with a major credit card,** if possible, so you can cancel payment or get reimbursed if there's a problem. Most shops will only give exchanges when merchandise is returned with the receipt. Refunds are rare, so ask before you buy. If you're doing business with a particular company for the first time, **contact your local Better Business Bureau and the attorney general's offices** in your state and (for U.S. businesses) the company's home state as well. Have any complaints been filed? Finally, if you're buying a package or tour, always **consider travel insurance** that includes default coverage(☞ Insurance, *below*).

➤ BBBs: **Council of Better Business Bureaus** (⊠ 4200 Wilson Blvd., Suite 800, Arlington, VA 22203, ☎ 703/276–0100, FAX 703/525–8277, WEB www.bbb.org).

CUSTOMS & DUTIES

When shopping, **keep receipts** for all purchases. Upon reentering the country, **be ready to show customs officials what you've bought.** If you feel a duty is incorrect or object to the way your clearance was handled, note the inspector's badge number and ask to see a supervisor. If the problem isn't resolved, write to the appropriate authorities, beginning with the port director at your point of entry.

IN AUSTRALIA

Australian residents who are 18 or older may bring home $A400 worth of souvenirs and gifts (including jewelry), 250 cigarettes or 250 grams of tobacco, and 1,125 ml of alcohol (including wine, beer, and spirits). Residents under 18 may bring back $A200 worth of goods. Prohibited items include meat products. Seeds, plants, and fruits need to be declared upon arrival.

➤ INFORMATION: **Australian Customs Service** (Regional Director, ⊠ Box 8, Sydney, NSW 2001, Australia, ☎ 02/9213–2000, FAX 02/9213–4000, WEB www.customs.gov.au).

IN CANADA

Canadian residents who have been out of Canada for at least seven days may bring home C$750 worth of goods duty-free. If you've been away fewer than seven days but more than 48 hours, the duty-free allowance drops to C$200; if your trip lasts 24–48 hours, the allowance is C$50. You may not pool allowances with family members. Goods claimed under the C$750 exemption may follow you by mail; those claimed under the lesser exemptions must accompany you. Alcohol and tobacco products may be included in the seven-day and 48-hour exemptions but not in the 24-hour exemption. If you meet the age requirements of the province or territory through which you reenter Canada, you may bring in, duty-free, 1.14 liters (40 imperial ounces) of wine or liquor *or* 24 12-ounce cans or bottles of beer or ale. If you are 19 or older you may bring in, duty-free, 200 cigarettes and 50 cigars. Check ahead of time with the Canada Customs Revenue Agency or the Department of Agriculture for policies regarding meat products, seeds, plants, and fruits.

You may send an unlimited number of gifts worth up to C$60 each duty-free to Canada. Label the package UNSOLICITED GIFT—VALUE UNDER $60. Alcohol and tobacco are excluded.

➤ INFORMATION: **Canada Customs Revenue Agency** (✉ 2265 St. Laurent Blvd. S, Ottawa, Ontario K1G 4K3, Canada, ☎ 204/983–3500 or 506/636–5064; 800/461–9999 in Canada, WEB www.ccra-adrc.gc.ca).

IN GERMANY

Since a single, unrestricted market took effect within the European Union (EU) early in 1993, there have been no restrictions on persons traveling among the 15 EU countries. However, there are restrictions on what can be brought in without declaration. For example, if you have more than 800 cigarettes, 90 liters of wine, or 10 liters of alcohol, it is considered a commercial shipment and is taxed and otherwise treated as such.

For anyone entering Germany from outside the EU, the following limitations apply: (1) 200 cigarettes or 100 cigarillos or 50 cigars or 250 grams of tobacco; (2) 2 liters of still table wine; (3) 1 liter of spirits over 22% volume or 2 liters of spirits under 22% volume (fortified and sparkling wines) or 2 more liters of table wine; (4) 50 grams of perfume and 250 milliliters of toilet water; (5) other goods to the value of €180.

Tobacco and alcohol allowances are for visitors age 17 and over. Other items intended for personal use can be imported and exported freely.

Dogs and cats can be brought into Germany if they have a veterinary certificate stating that they have been vaccinated against rabies not more than one year and not less than 30 days before entering the country. This certificate must be accompanied by a notarized German translation of the document.

➤ INFORMATION: **German Customs Service** (Zoll-Infocenter; ✉ Hansaallee 141, 60320 Frankfurt am Main, ☎ 069/4699–760, FAX 069/4699–7699, info@zoll-infocenter.de).

IN NEW ZEALAND

Homeward-bound residents 17 or older may bring back $700 worth of souvenirs and gifts. Your duty-free allowance also includes 4.5 liters of wine or beer; one 1,125-ml bottle of spirits; and either 200 cigarettes, 250 grams of tobacco, 50 cigars, or a combination of the three up to 250 grams. Prohibited items include meat products, seeds, plants, and fruits.

➤ INFORMATION: **New Zealand Customs** (Custom House, ✉ 50 Anzac Ave., Box 29, Auckland, New Zealand, ☎ 09/300–5399, FAX 09/359–6730), WEB www.customs.govt.nz.

IN THE U.K.

If you are a U.K. resident and your journey was wholly within the European Union (EU), you won't have to pass through customs when you return to the United Kingdom. If you plan to bring back large quantities of alcohol or tobacco, check EU limits beforehand.

➤ INFORMATION: **HM Customs and Excise** (✉ Dorset House, Stamford St., Bromley, Kent BR1 1XX, U.K., ☎ 020/7202–4227, WEB www.hmce.gov.uk).

IN THE U.S.

U.S. residents who have been out of the country for at least 48 hours (and who have not used the $400 allowance or any part of it in the past 30 days) may bring home $400 worth of foreign goods duty-free.

U.S. residents 21 and older may bring back 1 liter of alcohol duty-free. In addition, regardless of your age, you are allowed 200 cigarettes and 100 non-Cuban cigars. Antiques, which the U.S. Customs Service defines as objects more than 100 years old, enter duty-free, as do original works of art done entirely by hand, including paintings, drawings, and sculptures.

You may also mail or ship packages home duty-free: up to $200 worth of goods for personal use, with a limit of one parcel per addressee per day (except alcohol or tobacco products or perfume worth more than $5); label the package PERSONAL USE and attach a list of its contents and their retail value. Do not label the package UNSOLICITED GIFT or your duty-free exemption will drop to $100. Mailed items do not affect your duty-free allowance on your return.

➤ INFORMATION: **U.S. Customs Service** (✉ 1300 Pennsylvania Ave. NW, Room 6.3D, Washington, DC 20229, WEB www.customs.gov; inquiries ☎ 202/354–1000; complaints c/o ✉ 1300 Pennsylvania Ave. NW, Room 5.4D, Washington, DC 20229; registration of equipment c/o Office of Passenger Programs, ☎ 202/927–0530).

DINING

New eateries seem to be popping up all the time in Berlin, all heavy with renovated charm to cash in on the new capital's buzz. Conventional restaurants abound, as do cafés and bars, which often also serve light meals. Pubs (*Kneipen*) usually have a limited menu of traditional fare. An *Imbiss* is a stand-up place for a quick, cheap meal or snack. Most serve Turkish specialties, but you can also find German sausage stands and Asian dishes. Bakeries (*Bäckereien*) usually serve sandwiches and coffee as well as the usual range of sweet and savory baked goods, which can also be eaten on the premises. International chains have invaded, so you'll see a few familiar signs. Local chains include Nordsee (fast fish meals), Aschinger (traditional German) and Blockhaus (Argentinean steak house).

The restaurants we list are the cream of the crop in each price category. Properties indicated by an ✕☧ are lodging establishments whose restaurant warrants a special trip.

CATEGORY	COST*
$$$$	over €21
$$$	€16–€20
$$	€11–€15
$	under €10

per person for a main course at dinner, excluding drinks, tip, and 16% sales tax

MEALS & SPECIALTIES

Most hotels serve a buffet-style breakfast (*Frühstück*) of rolls, cheese, cold cuts, eggs, cereals, yogurt, and spreads, which is often included in the price of a room. Cafés offer a similar choice, accompanied by coffee, tea, or *Milchkaffee*—a milky coffee that is rarely available at other times of the day. If you just want a quick coffee and a pastry, go to a bakery. On weekends until midafternoon many cafés have all-you-can-eat brunch buffets, where you can choose from among cereal, salads, cheeses, cold cuts, hot dishes such as eggs and sausages, cake, and fruit. Orange juice and coffee are sometimes but not always included.

Lunch (*Mittagessen*) is generally light. You can get sandwiches from most cafés and from bakeries, or many restaurants have special lunch menus that are often cheaper than in the evenings. If you are buying bread to make your own lunch and don't want a whole loaf, you can ask for just half.

Going out for dinner (*Abendessen*) is a favorite pastime in Berlin. It's up to you whether you want a light meal or a extravagant spread—it is perfectly acceptable to just order an entrée or skip straight to dessert if you're not feeling hungry.

Berlin specialties are strongly meat focused. They include *Eisbein mit Sauerkraut* (knuckle of pork with pickled cabbage), *Rouladen* (rolled stuffed beef), *Spanferkel* (suckling pig), *Berliner Schüsselsülze* (potted meat in aspic), *Hackepeter* (ground beef), and *Kartoffelpuffer* (fried potato cakes). Spicy *Currywurst* is a chubby frankfurter that's served with thick tomato sauce, curry, and pepper. It's sold at *Bockwurst* stands all over the city. Turkish specialties are also an integral part of the Berlin diet. On almost every street you'll find stands selling *Döner kebab* (grilled lamb with salad in a flat-bread pocket).

MEALTIMES

Restaurants have quite long opening hours. At cafés you can often order breakfast until early afternoon. Lunch can run from 11 to 4, and dinner usually starts up again at 6. Most restaurants don't close until midnight or 1 AM. If you're invited to dinner, it will rarely be served before 8.

Unless otherwise noted, the restaurants listed in this guide are open daily for lunch and dinner.

PAYING

Credit cards are generally accepted only in moderate to expensive restaurants, even then some smaller places still only take cash. If you plan to pay with credit, always **check the stickers on the door** for credit card symbols (or ask a waiter) before ordering.

RESERVATIONS & DRESS

Reservations are always a good idea: we mention them only when they're essential or not accepted. Book as far ahead as you can, and reconfirm as soon as you arrive. We mention dress only when men are required to wear a jacket or a jacket and tie. Note, though, that even when Germans are in casual dress, the look is generally crisp and neat.

WINE, BEER & SPIRITS

Almost all restaurants have a range of wines, beers, and spirits on the menu. Local licensing laws are fairly relaxed, and there is no uniform closing time. Bars are often open until the wee hours of the morning, and clubs don't even stop at dawn. On weekends you can even participate in the local tradition of *Frühschoppen*—breakfast washed down with schnapps, beer, or sparkling wine. Drinking is permitted in public places, including on the street, in parks, and in public transport facilities. Wine, beer, and spirits can be bought cheaply from all supermarkets and from special drink stores (*Getränkemarkt*). For that after-hours bottle, head to your nearest gas station.

If you're from an inferior beer-brewing nation (i.e., the rest of the world), you could be forgiven for favoring the local drop. Those with more experience avoid any beer with "Berliner" in the name, particularly the local "specialty"—the Berliner Weisse, a sweet mixture of beer and red or green syrup—though many tourists and more than a few locals enjoy the combination. Brewed near Berlin,

Radeberger beer is one of the few East German products to survive reunification; taste it, and you'll see why. Locals also drink a lot of *Weizen*, wheat beer from southern Germany. The local spirit is *Korn*, but spirits from elsewhere in Germany are also readily available and shouldn't be neglected.

DISABILITIES & ACCESSIBILITY

Movado, the Berlin lobby for people with disabilities, gives the city a 7 out of 10 when it comes to providing for travelers with disabilities. Although many public buildings such as museums provide good access, the service industries and public transport could do more to improve the service to special-needs users. Movado has a great database that contains the results of an accessibility audit of more than 50,000 public buildings, hotels, tourist attractions, restaurants, bars, and clubs—a must for travelers with mobility restrictions. Travelers with disabilities looking for specific information should go to the Movado Web site or write to them requesting brochures in the . . . *without Barriers* series including *Hotels, Cinemas,* and *Excursions.* You can rent a wheelchair at minimal cost through the Association for the Disabled.

If you or a traveling companion have a disability but like to keep active, call the information line of the Informationsstelle für Sport behinderter Menschen (Sports Information Office for the Physically Restricted) to find out about sporting activities to suit your needs.

➤ LOCAL RESOURCES: **Movado** (✉ Langhanstr. 64, 13086, ☎ 030/471–5145, FAX 030/473–1111, WEB www.movado.de.) **Informationsstelle für Sport behinderter Menschen** (Sports Information Office for the Physically Restricted, ✉ Schwendener Str. 8, ☎ 030/824–3731). **Verband Geburts und andere Behinderte** (Association for the Disabled; ✉ Otto-Suhr-Alle 131, 10585, ☎ 030/341–1797, FAX 030/341–6216).

LODGING

The Movado brochure *Hotels without Barriers* recommends about 60 hotels and guest houses. Options are plentiful if you're looking at the top price range, but limited if you're traveling on a budget. Hotels listed below are suitable for wheelchair users.

➤ BEST CHOICES: **art'otel berlin-mitte** (✉ Wallstr. 70–73, D–10719 Mitte, ☎ 030/240–620, FAX 030/2406–2222, WEB www.artotel.de). **Hotel Adlon Berlin** (✉ Unter den Linden 77, D–10117 Mitte, ☎ 030/22610, FAX 030/2261–2222, WEB www.hotel-adlon.de). **Hotel Mondial** (✉ Kurfürstendamm 47, D–10707 Western Downtown, ☎ 030/884–110, FAX 030/8841–1150, WEB www.hotel-mondial.com). **Sorat Art'otel Berlin** (✉ Joachimstaler Str. 29, D–10719 Western Downtown, ☎ 030/884–470, FAX 030/884–47700, WEB www.SORAT-Hotels.com).

RESERVATIONS

When discussing accessibility with an operator or reservations agent, **ask hard questions.** Are there any stairs, inside *or* out? Are there grab bars next to the toilet *and* in the shower/tub? How wide is the doorway to the room? To the bathroom? For the most extensive facilities meeting the latest legal specifications, **opt for newer accommodations.**

➤ COMPLAINTS: **Aviation Consumer Protection Division**(☞ Air Travel, *above*) for airline-related problems. **Civil Rights Office** (✉ U.S. Department of Transportation, Departmental Office of Civil Rights, S-30, 400 7th St. SW, Room 10215, Washington, DC 20590, ☎ 202/366–4648, FAX 202/366–9371, WEB www.dot.gov/ost/docr/index.htm) for problems with surface transportation. **Disability Rights Section** (✉ U.S. Department of Justice, Civil Rights Division, Box 66738, Washington, DC 20035-6738, ☎ 202/514–0301 or 800/514–0301; 202/514–0383 TTY; 800/514–0383 TTY, FAX 202/307–1198, WEB www.usdoj.gov/crt/ada/adahom1.htm) for general complaints.

TRAVEL AGENCIES

In the United States, the Americans with Disabilities Act requires that travel firms serve the needs of all travelers. Some agencies specialize in working with people with disabilities.

➤ TRAVELERS WITH MOBILITY PROBLEMS: **Access Adventures** (✉ 206 Chestnut Ridge Rd., Scottsville, NY 14624, ☎ 716/889–9096, dltravel@prodigy.net), run by a former physical-rehabilitation counselor. **CareVacations** (✉ No. 5, 5110–50 Ave., Leduc, Alberta T9E 6V4, Canada, ☎ 780/986–6404 or 877/478–7827, FAX 780/986–8332, WEB www.carevacations.com), for group tours and cruise vacations. **Flying Wheels Travel** (✉ 143 W. Bridge St., Box 382, Owatonna, MN 55060, ☎ 507/451–5005 or 800/535–6790, FAX 507/451–1685, WEB www.flyingwheelstravel.com).

DISCOUNTS & DEALS

Be a smart shopper and **compare all your options** before making decisions. A plane ticket bought with a promotional coupon from travel clubs, coupon books, and direct-mail offers or on the Internet may not be cheaper than the least expensive fare from a discount ticket agency. And always keep in mind that what you get is just as important as what you save.

BERLIN'S STATE MUSEUMS COMBINED TICKET

Get discounted entry into 20 of Berlin's biggest and most popular museums with the Berlin State Museums combined ticket. Just some of the museums included are the Altes Museum, the Alte Nationalgalerie, the Pergamonmuseum, the Hamburger Bahnhof, the Gemäldegalerie, the Kupferstichkabinett, the Neue Nationalgalerie, the Ägyptisches Museum, and the Sammlung Berggruen. Entrance to these museums cost about €2–€4 each, so **consider the combined ticket if you're interested in more than one of Berlin's museum collections.** It's available at the cashier's desk of any participating museum; the cost is €4 for one day (€2 for seniors, students, and children), €8.18 for three consecutive days (€4 for seniors, students, and children).

FREE SUNDAY

All the state-run museums offer free admission on the first Sunday of the month.

WELCOMECARD

If you're in Berlin for three or four days, consider the Berlin Welcome-Card. It offers good value, especially if you're traveling as a family. For €16.36 this ticket allows one adult and up to three children 72 hours of unlimited travel in Zones A, B, and C, as well as free admission or reductions up to 50% for sightseeing trips, museums, theaters, and other events and attractions. WelcomeCards are available at all BVG ticket counters, Berlin Tourismus Marketing offices, and many Berlin hotels. Don't forget to **validate the card the first time you use public transportation.**

DISCOUNT RESERVATIONS

To save money, **look into discount reservations services** with toll-free numbers, which use their buying power to get a better price on hotels, airline tickets, even car rentals. When booking a room, always **call the hotel's local toll-free number** (if one is available) rather than the central reservations number—you'll often get a better price. Always ask about special packages or corporate rates.

When shopping for the best deal on hotels and car rentals, **look for guaranteed exchange rates,** which protect you against a falling dollar. With your rate locked in, you won't pay more, even if the price goes up in the local currency.

➤ AIRLINE TICKETS: ☎ **800/FLY– ASAP.**

➤ HOTEL ROOMS: **Hotel Reservations Network** (☎ 800/964–6835, WEB www.hoteldiscount.com). **International Marketing & Travel Concepts** (☎ 800/790–4682, WEB www. imtc-travel.com). **Players Express Vacations** (☎ 800/458–6161, WEB www.playersexpress.com). **Steigenberger Reservation Service** (☎ 800/ 223–5652, WEB www.srs-worldhotels. com). **Travel Interlink** (☎ 800/888– 5898, WEB www.travelinterlink.com). **Turbotrip.com** (☎ 800/473–7829, WEB www.turbotrip.com).

PACKAGE DEALS

Don't confuse packages and guided tours. When you buy a package, you travel on your own, just as though you had planned the trip yourself. Fly/drive packages, which combine airfare and car rental, are often a good deal. In cities, ask the local visitors' bureau about hotel packages that include tickets to major museum exhibits or other special events.

ELECTRICITY

To use electric-powered equipment purchased in the U.S. or Canada, **bring a converter and adapter.** The electrical current in Germany is 220 volts, 50 cycles alternating current (AC); wall outlets take Continental-type plugs, with two round prongs.

If your appliances are dual-voltage, you'll need only an adapter. Don't use 110-volt outlets marked FOR SHAVERS ONLY for high-wattage appliances such as blow-dryers. Most laptops operate equally well on 110 and 220 volts and so require only an adapter. Australian and U.K. (240V) appliances just need an adapter to fit the local two-prong socket.

EMBASSIES

➤ AUSTRALIA: (✉ Friedrichstr. 200, D–10117, ☎ 030/880–0880).

➤ CANADA: (✉ International Trade Center, Friedrichstr. 95, 23rd floor, D–10117, ☎ 030/203–120).

➤ IRELAND: (✉ Friedrichstr. 200, D–10117, ☎ 030/220–720).

➤ NEW ZEALAND: (✉ Friedrichstr. 60, D–10117, ☎ 030/206–210).

➤ SOUTH AFRICA: (✉ Friedrichstr. 60, D–10017, ☎ 030/220–730).

➤ UNITED KINGDOM: ✉ Wilhelmstr. 70–71, D–10117, ☎ 030/204–570.

➤ UNITED STATES: ✉ Neustädtische Kirchstr. 4–5, D–10117, ☎ 030/830– 50.

EMERGENCIES

For emergency medical treatment you can go to the emergency department of any hospital. Generally, someone will speak enough English to help you, and you will be seen promptly. You will generally have to pay for your treatment at the time of service, and then you can make a claim with your insurance company at a later time. The 24-hour American Hotline provides referrals to English-speaking medical services and can also help with other problems.

Pharmacies in Berlin offer late-night service on a rotating basis. Every pharmacy displays a notice indicating the location of the nearest shop with evening hours.

➤ DOCTORS & DENTISTS: **After-hours doctor** (☎ 030/3100–3399).

➤ EMERGENCY SERVICES: **Ambulance/ fire** (☎ 112).**Police** (☎ 110). **Emergency dentist** (*Notzahnarzt*; ☎ 030/ 8900–4333). **Emergency doctor** (*Notarzt*; ☎ 030/310–031). **Emergency pharmaceutical assistance** (*Apotheken-Notdienst*; ☎ 01189).

➤ HOSPITALS: **Charite** (✉ Schumannstr. 20–21, Mitte, ☎ 030/ 28020). **Krankenhaus Am Urban** (✉ Dieffenbachstr. 1, Kreuzberg, ☎ 030/ 6970). **Krankenhaus Prenzlauer Berg** (✉ Fröbelstr. 15, Prenzlauer Berg, ☎ 030/42420). **Städtisches Krankenhaus** (✉ Landsberger Allee 49 Friedrichshain, ☎ 030/42210).

➤ HOT LINES: **Alcoholics Anonymous** (☎ 030/787–5188) **American Hotline** (☎ 0177/814–1510). **Crisis Line** (☎ 0800/1110–111). **Emergency Drug Service** (☎ 030/19237). **International Emergency Hotline** (☎ 030/ 3100–3222 or 030/3100–3243). **Poisons Center** (☎ 030/19240).

ENGLISH-LANGUAGE MEDIA

NEWSPAPERS & MAGAZINES

Berlin is a major international tourist destination, so it's not difficult to find English-language newspapers. For the best selection visit one of the main stations or the International Presse newsagents. Even smaller newsstands may stock international press, especially in touristy areas such as Checkpoint Charlie and the Ku'damm. Major bookstores like Kiepert and Dussman also stock international press.

RADIO & TELEVISION

You can pick up the BBC World Service in Berlin at 90.2 FM, and for the younger listener, local station Rock Star FM (at 87.9 FM) has regular news bulletins, current affairs reports, and music programs from American networks.

Most hotels have a range of American cable TV channels on offer including CNN, NBC, and MTV. BBC World broadcasts free, airing on Channel 41.

ETIQUETTE & BEHAVIOR

Berlin is a big city, and big-city manners prevail. Berliners are generally forthright, and if you upset them a sharp comment or glare will let you know you're out of line. The waiter who remarks, "You'll just have to wait your turn," and the bus driver who snaps because you don't have the correct change ready aren't being rude as such; they're just going about their business in a city where pleasantries are not always extended to strangers, even when those strangers are customers.

Always **address acquaintances as Herr (Mr.) or Frau (Mrs.) plus their last name** and do not call them by their first name unless invited to do so. A handshake is always appropriate for greeting or saying goodbye. A kiss is too intimate in most situations, and it is not necessary, as both men and women will prefer to shake hands. The home is a private space for most Germans, and the first time you are invited to eat or take coffee at someone's home is likely to be a special occasion. As a guest you can expect to be amply provided for, but if invited for a meal it is a polite gesture to **bring a small gift (such as wine or chocolate) for the host.** Before drinking it is customary to look your company in the eye and say *"Prost"* (cheers). Before eating, wish those sitting down with you a *"Guten Appetit."* Putting your shoes on the furniture is considered bad form in most countries, but it is extremely so in Germany, where even resting your shod feet on a park bench is frowned upon. If you take your shoes off, however, you can put your smelly socks on the seats in trains and buses without anyone batting an eyelid. In summer it is not unusual to see nude sunbathers in many of the city's public parks and gardens.

GAY & LESBIAN TRAVEL

As the capital of Germany's (and Europe's) gay cultural and nightlife scene, Berlin has a reputation for tolerance. The gay community is an integral part of Berlin society and same-sex couples are just as accepted as any other couples in the central districts. In summer relaxed attitudes toward nudity make parks and beaches a favorite haunt of sun-loving couples and singles, both gay and straight. You should **be more circumspect in the outer eastern suburbs,** where right-wing thugs have sometimes been known to target gays.

Hotels are happy to accommodate same-sex couples, but if you would prefer to lodge with other gays, contact Enjoy Bed & Breakfast, a private agency that finds rooms in Berlin and elsewhere in Europe. Timmy's Bed and Breakfast, in Tiergarten, has a mostly gay male clientele and offers discounts for longer stays. Women, hetero or gay, who prefer to lodge in an all-female environment, can book a room at the Artemisia hotel, in Charlottenburg.

The gay and lesbian community in Berlin organizes a number of high-profile events throughout the year. In mid-June, the Gay and Lesbian Street Party is a two-day festival centered around Nollendorfplatz. Streets, bars, and clubs fill with food stands and entertainers as a kind of a warm-up for the Christopher Street Day parade, usually held a week later. This is the most flamboyant parade of the summer, when hundreds of thousands of gays, lesbians, and friends flaunt their stuff from Kurfürstendamm to the Victory Column, commemorating the 1969 Stonewall riots on Christopher Street in New York, which kicked off the gay liberation movement. If you're a film aficionado, the Queer Film Festival runs for a week in late November, showing international features and shorts. The Lesbian Film Festival is one of the three largest in Europe and runs for a week in October. Both festivals are hosted by the Hackesche Höfe cinemas.

Schöneberg is the traditional home of Berlin's gay and lesbian community and has a bewildering array of bars, cafés, clubs, shops, and support organizations. Neighboring Kreuzberg is home to a less polished scene, including the majority of the gay Turkish community. Mitte has plenty of clubs that host gay or lesbian one-nighters. A working-class suburb during Socialist times, Prenzlauer Berg had a nascent gay and lesbian scene before reunification, which the forces of gentrification have made slicker but also more diverse. Friedrichshain also has a small but growing community, reinforced by some of the biggest clubs in Berlin and an increasing number of cafés and bars.

To find out what's on during your stay in Berlin, pick up a free copy of *Sergej* or *Siegessäule* in any café or bar. Mann-O-Meter is an all-purpose advice center in Schöneberg that also has a help line. Staff members speak English and can help with anything from counseling to finding a room or providing directions to clubs. The Gay Museum, Archive and Library can provide you with more background on the history of the Berlin scene, and the staff speaks English. For women, the Schokofabrik is a resource center with a café, a women's hammam (steam room), and space for self-help groups. It also runs regular cultural events. A relic of the underground scene in the East, the Sonntags Club is a bar–café that also has counseling and information services.

➤ LODGINGS: **Artemisia** (☎ 030/873–8905, FAX 030/861–8653). **Enjoy Bed & Breakfast** (✉ Motzstr. 5, Schöneberg, D–10777, ☎ 030/215–1666, FAX 030/2175–2219, WEB www.ebab. de). **Timmy's Bed and Breakfast** (✉ Perlebergerstr., Tiergarten, D–10559, ☎ 030/8185–1988, FAX 030/8185–1989, WEB www.gaybed.de).

➤ LOCAL RESOURCES: **Gay Museum, Archive and Library (Schwules Museum;** ✉ Mehringdamm 61, Kreuzberg, ☎ 030/693–1172, FAX 030/693–4037, WEB www.schwulesmuseum.de). **Mann-O-Meter** (✉ Motzstr. 5, Schöneberg, ☎ 030/216–8008, FAX 030/215–7078, WEB www.mann-o-meter.de). **Schokofabrik** (✉ Mariannenstr. 6, Kreuzberg, ☎ 030/615–2999). **Sergej** (WEB www.sergej.de). **Siegessäule** (WEB www.siegessaeule.de). **Sonntags Club** (✉ Greifenhagener Str. 28, Prenzlauer Berg, ☎ 030/449–7590).

► GAY- & LESBIAN-FRIENDLY TRAVEL AGENCIES: **Different Roads Travel** (✉ 8383 Wilshire Blvd., Suite 902, Beverly Hills, CA 90211, ☎ 323/651–5557 or 800/429–8747, FAX 323/651–3678, lgernert@tzell.com). **Kennedy Travel** (✉ 314 Jericho Turnpike, Floral Park, NY 11001, ☎ 516/352–4888 or 800/237–7433, FAX 516/354–8849, WEB www.kennedytravel.com). **Now Voyager** (✉ 4406 18th St., San Francisco, CA 94114, ☎ 415/626–1169 or 800/255–6951, FAX 415/626–8626, WEB www.nowvoyager.com). **Skylink Travel and Tour** (✉ 1006 Mendocino Ave., Santa Rosa, CA 95401, ☎ 707/546–9888 or 800/225–5759, FAX 707/546–9891, WEB www.skylinktravel.com), serving lesbian travelers.

HEALTH

Medical care in Germany is generally of a very high quality and quite affordable. A doctor's appointment will set you back around €25–€35, and a visit to the emergency department including necessary drugs around €40, which may well be less than the minimum amount you can claim on your travel insurance. Prescription drugs are quite expensive—it is not unusual for a small box of tablets to cost €50. Alternative and homeopathic remedies are widely accepted in Germany, to the point that you may have a hard time convincing a doctor that antibiotics are really going to be of more use than a cup of chamomile tea. Most doctors can speak passable English. **Call your embassy for a list of English-speaking practitioners.**

FOOD & DRINK

There are stringent health and hygiene regulations in Germany. The water may not taste great, but it is perfectly safe to drink. The only exception is if you happen to be staying in an older unrenovated building in the former East, where some of the plumbing may still contain lead piping.

OVER-THE-COUNTER REMEDIES

For aspirin, cough remedies, and other common over-the-counter drugs, you will need to go to a pharmacy (*Apotheke*). You will not be able to find Tylenol—ask for *Paracetamol* instead. Pharmacists in Germany are highly qualified and can advise you on the appropriate remedies for minor complaints as well as provide simple first aid. Most of them speak English; if not, they will refer you to someone who can.

HEALTH WARNINGS

Mad cow disease (or BSE) is a neurological disorder that affects cattle. It is transmissible to humans and causes a fatal deterioration of the central nervous system. There is no known cure or vaccination. The disease is very rare, but its appearance in beef and dairy stock in recent years has caused many Germans to reconsider their meat consumption. Current evidence suggests that it is only the brain, central nervous system, eyes, and intestine of infected cows that contain the contagious agent. As of December 2000, BSE testing is compulsory before any cow is slaughtered. For the latest updates on the situation, see www.mad-cow.org.

HOLIDAYS

The following national holidays are observed in Berlin: January 1; Good Friday; Easter Monday; May 1 (Labor Day); Ascension; Pentecost Monday; October 3 (German Unity Day); November 1 (All Saints' Day); December 24–26 (Christmas).

INSURANCE

The most useful travel-insurance plan is a comprehensive policy that includes coverage for trip cancellation and interruption, default, trip delay, and medical expenses (with a waiver for pre-existing conditions).

Without insurance you will lose all or most of your money if you cancel your trip, regardless of the reason. Default insurance covers you if your tour operator, airline, or cruise line goes out of business. Trip-delay covers expenses that arise because of bad weather or mechanical delays. Study the fine print when comparing policies.

If you're traveling internationally, a key component of travel insurance is coverage for medical bills incurred if you get sick on the road. Such expenses are not generally covered by Medicare or private policies. U.K. residents can buy a travel-insurance policy valid for most vacations taken during the year in which it's purchased (but check pre-existing-condition coverage). British and Australian citizens need extra medical coverage when traveling overseas.

Always **buy travel policies directly from the insurance company**; if you buy them from a cruise line, airline, or tour operator that goes out of business you probably will not be covered for the agency or operator's default, a major risk. Before making any purchase, **review your existing health and home-owner's policies** to find what they cover away from home.

➤ TRAVEL INSURERS: In the U.S.: **Access America** (✉ 6600 W. Broad St., Richmond, VA 23230, ☎ 800/284–8300, FAX 804/673–1491, WEB www.etravelprotection.com), **Travel Guard International** (✉ 1145 Clark St., Stevens Point, WI 54481, ☎ 715/345–0505 or 800/826–1300, FAX 800/955–8785, WEB www.noelgroup.com).

➤ INSURANCE INFORMATION: In the U.K.: **Association of British Insurers** (✉ 51–55 Gresham St., London EC2V 7HQ, U.K., ☎ 020/7600–3333, FAX 020/7696–8999, WEB www.abi.org.uk). In Canada: **RBC Travel Insurance** (✉ 6880 Financial Dr., Mississauga, Ontario L5N 7Y5, Canada, ☎ 905/791–8700, 800/668–4342 in Canada, FAX 905/816–2498, WEB www.royalbank.com). In Australia: **Insurance Council of Australia** (✉ Level 3, 56 Pitt St., Sydney NSW 2000, ☎ 02/9253–5100, FAX 02/9253–5111, WEB www.ica.com.au). In New Zealand: **Insurance Council of New Zealand** (✉ Box 474, Wellington, New Zealand, ☎ 04/472–5230, FAX 04/473–3011, WEB www.icnz.org.nz).

LANGUAGE

You'll often read that nearly all Germans speak some English. This is not the case in Berlin. Berliners who hail from the former West Germany will most likely have had English classes in school, but one legacy of the former Communist regime is that until 1989, East Berliners learned Russian, not English, as a second language. Whereas people who deal with tourists will generally speak English, shop assistants, waitstaff, and many public officials who grew up in the East might not. If you are in Berlin for any length of time, **be prepared with some basic German.**

When reading German, be aware of the following characters peculiar to German. "ß" as in Straße (street) is pronounced "ss" (thus "Strasse"). The vowels a (ä), o (ö), and u (ü) can each be written with or without the two dots above the letter. These are called umlauts and signify a change in how the vowel is pronounced. Some other letters to be aware of are the German z, which is pronounced "tz"; the j, pronounced "y"; the sch," pronounced "sh"; and the ch, pronounced like the "ch" in loch.

LANGUAGES FOR TRAVELERS

A phrase book and language-tape set can help get you started. *Fodor's German for Travelers* (available at bookstores everywhere) is excellent.

LODGING

Berlin has a wide range of accommodations from simple pensions to world-class hotels. The lodgings we list are the cream of the crop in each price category. Properties marked ✕⌂ are lodging establishments whose restaurants warrant a special trip. Standards in German hotels are generally high, and you can nearly always **expect courteous and polite service and clean and comfortable rooms.** During tourist season (May–October), room rates are fairly inflexible because of the high demand, particularly at the budget end of the market. Rates often drop in winter, and you may find it easier to negotiate a discount. We always list the facilities that are available—but we don't specify whether they cost extra: when pricing accommodations, always ask what's included and what costs extra. All taxes are included in a hotel's advertised price.

A list of more than 7,000 lodgings is available from the Deutsche Hotel- und Gaststättenverband (DEHOGA). Although there is no nationwide grading system for hotels in Germany, the DEHOGA's guide has one- to five-star ratings based on amenities offered. Most of their publications are in German.

CATEGORY	COST*
$$$$	over €250
$$$	€150–€250
$$	€75–€150
$	under €75

*All prices are for a standard double room, including tax and service

➤ LODGING LISTINGS: **Deutsche Hotel-und Gastättenverband** (DEHOGA; ✉ (An Weidendamm 1, D–10117 Berlin WEB www.dehoga.de).

APARTMENT RENTALS

The international staff at fine+mine can arrange apartments or private rooms for both short- and longer-term visits. Freiraum runs a guest house that has two apartments for short-term rentals, and and it can locate apartments elsewhere in Berlin for stays of of more than a month. The weekly listings magazines *Tip* and *Zitty* also have rental listings (in German). Look in the classified section at the back of the magazine under *"auf Zeit."*

➤ INTERNATIONAL AGENTS: **Interhome** (✉ 1990 N.E. 163rd St., Suite 110, N. Miami Beach, FL 33162, ☎ 305/940–2299 or 800/882–6864, FAX 305/940–2911, WEB www.interhome.com). **Villas International** (✉ 950 Northgate Dr., Suite 206, San Rafael, CA 94903, ☎ 415/499–9490 or 800/221–2260, FAX 415/499–9491, WEB www.villasintl.com).

➤ LOCAL AGENTS: **fine+mine** (✉ Neue Schönhauserstr. 20, 10178 Berlin-Mitte, ☎ 030/2355–120, FAX 030/2355–1212, WEB www.fineandmine.de). **Freiraum** (✉ Wienerstr. 14, 10999 Berlin-Kreuzberg, ☎ 030/618–2008, FAX 030/618–2006, WEB www.freiraum-berlin.com).

B&BS

B&Bs are not common in Berlin. Either of the local agents listed above can find something, and Berlin Tourismus Marketing also has information on a few individuals who offer private rooms.

HOME EXCHANGES

If you would like to exchange your home for someone else's, **join a home-exchange organization,** which will send you its updated listings of available exchanges for a year and will include your own listing in at least one of them. It's up to you to make specific arrangements.

➤ EXCHANGE CLUBS: **HomeLink International** (✉ Box 47747, Tampa, FL 33647, ☎ 813/975–9825 or 800/638–3841, FAX 813/910–8144, WEB www.homelink.org; $98 per year). **Intervac U.S.** (✉ Box 590504, San Francisco, CA 94159, ☎ 800/756–4663, FAX 415/435–7440, WEB www.intervacus.com; $93 yearly fee includes one catalogue and on-line access).

HOSTELS

No matter what your age, you can **save on lodging costs by staying at hostels.** In some 4,500 locations in more than 70 countries around the world, Hostelling International (HI), the umbrella group for a number of national youth-hostel associations, offers single-sex, dorm-style beds and, at many hostels, rooms for couples and family accommodations. Membership in any HI national hostel association, open to travelers of all ages, allows you to stay in HI-affiliated hostels at member rates; one-year membership is about $25 for adults (C$26.75 in Canada, £9.30 in the U.K., $30 in Australia, and $30 in New Zealand); hostels run about $10–$25 per night. Members have priority if the hostel is full; they're also eligible for discounts around the world, even on rail and bus travel in some countries.

Although Berlin has three official HI hostels, none of them are central, rates are relatively expensive, and they tend to be booked solid most of the year by German school groups. Luckily, there is also an increasing number of independent hostels. These are more central, with cheaper prices, no membership requirements, and a more flexible setup—no curfews, mixed dorms, and extra facilities such as kitchens, Internet access, or bars. They generally have a range of rooms, from dorm beds to rooms for couples or families. The price depends on how many beds are in the room, with single rooms around €25–€35 and dorm beds from €12. Staff members are young and international and will help to find you a bed elsewhere if they are full. It's wise to reserve at least two weeks in advance, especially in summer. Many of Berlin's independent hostels are listed on www. hostelseurope.com.

➤ BEST OPTIONS: **Circus–the hostel** (⌧ Rosa-Luxemburg-Str. 39–41, Mitte, D–10117, ☎ 030/2839–1433, FAX 030/2839–1484, WEB www. circus-berlin.de).**Die Fabrik** (⌧ Schlesische Str. 18, Kreuzberg, D–10997, ☎ 030/611–7116 or 030/617–5104, FAX 030/618–2974, WEB www. diefabrik.com). **Odyssee Globetrotter Hotel** (⌧ Grünberger Str. 23, Friedrichshain, D–10243, ☎ FAX 030/ 2900–0081, WEB www.hostel-berlin. de).

➤ IN GERMANY: **DJH Service GmbH** (⌧ Postfach 1462, D–32704 Detmold, ☎ 05231/74010, FAX 05231/ 74010, WEB www.djh.de).

➤ ORGANIZATIONS: **Hostelling International—American Youth Hostels** (⌧ 733 15th St. NW, Suite 840, Washington, DC 20005, ☎ 202/783–6161, FAX 202/783–6171, WEB www. hiayh.org). **Hostelling International—Canada** (⌧ 400–205 Catherine St., Ottawa, Ontario K2P 1C3, Canada, ☎ 613/237–7884, FAX 613/237–7868, WEB www.hostellingintl.ca). **Youth Hostel Association of England and Wales** (⌧ Trevelyan House, 8 St. Stephen's Hill, St. Albans, Hertfordshire AL1 2DY, U.K., ☎ 0870/ 8708808, FAX 01727/844126, WEB www.yha.org.uk). **Australian Youth Hostel Association** (⌧ 10 Mallett St., Camperdown, NSW 2050, Australia, ☎ 02/9565–1699, FAX 02/9565–1325, WEB www.yha.com.au). **Youth Hostels Association of New Zealand** (⌧ Level 3, 193 Cashel St., Box 436, Christchurch, New Zealand, ☎ 03/379–9970, FAX 03/365–4476, WEB www.yha. org.nz).

HOTELS

Berlin has a wide range of hotels, from small family-run affairs to large international chains. As there is no government star-rating system, price is the best guide to quality—generally you get what you pay for. Expensive hotels and international chains usually have air-conditioning (*Klimatisierung*), but smaller establishments may not, so ask in advance if it's important to you. All hotels listed have private bath (*Bad*) unless otherwise noted. Most just have showers (*Duschen*) in the bathrooms—ask for a tub (*Badewanne*) if you'd prefer one. Washcloths are usually not provided. When you reserve, specify if you want a double bed (*Doppelzimmer*) or two single beds (*Zweibettzimmer*). Queen and king beds (*extra gross*) are rare.

To be sure of getting the best and cheapest accommodations, **reserve early.** Berlin's hotels tend to fill up, particularly in summer and around major events. Take local events into account when planning your travel—sometimes lodging may be more scarce in the immediate vicinity of an event, but easier to find elsewhere. You may have to settle for a hotel farther out of the center at peak times, but the efficient public transportation system means this is not such a hardship. If you are concerned about noise, book a hotel room in a residential neighborhood. In areas in the former East Berlin, check whether there are tramlines running past the building, as this can be a source of annoyance. Many smaller hotels are in older buildings that may not have adequate sound insulation; **ask for a room facing the courtyard (***Hof***).**

➤ RESERVING A ROOM: Although most hotels will be able to cope with a reservation request in English, here is a sample text that may be useful if you run into any problems:

Sehr geehrte Damen und Herren (Dear Sir/Madam)!

Ich möchte ein Doppelzimmer / Zweibettzimmer mit Bad reservieren (I would like to reserve a double/twin room with bath) *und zwar vom. . . bis. . .* (from. . . until. . . [dates are written day/month/year] *Ich hätte gern ein Zimmer auf der oberen Etage / auf der unteren Etage / mit Ausblick / in ruhiger Lage* (I would like a room on a high floor / a low floor / with a view / a quiet room).

Können Sie mir bitte weitere Informationen auf Englisch über Ihr Hotel zuschicken (Please send me more information in English about your hotel). *Mit freundlichen Grüssen* (Kind regards).

➤ TOLL-FREE NUMBERS: **Best Western** (☎ 800/528–1234, WEB www. bestwestern.com). **Choice** (☎ 800/ 221–2222, WEB www.hotelchoice. com). **Clarion** (☎ 800/252–7466, WEB www.hotelchoice.com). **Comfort** (☎ 800/228–5150, WEB www.comfortinn.com). **Four Seasons** (☎ 800/ 332–3442, WEB www.fourseasons. com). **Hilton** (☎ 800/445–8667, WEB www.hilton.com). **Holiday Inn** (☎ 800/465–4329, WEB www. basshotels.com). **Hyatt Hotels & Resorts** (☎ 800/233–1234, WEB www. hyatt.com). **Inter-Continental** (☎ 800/327–0200, WEB www.interconti. com). **Quality Inn** (☎ 800/228– 5151, WEB www.qualityinn.com). **Ritz-Carlton** (☎ 800/241–3333, WEB www. ritzcarlton.com). **Westin Hotels & Resorts** (☎ 800/228–3000, WEB www. westin.com).

MAIL & SHIPPING

Post offices (*Deutsche Post*) are scattered throughout the city and are recognizable by the postal symbol, a black bugle on a yellow background. Stamps (*Briefmarken*) can also be bought at some news agencies and souvenir shops. Letters take approximately 3–4 days to the United Kingdom, 7–8 days to the United States, and 7–10 days to Australia and New Zealand. Post offices are generally open weekdays 8–6, Saturday 8–1. Some have extended opening hours; the Zoo station branch is open from Monday to Saturday 6 AM–midnight and Sunday 8 AM–midnight; Tegel Airport is open weekdays 6 AM–9 PM, weekends 8–8; Schönefeld Airport is open weekdays 8–7, weekends 8–3.

➤ POST OFFICES: **Zoo Station** (✉ Joachimsthaler Str. 7, Charlottenburg D–10623. ✉ Dorotheenstr. 97, Mitte D–10117;✉ Georgenstr. 12, Mitte D–10117; ✉ Rathausstr. 5, Mitte D–10178.

OVERNIGHT SERVICES

The Deutsche Post has an express international service that will deliver your letter or package the next day to countries within the EU, within 1–2 days to the United States, and slightly longer to Australia. A letter or package to the United States weighing less than 200 grams costs €50. You can drop off your mail at any post office, or it can be picked up for an extra fee. International carriers tend to be slightly cheaper (€35–€45 for the same letter) and provide more services.

➤ MAJOR SERVICES: **Deutsche Post Express International** (☎ 08105/ 2711, WEB www.deutschepost.de). **DHL** (✉ Schönefeld Airport, Gebäude G 005, ☎ 01803/258–258, FAX 030/6091–4221, WEB www.dhl.de). **FedEx** (☎ 0800/123–0800, WEB www. fedex.com). **UPS** (✉ Industriestr. 4–9 Tempelhof, ☎ 0800/822–6630, FAX 02131/947–222, WEB www.ups.com).

POSTAL RATES

Airmail letters to the United States, Canada, Australia, and New Zealand cost €1.50; postcards, €1. All letters to the United Kingdom and other European countries including Germany cost €.55; postcards, €.50. Letters heavier than 20 grams (7 ounces), or outside the standard dimensions of 5½–9¼ inches by 3½–5 inches by ⅕ inch are more expensive. Make sure you pay sufficient postage, or your letter may be downgraded to sea mail.

RECEIVING MAIL

You can arrange to have mail sent to you in care of any post office in Berlin; **have the envelope marked "Postlagernd" and with a short password.** They will hold the mail for you for 14 days. This service is free. Or you can have mail sent to an American Express office, which will hold your mail for up to 30 days. There's no charge to cardholders, holders of American Express traveler's checks, or anyone who has booked a vacation with American Express; otherwise the cost is €1 per letter.

SHIPPING PARCELS

Most major stores that cater to tourists will also ship your purchases home. You should check your insurance for coverage of possible damage. The companies listed under ☞

Overnight Services also have international shipping services, although these are quite expensive.

If you are sending goods *to* Germany by mail, be aware that the recipient will have to pay a 25% duty charge if the value stated on the customs slip is greater than €50.

MONEY MATTERS

Berlin has a high standard of living, but prices for hotels, food, and drink are less expensive than in other major European capitals, such as Paris, Rome, and, particularly, London. Some things—gas, food, hotels, and trains, to name but a few—are more expensive than in the United States, but in 2001 the strong dollar was a benefit to American travelers.

Prices throughout this guide are given for adults. Substantially reduced fees are almost always available for children, students, and senior citizens. For information on taxes, *see* Taxes, *below*.

ATMS

Twenty-four-hour ATMs (*Geldautomaten*) can be accessed with PLUS or Cirrus credit and banking cards. Some German banks exact €2–€5 fees for use of their ATMs. Your PIN number should be set for exactly four digits; if it's not, go to your bank and change it for your trip. Because some ATM keypads show no letters, **know the numeric equivalent of your password.**

CREDIT CARDS

Though major U.S. credit cards are accepted in Germany, they are not used as widely as they are in the English-speaking world. Keep some cash at hand, as small retailers and service providers may not accept credit. If your card has a four-digit PIN number, you can use it at German ATMs.

Throughout this guide, the following abbreviations are used: **AE,** American Express; **DC,** Diner's Club; **MC,** MasterCard; and **V,** Visa.

➤ REPORTING LOST CARDS: **American Express** (☎ 01805/840–840 or 069/9797-1000). **Diners Club** (☎ 05921/861–234 or 0180/234–5454).

MasterCard (☎ 0130/819–104 or 069/7933–1910). Visa (☎ 0800/814–9100).

CURRENCY

2001 was the last year of the deutsche Mark, the currency that sustained Germany's economic power for nearly the whole postwar period. Euro (€) notes and coins were issued on January 1, 2002. Until February 28, 2002, you will be able to use both deutsche Marks and euros; and as of March 1, Germany along with France, Austria, Belgium, the Netherlands, Luxembourg, Spain, Portugal, Ireland, Finland, and Italy will have a single currency. During the transition you may get your change in euros even if you pay in Marks. Until the withdrawal of the Mark, stores, restaurants, and other businesses are legally obliged to show prices in both currencies. Read prices carefully (there are about DM 2 to the euro) and be sure that bills, credit-card charges, and other monetary transactions indicate whether the price is in euros (€) or Marks (DM). The euro is divided into 100 eurocents (€.01). There are 500-, 200-, 100-, 50-, 20-, 10-, and 5-euro bills. Coins are minted in different designs (but in the same size and shape) by each of the participating countries. They exist in denominations from 1 eurocent to 2 euros. At press time the euro stood at €1.09 to the U.S. dollar, €.69 to the Canadian dollar, €1.59 to the British pound sterling, and €.53 to the Australian dollar.

CURRENCY EXCHANGE

For the most favorable rates, **change money through banks.** Although ATM transaction fees may be higher abroad than at home, ATM rates are excellent because they are based on wholesale rates offered only by major banks. You won't do as well at exchange booths in airports or rail and bus stations, in hotels, in restaurants, or in stores. To avoid lines at airport exchange booths, **get a bit of local currency before you leave home.**

➤ EXCHANGE SERVICES: **International Currency Express** (☎ 888/278–6628 for orders, WEB www.foreignmoney.com). **Thomas Cook Currency Services** (☎ 800/287–7362 for telephone

orders and retail locations, WEB www.
us.thomascook.com).

TRAVELER'S CHECKS

With few exceptions, Berlin retailers
do not accept traveler's checks. **Cash
your traveler's checks with the agency
that issued them** (Amex, Thomas
Cook, etc.) to save on fees. Lost or
stolen checks can usually be replaced
within 24 hours. To ensure a speedy
refund, buy your own traveler's
checks—don't let someone else pay
for them; irregularities like this can
cause delays. The person who bought
the checks should make the call to
request a refund.

PACKING

What you pack depends more on the
time of year than on any particular
dress code. Winters can be bitterly
cold; summers are warm but with
days that suddenly turn cool and
rainy. Pack dressy outfits for formal
restaurants and performances, casual
clothes for elsewhere. Jeans are as
popular in Germany as anywhere else
and are perfectly acceptable for
sightseeing and informal dining. In
the evening men will probably feel
more comfortable wearing a jacket
and tie in more expensive restaurants,
although it is almost never required.
Many Berlin women are extremely
fashion-conscious and wear stylish
outfits to restaurants and the theater.

To discourage purse snatchers and
pickpockets, **carry a handbag with
long straps** that you can sling across
your body bandolier style and that
has a zippered compartment for
money and other valuables.

For stays in budget hotels, **take your
own washcloth and soap.** Many
provide no soap at all or only a small
bar.

If you are traveling with a wine
opener, pocketknife or any other kind
of knife, or toy weapons, **pack them
in check-in luggage.** These are considered potential weapons and are not
permitted as carry-on items.

In your carry-on luggage, **pack an
extra pair of eyeglasses or contact
lenses and enough of any medication**
you take to last the entire trip. You
may also ask your doctor to write a

spare prescription using the drug's
generic name, since brand names may
vary from country to country. In
luggage to be checked, **never pack
prescription drugs or valuables.** To
avoid customs delays, carry medica-
tions in their original packaging. And
don't forget to carry with you the
addresses of offices that handle refunds of lost traveler's checks. Check
Fodor's How to Pack (available in
bookstores everywhere) for more tips.

CHECKING LUGGAGE

How many carry-on bags you can
bring with you is up to the airline.
Most allow two, but not always, so
make sure that everything you carry
aboard will fit under your seat or in
the overhead bin, and get to the gate
early.

If you are flying internationally, note
that baggage allowances may be
determined not by piece but by
weight—generally 88 pounds (40
kilograms) in first class, 66 pounds
(30 kilograms) in business class,
and 44 pounds (20 kilograms) in
economy.

Airline liability for baggage is limited
to $1,250 per person on flights within
the United States. On international
flights it amounts to $9.07 per pound
or $20 per kilogram for checked
baggage (roughly $640 per 70-pound
bag) and $400 per passenger for
unchecked baggage. You can buy
additional coverage at check-in for
about $10 per $1,000 of coverage,
but it excludes a rather extensive list
of items, shown on your airline ticket.

Before departure, **itemize your bags'
contents** and their worth, and label
the bags with your name, address,
and phone number. (If you use your
home address, cover it so potential
thieves can't see it readily.) Inside
each bag, **pack a copy of your
itinerary.** At check-in, **make sure that
each bag is correctly tagged** with the
destination airport's three-letter code.
If your bags arrive damaged or fail to
arrive at all, file a written report with
the airline before leaving the airport.

PASSPORTS & VISAS

When traveling internationally, **carry
your passport** even if you don't need
one (it's always the best form of I.D.)

and **make two photocopies of the data page** (one for someone at home and another for you, carried separately from your passport). If you lose your passport, promptly call the nearest embassy or consulate and the local police.

ENTERING GERMANY

U.S., Canadian, British, Australian, and New Zealand citizens need only a valid passport to enter Germany for stays of up to 90 days.

PASSPORT OFFICES

The best time to apply for a passport or to renew is in fall and winter. Before any trip, check your passport's expiration date, and, if necessary, renew it as soon as possible.

➤ AUSTRALIAN CITIZENS: **Australian Passport Office** (☎ 131–232, WEB www.dfat.gov.au/passports).

➤ CANADIAN CITIZENS: **Passport Office** (☎ 819/994–3500; 800/ 567–6868 in Canada, WEB www. dfait-maeci.gc.ca/passport).

➤ NEW ZEALAND CITIZENS: **New Zealand Passport Office** (☎ 04/494– 0700, WEB www.passports.govt.nz).

➤ U.K. CITIZENS: **London Passport Office** (☎ 0870/521–0410, WEB www. ukpa.gov.uk) for fees and documentation requirements and to request an emergency passport.

➤ U.S. CITIZENS: **National Passport Information Center** (☎ 900/225– 5674; calls are 35¢ per minute for automated service, $1.05 per minute for operator service; WEB www.travel. state.gov/npicinfo.html).

PUBLIC TRANSPORTATION

Berlin has one of the most efficient public-transportation systems in Europe. Known as the BVG, the system includes subway (U-Bahn) and suburban (S-Bahn) train lines, buses, trams (in eastern Berlin only), and even a number of ferry services on the Spree and Havel rivers, all of which are integrated to make every part of the city easily accessible. **Get a route map off the Internet or from any BVG information booth.** There's a main BVG information office on Hardenbergplatz, right in front of the Bahnhof Zoo train station.

BUS & TRAM

Berlin's trams and double-decker buses are comfortable, efficient, and only rarely overcrowded, but they are slower than the subway. Worth a trip just for the sights en route is Bus 100. A regular BVG public bus, Bus 100 runs from Zoo station to Prenzlauer Berg and back, passing many landmarks, such as Unter den Linden, the Reichstag, Alexanderplatz, and the Brandenburg Gate. If you're lucky, you'll step on board with an enthusiastic driver who provides impromptu commentary for the tourists. Buses run every 5–10 minutes on this busy route.

Bus and tram stops are marked by a green *H* on a yellow background. If you've lost, **seek out one of the larger stops, which will have a neighborhood map marked with a conspicuous blue circle to tell you where you are.** Posted schedules are easy to read and fairly reliable. Buses are often a more direct means of travel to attractions than the subway, so don't shy away from them.

The farther you go from the center of town, the more buses and trams replace the subway as the main form of transport. For a taste of the Communist architecture of former East Berlin, **hop on any of the trams at Hackescher Markt (1–5) and head toward the rarely touristed districts of Hohenschönhausen or Weissensee.** Between about 12:30 AM and 5:30 AM, night trams and buses run on many routes. You will recognize these by the *N* that precedes the route number. Buses and trams on night routes run only once or twice an hour, so check the timetable to avoid a long, lonely wait at the bus stop.

U- & S-BAHN—THE SUBWAY

Two networks, the S-Bahn and the U-Bahn, make up Berlin's metropolitan rail system and are the fastest way to get around Berlin.

Each line is color coded, and platform signs tell you the line number and destination of the next train. If you want to use public transport after midnight, **check when the last train leaves.** S-Bahn trains run every 10–20 minutes from around 5 AM to 12:30 AM, with additional services every hour on weekend mornings from 12:30 AM to 5:00 AM. U-Bahn trains run more frequently. Generally speaking, they run every 5–10 minutes from around 5 AM to 12:30 AM, with services running until 1:30 AM on weekend mornings. The only U-Bahn lines that run 24 hours are the U–12 and U–9, both of which run every 15 minutes through Friday and Saturday nights.

FERRY

Berlin is crisscrossed by arms of the Rivers Havel and Spree, and there are six ferries that form part of the public transport system. As a visitor you probably won't have to use them, as they don't cover any of the major points of interest. If you want to get a taste of Berlin's waterways without paying the price of a boat tour, your BVG public transport ticket allows you to travel on the ferry lines at no extra cost. Ferry lines F–10, F–11, and F–12 run during daylight hours all year round. Ferry lines F–21, F–23, and F–24 run only from Tuesday to Sunday during the tourist season (from Good Friday until the beginning of October).

FARES & SCHEDULES

If you are just making a short trip, buy a *Kurzstreckentarif;* this ticket allows you to ride six bus stops or three U-Bahn or S-Bahn stops for €1.20. For €2.10, an *Einzelfahrausweis,* or single journey ticket, covers all but the outlying suburban areas and allows you to make an unlimited number of changes between trains, buses, and trams within two hours. If you're going to cover the city extensively within a day, **buy the day ticket** (*Tageskarte*) for €6.10; it is good on all trains and buses in Zones A and B until 3 AM on the day after validation. The group day ticket, €10.75, offers the same benefits as the day card but for up to five people (adults or children) traveling together. A seven-day tourist pass costs €22 and allows unlimited travel on all city buses and trains for fare Zones A and B. The above tickets are all available in a version that allows travel in Zones A, B, and C. These cost around 10% more than the Zone A–B ticket; only buy one if you are going to outlying areas such as Potsdam, the Sachsenhausen concentration camp, or the Schönefeld airport.

If you're in Berlin for three or four days, **consider the Berlin Welcome-Card.** It offers good value, especially if you're traveling as a family. For €16.35 this ticket allows one adult and up to three children 72 hours of unlimited travel in Zones A, B, and C as well as free admission or reductions of up to 50% for sightseeing trips, museums, theaters, and other events and attractions. WelcomeCards are sold at all BVG ticket counters, Berlin Tourismus Marketing offices, and many Berlin hotels.

BVG tickets are available from vending machines at U-Bahn and S-Bahn stations, bus stops, from bus drivers, as well as from authorized retail outlets. Tickets must be validated before travel. To validate, insert your ticket into the machines on S- and U-Bahn platforms or on-board buses and trams. Ticket inspections are not uncommon. The inspectors (known as *Controletti*) can be in or out of uniform, and they're hard to avoid because they board trains, buses, and trams in groups of three or more. There are signs up everywhere explaining the ticketing system in English and German, so feigning ignorance of the local fare scheme or language probably won't help you wheedle your way out of a €30 fine.

➤ INFORMATION: **BVG** (✉ Hardenbergpl., opposite Zoo station ☎ 030/19449 [24-hr service] or 030/752–7020, 🕸 www.bvg.de).

REST ROOMS

German public toilets are usually kept clean and hygienic by white-coated attendants, to whom you should leave some change as a tip. The cylindrical city toilets around the city are coin-operated (€1) and self-cleaning. Public toilets in major railway stations usually cost €.50–€1. Restaurants that have seating must legally also have free rest-room facilities and must let you use them, although they may get annoyed if groups come through without ordering anything. Department stores and museums have rest rooms with attendants. At gas stations ask the cashier for the key to the bathroom.

SAFETY

You are unlikely to be troubled with problems of personal safety in Berlin. Do be sensible, though—as in most major cities, pickpockets sometimes operate in crowded locations, so keep your valuables in inside pockets at all times or leave them in the hotel safe. Thieves have also been known to target cafés and bars popular with tourists, for example, along Oranienburgerstrasse, where the constant flux of patrons make it easy to walk off with a bag unnoticed. Make sure you **know where your personal belongings are at all times.** Walking around the central districts is safe for both men and women, even late at night. There have been some incidents of right-wing violence in the outer eastern suburbs such as Lichtenberg and Marzahn, so if you look noticeably non-German or gay, it's best to avoid these areas, particularly at night. If you do run into trouble, Berlin has a large police presence, and they will do their best to help.

SENIOR-CITIZEN TRAVEL

German wanderlust doesn't end with retirement. You'll see plenty of older couples traveling together, socializing over their beers with gusto.

The German railways offer a special senior pack to people over 55. For €10 you get return seat reservations, a voucher for a free drink or snack, and numerous discounts on travel-related goods and accommodations in tourist destinations. In addition, railway staff will be on hand to help and carry your luggage when you board, change trains, or disembark. The offer is not currently available in all of Germany, so check first at any railway station.

To qualify for age-related discounts, **mention your senior-citizen status up front** when booking hotel reservations (not when checking out). When renting a car, ask about promotional car-rental discounts, which can be cheaper than senior-citizen rates.

➤ EDUCATIONAL PROGRAMS: **Elderhostel** (✉ 11 Ave. de Lafayette, Boston, MA 02111-1746, ☎ 877/426–8056, FAX 877/426–2166, WEB www.elderhostel.org). **Interhostel** (✉ University of New Hampshire, 6 Garrison Ave., Durham, NH 03824, ☎ 603/862–1147 or 800/733–9753, FAX 603/862–1113, WEB www.learn.unh.edu).

SHOPPING

Shopkeepers in Berlin are very competent and knowledgeable about their wares. Leather goods are very stylish here, but check to see that your business cards fit into a European-made wallet before buying one. As for clothing, even affordable fashions can have a distinct flair not found in the many retail chains in the United States.

SIGHTSEEING TOURS

BIKE TOURS

As the city is mostly flat and equipped with well-respected bicycle paths, a bike tour can be an efficient and fun way of getting around the far-flung sights. Insider Tours(☞ Walking Tours, *below*) offers a four-hour tour in English for €18. Bike rentals can also be arranged for €8. Fahrradstation runs tours in German, but the guides will provide some commentary in English if you ask. Tours last 2–3 hours and cost €10. All tours depart from the Friedrichstrasse station.

➤ TOUR OPERATORS: **Fahrradstation** (✉ Friedrichstr. station, ☎ 030/2045–4500).

BOAT TOURS

Berlin has more bridges than Venice, and a boat tour of the canals can be a pleasant way to see the sights. Three companies offer very similar 3- to 3½-hour tours for around €10. Departure points include Schlossbrücke, Hansabrücke, Märkisches Ufer, Kottbusser Brücke, and Corneliusbrücke. In summer these companies run longer tours, to Postdam, the Havel lakes, and Brandenburg. Cruising through the lakes past forests and historic palaces is a delightful way to spend a sunny day.

➤ TOUR OPERATORS: **Reederei Bruno Winkler** (☎ 030/349–9595, WEB www.reedereiwinkler.de). **Reederei Heinz Riedel** (☎ 030/693–4646). **Stern- und Kreisschiffahrt** (☎ 030/536–3600).

BUS TOURS

For the cheapest bus tour in town, **take Bus 100 from Alexander Platz to Zoo station** (or vice versa). For the price of a public transport ticket you will be driven past many of the major sights. More or less identical live or taped bus tours in English are offered by several companies. Most of them are organized on a hop-on, hop-off basis and cover all the major sights. Tours cost €10–€20 and depart from clearly marked stops on the Kurfürstendamm near Zoo station.

➤ TOUR OPERATORS: **Berolina Berlin-Service** (☎ 030/8856–8030, WEB www.berolina-berlin.com). **Berliner Bären Stadtrundfahrten** (BBS; ☎ 030/3519–5270). **Bus Verkehr Berlin** (BVB; ☎ 030/885–9980, WEB www.bvb.net). **Severin & Kühn** (☎ 030/880–4190, WEB www.severin-kuehn-berlin.de). **Sightseeing Berlin** (Stadtrundfahrtbüro Berlin; ☎ 030/261–2001). **Top Tour Berlin** (☎ 030/2562–4720).

PRIVATE GUIDES

Both Insider Tours and Berlin Walks (☞ Walking Tours, *below*) can arrange private, customized tours, as can Berlin Starting Point. In addition to a variety of customized theme tours, City Guide Berlin can show you the city from a helicopter, motorcycle, biplane—you name it!

➤ TOUR OPERATORS: **Berlin Starting Point** (☎ 030/6272–1303, WEB www.berlin-starting-point.de). **City Guide Berlin** (☎ 03329/614–397, WEB www.c-g-b.de).

WALKING TOURS

A walking tour is one of the best ways to familiarize yourself with Berlin's history and sights. Insider Tours' general tour of the city lasts just over three hours and takes in the sights from Zoo station to Alexanderplatz. The guides, all native English speakers who are long-term Berliners, will not only share their inside knowledge of the city and its turbulent history but will also provide you with a host of tips to help you get the most out of your stay. For more handy hints **ask your guide for a copy of their helpful information booklet.** Terry Brewer was stationed in Berlin

with the British Forces and later with the diplomatic service. His firsthand accounts of divided and reunified Berlin are a highlight of the six-hour "Brewer's Best of Berlin" tour, which takes in the old Jewish quarter, the Third Reich government area, the remnants of the divided city, and the legacy of the Prussian kings. Berlin Walks offers theme tours (Third Reich sites, Jewish life, Potsdam) in addition to their introductory "Discover Berlin" tour. All tours cost around €8–€10; discounts are available to students and WelcomeCard holders.

➤ TOUR OPERATORS: **Insider Tours** (✉ meet at McDonald's at Zoo station, ☎ 030/692–3149, WEB www.insidertour.de). **Brewer's Best of Berlin** (✉ meet at New Synagogue, ☎ 030/2839–1433). **The Original Berlin Walks** (✉ meet at taxi stand outside Zoo station and west end of Hackescher Markt S-Bahn station, ☎ 030/301–9194, WEB www.berlinwalks.com).

STUDENTS IN BERLIN

Before coming to Berlin, **make sure you have a current International Student Identity Card (ISIC).** You will save lots of money with an internationally recognized student card. Students are eligible for discounts of up to 50% in most museums, theaters, and tourist attractions on presentation of a student card. You will have to pay full price on public transport—the advertised student tickets are only for local students. However, if you are under 26, you can take advantage of the German railways' TwenTicket (*twen*, like 20) for longer journeys. This gives you a 20% discount on rail travel within Germany and 20%–60% off for international travel. The ISIC Web site has a list of student travel agents worldwide that can issue the ISIC card, as well as a detailed list of student discounts available in Berlin.

➤ IDs & SERVICES: **Council Travel** (CIEE; ✉ 205 E. 42nd St., 15th floor, New York, NY 10017, ☎ 212/822–2700 or 888/268–6245, FAX 212/822–2699, WEB www.councilexchanges.org), for mail orders only, in the U.S. **ISIC** (WEB www.isic.org). **Travel Cuts**

(✉ 187 College St., Toronto, Ontario M5T 1P7, Canada, ☎ 416/979–2406 or 800/667–2887 in Canada, FAX 416/979–8167, WEB www.travelcuts.com).

TAXES

All airport taxes are included in the price of your ticket. There is no special hotel tax in Germany; VAT is included in the room rate.

VALUE-ADDED TAX

Germany has a 16% value-added tax (VAT) on most goods and services. In German it is called *Mehrwertsteuer,* and you will see it abbreviated as MWST on bills and receipts. Generally, prices of goods already include VAT, but services often don't—for example, VAT will be added to the price the mechanic quotes to repair your car. When traveling to a non-EU country, you are entitled to a refund of the VAT you pay (multiply the price of an item by 13.8% in Germany to find out how much VAT is embedded in the price). Some goods, like books and antiquities, carry a 6.5% VAT as a percentage of the purchase price.

Global Refund is a VAT refund service that makes getting your money back hassle-free. The service is available Europe-wide at 130,000 affiliated stores. In participating stores **ask for the Global Refund refund form** (called a Shopping Cheque). If a store is not a participating member of Global Refund, they'll probably have a form called an *Ausfuhr-Abnehmerbescheinigung,* which Global Refund can also process, for a higher fee.

When you leave the European Union, you must be prepared to **show your purchases to customs officials** before they will stamp your refund form.Go to the "Zoll" or customs office before checking your luggage at the airport (at Tegel, it's behind the information office). Present your VAT forms and original receipts. The customs office will give you a stamped export certificate, which you then bring to a refund counter for an on-the-spot cash refund in the form of cash, check, or a refund to your credit-card account, minus a charge for processing. For example, if you bought clothes worth €250, you would get back approximately €25 instead of €35.

There are Global Refund counters at every major airport and border crossing, as well as at the major railway stations in Berlin. At Tegel airport, the Global Refund desk is around the corner from the customs office.

➤ VAT REFUNDS: **Global Refund** (✉ 99 Main St., Suite 307, Nyack, NY 10960, ☎ 800/566–9828, FAX 845/348–1549, WEB www.globalrefund.com).

TAXIS

Taxi drivers in Berlin aren't known for their high spirits, but they are honest enough, and the cars are clean. Even late at night it's not unusual to see a woman driving a taxi, which is an indication of just how safe the city is. You don't have to search too hard to find a taxi in the inner districts. Cabs are painted beige and have a lighted taxi sign on the roof. You can hail a taxi on the street, hop into any car at a stand, or place an order with one of the companies listed below. Not all dispatchers speak German, so it may be easier if you ask a staff member at a hotel or restaurant to call one for you.

FARES

Taxi fares are calculated on the basis of a flagfall (€2.05) and a per-kilometer rate (€0.92–€1.23). An additional €1.02 is charged if you order a taxi. If you are only traveling a short distance, ask the driver for a *Kurzstreckentarif* as soon as you enter the cab. For just €3, this deal buys you a short ride of less than 2 km (1 mi) or five minutes. You can take advantage of this fare only if you hail a cab on the street. It's not necessary to tip the driver, but it's normal to round the fare up a mark or two. Here's a service worth knowing about: employees of the public transport company, BVG, will call a taxi to meet you at the station if it's after 8 PM.

In the tourist season students operate *Velotaxis,* a rickshaw service system, along Kurfürstendamm, Unter den Linden, and other touristy areas. Just hail one on the street or look for the VELOTAXI-STAND signs along the boulevards mentioned. The fare is €.50 for up to 1 km (½ mi), €2.56 for a tour between sightseeing landmarks (for example, from the Europa-Center to the Brandenburger Tor), and €7.65 for 30 minutes of travel. Velotaxis operate April–October, daily 1–8.

➤ TAXI COMPANIES: **Cityfunk** (☎ 030/ 210–202). **Funktaxi** (☎ 030/261– 026). **Taxifunk** (☎ 030/443–322). **Würfelfunk Berlin** (☎ 030/210–101).

TELEPHONES

AREA & COUNTRY CODES

The country code for Germany is 49. The city code for Berlin is 030. When dialing any German number from abroad, drop the initial 0 from the area or city code. Within Berlin, you do not have to dial 030. The country code is 1 for the United States and Canada, 61 for Australia, 64 for New Zealand, and 44 for the United Kingdom.

DIRECTORY & OPERATOR ASSISTANCE

The German telephone system is fully automatic, and it's unlikely you'll have to employ the services of an operator unless you're seeking information. In case of service difficulties call 0180/200–1033. You can also make national and international collect calls through this number. For English language directory assistance dial 11837 and for international directory assistance, 11834. All international operators speak English. Try to locate the number you're after in the phone book or on the Web (www.teleauskunft.de), because directory assistance is costly. Calls to 11837 cost €0.74 and to 11834 €1.40 per minute, respectively.

INTERNATIONAL CALLS

International calls can be made from just about any telephone booth in Germany. It costs only €.24 per minute to call the United States, day or night, no matter how long the call lasts. If you have access to a private telephone, ask your host for a cheap call-by-call prefix, which can be used to make calls at less than 20% of the rate you'd pay at a phone booth. Otherwise, use a phone card or make international calls from post offices, where you pay the clerk the cost of

the call plus a €1 connection fee. If you don't have a good deal with a calling card, there are many stores that offer international calls at rates well below that which you would pay from a phone booth. At a hotel, rates will be at least double the regular charge, so **never make international calls from your room.**

LOCAL CALLS

A local call costs minimum €0.10 for between 1½ and 4 minutes, depending on the time of day.

LONG-DISTANCE SERVICES

AT&T, MCI, and Sprint access codes make calling long distance relatively convenient, but you may find the local access number blocked in many hotel rooms. First ask the hotel operator to connect you. If the hotel operator balks, ask for an international operator, or dial the international operator yourself. One way to improve your odds of getting connected to your long-distance carrier is to travel with more than one company's calling card (a hotel may block Sprint, for example, but not MCI). If all else fails, call from a pay phone.

➤ ACCESS CODES: In Germany: **AT&T Direct** (☎ 0130–0010 or 0800/225–5288). **MCI WorldPhone** (☎ 0130–0012). **Sprint International Access** (☎ 0130–0013).

MOBILE PHONES

Germany has a GSM cell-phone network, which is compatible with digital mobile phones from Australia, New Zealand, the United Kingdom, and the United States. Your home network will be able to advise you on how to use your cell phone or pager while in Germany.

PUBLIC PHONES

Most telephone booths in Germany now are card-operated, and it's risky to assume you'll find a coin-operated booth when you need one, so **buy a phone card.** You can purchase one at any German post office (also available at many newsstands). They come in denominations of €6 and €25. Most phone booths have instructions in English as well as German. Another advantage of the card is it charges only what the call cost. Coin-operated phones don't make change. If you have a cell phone, bring it, because even having a phone card in hand won't help the fact that phone booths aren't particularly widespread.

TIME

Berlin (like the rest of Germany) is on Central European Time (+0100 UTC/ GMT)—the same time zone as Paris, Rome, Vienna, and many other central and western European cities. It is one hour ahead of London, six hours ahead of New York, seven hours ahead of Chicago, and nine hours ahead of Los Angeles. As in the United States, Germany and most other European countries move their clocks forward one hour for daylight saving during the warmer months. For this reason the time difference between Berlin and Sydney is eight hours when Germany is on daylight saving time (from April to October), and 10 hours when Australia is (from October to April). Germans use military time (1 PM is indicated as 13:00) and write the date before the month, so October 3 will appear as 03.10.

TIPPING

Generous tipping is not a feature of German culture. The service charge on bills is sufficient for most tips in your hotel, though you might **tip bellhops and porters**; €1 per bag or service is ample. It's also customary to **leave a small tip for the cleaning staff** (a euro per night will do). Whether you tip the desk clerk depends on whether he or she has given you any special service. Concierges hold a prestigious position and they don't expect tips for small services. If one does go above the call of duty for you, a €10 tip is appreciated.

Service charges are included in all restaurant checks (listed as *Bedienung*), as is tax (listed as *MWST*). Nonetheless, it is customary to **round up the bill to the nearest euro or to leave about 5%** (give it to the waiter or waitress as you pay the bill; don't leave it on the table, as that's considered rude). Bartenders and servers also expect you to round the bill up a euro or so.

In taxis **round up the fare to the nearest euro** as a tip. Only give more

if you have particularly cumbersome or heavy luggage.

Public toilets may have attendants, or you may see a small plate for coins on the wash basin or bench. In either case you are expected to leave a small tip (less than €1) for the cleaner.

TOURS & PACKAGES

Because everything is prearranged on a prepackaged tour or independent vacation, you spend less time planning—and often get it all at a good price.

BOOKING WITH AN AGENT

Travel agents are excellent resources. But it's a good idea to collect brochures from several agencies as some agents' suggestions may be influenced by relationships with tour and package firms that reward them for volume sales. If you have a special interest, **find an agent with expertise in that area**; ASTA(☞ Travel Agencies, *below*) has a database of specialists worldwide.

Make sure your travel agent knows the accommodations and other services of the place being recommended. Ask about the hotel's location, room size, beds, and whether it has a pool, room service, or programs for children, if you care about these. Has your agent been there in person or sent others whom you can contact?

Do some homework on your own, too: local tourism boards can provide information about lesser-known and small-niche operators, some of which may sell only direct.

BUYER BEWARE

Each year consumers are stranded or lose their money when tour operators—even large ones with excellent reputations—go out of business. So **check out the operator**. Ask several travel agents about its reputation, and try to **book with a company that has a consumer-protection program**. (Look for information in the company's brochure.) In the United States, members of the National Tour Association and the United States Tour Operators Association are required to set aside funds to cover your payments and travel arrangements in the event that the company defaults. It's also a good idea to choose a company that participates in the American Society of Travel Agents' Tour Operator Program (TOP); ASTA will act as mediator in any disputes between you and your tour operator.

Remember that the more your package or tour includes the better you can predict the ultimate cost of your vacation. Make sure you know exactly what is covered, and **beware of hidden costs.** Are taxes, tips, and transfers included? Entertainment and excursions? These can add up.

➤ TOUR-OPERATOR RECOMMENDA-TIONS: **American Society of Travel Agents** (☞ Travel Agencies, *below*). **National Tour Association** (NTA; ✉ 546 E. Main St., Lexington, KY 40508, ☎ 859/226–4444 or 800/682–8886, WEB www.ntaonline.com). **United States Tour Operators Association** (USTOA; ✉ 342 Madison Ave., Suite 1522, New York, NY 10173, ☎ 212/599–6599 or 800/468–7862, FAX 212/599–6744, WEB www.ustoa.com).

TRAIN TRAVEL
TO AND FROM BERLIN

Unlike other major German cities, Berlin lacks a central station, or *Hauptbahnhof*. Instead, there are a number of main stations, each of which serves one or more lines. Most trains to major cities pass through the stations Zoo and Ostbahnhof; regional services may stop at Alexanderplatz and/or Friedrichstrasse. Other trains (particularly those to the north and east) stop only at Lichtenberg. You can continue your journey on Berlin's S-Bahn network free of charge if you have a valid Deutsche Bahn (DB) train ticket.

Germany's national railway, the Deutsche Bahn, provides comprehensive service from Berlin to German and European destinations. Tickets are expensive if you pay full fare, but you can get a good deal if you **take advantage of a range of specials.**

CUTTING COSTS

Some specials to watch out for: For €20 the Schönes Wochenende ticket

gives you unlimited travel for up to five adults on any local (slow) train in Germany on Saturday or Sunday; also for €20 the Brandenburg ticket entitles up to five adults to one day of travel within Berlin and Brandenburg (express trains excluded); for €35 the Guten Abend ticket gives you unlimited travel on all trains in Germany between 7 PM and 3 AM Sunday–Friday, or for €43 between 2 PM and 3 AM on Saturday. Current specials are published on the DB Web site; click on "international guests" for English-language information.

➤ TRAIN INFORMATION: **Deutsche Bahn** (☎ 01805/996–633, WEB www.bahn.de).

TRAVEL AGENCIES

A good travel agent puts your needs first. Look for an agency that has been in business at least five years, emphasizes customer service, and has someone on staff who specializes in your destination. In addition, **make sure the agency belongs to a professional trade organization.** The American Society of Travel Agents (ASTA), with more than 26,000 members in some 170 countries, is the largest and most influential in the field. Operating under the motto "Without a travel agent, you're on your own," it maintains and enforces a strict code of ethics and will step in to help mediate any agent-client disputes if necessary. ASTA also maintains a Web site that includes a directory of agents.(If a travel agency is also acting as your tour operator, *see* Buyer Beware *in* Tours & Packages, *above*.)

➤ LOCAL AGENCIES: **Euroaide** (✉ Hardenbergpl., inside the Zoologischer Garten train station, ☎ 030/2974–9241). **Reiseland American Express Reisebüro** (✉ Wittenbergerpl., Bayreuther Str. 37 D–10787, ☎ 030/2149–8363; Friedrichstr. 172 D–10017, ☎ 030/238–4102, WEB www.reiseland-american-express.de).

➤ LOCAL AGENT REFERRALS: **American Society of Travel Agents** (ASTA; ✉ 1101 King St., Suite 200, Alexandria, VA 22314 ☎ 800/965–2782 24-hr hot line, FAX 703/739–7642, WEB www.astanet.com). **Association of British Travel Agents** (✉ 68–71

Newman St., London W1T 3AH, U.K., ☎ 020/7637–2444, FAX 020/7637–0713, WEB www.abtanet.com). **Association of Canadian Travel Agents** (✉ 130 Albert St., Suite 1705, Ottawa, Ontario K1P 5G4, Canada, ☎ 613/237–3657, FAX 613/237–7052, WEB www.acta.net). **Australian Federation of Travel Agents** (✉ Level 3, 309 Pitt St., Sydney NSW 2000, Australia, ☎ 02/9264–3299, FAX 02/9264–1085, WEB www.afta.com.au). **Travel Agents' Association of New Zealand** (✉ Level 5, Paxus House, 79 Boulcott St., Box 1888, Wellington 10033, New Zealand, ☎ 04/499–0104, FAX 04/499–0827, WEB www.taanz.org.nz).

VISITOR INFORMATION

For information in English on all aspects of the city, pick up a copy of *Berlin—the magazine* (€1.75) from any tourist office.

Berlin's tourist office (Berlin Tourismus Marketing) is a privatized service. Its local number (030/250–025) is for hotel bookings only. Calls to the information line cost €1.21 a minute. However, another phone number is designated for calls from abroad, and callers need only pay their home phone rate to obtain both information and hotel bookings. The main office is in the heart of western downtown in the Europa-Center and is open Monday–Saturday 8:30 AM–8:30 PM, Sunday 10–6:30. Other offices are found at the Brandenburg Gate, open daily 9:30–6, and at Tegel Airport, open daily 5 AM–10:30 PM. The Brandenburg Gate office functions more as a souvenir shop than an information center. Request for brochures and information on Berlin can also be sent to any of the German National Tourist offices.

➤ BERLIN TOURIST OFFICES: **Berlin Tourismus Marketing** (✉ Europa-Center, Budapester Str. 45; Pariser Pl., south wing of Brandenburg Gate, ☎ 0190/016–316 [€1.21 per min]; 030/250–250 for hotel reservations only; 180/575–4040 from outside Germany for information and hotel reservations, WEB www.berlin-tourism.de).

➤ GERMAN NATIONAL TOURIST OFFICES ABROAD: **Australia** (✉ Box A980, Sydney South NSW 1235, ☎ 2/9267–8148, FAX 2/9267–9035). **Canada** (✉ 175 Bloor St. E, Suite 604, Toronto, Ontario M4W 3R8, ☎ 877/315–6237). **United Kingdom** (✉ Box 2695, London W1A 3TN, ☎ 020/7317–0908; 09001/600–100 for automated brochure requests [costs 60p per minute], FAX 020/7495–6129). **United States** (German National Tourist Office, ✉ 122 E. 42nd St., New York, NY 10168, ☎ 212/661–7200 or 877/315–6237, FAX 212/661–7174).

➤ U.S. GOVERNMENT ADVISORIES: **U.S. Department of State** (✉ Overseas Citizens Services Office, Room 4811 N.S., 2201 C St. NW, Washington, DC 20520, ☎ 202/647–5225 for interactive hot line, WEB http://travel.state.gov/travel/html); enclose a self-addressed, stamped, business-size envelope.

WEB SITES

Do check out the World Wide Web when planning your trip. You'll find everything from weather forecasts to virtual tours of famous cities. Be sure to **visit Fodors.com** (www.fodors.com), a complete travel-planning site. You can research prices and book plane tickets, hotel rooms, rental cars, vacation packages, and more. In addition, you can post your pressing questions in the Travel Talk section. Other planning tools include a currency converter and weather reports, and there are loads of links to travel resources.

Berlin's official city site is www.berlin.de, which includes, but isn't limited to tourist information. The useful tips and recommendations at www.berlinfo.com is gathered from local residents. To save money by not using your phone card or operator assistance, **check the German telephone directory assistance page,** www.teleauskunft.de. The Berlin state museums site is www.smb.spk-berlin.de. The most comprehensive list of Berlin links on the net is compiled by an unwieldy university site, userpage.chemie.fu-berlin.de/BIW/e_berlin-info.html—its links don't always have an English-language option. The German

National Tourist Office's website is www.visits-to-germany.com, which is best for general information about travel in Germany. Berlin Tourism's site is www.berlin-tourism.de.

WHEN TO GO

The tourist season in Berlin runs from May to late October, when the weather is at its best. People are more relaxed, cafés and bars spill over into the streets in the long evening sunlight, and parks and lakes fill with scantily clad Berliners desperate to cheat the solariums. This is also the time when many of Berlin's most popular events are held, including the Berlin Marathon, Christopher Street Day, and the Love Parade. More than a million people attend the Love Parade each year, so budget accommodations tend to be scarce on that July weekend. If you're a theater buff, don't come in July and August, when the big ensembles are on break.

In fall the city's parks and forests put on their brightest colors, and the cool but sunny weather makes for ideal day trips to the countryside. In winter Germans are a breed apart, hurrying from overheated house to overheated office, pausing only to snap at tourists breaking road rules. The smoke from the coal stoves that are still the principal method of heating in the former East hangs over the city, giving the air a distinctive odor. Museums and tourist attractions are relatively empty in winter, and accommodations are easy to find. An abundance of cozy bars and restaurants will warm you up after a day of sightseeing. The theater and concert seasons are in full swing, Christmas markets dispense good cheer for most of December, and in February the city plays host to the Berlinale, one of the three biggest film festivals in the world.

CLIMATE

Berlin's climate is temperate, although cold spells, rainy weather, and many overcast days can make temperate seem a lot worse than it sounds. The weather is fairly stable and often doesn't change for weeks at a time—lovely if that means weeks of blue skies, less so when it's constant drizzle. Summers are usually sunny and warm, though you should **be prepared for a few cloudy and wet days.** Umbrellas are hard to find outside of department stores. Except in upmarket hotels and department stores, air-conditioning is not the norm. This can make your Berlin experience rather unpleasant if you happen to visit during a hot spell. Winters are quite cold, with temperatures a few degrees below freezing common. The infrequent snowfalls make smaller streets and uncleared sidewalks hazardous to navigate. Spring and fall tend to be cool but sunny, with the occasional day of rain. Germans measure temperature in Celsius not Fahrenheit.

➤ FORECASTS: **Weather Channel Connection** (☎ 900/932–8437, 95¢ per minute, WEB www.weather.com).

The following are the average daily maximum and minimum temperatures for Berlin.

BERLIN

Jan.	35F	2C	May	66F	19C	Sept.	68F	20C
	26	− 3		47	8		50	10
Feb.	37F	3C	June	72F	22C	Oct.	56F	13C
	26	− 3		53	12		42	6
Mar.	46F	8C	July	75F	24C	Nov.	45F	7C
	31	0		57	14		36	2
Apr.	56F	13C	Aug.	74F	23C	Dec.	38F	3C
	39	4		56	13		29	− 1

1 DESTINATION: BERLIN

Where History Is Bitter and the Beer Is Sweet

What's Where

Pleasures and Pastimes

Great Itineraries

Fodor's Choice

Festivals and Seasonal Events

WHERE HISTORY IS BITTER AND THE BEER IS SWEET

ERLIN IS A CITY BUILT ON SAND; and we're not talking the metaphorical shifting sands of history, though Berliners have found themselves shipwrecked on those often enough. Just under the mosaic of small stones paving the city sidewalks, painstakingly hammered into place by workmen down on their knees, dug up time and again by angry demonstrators, lies the debris of the Ice Age, ground by the glaciers to a grayish powder that will support little more than scraggly spruce and scrub. To strike roots in this inhospitable soil, you have to be hardy, and Berliners have a toughness to them, a rough edge bordering on impoliteness, of which they are strangely proud. *Herz mit Schnauze* is how Berliners describe themselves: a big heart hidden behind a big mouth. Willy Brandt, the mayor of West Berlin when the Communists erected the Wall in 1961, is a prime example—even though, like many Berliners, he wasn't born here. Hard-nosed and rhetorically brilliant, Brandt is still best remembered for the moment in 1970 when, as chancellor of West Germany, he visited the site of the Warsaw Ghetto and fell to his knees, for once at a total emotional loss for words. Today you might find yourself bewildered by the gruffness of one of the notoriously bad-tempered bus drivers, only to have a fellow passenger take pity on you and give you an impromptu tour of the town.

And what a beautiful city it is, in spite of the ravages of war. Berlin, a latecomer and upstart among Germany's historic cities, rose to preeminence as capital of Prussia in the 18th and 19th centuries. The sense of proportion, love of understatement, simplicity, and clarity that characterized Prussian classicism have left their mark on the townscape that extends from the Brandenburg Gate down Unter den Linden, where aristocrats, officers, and common citizens used to take the air, past Karl Friedrich Schinkel's Gendarmenmarkt—arguably the finest square in Europe—to the State Opera House and the treasures of Museum Island.

In the 20th century Berlin became a laboratory of modern and postmodern architecture, and the process of building and rebuilding is still underway. Berliners never tire of sightseeing in their own city. Join them in line to climb up into the glass dome atop the Reichstag and view the new government district. Around Potsdamer Platz, a desolate no-man's-land between East and West until reunification, modern office and entertainment architecture struts its stuff, crowned by the steel-and-glass spaceship of Helmut Jahn's Sony Center. Go on a shopping spree in the glass-and-marble temples to consumerism on Friedrichstrasse—where most locals can only afford to browse, or visit the Jüdisches Museum, Daniel Libeskind's deconstructionist silver-skinned snake and once Berlin's most hotly debated museum. Two dictatorships have left their architectural mark on the city, too. Berlin's soccer heroes, Hertha BSC, play in the Olympic Stadium, where Hitler hosted the 1936 Olympics and Leni Riefenstahl shot *Triumph of the Will*. A ride down the wide expanse of Karl-Marx-Allee will show you some of the best examples of Stalinist neo-Renaissance sugar-icing style this side of Moscow.

But under all this architectural finery is that gray sand. Berlin has a gritty, proletarian, slightly vulgar charm, and if you associate Paris with oysters washed down by Dom Perignon, Berlin's claim to culinary fame is the meaty Currywurst and Döner Kebab, and the garishly colorful Berliner Weisse—weak beer served with a shot of raspberry or woodruff syrup. Take time off from sightseeing to get acquainted with the real Berlin: a sea of apartment blocks jerry-built by get-rich-quick investors during the boom years of the late 19th century—all four stories high, a uniform sand-brown color, built around courtyards that barely let in enough light to see or enough air to breathe. Stroll around Kreuzberg or Prenzlauer Berg on a summer evening when the sky is Prussian blue and the light of the street lamps filters down through the leaves of the chestnut and linden trees, giving the broad side-walks a submarine feeling. Older folk will have propped their elbows on cushions on their windowsills, forgetting television while they watch the scenes unfolding below. Customers finger the produce at a Turkish greengrocer's store; a multilingual group of kids, whose parents may have come from such exotic places as Sarajevo, Beirut, or even Bonn, kick a ball around; young would-be artists in obligatory neoexistentialist black and go-getters in business suits drink Bavarian *Weissbier* and Italian Pinot Grigio at long trestle tables outside a restaurant that serves Brazilian cuisine. From the corner *Kneipe* comes the whir of slot machines, the muffled roar of a soccer stadium, working-class voices raised in Schnaps-laden disagreement over the merits of a player or local politician. The air is a muddle of aromas: the musty, mushroom smell of old brick and plaster, the tang of fresh vegetables, ventilator blasts of warm air and stale beer, a whiff of frying onions—all laced with hot asphalt and the heady sexual attack of the linden blossoms.

Take the red-and-mustard S-Bahn out to Wannsee, in the southwest, or Köpenick, in the southeast. If you're lucky, you'll find yourself in one of the old trains that pull out of the station with the slam of doors and the distinctive electric groan that's embedded in the subconscious of every denizen of the city. Find a shady beer garden next to a lake, order a pinkish Bockwurst and a glass of the bitterish Berlin brew everyone except the Berliners despises. As the setting sun turns the bark of the spruce trees blazing red, mothers tug sunburned children home, and swans and ducks waddle up from the greenish water to reclaim the deserted beach. The colorful brochures distributed by Berlin's tourist authority stress the vibrancy, cultural treasures, and urban zest of the city, so breathless tourists often miss out on what is perhaps Berlin's greatest asset: the hundreds of lakes, large and small—gouged out by those Ice Age glaciers—and the extended forests that surround the city and give its dwellers space to breathe. After all, Berlin started its career some 760 years ago as a fishing village.

AND WHAT A CAREER IT'S BEEN. That's why you're here, of course. Other cities have a history. Berlin *is* history, a book awaiting a reader. The city's most famous landmark, the Brandenburg Gate, is a perfect illustration. Built by order of war hawk King Frederick the Great, it was completed in 1791 as one of the gates into the city. Atop the rather squat structure, the Goddess of Peace rides a four-horse chariot—the quadriga—into Prussia's capital. But Berlin was not to know lasting peace for another two centuries. Napoléon marched through the Brandenburg Gate after humiliating Prussia in 1806 and ordered the statue taken down and brought to Paris. When the "Corsican horse thief" was defeated and the quadriga returned in triumph in 1814, the edifice became a symbol of national rebirth. Prussia's King Wilhelm rode out through the gate to the troops fighting France in 1870 and returned as German emperor, bringing with him the cannons of the Paris Communards, which to this day adorn the Siegessäule (Victory Column), just down the road. In 1914 soldiers on their way to France and death in the mud of the Western Front marched singing through these classical columns, as did Adolf Hitler's Brown Shirts in a torchlight parade on January 30, 1933, to mark the beginning of the "Thousand-Year Reich." Twelve years later it was all over, and Red Army soldiers clambered up the gate to hoist the Red Flag as bullets whined past their heads. When the cold war divided the city and East Berlin's Communist leadership had bricked itself and millions of its sullen citizens into the "Workers' paradise," the gate made impassable by the Berlin Wall symbolized the dead-end of the idea of heaven on earth. Finally, on November 10, 1989, West Berliners stood atop the Wall and danced as bewildered Communist border guards waved their fellow citizens through to the promised land of freedom and consumerism.

Within sight of the Brandenburg Gate, keeper of Berlin's chronology, are monuments that bear witness to Berlin's role in world history. In the Reichstag, now housing the parliament of democratic Germany, a suspicious fire in 1933 gave Hitler the opportunity to initiate the reign of terror that was to engulf all of

Europe. A nondescript patch of land just off the gate, soon to be covered with a field of steles reminiscent of a grave-yard, is the memorial to the 6 million Jews murdered by Germans. That crime was planned in Berlin, in a beautiful villa out on the idyllic lakeshore of Wannsee; it was executed in Berlin, in the destroyed offices of the SS and Gestapo head-quarters, whose cellars now house a per-manent exhibition; and by what is, according to your point of view, either a felicitous or macabre coincidence, Hitler himself ended his life near this very spot, in a bunker within 100 yards of the memorial to his victims.

Berlin is condemned by fate "forever to become and never to be," wrote Karl Scheffler in 1910. These prophetic words are still true. Even while cranes wheel and concrete pours into the huge build-ing projects surrounding the shift of the German government from sleepy Bonn to sleepless Berlin, the city is looking be-yond its function as the capital of an al-most obsolete nation-state to a new role. In the 20th century it was the testing ground of the totalitarian experiments that wanted to create a New Man and brought forth monsters. At this junction the city is a laboratory for the difficult task of unifying a free and freed society. Else-where in Germany, and in Europe, East is East and West is West. Only here do the twain meet. In the 21st century Berlin will be at the center of a multicultural con-tinent that must embrace both Eastern and Western European traditions. Rest assured, the people of Berlin will keep any lofty goals in check with their down-to-earth cynicism and burst any philo-sophical bubbles with the bite of their wit. The pace of change is exhilarating, whatever the outcome may be.

— Alan Posener

WHAT'S WHERE

Western Downtown Berlin
The best way to understand western down-town is to follow its most famous av-enue, the Ku'damm, or Kurfürstendamm as it is properly called. This is 5th Avenue Berlin style. The city's most upscale de-signer stores rub their silken shoulders with some of its grimiest sleaze, the most respectable and accepted of which is the Beate Uhse Erotic Museum, near the gritty Zoologischer Garten train station. Un-like other cities, Berlin wears its underbelly on the outside.

Around the bombed-out remains of the Kaiser Wilhelm church, you might get hit up for change by spiky-hair punks in need of a shower. A few blocks away you can sit under the awning of a centuries-old café and order a cappuccino from a tuxedo-clad waiter. Named for the Prussian Kur-fürst (elector), the Ku'damm was *the* shopping promenade of the old West Berlin. Downtown has two main com-mercial centers, the Europa-Center, a 1960s-style mall with about 100 stores, and the Kaufhaus Des Westens (KaDeWe), with its dazzling food halls.

Quieter but still vibrant are Savignyplatz, just a couple of blocks north of Ku'damm, and the Nollendorfplatz area in Schöneberg—historically, and still, a hub of gay life. Schöneberg veers toward the alternative, but with a distinctly upscale twist. Packed with fun bars and a few racy dance clubs, and blessed with a large number of roomy 19th-century apart-ments, it has become the favorite neigh-borhood of thirty-something singles and couples. You can sit all day here and watch people watch you.

Charlottenburg and Spandau
Once the undisputed center of West Berlin, radiant Charlottenburg bubbled with a curious mixture of chic cafés, health-food stores, antiques dealers, posh hotels, fab-ulous museums, and discos. Tourists often came and left Berlin without ever leaving the district. A few still do, but since the Wall fell the area has lost much of its spunk, as young people emigrated to the edgier, cheaper neighborhoods in Mitte and Pren-zlauer Berg. Nonetheless, Charlottenburg remains the classiest district in the city and rolls out the most fashionable streets and boutiques. Unlike those in eastern Berlin, its institutions have withstood the test of time, and everything—from the size of its 50-year-old linden trees to the familiarity and quality of its mom-and-pop stores—feels solid. The neighborhood gets its name from the gorgeous lemon-color baroque summer palace of Queen Sophie-Charlotte, which sits in a lovely park sur-rounded by terrific museums and galleries.

The palace, built as Berlin's response to Versailles, is a must-see.

Straddling the Havel River to the northwest is Spandau, one of the few places in Berlin where you'll find that the city is older than its high-rises suggest. An early 19th-century and even medieval atmosphere is preserved among Spandau's cobblestone streets and in its citadel.

Tiergarten and the Government District

The Tiergarten began as a hunting ground for local princes, but today is a highly beloved public park. When the weather is even moderately warm, its pathways and meadows fill with cyclists, joggers, soccer players, families pushing baby carriages, and Turkish barbecues. Berlin's main east-west thoroughfare—Strasse des 17. Juni—runs straight through the Tiergarten to the Brandenburg Gate. The area around the gate, once the no-man's-land between East and West Berlin, is quickly developing into the government district, but is still a maze of construction sites. One of those lots will one day hold Europe's largest train station.

However, there are sights to see in finished form. Climb up into the Reichstag's glass dome for an exhilarating view of the city, and judge which corporate giant earns pride of place at Potsdamer Platz, where world-renowned architects had a field day building headquarters among shopping and entertainment complexes. Sandwiched between the park and Potsdamer Platz are cultural centers and art museums.

Mitte

The pulse of the city is unmistakable in Mitte. Newly restored and painted in colorful tones, Mitte (which means "middle") is the hub of the city's cultural, intellectual, and social life, and you're likely to spend most of your sightseeing hours here. It is on these streets that the city first began as a trade center in the 13th century. Culture blossomed between 1740 and 1770, when Frederick the Great laid out stridently Prussian Unter den Linden with the Forum Fridericianum and the State Opera, and had classic Gendarmenmarkt built and centered by a theater. By 1810 Humboldt University would establish itself next to these baroque and classical monuments and become an intellectual center of Europe.

The division of Berlin gave the parade of landmarks on Unter den Linden as well as glorious Museum Island to the East Germans. After the Wall fell, Mitte became the meeting point of East and West. Today's delightfully strange mix merges past with present, capitalism with communism, and young with old. Star architects have revamped Friedrichstrasse with shopping emporiums. In the Scheunenviertel, north of Unter den Linden, narrow alleyways and interlocking courtyards are packed with sleek boutiques, cafés, small theaters, and antiques and ethnic shops. On weekend nights the neighborhood's streets throb with activity, and its bars and clubs buzz with frenetic energy.

Prenzlauer Berg

Close to Mitte, yet far enough away to maintain artistic aloofness, Prenz'lberg (as its inhabitants call it) is unquestionably the hippest part of town, where the footloose and fancy-free can while away time in cafés, small galleries, and dance clubs. Built up as a workers' district in the late 1800s, it is blessed with wide streets and sidewalks and numerous grassy parks. Since the Wall fell, its gorgeous old buildings have been scrubbed, restored, and repainted, giving the formerly dreary eastern neighborhood a rich 19th-century charm. Many buildings are still owned by the state, and as a result rents remain fairly low. Artists, yuppies, well-funded bohemians, and quite a few foreigners have joined the East German families living here, giving the area a distinctly youthful energy, particularly around Kollwitzplatz.

Friedrichshain and Lichtenberg

For a fleeting glimpse of the Communist era, head to Friedrichshain and Lichtenberg, where an array of of monuments, parks, and museums evoke the former glory of "Papa Joe." Friedrichshain ("hain" means "small forest" in German) was a pile of rubble after World War II and when the Russians took over, they erected a Communist-style parade boulevard. The result was Karl-Marx-Allee (originally named Stalin Allee), a thoroughfare lined with monolithic and monochromatic concrete housing blocks that the GDR considered the epitome of glamour. Friedrichshain's park is also loaded with Communist propaganda. A 1972 statue commemorates German-Polish solidarity in the fight against fascism, a monument honors Berliners who died during the Communist-led November revolutions of 1918–19, and a 1968 monument remembers the 3,000 Germans who died in the Spanish war against Franco from 1936–39. If you are tired of human trials and tribulations, head to the lovely zoo and visit its adjacent Prussian-style castle.

Köpenick

A stroll through Köpenick's Old Town is as close you can come to a trip back in time in Berlin. It is also one of the few sections of the city that has a uniform architectural style. Most buildings date from the 18th century and miraculously survived both World War II bombs and East German developers. It is eastern Berlin's ritziest section and is a perfect place for window-shopping and a late-afternoon Sunday stroll. At the confluence of the Spree and Dahme rivers, its tiny island with a castle was used by members of the Hohenzollern dynasty. Nearby, narrow streets with small cramped houses are filled with art galleries and antiques dealers.

Kreuzberg

Southern Berlin is the most ethnically mixed section of the city. Some call Kreuzberg "Little Istanbul" because of its large number of Turkish residents. On Friday and Tuesday wander through the Turkish market along the canal, and on a sunny weekend peek into Görlitzer Park and observe the gaiety of a Turkish barbecue. The area became famous in the 1970s and 1980s, when squatters, anarchists, and punky, draft-dodging youths took over its decaying tenements. When the Wall fell, Kreuzberg became prime real estate, and rents skyrocketed. The alternative scene picked up and moved to Mitte and Prenzlauer Berg. Nonetheless, much of the old feel-good atmosphere remains. Earthy cafés, great bars, and independent movie houses abound on Oranienstrasse, and in many corners the smell of hashish still hangs in the air. Checkpoint Charlie and the new Jüdisches Museum are the big tourist draws.

Zehlendorf

The district of Zehlendorf holds the Wannsee, a huge lake, and the southern half of the Grunewald, the largest of Berlin's many forests. The Grunewald is easily accessible by the S-Bahn and has enough activities to keep the whole family occupied: paths for cycling, lakes for swimming, trails for horseback riding, and sand for sunbathing. There are plenty of sit-down restaurants and ice-cream stands at which to take a break. Nude sunbathing is fairly common in Germany, and a few of the lakes—particularly the tiny Teufelssee (Devil's Lake)—are well-known nudist spots. Krumme Lanke and Schlachtensee are calm lakes that cater to kids and offer scenic spots for picnics and rowing. The Jagdschloss is a fine example of the kind of hunting lodge used by the Prussian landed gentry in the 16th century, and a trip to the Brücke Museum could add a little culture to the day. All in all, with other sights like open-air museums of farms and medieval villages, arts-and-crafts and ethnological museums, and the city's botanic gardens, Zehlendorf makes for a day of reconnecting to nature.

PLEASURES AND PASTIMES

Architecture

Architects have always packed up their slide rules and drawing papers to descend on Berlin—and the marvelous thing is, they're still coming. From ground zero, Potsdamer Platz has sprung up in the past five years, benefiting from such modern geniuses as Renzo Piano and Helmut Jahn. Next door, the Kulturforum dons the golden tentlike structure and outstanding acoustics of Hans Scharoun's Philharmonic and the severe purity of Ludwig Mies van der Rohe's New National Gallery. Unlike any other European capital, Berlin has had the good and bad luck to rebuild itself every second generation. The result is a wild and often cacophonous hodgepodge of styles that ranges from 1960s abominable to 21st-century sublime.

Few major public buildings survived the Allies' relentless bombing at the end of World War II, but many apartments did—especially in the former East—and have been beautifully restored. Neoclassical, baroque, and rococo buildings commissioned by philosopher-king Frederick the Great lend a grandeur and pomp to Mitte. Some of the best are the colonnaded Altes Museum, the Neue Wache, and the Schauspielhaus, all by revered Prussian architect Karl Friedrich Schinkel.Outstanding new architecture includes the Jüdisches Museum, by Daniel Libeskind, the Hamburger Bahnhof, by Joseph P. Kleihues, and the glass-domed Reichstag, by Sir Norman Foster. Because of building restrictions, some world-class architects have been forced to turn their talents inward to designing interiors. Be sure to peek inside the Dresdner (Gerkan, Marg and Partners) and DG (Frank O. Gehry) banks, on Pariser Platz, and the Galeries Lafayette (Jean Nouvel) and its accompanying shopping arcade.

Museums

When it comes to museums, Berlin has an advantage most cities can't top: it has two cities' worth of treasures. In the east there is Museumsinsel, which houses the most outstanding collection of antiquities in the world in the breathtaking Pergamonmuseum. In the west are the royal suites and galleries of Schloss Charlottenburg, Queen Nefertiti's bust in the Ägyptisches Museum, the art nouveau arts and crafts of the Bröhan Museum, and numerous galleries. The Gemäldegalerie has an astonishing collection of old French, English, Dutch, Italian, and, of course, German masters. The Hamburger Bahnhof is worth a look just to see the architecture and the Anselm Kiefer installations, but it also houses a wing dedicated to Joseph Beuys. The more arcane museums include those devoted to East German design (Sammlung Industrielle Gestaltung) and the former East German Secret Security Service (Forschungs- und Gedenkstätte Normannenstrasse). If you prefer small, single-themed museums, head for the Käthe Kollwitz Museum, in a four-story villa on one of Berlin's most elegant streets.

Nightlife

Berlin is party central. Bartenders don't know the meaning of last call, and most places just begin to rock around 2 AM. Nightclubs, dance clubs, bars, and late-night lounges abound and pop with energy. The newer, edgier clubs tend to be in Mitte and Prenzlauer Berg, while the established favorites still pack crowds into Kreuzberg, Schöneberg, and Charlottenburg. People in their forties, fifties, and sixties still sit at the bar next to twentysomethings and don't look or feel out of place. The favorite drink is beer, but lately 1930s-style cocktail bars have become fashionable, as has sipping whiskey and scotch. If you don't quite know what you are after but want to dive into a lively scene, head for Oranienburger Strasse and the Hackesche Höfe.

20th-Century History

No city in the world rivals Berlin for 20th-century history. For more than 100 years the city was the hot spot for the world's trends and tragedies. In the 1920s its cabarets ignited the world with their wit and decadence and debuted the talent of stars like Marlene Dietrich and the vulgarity of adept stripteasers like Anita Berber. In the 1930s and 1940s the Nazis turned the wayward city into the capital of their war machine, and from it they unleashed their brutality on Europe. Nazi-era buildings—the Bundesfinanzministerium (former air force ministry), Tempelhof Airport, and the Olympic Stadium (where sprinter Jesse Owens made world history in 1936)—still stand, some still pocked with bullet holes. The "Topography of Terror" exhibit resides among the ruins of the Gestapo and SS headquarters and traces Nazi atrocities. Allied bombers left much of the city in ruins, and the spoils—and the city's neighborhoods—were divided among the four conquering powers. As relations with Stalin deteriorated, Berlin again became a flash point, a lawless zone of espionage, double agents, and John Le Carré–style secret deals. You can still visit bridges (like Glienicker Brücke) where spies were traded and information exchanged. In 1961 one of the strangest phenomena of 20th-century history occurred when the Berlin Wall went up, dividing the city and its residents into two separate nations. In the West capitalism thrived; in the East communism took root. It was the tumbling Wall in 1989 that signaled the "peaceful revolution" of Eastern-bloc peoples against their totalitarian governments. More than a decade after reunification, Berlin and its people still struggle to forge forward as one.

GREAT ITINERARIES

In a sprawling city with as many richly stocked museums and curiosities as Berlin, you really can't go wrong, but it helps to have an idea of what you would like to experience in advance. Whether you're a manic tourist, covering landmarks at a memory-erasing pace, or a hopelessly relaxed traveler who somehow becomes acquainted with the best cafés but never makes it to the sights you read about while sipping espresso, browse these time- and theme-based tours for a guideline.

If You Have 3 Days

Tour **Schloss Charlottenburg** and any of the nearby museums. By taking the U-Bahn next to Adenauerplatz, you can browse the most elegant of the **Kurfürstendamm** boutiques before reaching the grittier scene of **Breitscheidplatz,** where locals and street performers gather. Stop inside the **Kaiser-Wilhelm-Gedächtniskirche,** a war memorial, before picking out a gourmet snack at the **Kaufhaus des Westens** department store just a bit farther down Tauentzienstrasse.

Start the next morning surveying the city from the dome of the **Reichstag,** then head south along Ebertstrasse, passing the **Brandenburg Tor** and leafy **Tiergarten** on your way to the architectural feast of **Potsdamer Platz.** Beyond the showy corporate and commercial buildings is the Kulturforum's **Gemäldegalerie,** an outstanding fine arts museum. Next head east to Friedrichstrasse for a look at the cold-war hot spot **Checkpoint Charlie** and some window-shopping. At Unter den Linden, turn east for an eyeful of imperial architecture. Spend the evening around the Hackesche Höfe in Mitte.

Eastern Berlin holds still more attractions for your third day. Visit the museums on the Spree canal's **Museumsinsel** (especially the Pergamonmuseum), and explore the courtyards and shops around Oranienburger Strasse. Further north, at the **Gedenkstätte Berliner Mauer-Dokumentationszentrum,** you can inspect the last original remains of the Berlin Wall.

If You Have 5 Days

A five-day visit is really the only way to experience the electrifying atmosphere of the city, and to visit sights off the beaten track. Follow the three-day itinerary above, but continue east to the old working-class district of Prenzlauer Berg. Finish your day at a café near **Kollwitzplatz,** or with evening entertainment at the old **Kulturbrauerei.**

Begin your fourth day in the district of Kreuzberg. See if the current exhibit interests you at the **Martin-Gropius-Bau** and then head next door to the **Prinz-Albrecht-Gelände,** where former Nazi prison cellars were excavated. Make the new **Jüdisches Museum** your last stop before hitting the heart of Kreuzberg via Oranienstrasse.

Spend your last day either in Zehlendorf, a green district of lakes, forest, and a few standout museums, or in Potsdam and the summer-palace grounds of Schloss Sanssouci.

New Berlin

Berlin is changing at such a fast rate that describing what is new becomes a Sisyphean task. For an overview of the new old capital, head for the **Reichstag** and climb up its glass dome, designed by Sir Norman Foster. From here head toward the Brandenburger Tor, where on adjoining plots you'll see the planned American embassy and the Holocaust memorial, **Denkmal für die ermordeten Juden Europas.** Nearby is the "downtown of the future," **Potsdamer Platz.** Though it looks purely commercial, there's actually housing within the complexes. From here hop the S-Bahn eastward to Hackescher Markt and the bustling area around the **Hackesche Höfe.** Meander through the charmingly renovated streets of Mitte's Scheunenviertel and take a coffee break in the formerly working class—and now terrifically chic—interlocking courtyards. A few galleries exhibit work of young artists from across Europe. From here you will have to jump a bit around town. The **Jüdisches Museum** is Berlin's newest museum and a stunning example of modern architecture. Browse through the shopping arcades on **Friedrichstrasse** and have a look at the conical-shape core of the Galeries Lafayette. At the **Hamburger Bahnhof** architect Joseph Kleihues did a brilliant job of transforming an old train station and transport museum into a glorious showcase for modern art. Finally, for a taste of the low-key sophistication of new Berliners, settle down with a meal on **Kollwitzplatz** in Prenzlauer Berg. Here you can watch life in the new city unfold.

Old Berlin

Berlin is such a young city that looking for the old can sometimes be a challenge. What wasn't bombed was often destroyed and replaced by horrid modern structures. Still, a few treasures did survive and several others were rebuilt. If you must see cobblestone alleys to satisfy your Old World nostalgia, head to Berlin's oldest neighborhood, **Spandau,** in the northwest, or to 18th-century **Köpenick** in the southeast. In the center of the city, the medieval **Nikolaiviertel** (rebuilt in 1987 by the GDR in an attempt to outdo the West on Berlin's 750th birthday) has the reconstructed churches **Nikolaikirche** and **Marienkirche,** both used by traders and fisherman in the 13th century. From the Nikolaiviertel it's just a short walk to **Museumsinsel,** where Berlin began as a small trading post. Under the Prussian kings, Otto von Bismarck, and emperors Wilhelm I and II, the city was transformed into a world power. The most striking building on the island is the Lustgarten's **Altes Museum,** built in 1830 by Karl Friedrich Schinkel to house the royal art treasures. Also of note are the neobaroque Bodemuseum (1904), the magnificent Pergamonmuseum (1902–30), and the bombastic neobaroque **Berliner Dom** (1905). These classically inspired buildings helped give Berlin its prewar nickname of "Athens on the Spree." Berliners are currently debating whether to rebuild the Prussian royal palace that stood across from the Lustgarten on Schlossplatz before the GDR dynamited it.

Proceed down **Unter den Linden** and take a look at **Humboldt University** and the dramatic bronze statue of Frederick the Great on horseback. Across the street, visit the former royal opera, now the **Staatsoper Unter den Linden,** and the **Kronprinzenpalais** and **Opernpalais.** Two blocks south is the **Gendarmenmarkt,** one Berlin's most beautiful plazas, with domed museums, a concert house, and sidewalk cafés. From here jump on the U-2 U-Bahn at Stadtmitte and get off at Sophie-Charlotte-Platz to be dazzled by the sprawling 17th-century **Schloss Charlottenburg,** the summer palace of King Friedrich I's wife, Queen Sophie Charlotte. Southwest of Berlin, Potsdam and Schloss Sanssouci have a wealth of royal palaces and baroque buildings.

The East

The best way to start a tour of what was East Berlin is with what defined it—the Wall. The most intact sections are a bit out-of-the-way (which is how most Berliners like it). The **East Side Gallery,** a 3-km-long (2-mi-long) strip in Friedrichshain, was painted by artists just after the Wall fell. A more accurate depiction of the cement border system is the **Gedenkstätte Berliner Mauer-Dokumentationszentrum,** in northern Mitte. Bookstores have detailed maps tracing exactly where the Wall divided the city. **Checkpoint Charlie** gives a dramatic feel for what it meant to cross from East to West. Remnants of the Wall are nearby on Niederkirchnerstrasse. From Checkpoint Charlie walk north along Westernized and commercial **Friedrichstrasse,** one of the GDR's central thoroughfares. When you reach **Under den Linden,** the **Brandenburger Tor,** most famously photographed with exuberant celebrants atop the obsolete Wall in front of it, is to your left. At the end of the boulevard to your right is the metallic **Palast der Republik,** where the former GDR parliament met. It's nearly universally considered an eyesore. Beyond the bridge crossing the Spree is the **Marx-Engels-Forum** and its statue of Karl Marx and Friedrich Engels. Further on is **Alexanderplatz,** the dreary, windswept plaza that came to epitomize the East. For a good look at the city, take a trip to the top of the **Berliner Fernsehturm** and have coffee or a drink in the revolving restaurant. The TV tower was the pride of Socialist architecture. Around the plaza note the rows of Communist-bloc housing and the dull-colored murals depicting good party members working together.

In Prenzlauer Berg, the **Sammlung Industrielle Gestaltung** (Industrial Design Museum) shows you East German products and packaging now disappeared from reunited Germany. Farther southeast in Lichtenberg, the **Forschungs- und Gedenkstätte Normannenstrasse** (the East German secret-service museum) is where the East German equivalent of the KGB worked. Walk through the former office of secret police chief Erich Mielke, view bugging devices, and see loads of Communist kitsch. **Treptower Park** holds the immense Soviet war memorial, which was built with red marble that came from Hitler's chancellery. If you want to continue your tour into the night, head for the former border checkpoint, the **Tränenpalast** (Palace of Tears). It was where West Germans lucky enough to receive a visiting pass said goodbye to their loved ones in East Berlin. Today it's a nightclub.

World War II Era

Begin at **Bebelplatz,** on Unter den Linden between the Alte Bibliothek of Humboldt University and the Deutsche Staatsoper. It was there that Nazi students burned thousands of books on May 10, 1933. Set flush in the ground you will see the Empty Library installation by Israeli artist Micha Ullman. From here walk to Stresemannstrasse and view the outdoor "Topography of Terror" exhibit at the **Prinz-Albrecht-Gelände,** which chronicles the Nazis' rise to power. The exhibit is propped up against the ruins of Gestapo prison cells and is in what was the heart of the Nazi war machine. Hitler's bunker, where he spent his last days and committed suicide, is closed to the public; it is under a parking lot and a grassy plot behind Wilhelmstrasse 90–92. The **Bundesfinanzministerium,** on Wilhelmstrasse, is a prime example of Nazi architecture and originally served as the air force ministry occupied by Hermann Göring.

Walk to the Mohrenstrasse subway station to see the cranberry-color marble that came from the inner chambers of Hitler's chancellery and offices. Take the subway to Zoologischer Garten to view the remains of the **Kaiser-Wilhelm-Gedächtniskirche,** on Breidtscheidplatz. Built in the late 19th century, the neo-Romanesque church was badly destroyed by air raids in 1943 and then left as a reminder of the brutality of war. From here hop back on the U-2 subway and head to the **Olympiastadion,** which was built as a showcase for the Nazis in 1936 and is a stunning example of the Nazi penchant for monumental architecture.

Two other sites are worth visiting but best done on separate day trips. **Sachsenhausen Memorial,** north of the city in Oranienburg, was one of the first concentration camps established by the Nazis. At **Bildungs- und Gedenkstätte Haus der**

Wannsee-Konferenz (Wannsee Conference Memorial Site), a lovely lakeside resort in southwest Berlin, you can tour the villa where Adolf Eichmann, Reinhard Heydrich, and other top Nazi officials planned the extermination of European Jewry.

FODOR'S CHOICE

Dining

Borchardt. Go back to the 1920s and as far away as the Mediterranean at this art nouveau celebrity haunt in Mitte. *$$$$*

Margaux. The city's new gourmet star is also one of the most stylish restaurants in town. German-French nouvelle cuisine is celebrated here, while the rich and beautiful enjoy trading glances. *$$$$*

VAU. Designer restaurant VAU was Mitte's first name in hip when the district's restaurant scene boomed, and it continues to reign. The lunchtime *Mittagskarte* is a good choice if dinner is out of your range. *$$$$*

Schwarzenraben. The new East celebrates nights out with new Italian cooking at this narrow little restaurant. *$$$*

Grossbeerenkeller. Come to this cellar restaurant for Old Berlin atmosphere, where Berliners unwind over beer and Frau Zinn-Baier's fried potatoes. *$–$$*

April. This unpretentious restaurant in Schöneberg serves consistently good cuisine, be it Italian, Turkish, German, or French, and at extremely reasonable prices. *$*

Lodging

Four Seasons. For the ultimate in turn-of-the-20th-century luxury, check into the still large, but most intimate-sized of Berlin's finest hotels. The chandeliers and open fireplace in the dining room win repeat guests. *$$$$*

Hotel Adlon Berlin. No other hotel in Berlin can match the Adlon's prestigious history or location near the Brandenburg Gate, and nothing is overdone in the streamlined 1920s-style rooms. The international staff is not only the most personable in town, but also the most professional. *$$$$*

Dorint am Gendarmenmarkt. Overlooking the stunning Gendarmenmarkt and its cathedrals and theater, this designer Dorint hotel is just as elegant as the historic square in front of it. The service is excellent. *$$$–$$$$*

DeragResidenzhotel Henriette. With a historic look, this new hotel is a gem of old-style European hospitality, both in the traditionally furnished rooms and the impeccable yet warm service. *$$$*

Brandenburger Hof Relais & Chateau. Bauhaus-designed furniture by Mies van der Rohe, Le Corbusier, and Eileen Gray, as well as original prints, decorate the guest rooms here. When the day has become too long, you can retire to the spa for facials and shiatsu massage. *$$$*

art'otel berlin-mitte. Art is central to this rococo city mansion, and the abstract works of Georg Baselitz hang throughout the hotel. The dining rooms are a rare juxtaposition of the historic and the modern, creating a near-theatrical setting. *$$–$$$*

Hotel Künstlerheim Luise. If you're fantasy is to become an artist in Berlin, take your pick of one of the 30 individually designed rooms in this early 19th-century house, each a commissioned work. The reasonably priced hotel is centrally located in Mitte. *$–$$*

Museums

Ägyptisches Museum. One of the premier museums of ancient Egyptian art and history, the Ägyptisches Museum presents works of art from all major eras and has some of the best-preserved mummies outside Cairo. Archaeologists swoon over the 3,300-year-old bust of Queen Nefertiti and the "green-headed Berliner" from 500 BC.

Checkpoint Charlie. With actual escape vehicles, photographs, and documents, the museum at this famous border crossing captures the resourcefulness and ingenuity of those who braved escaping East Berlin and East Germany.

Gemäldegalerie. Pace yourself through this extensive selection of European paintings from the 13th to the 18th centuries, and leave time for the particularly strong French and Italian collections.

Pergamonmuseum. Awesome monuments of antiquity, from an ancient Greek temple to a Persian portal, fill this treasure trove on Museum Island.

Sammlung Berggruen. Once a private collection, Berlin's favorite small art museum features van Gogh, Cézanne, Picasso, Giacometti, and Klee.

Schloss Sanssouci. Walk the grounds of fountains, teahouses, and orangeries at Frederick the Great's rococo palace in Potsdam, and be dazzled by the interior's marble cupolas, gilding, and paintings by Caravaggio, Rubens, and Van Dyck.

Quintessential Berlin

Breitscheidplatz. Berliners, tourists, and transients all cross paths on this busy western downtown plaza to watch with interest how the other half lives. Join those cooling their feet at the Wasserklops fountain.

Gendarmenmarkt. The classic square is one of Europe's great piazzas and is watched over by the German and French cathedrals and Schinkel's Schauspielhaus. Surrounding it is a thriving restaurant and nightlife scene.

Kaufhaus des Westens. Europe's largest department store will tempt you to its upper floors with classy champagne bars, bread and cheese stations, and gourmet buffets.

Reichstag. Start a morning within the parliament building's huge glass dome, surveying the evolving city before you—or come before closing for a brilliant view of the night skyline.

Scheunenviertel Courtyards. Cafés, bars, theaters, galleries, and shops are ensconced within the courtyards and passageways of Mitte. The art nouveau Hackesche Höfe is the most popular, but Heckmann's Höfe is fun for shopping, and the redbrick Sophiensäle dates to the early 19th century.

Tiergarten. Stroll the pebbly pathways of this central, 630-acre park and settle down under the chestnut trees at the lakeside beer garden, Café am Neuen See.

FESTIVALS AND SEASONAL EVENTS

WINTER

LATE NOV.-LATE DEC.➤ **Christmas markets** selling traditional decorations and seasonal food spring up all around the city the month before Christmas. The principal ones are held on Alexanderplatz, on Unter den Linden near the Opera House, next to the Kaiser Wilhelm Memorial Church, and in the old town of Spandau.

NEW YEAR'S➤ **Sylvester** (New Year's Eve) brings thousands of Berliners onto the streets concentrated on both sides of the Brandenburg Gate. The public fireworks display is supplemented by random ones by neighborhood inhabitants, making the streets irksome for nervous children, pets, and cyclists.

JAN.➤ **Internationale Grüne Woche** (Green Week; ☎ 030/30380) is ostensibly a 10-day farm show, but the focus is firmly on the produce. Visitors from all over Germany and the rest of the world come to see and taste-test the best fresh food the country has to offer.

During the last week in January or beginning of February, Berlin's state museums stay open until well after midnight for the **Long Night of the Museums** (☎ 030/2839–7444). Musical performances, tours, and readings complement the usual displays.

FEB.➤ The two-week **Berlinale** (☎ 030/2592–

0351, WEB www. berlinale.de) is the third-biggest European film festival after Cannes and Venice. Starting on the first Thursday in February, the festival brings films from around the world to the city.

EARLY MAR.➤ The **International Tourist Fair** (☎ 030/3038–4444) attracts more than 100,000 visitors to the Berlin International Congress Center. Most visitors work in the tourism trade, but the fair also offers a variety of resources for those planning their next trip.

SPRING

MAY➤ Leave it to Berlin for scheduled rioting. The traditional day of workers' solidarity, May 1, has been marked by the **May Day riots** in Berlin since 1987. Clashes between the police and protesters are usually concentrated in the Kreuzberg district. The Women's Tennis Association tour comes to Berlin in early May for the **German Open** (☎ 030/8957–5520). With more than $1 million in prize money, some of the biggest names in women's tennis compete.

SUMMER

JUNE➤ The two-day **Karnaval der Kulturen** (Carnival of Cultures;

☎ 030/622–4232) takes place over the Whitsun weekend (late May or early June, depending on when Easter falls) and is a celebration of Berlin's diverse population. At the center of festivities is a parade in which people from more than 70 different cultures dance their way through Kreuzberg, but there are also stages and food stalls scattered throughout the area.

MID-JUNE➤ **World Music Day (La Fete de la Musique)** takes place on the summer solstice, June 21. Outdoor stages all over the city present a wide variety of music, and much of it is free. The **Gay and Lesbian Street Party** (☎ 030/216–8008) is a weekend of food and entertainment centered around Nollendorf Platz, the heart of the gay community. Events include club nights, street entertainment, and parties galore. One week later the **Christopher Street Day Parade** (☎ 0177/277–3176) commemorates the 1969 Stonewall riots in New York, the impetus behind the gay liberation movement. Thousands of participants prance their way from the Kurfürstendamm to the Siegessäule, intoxicating spectators with outrageous costumes and floods of champagne.

MID-JULY➤ For four evenings, **Classic Open Air Berlin** (☎ 030/315–7540) presents peformers from Chaka Khan to José Carreras on the Gendarmenmarkt. The **Love Parade** (WEB www. loveparade.de) is the single largest event of the year in Berlin, and the largest dance party in the world, attracting more than 1 million participants and spectators. Hundreds of floats pound out mainstream techno to the masses as the parade slowly progresses down Strasse des 17. Juni in Tiergarten on a Saturday in July. Many parties continue for the entire weekend.

JULY–AUG.➤ **Heimat-klänge** (Sounds Like Home ⊠ Tempodrom am Ostbahnhof, ☎ 030/318–6140) brings international music to Berlin in summer. Each year has a different theme; previous years have presented music from Brazil and Japan and Afro-American blends. A different band is on show every week from Wednesday to Sunday for a nominal entry fee. In Zehlendorf, the three-week **German-American Festival** (⊠ Argentinischer Allee and Clayallee, ☎ 0172/390–0930) turns Truman Plaza into a rodeo and carnival of rides, sideshows, and American-style food. The tradition began when the United States was an occupying military presence in Berlin.

The **International Berlin Beer Festival** (☎ 030/508–6822) showcases the local brews as well as more than 1,000 beers from more than 60 countries. Held along Karl-Marx-Allee in Mitte, the festival also has plenty of beer-hall fare on offer with musical accompaniment.

LATE AUG.➤ Usually the last of the summer parades, the **Hemp Parade** (☎ 030/2472–0233) attracts a group of people campaigning for full legalization of marijuana. The last week in August Berlin's state museums stay open until well after midnight for the **Long Night of the Museums** (☎ 030/2839–7444). Musical performances, tours and readings complement the usual displays.

AUTUMN

SEPT.➤ The **Berlin Marathon** (☎ 030/302–5370) is Germany's most popular race. Around 30,000 participants from around the world join in to run, walk, skate, or ride the 42-km (26-mi) course, which ends on the Kurfürstendamm.

The **Berliner Festwochen** (Kartenbüro, ⊠ Budapester Str. 50, D–10787, ☎ 030/254–890, FAX 030/2548–9111) bring nearly two weeks of international theater, dance, and classical music to the city's performance venues.

Art lovers have their chance in late September or early October when the **Art Forum** (☎ 030/8855–1643/44) comes to town. More than 140 galleries from all over the world display their wares to collectors, curators, and the curious public.

OCT.➤ **German Unity Day,** October 3, is celebrated with fireworks, concerts, and other cultural activities in the streets around the Brandenburg Gate and the Reichstag, marking the day East and West Germany reunited in October 1990. **Womex** (☎ 030/397–870), the international world music expo, is held in a different venue each year, and returns to Berlin in 2002. Bands and industry professionals from around the world gather for a festival of information sharing and cultural performances.

OCT.–NOV.➤ In even-numbered years the **Berlin Motor Show** (☎ 030/3038–2014) provides five days of information and entertainment for those in the industry and other motor fans in late October and early November. **Jazz Fest Berlin** (☎ 030/2548–9100) calls in jazz musicians from around the globe. The festival dates from 1964 and has an enviable track record of attracting some of the big names in jazz. Dates change year to year, but the festival usually runs in late October and early November.

NOV.➤ Berlin celebrates its Jewish heritage each year in November during the **Jüdische Kulturtage** (Jewish Culture Days; ☎ 030/8802–8252). The theme changes each year but generally includes a mixture of films, musical events, and art exhibitions.

2 EXPLORING BERLIN

In this truly international metropolis the pace
of change is staggering. Walking the streets
of bustling downtown centers and quaint,
quiet neighborhoods is a thrilling study of
urban development. The winds of change
have swept away the old rules that once
had their grip on both West and East Berlin,
and have made the city's famous air giddy
with high hopes, which attracts an ever-
growing cadre of young entrepreneurs,
artists, and policy-makers.

By Jürgen
Scheunemann

AT THE DAWN OF THE NEW CENTURY, BERLIN faces an exciting and promising future as one of Europe's great cosmopolitan cities. Since the fall of the infamous Berlin Wall on November 9, 1989, the city-state has slowly recovered from its division of almost three decades. Today, as 3.5 million citizens are still grappling with the rapid changes surrounding them, the capital is regaining its status as Germany's leading cultural, political, and social center. The capital looks forward to becoming the center of a Europe whose borders are moving ever more eastward.

News to most visitors is that the most famously divided city actually has its roots in two separate settlements, Cölln and Berlin. Both began more than 760 years ago on the Spree River, around what is known today as the Museum Island. As a Prussian (1701) and then German (1871) capital, the city underwent dramatic changes in its architecture, urban development, and street layout, as each king, chancellor, and emperor left his mark. The Greater Berlin of today didn't come into existence until 1920, when seven cities (including Charlottenburg, Neukölln, and Spandau) and 59 towns and communities, as well as 27 farm districts and counties, were all integrated into a new entity called Gross-Berlin. This accounts for Berliners' strong allegiance to their particular *Kiez* (neighborhood or district) and for their general, occasionally harsh dislike of other boroughs.

The city's patchwork development has resulted in several "downtowns." Most famous are the western downtown neighborhoods of Charlottenburg, Wilmersdorf, and Schöneberg, with the Kurfürstendamm running through them, and the eastern, more historic downtown section between Unter den Linden and Alexanderplatz.

Though its tree-lined streets and boulevards are charming to stroll, Berlin, covering an area of 889 square km (355 square mi), is laid out on an epic scale—western Berlin alone is four times the size of Paris. Of its 12 present boroughs (the former 20 were reorganized in a major administrative reshuffling in early 2001), seven are of real interest: Charlottenburg-Wilmersdorf, in the west; Tiergarten (a district of the Mitte borough), Kreuzberg, and Schöneberg, in the downtown western area; the historic eastern part of town in Mitte; and Prenzlauer Berg, in the northeast. Southwest and southeast Berlin have lovely parks, and secluded forests and lakes in Zehlendorf's Grünewald and Köpenick's Müggelsee areas, respectively. The eastern districts of Friedrichshain and Lichtenberg hold a few scattered points of interest as well.

A Tageskarte (day card) is available for €4 and covers 1-day admission to all of Berlin's state museums; a Dreitageskarte (3-day card) costs €8.18. Both tickets are available at all state museums. State museums, which include those on Museumsinsel and the Kulturforum, are free the first Sunday of the month.

WESTERN DOWNTOWN BERLIN

Ku'damm, as Berliners affectionately call the tree-lined Kurfürstendamm, stretches for 3 km (2 mi) through the heart of the western downtown, spilling over with shops, department stores, art galleries, movie theaters, and hotels, as well as restaurants, bars, clubs, and sidewalk cafés. The grand boulevard crosses the boroughs of Charlottenburg and Wilmersdorf and touches Schöneberg at its eastern end. This route and its chichi side streets such as Fasanenstrasse or Uhlandstrasse, is the most fashionable area in western Berlin and passes through the

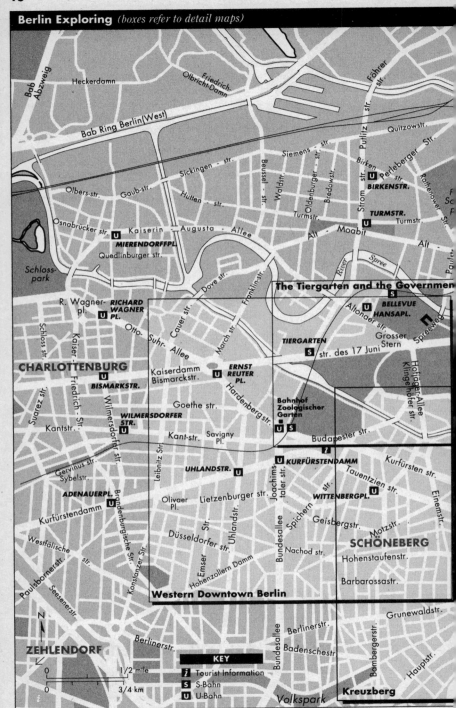

Bab Abzweig

Heckerdamm

Friedrich-Olbricht-Damm

Föhrer str.

Bab Ring Berlin (West)

Sickingen - str.

Siemens - str.

Quitzowstr.

Pulitz

Perleberger Str.

Birken str.

Rathenower str.

BIRKENSTR.

Olbers-str.

Gaub-str.

Hutten - str.

Beussel - str.

Waldstr.

Oldenburger - str.

Bredowstr.

Strom str.

Turmstr.

TURMSTR.

Turmstr.

Osnabrücker str.

Kaiserin - Augusta - Allee

Alt - Moabit

Alt

MIERENDORFFPL

Quedlinburger str.

Dove str.

Franklin str.

River Spree

Schloss park

R. Wagner-pl.

RICHARD WAGNER PL.

Otto- Suhr- Allee

Cauer str.

March str.

Altonaer str.

The Tiergarten and the Governmen

BELLEVUE HANSAPL.

Grosser Stern

Spreeweg

TIERGARTEN

str. des 17 Juni

Hofjäger-Allee

Klingelhöfer str.

CHARLOTTENBURG

Schloss str.

Kaiser- Friedrich- Str.

Suarez str.

Wilmersdorfer - str.

BISMARCKSTR.

Kaiserdamm Bismarckstr.

ERNST REUTER PL.

Goethe str.

Hardenberg str.

Bahnhof Zoologischer Garten

WILMERSDORFER STR.

Kant-str.

Savigny Pl.

Leibnitz Str.

Budapester str.

Gervinus str.

Sybelstr.

Kantstr.

UHLANDSTR.

KURFÜRSTENDAMM

Joachims taler str.

Kurfürsten str.

Tauentzien str.

Einemstr.

ADENAUERPL.

Kurfürstendamm

Westfälische str.

Olivaer Pl.

Lietzenburger str.

Uhlandstr.

Spichern

Bundesallee

WITTENBERGPL.

Geisbergstr.

Motzstr.

SCHÖNEBERG

Paulsbornerstr.

Düsseldorfer str.

Str.

Emser

Hohenzollern Damm

Nachod str.

Hohenstaufenstr.

Barbarossastr.

N

ZEHLENDORF

Berlinerstr.

Seesenerstr.

Kоyslav

Brandenburgische Str.

Bundesallee

Berlinerstr.

Badenschestr.

Grunewaldstr.

Bambergerstr.

Hauptstr.

0   1/2 mile

0   3/4 km

Western Downtown Berlin

KEY

i Tourist Information

S S-Bahn

U U-Bahn

Kreuzberg

Volkspark

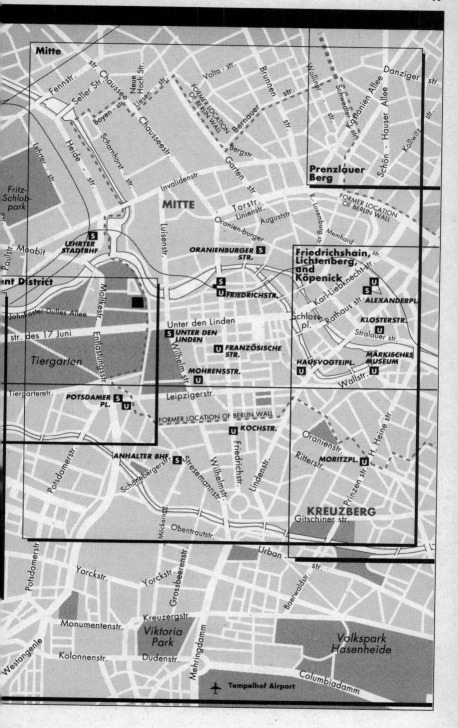

Mitte

Fennstr.

Seller Str. Chaussee

Neue Hoch Str.

Volta - str.

Brunnen

str.

Wolliner str.

Danziger str.

Schwedler str.

Kastanien Allee

Schön - Hauser Allee

Kollwitz

Boyen str.

Liesen str.

Bernauer

FORMER LOCATION OF BERLIN WALL

Bergstr.

Scharnhorst str.

Chausseestr.

Garten str.

Prenzlauer Berg

Heide str.

Lehrter str.

Fritz-Schlob-park

Moabit

Paulstr.

Invalidenstr.

MITTE

Torstr.

Linienstr.

Oranien-burger

Auguststr.

R. Luxemburg str.

Memhard

FORMER LOCATION OF BERLIN WALL

Luisenstr.

S **LEHRTER STADTBHF**

ORANIENBURGER STR. **S**

Friedrichshain, Lichtenberg, and Köpenick

Karl-Liebknecht-str.

Rathaus str.

U **ALEXANDERPL.**

ent District

Moltkestr.

Entlastungsstr.

S
U **FRIEDRICHSTR.**

Schloss-pl.

Stralauer str.

U **KLOSTERSTR.**

John Foster-Dulles Allee

str. des 17 Juni

Tiergarten

Unter den Linden

S **UNTER DEN LINDEN**

Wilhelm str.

U **FRANZÖSISCHE STR.**

U **MOHRENSSTR.**

HAUSVOGTEIPL. **U**

MÄRKISCHES MUSEUM

Wallstr.

U

Tiergartenstr.

POTSDAMER PL. **S** **U**

Leipzigerstr.

FORMER LOCATION OF BERLIN WALL

U **KOCHSTR.**

Oranienstr.

Ritterstr.

H. Heine str.

MORITZPL. **U**

Potsdamerstr.

ANHALTER BHF. **S**

Stresemannstr.

Schönebergerstr.

Wilhelmstr.

Friedrichstr.

Lindenstr.

Prinzen str.

KREUZBERG

Gitschiner str.

Möckernstr.

Obentrautstr.

Urban str.

Baenwaldstr.

Potsdamerstr.

Yorckstr.

Yorckstr.

Grossbeerenstr.

Kreuzergstr.

Monumentenstr.

Viktoria Park

Dudenstr.

Mehringdamm

Volkspark Hasenheide

Westangenle

Kolonnenstr.

✈ **Tempelhof Airport**

Columbiadamm

younger parts of Charlottenburg and Wilmersdorf, which evolved early in the 20th century as the "New West" to contend with the historic downtown area between Unter den Linden and Alexanderplatz. The older parts of proud Charlottenburg, then a big city in its own right and the richest in all of Prussia, are north and west of the Kurfürstendamm area.

Numbers in the text correspond to numbers in the margin and on the Western Downtown Berlin map.

A Good Walk

Start an eastward stroll along **Kurfürstendamm** ①, at Adenauerplatz. If at any time you get tired of walking, Buses 119, 109, and 129 can speed you along. At the corner of Leibnizstrasse is the Iduna-Haus—the most beautiful old mansion still standing on the boulevard. The next corner at Wielandstrasse comes closest to having nearly perfectly preserved its original appearance. Its owners and the city have gone to great expense to do so. For example, the extraordinarily elegant building at No. 185 burned to the ground in 1988, right after it had been renovated. It was decided to painstakingly restore its facade and to erect a new building behind it. This project was undertaken by Wolf-Rüdiger Borchardt, the same architect who had restored the U-Bahn station on Wittenbergplatz five years earlier.

Kurfürstendamm slowly changes its face as you proceed farther east, with smaller shops and boutiques beckoning, many representing the top names of Paris, Milan, New York, and London. Haus Cumberland (Nos. 193–194), a gray and gloomy building, first opened as a hotel in the late 19th century. Next up are the theater and shopping mall known as the Ku'damm-Karree (Nos. 207–208); it houses the multimedia attraction **The Story of Berlin** ②. The boulevard now crosses Uhlandstrasse and opens into a squarelike area. Its southern end is one of the most historic parts of Ku'damm, dominated by the massive bright-white columns of the Galerie Brusberg (No. 213), one of the city's premier art galleries and dealers. Directly opposite is the Maison de France (No. 211), a French cultural institution, which contains a library, bookstore, and movie theater. Further on is another one of west Berlin's fixtures, King's Teagarden (No. 217), one of the country's best tea specialty shops. In the same building Austrian writer Robert Musil wrote his best-selling modernist novel *The Man Without Qualities*. Next to it at narrow No. 218 is the former Chinese embassy, now occupied by the chocolates purveyor Café Leysieffer. The tiny second-floor balcony offers a rare vantage point of the street scene.

Detour north on Grolmanstrasse for more window browsing until you reach the shops and sidewalk eateries bordering the greenery of **Savignyplatz** ③. Return to Kurfürstendamm via Kantstrasse and Uhlandstrasse and continue east to **Fasanenstrasse** ④, one of the boulevard's nicest side streets. On the north side of Ku'damm, the columned Haus Wien (Vienna House) has seen many different occupants, including a movie theater, clothing stores, and—today—a junk shop. To the south on Fasanenstrasse is the **Käthe-Kollwitz-Museum** ⑤. Follow Fasanenstrasse north, passing the **Jüdisches Gemeindehaus** ⑥ on your right. At Kantstrasse is the 11-story Kantdreieck, designed by Berliner Paul Kleihues. The giant aluminum sail on the roof slowly changes its direction with the wind and was one of Charlottenburg's most disputed new architectural features in the 1990s. To the right is the **Theater des Westens** ⑦, Berlin's most beautiful theater. Continue east on Kantstrasse to the corner of Joachimsthaler Strasse, where the **Erotik-Museum** ⑧ presents an exhibition on the art and culture of sexuality. Just ahead is **Breitscheidplatz** ⑨, the crossroads where hippies, homeless people, tourists, and street musicians mingle around the ruin of the **Kaiser-Wil-**

helm-Gedächtniskirche ⑩. Across the plaza is the **Europa-Center** ⑪, a shopping mall; the Berlin tourist information office is at its back on Budapester Strasse. Across from the tourist office is the Elefantentor (Elephant Gate), the main entrance to the **Zoologischer Garten** ⑫, western Berlin's zoo and aquarium. The boulevard **Tauentzienstrasse** ⑬ runs southeast from the corner of the Europa-Center straight to Europe's largest and Germany's most elegant department store, the **Kaufhaus des Westens** ⑭, nicknamed KaDeWe. The soaring structure watches over modern **Wittenbergplatz** ⑮ and its magnificent 1913 art nouveau metro station. Tauentzienstrasse continues as Kleiststrasse to the heart of the Schöneberg district, **Nollendorfplatz** ⑯, a square that is also the center of the gay community (instead of walking the fairly dull stretch, you could take the U-Bahn one stop from Wittenbergplatz). Motzstrasse, full of gay bars and restaurants, leads southeast away from Nollendorfplatz to lovely Viktoria-Luise-Platz, which has outdoor cafés. If your legs are leaving you at this point, you could take the U-4 subway from either Nollendorfplatz or Viktoria-Luise-Platz (direction Innsbrucker Platz) to the Rathaus Schöneberg station. Just outside it, **Schöneberger Rathaus** ⑰, West Berlin's town hall when the city was divided, is where U.S. president John F. Kennedy gave his famous *"Ich bin ein Berliner"* ("I am a Berliner") speech.

TIMING

This area is meant for leisurely browsing, and how long your walk takes will depend on your interest in the various shops and cafés you'll pass. Even without stepping into any of the museums or attractions, you can expect to spend three hours here. The admirable zoo and aquarium—watching feeding times and monkey play is worth skipping some shopping—will take about three hours to enjoy. The Ku'damm and Tauentzien are extremely crowded on Saturday morning, so if you're planning to do some serious shopping, visit on a weekday.

Sights to See

★ ❾ **Breitscheidplatz** (Breitscheid Square). Always-bustling Breitscheidplatz is the heart and soul of western Berlin. The vast square is dominated by the Kaiser-Wilhelm-Gedächtniskirche and is flanked by the Europa-Center. Its southern end marks the confluence of Kurfürstendamm and Tauentzienstrasse. The plaza is named after Social Democrat Rudolf Breitscheid, who died in a concentration camp during World War II. The square hardly resembles its prewar design—gone are the trams and the historic buildings and cafés frequented by the likes of director Billy Wilder. But street life has probably never been more energetic and colorful than today. Even at 1 AM or 2 AM the square is crowded with people. In December the Christmas market with its merry-go-rounds arrives. In summer, street and con artists, vendors, Berliners, and tourists alike enjoy the carnivalesque atmosphere. Vietnamese artists advertise with their sketches of American celebrities—they can paint or draw a portrait of you in less than 20 minutes.

The square also serves as a stage for all kinds of political groups and demonstrators. Among the street artists is an older lady, usually standing on the steps at the southern end of the Memorial Church, surrounded by hordes of tourists. She's Helga Goetze, who lives in Charlottenburg and has been a peculiar fixture on the square for more than 20 years, crying out her solutions to the world's hardships ("Make as much love with each other as possible!") and by displaying her thoughts on billboards. She often peppers her remarks with profanity, and at times will approach someone to explain her cause personally.

In the summer exhausted Berliners and tourists refresh their tired feet in the cool water of the imaginative **Weltkugelbrunnen** (Globe Foun-

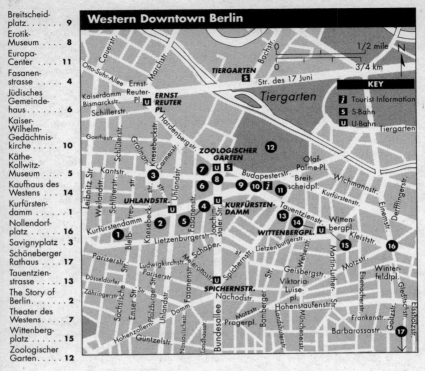

tain), in front of the Europa-Center. Berliners didn't take to the fountain's name, and simply call it *"der Wasserklops"* (the water meatball). Designed by German artist Joachim Schmettau and built in 1983, the fountain pours water over several levels, where it bubbles through many openings and playfully flows over the little bronze sculptures that decorate the granite construction. One little detail is an abandoned beer bottle rendered in bronze (Berliners love to drink in public).

While strolling on Breitscheidplatz, you might notice a police presence, but there is no reason to worry. The square is absolutely safe, even in the wee hours of the morning. Because of some drug dealing behind the Memorial Church and some hustling in the underground bathrooms in front of the Europa-Center, police officers are necessary. The police also look for illegal immigrants here.

⓼ Erotik-Museum. The culture and art of human sexuality in all its manifestations are exhibited here, though primarily in paintings and other works of art from Europe and Asia. Outstanding exhibits document the history of German scientist Magnus Hirschfeld, whose institute for sexuality was destroyed by the Nazis, and Berliner Heinrich Zille's humorous early 20th-century cartoons of sexual behavior in the city's working-class tenements. The museum is extremely tasteful, but it is owned and run by the Beate Uhse company, Germany's largest retailer of X-rated videos and other bedroom paraphernalia. Only adults over 18 years of age are admitted. ⊠ *Kantstr. (corner Joachimsthaler Str.),* ☎ *030/886–0666.* 🎟 *€5.* ⊘ *Daily 9 AM–midnight.*

⓫ Europa-Center. This vast shopping and business complex was erected on the site of the renowned Romanisches Café, the hot spot for writers and actors during the Roaring '20s. The 22-story tower, built in the 1960s—nicknamed "Pepper's Manhattan" after its owner—is a somewhat depressing leftover from the good old days of West Berlin, when the city was pampered with federal money and business boomed around Kurfürstendamm. Any past glamour has faded into shabbiness. The center houses more than 100 shops, restaurants, and cafés, two cinemas, a comedy club, and the tourist information center. Two pieces of the Berlin Wall stand by the Tauentzienstrasse entrance. The **Uhr der fliessenden Zeit** (Clock of Flowing Time) is an ingenious artwork constructed by French physicist Bernard Gitton. The 13-m-high (42-ft-high) sculpture with various colored liquids demonstrates drop by drop how quickly time passes. Some Berliners jokingly refer to it as *"der Fruchtsaftautomat"* (the fruit-juice machine). ⊠ *Breitscheidpl.,* ☎ *030/3480–088,* WEB *www.europa-center-berlin.de.*

❹ **Fasanenstrasse.** Regarded as western Berlin's most fashionable street, subdued and narrow Fasanenstrasse is bisected by bustling Kurfürstendamm: the southern part has many small boutiques and three impressive old villas, including the Käthe-Kollwitz-Museum, the adjoining **Villa Grisebach**, an art auction house, and the **Literaturhaus Berlin** (Center for Literature Berlin). The latter is set in a lovely garden and is not only home to readings, literary exhibits, and a bookstore, but also to the Café Wintergarten, with a greenhouselike glass porch.

The massive Kempinski Hotel Bristol Berlin, once western Berlin's flagship grand hotel, marks the north side of Fasanenstrasse. Opposite that is the **Bankhaus Löbbecke & Co,** one of Germany's most renowned private banking houses, whose company headquarters is an excellent example of how a historic city villa can be integrated into a modern architectural ensemble—the glass-and-steel pedestrian bridge connecting the two buildings is a stunning sight. Farther up the street is the **Jüdisches Gemeindehaus** (Jewish Community Center), a reminder of the once-thriving Jewish community in this part of town.

North of Kanststrasse, Fasanenstrasse becomes less elegant. One of the city's most spectacular new buildings, the **Ludwig-Erhard-Haus**, lies amid the historic buildings like a giant lizard creeping through the urban jungle. Completed in 1998 by English architect Nicholas Grimshaw, the arched, silver construction houses the stock exchange and the Chamber of Commerce and Industry.

On the street's south side, **Fasanenplatz** is a quaint square with an illustrious past. In the 1920s leading German writers such as Bertolt Brecht, Heinrich Mann, Erich Kästner, and Erich Maria Remarque either had an apartment here or lodged at one of the small hotels.

❻ **Jüdisches Gemeindehaus** (Jewish Community Center and Synagogue). The religious center of western Berlin's Jewish community is a modern yet unspectacular postwar edifice, not at all reminiscent of what was once Germany's largest and most beautiful synagogue. The original 1912 synagogue was built in a Roman-Byzantine style by architect Ehrenfried Hessel. Like most Jewish houses of worship in Germany, it was heavily damaged by the Nazis on *"Kristallnacht"* ("the Night of Broken Glass"), November 9, 1938, the Nazis's first open and direct attack on Jewish German citizens. (The evening is less euphemistically referred to as the *"Reichspogromnacht"*—"Reich's night of pogroms.") Synagogues and Jewish-owned stores were burned or destroyed, several thousand Jews were arrested or wounded, and many were deported. Most Germans who witnessed the terror (even the police) only watched, not daring to intervene. The synagogue was again hit hard by Allied bombardments in 1943. After the war it was demolished to make way for an entirely new house of worship, built between 1957 and 1959. Only the reddish sandstone arch of the old entrance gate was preserved, integrated into the new facade.

In front of the gate you can see a bronze statue of a broken torah scroll, which stands as a reminder of all the Jewish religious writings destroyed in 1938. Today the synagogue houses a kosher restaurant, a Jewish community college, and a research library, and hosts frequent cultural and political events. The heavy police presence in front of the synagogue—and at all Jewish institutions in Germany—is a sobering reminder of persisting anti-Semitism. ⊠ *Fasanenstr. 79–80,* ☎ *030/8862–7663,* WEB *www.jg-berlin.org.*

★ ❿ **Kaiser-Wilhelm-Gedächtniskirche** (Kaiser Wilhelm Memorial Church). Though referred to unsolemnly as the "hollow tooth," this ruin stands as a dramatic reminder of World War II's destruction. The bell tower is all that remains of the once-imposing church, which was built between 1891 and 1895 and dedicated to the emperor, Kaiser Wilhelm I. On the hour the tower chimes out a melody composed by the last emperor's great-grandson, the late Prince Louis Ferdinand von Hohenzollern.

In stark contrast to the ruin are the adjoining Memorial Church and Tower, erected by the noted German architect Egon Eiermann in 1959–61. These ultramodern octagonal structures, with their myriad honeycomb windows, are aptly described by their nicknames: "the lipstick" and "the compact." The interior is dominated by the brilliant blue of its stained-glass windows, imported from Chartres. Church music and organ concerts are presented in the church regularly.

An exhibition inside the old tower focuses on the devastation of World War II, with a cross constructed of nails recovered from the ashes of Coventry Cathedral in England, destroyed in a German bombing raid in November 1940. ⊠ *Breitscheidpl.,* ☎ *030/218–5023,* WEB *www.gedachtniskirche.com.* ◻ *Free.* ☉ *Old Tower: Mon.–Sat. 10–4; Memorial Church: daily 9–7.*

❺ **Käthe-Kollwitz-Museum.** The suffering and desperation of poverty-stricken Berliners, portrayed by artist Käthe Kollwitz (1867–1945) in her drawings, woodcuts, and sculptures, seem a world away from the museum dedicated to her on chic Fasanenstrasse. The works give a poignant glimpse into the daily hardships of the working-class populace in the first half of the 20th century. They also assert the artist's pacifist beliefs. The small private museum, in a neoclassic villa, holds some 200 of her paintings and engravings, many of her self-portraits and sculptures, and personal documents and letters. ⊠ *Fasanenstr. 24,* ☎ *030/ 882–5210,* WEB *www.kaethe-kollwitz.de.* ◻ €4. ☉ *Wed.–Mon. 11–6.*

★ ⓮ **Kaufhaus des Westens** (Department Store of the West). KaDeWe isn't just Berlin's classiest emporium—it's also Europe's largest. Covering 60,000 square meters over eight floors, the store holds an enormous selection, but it's best known for its top two floors of delicatessens, restaurants, and bars. Crowning the building is a lovely winter garden.

The opening of KaDeWe in 1907 marked the birth of the Neuer Westen (New West) around the Kurfürstendamm: in those days Berlin's grand boulevard had been Unter den Linden, and only the nouveau riche dared to move to Charlottenburg. The KaDeWe catered to this upwardly mobile crowd, served them well, and gained quite a reputation. Despite heavy destruction during World War II, KaDeWe quickly reopened in 1950, selling wares only on the first two floors. In the early 1990s the building was given a complete face-lift, and the main lobby was carefully restored to its original appearance. The two eight-story atria, which lead to a glass ceiling, are awe-inspiring. The best way to see all the floors in a blink of an eye is via one of the four glass elevators.

The KaDeWe staff (and proud locals, for that matter) never tire of bragging about the nutritious (although not necessarily healthy) superlatives that can be seen, smelled, and sampled on the gourmet floors: more than 33,000 different items are on display, including 1,300 cheeses, 400 kinds of breads and rolls, 1,200 types of sausages, and a selection of 2,400 wines from all corners of the earth. ⊠ *Tauentzienstr. 21,* ☎ *030/ 21210,* WEB *www.kadewe.de.*

★ ❶ **Kurfürstendamm.** This grand boulevard, nicknamed the Ku'damm, is the liveliest stretch in all of Berlin. The busy thoroughfare was first laid out in the 16th century, when it was still known as Knüppeldamm (Log Road), the path by which the elector Joachim II of Brandenburg traveled from his Spree River palace to his hunting lodge in Grunewald. The Kurfürstendamm (Elector's Causeway) developed into a major route in the late 19th century, thanks to the initiative of Bismarck, Prussia's Iron Chancellor. He had seen the Champs Élysées in Paris and longed for a similar boulevard in the imperial German capital. Bismarck specified that it be 3.8 km (2.3 mi) long, 56 m (184 ft) wide, and have a riding path in the middle. The boulevard was designed according to his wishes (even though Bismarck couldn't persuade the stubborn Berlin magistrate to honor him with a statue), becoming the western downtown center after the turn of the 20th century.

It was only in the Roaring '20s that Kurfürstendamm rose to its status as one of Germany's few grand boulevards. The capital's bustling entertainment strip, lined with movie theaters, variety shows, bars, and restaurants, joined ranks with the world's other great avenues: the Champs Élysées, Oxford Road, and Broadway. But in World War II nearly half of Ku'damm's 245 late-19th-century villas burned to the ground during Allied bombardments, and the remaining buildings suffered damage in varying degrees. Any surviving glimmer of grandeur was lost in the bitter house-to-house fighting that took place during the Battle of Berlin in April 1945. Remarkably, most facades survived the war (thanks to their inner steel structures), and the Ku'damm quickly reassumed its old role as early as the fall of 1945. By the time of the "economic miracle" of the Marshall Plan–aided recovery, in the 1950s, it was as international and attractive as ever before, regardless that most businesses operated out of ruins. But during this decade most of the surviving historic buildings were torn down, and—over the course of the next 20 years—replaced by cheap and quickly erected ones.

With the advent of radical changes in German society in 1968, the nation's eyes focused on Kurfürstendamm as a stage for revolutionaries and demonstrations. Kurfürstendamm became a kind of parade route for all sorts of political protesters—a reputation it still has today. By the early 1980s many claimed that the boulevard was, in fact, dead because most restaurants and cafés had closed their doors. As more tourists were drawn to Ku'damm, hoping to see what had made it legendary, shops and restaurants catered to their lower budgets and fewer upscale shops remained. Thus began the exodus of the chic boutiques to the far western end of the boulevard, where they have mostly stayed. Reunification seemed to deliver the death blow to the Ku'damm, as developers envisioned new shopping and entertainment centers reclaiming the east. But like a phoenix, the Ku'damm was back five years later with new shops and ultramodern buildings. Today there is no doubt the Ku'damm is Berlin's premier boulevard.

If you start a stroll down Ku'damm at its far western end, don't look for house Number 1—when the Ku'damm was relocated in the early 1920s the first 10 address numbers were simply dropped. This west end begins with an ironic commentary on all the commercial frenzy the Ku'-

damm epitomizes: on **Rathenauplatz** a sculpture by Berlin artist Wolf Vostell includes several old up-ended Cadillacs, noses embedded in concrete—a reminder of the disposability of all goods. Behind Rathenauplatz, the quiet and upscale residential areas of Grunewald begin.

The center of Kurfürstendamm is the corner of Joachimsthaler Strasse, which has always been western Berlin's display window, a place where the rich and beautiful admire one another. However, the crossing has changed dramatically in the last two years: with the construction of the massive Swissôtel and the soaring glass-and-steel Neues Kranzler-Eck across the street, the old gentility is gone. The Neues Kranzler-Eck, a sleek shopping center and office complex designed by German-American star architect Helmut Jahn, opened in 2000. It had to integrate the historic rotunda of the famous **Café Kranzler,** whose ornate red sign was lost amid the many flashing neon lights here. For more than 40 years the café had been the epitome of West Berlin's coffeehouse culture.

NEED A BREAK?

The **Kurfürstendamm 195** (✉ Kurfürstendamm 195) is a somewhat hidden *Imbiss* on the south side of the boulevard. Though it doesn't serve the city's best *Currywurst,* it certainly serves it to the most elegant Berliners. This is probably the only Imbiss in Germany where you can observe fur-clad ladies sipping champagne between nibbles on spicy sausages.

---

⑯ Nollendorfplatz. Clearly the center of Schöneberg's gay nightlife, Nollendorfplatz is bounded by two large structures, the metro stop **U-Bahnhof Nollendorfplatz** and the **Metropol.** The latter was built in 1906 by architect Albert Fröhlich and first served as a stage for dramatic productions. It was not until 1927 that the theater gained renown, when legendary German director Erwin Piscator started his radical *Proletarisches Theater* (proletarian theater) here, a new form of interpretive drama for social revolutionary purposes, primarily aimed at the working class. The building suffered much damage during the war, and restoration of the theater began in the late 1970s. Upon completion, it reopened as a dance club. Behind the restored walls, Metropol Tanztemple is notorious for its outrageous parties.

Nollendorfplatz has always been known as an eccentric area, especially among the gay community. Schöneberg's two major "gay" streets, **Motzstrasse** and **Eisenacher Strasse,** are just two minutes west of Nollendorfplatz, with antiques stores, bars, a few nightclubs, gay community centers and other services, as well as restaurants, *Imbisse,* and clothing stores that cater to a mostly gay, young, and stylish crowd.

Christopher Isherwood (1904–86), the British writer who later became world famous thanks to the smash musical hit *Cabaret,* lived just south of the square, at Nollendorfstrasse 17. A plaque recognizes the writer, who resided there from 1929 to 1933. His *Berlin Diaries,* which served as the basis for the musical, chronicles the last days of a wild and tolerant Berlin, before the Nazis crushed it. Isherwood, who was himself homosexual, took part in the thriving gay nightlife of the Roaring '20s with his friend W. H. Auden (later husband of essayist and activist Erika Mann) and occasional visitors Paul Bowles and Aaron Copland. Many residents of this house later became figures in his novel. The musical's main character, dancer Sally Bowles, was based on Jean Ross, an Englishwoman whom he met during his stay in Berlin, and Fräulein Schneider from *Cabaret* was cast after his own landlady, Ms. Meta Thurau.

NEED A BREAK?

Upscale Viktoria-Luise-Platz offers many cafés and restaurants. One of the coffee-and-cake institutions is **Montevideo** (✉ Viktoria-Luise-Pl.

Close-Up

GAYER THAN GAY PARIS

SOME OF BERLIN'S MOST PROMINENT MEN over the centuries are said to have been gay, including Frederick the Great, Heinrich von Kleist, and Alexander von Humboldt. Beginning in the 19th century, the city had a vibrant, if underground, gay scene, equivalent to that of much larger cities like Paris or London. In the 1920s, after a series of discriminating laws were abolished, gays became more open and could choose to meet at more than 100 bars, cafés, and clubs that were in essence openly gay. One of the most popular cruising areas was around Nollendorfplatz. However, with the victory of National Socialism in January 1933, tolerance came to a sharp end. More than 5,000 homosexuals were sent to concentration camps, and others were brutally castrated or sent to prison.

Today Berlin is the most prominent gay community in Europe, making the city a gay mecca for Germans and tourists alike. Many establishments around Nollendorfplatz today not only display the international gay emblem—the rainbow flag—but also a particular historical symbol for gays, the *Rosa Winkel* (pink triangle), an insignia that gay inmates had to wear on their clothing in the Nazi concentration camps. The marking that once symbolized oppression and violence has now been appropriated as a declaration of freedom and pride. Just outside the Nollendorfplatz U-Bahn station, on the building's wall (to your right when you enter from Nollendorfplatz), are a triangle and the inscription TOTGESCHLAGEN. TOTGESCHWIEGEN (Beaten to death. Silenced to death), commemorating the gay victims of the Third Reich.

6, ☎ 030/213–1020), an odd mixture of Berlin café and American restaurant, but buzzing with people enjoying the delicious breakfasts and appetizers at the sunny sidewalk tables.

❸ Savignyplatz (Savigny Square). This charming square is the epitome of the bohemian Charlottenburg social scene. At the convergence of three streets—Grolman-, Knesebeck-, and Carmerstrasse—and bisected by Kantstrasse, the green lawns of the square with their private bowers are less the attraction than the residential neighborhood around them. Many grand mansions here were homes to famous writers and artists. One of Germany's best satirical cartoonists, George Grosz, once lived at Savignyplatz 5. Most of the good eateries and pubs are not on the square itself but on nearby streets and under (as well as along) the redbrick S-Bahn viaduct south of the square. You'll find the best places between the square and Bleibtreustrasse, as well as between the square and Grolman- and Uhlandstrasse. Some fine bookstores and interior-design shops nest under the viaduct.

The streets around Savignyplatz, including Goethestrasse, and **Steinplatz** (Stein Square), which is only a stone's throw from Savignyplatz via Carmerstrasse, make up one of the nicest quarters in all of Charlottenburg. The small Steinplatz is overshadowed by the neoclassical, column-decorated **Hochschule der Künste** (University of Fine Arts), shortened to "HdK" by its more than 5,000 students. Hidden in the bushes of Steinplatz is a field stone with an inscription commemorating the victims of National Socialism—one of the many small memorials to be found throughout Berlin.

⑰ **Schöneberger Rathaus** (Schöneberg City Hall). If not for the administrative division of Berlin in 1948–49, this unremarkable city hall, one
of many in amalgamated Berlin, would have remained obscure. But
after the city was divided the West Berlin Senat (the city-state's government) and the Abgeordnetenhaus (state parliament) relocated here.
Since then the city hall, which dates from 1911, has seen many highlights of cold war history. The most memorable of these events was a
visit from U.S. president John F. Kennedy in July 1963, who traveled
to West Berlin to assure its citizens of American support. During his
speech on the balcony, in front of a huge, cheering crowd, the young
president spoke what would become the famous words *"Ich bin ein
Berliner"* ("I am a Berliner"). Though he meant to express his solidarity
with Berliners, his attempt at a grandiose and political statement was
also the equivalent of declaring, "I am a doughnut!" Grammatically
speaking, using an article (*ein*) before the word *Berliner* essentially describes a particular type of doughnut usually eaten on New Year's Eve.
Berliners, however, got the point—after all, the same doughnut in
Berlin is called *Pfannkuchen.*

Inside the city hall tower is the **Freiheitsglocke** (Liberty Bell), a replica
of the American Revolution–era Liberty Bell in Philadelphia. The bell
was financed by 16 million American citizens and presented to the city
in 1950. The bell and its inscription, THAT THIS WORLD UNDER GOD SHALL
HAVE A NEW BIRTH OF FREEDOM, was a gesture of friendship from Americans to West Germans. It rings every day at noon and on special occasions. The signatures of the Americans who funded the bell are still
stored in the city hall. The square in front of city hall was renamed
John-F.-Kennedy-Platz in November 1963. ⊠ *John-F.-Kennedy-Pl.,*
☎ *030/75600.* ⊠ *Free.* ⊙ *Weekdays 8–6.*

⑱ **Tauentzienstrasse** (Tauentzien Street). Many visitors don't realize that
Kurfürstendamm ends at Breitscheidplatz and that the short boulevard
leading to the Wittenbergplatz is an avenue in its own right. "Der Tauen-
zien," as Berliners call it, has always been a cheaper version of its big
brother, the Ku'damm. But the street has seen a rise in brand-name stores
over the past decade: Nike, Salamander, Peek und Cloppenburg, and
Levi's have all built flagship stores here. Close to Wittenbergplatz is
the legendary **Kaufhaus des Westens**, Berlin's temple of consumerism.

A shimmering silver statue representing two broken links of a chain
dominates Tauentzienstrasse. Simply called *BERLIN*, the large piece
by the artist couple Matschinsky-Denninghoff is the last reminder of
the *Skulpturenboulevard* (Sculpture Boulevard), a series of sculptures
in the western downtown area, erected during Berlin's 750th anniversary in 1987.

❼ **Theater des Westens** (Theater of the West). This premier musical stage
was built in an unusual mixture of neoclassical and art nouveau styles
in 1895–96 by Bernhard Sehring. Peek into the rather small entrance
hall to catch a glimpse of late-19th-century glamour. The theater
started out as an *Operettenhaus*, presenting the light German opera
that gave rise to the musical, and later became a variety theater. During the 1920s it welcomed stars from around the world. One of the
most famous performers was Josephine Baker, who in 1926 thrilled
Berliners with her legendary banana dance. Unlike British and American audiences, open-minded Berliners were more interested in her fast
footwork than her lack of clothing.

Since 1978 the Theater des Westens—a name referring to Charlottenburg's turn-of-the-20th-century designation as the "New West"—has
hosted musicals, and in-house productions have included smash hits

like *Cabaret* and *Porgy and Bess.* ✉ *Kantstr. 9–12,* ☎ *030/882–2888,* WEB *www.tdw.de.*

2 **The Story of Berlin.** In a city with such a turbulent past, this multimedia show and museum built over a nuclear shelter (which is the eeriest part of the exhibition) has a wealth of historic events to depict. The odd mixture of history museum, theme park, and movie theater covers 800 years of city history, from the first settlers to the fall of the Wall, with displays on four floors. Many original objects are woven together in an interactive design, making the exhibits both entertaining and informative. Descriptions are written in both German and English, and self-guided audio tours in English are available. ✉ *Ku'damm Karree, Kurfürstendamm 207–208,* ☎ *030/8872–0100,* WEB *www.story-of-berlin.de.* 🎫 *€9.* 🕐 *Daily 10–8 (last admission at 6).*

15 **Wittenbergplatz** (Wittenberg Square). At the eastern end of western Berlin's shopping drag is Wittenbergplatz—a well known and architecturally interesting site. The square's two halves are separated by the traffic lanes of the **Tauentzien.** Standing directly in the middle is the boxy, sandstone **U-Bahnhof Wittenbergplatz** (Wittenbergplatz subway station). The neoclassical station, designed by one of the city's most important early 20th-century architects, Alfred Grenander, dates from 1910–13 and is one of the oldest metro stations in Berlin. It was almost completely destroyed in World War II, and it was only in 1983 that a historically accurate reconstruction was completed by Wolf-Rüdiger Borchardt. Apart from the clock tower and the vintage billboards, every detail has been painstakingly replicated. Today the U-1, U-2, U-12, and U-15 subway lines stop here. In front of the station a simple plaque with the names of 12 Nazi concentration camps and the inscription PLACES OF TERROR WE SHALL NEVER FORGET is a reminder that the Holocaust was administered from a (now-destroyed) building a few hundred yards north of here.

Two shallow, bowl-shape fountains on the square invite passersby to loiter and enjoy the sun. They were designed by Waldemar Grzimek and integrated into the square's reconstruction in 1983. Yet due to the traffic and uninspired buildings flanking it, Wittenbergplatz never gained the popularity of Breitscheidplatz, farther west. A highlight, however, is the soaring **Kaufhaus des Westens** on the southwest corner of the square. Twice a week (Tuesday and Friday 8–2), the northern half of the square is home to a *Wochenmarkt* (farmers' market), one of the largest in western Berlin.

★ **12** **Zoologischer Garten** (Zoological Gardens). Germany's oldest zoo opened in 1844, and today it is the world's largest. More than 14,000 animals representing 1,400 species live in enclosures designed to closely resemble their natural habitats. The zoo has been able successfully to breed various rare and endangered species on its grounds. The main entrance to the zoo is marked by the impressive Asian-style **Elefantentor** (Elephant Gate).

A visit is always more enjoyable when the weather allows you to enjoy the sophisticated open-air ranges. The most popular places to visit are the **Affenhaus** (monkey house), the **Elefantenhaus** (elephant house), and the **Löwenfreianlage** (open-air lion habitat). Feeding times are always a crowd pleaser. Primates are fed at 3:30 daily, all other monkeys at 11, 2, and 3:30 daily; lions and other wild cats eat daily at 2:30 in summer, 3:30 in winter.

Even in this rough-edged city, the zoo's more endearing animals make headlines in the city's tabloids when they become ill or die. The zoo's most celebrated resident lived here between 1927 and 1935, a gorilla named Bobby. He later became the zoo's official mascot and is commemorated by a stone statue at the monkey house.

Not to be missed is the aquarium, next to the Elefantentor entrance. Marine life from all climates inhabit tanks and basins large and small. Among the main attractions are the shark tank, with black reef and hammer sharks, and the several tanks with rare and unusual fish. One of the curiosities here is the *Zitteraal*, a kind of eel that can generate an electric charge up to 800 volts when it fights, creating a lightning-like flash. At the small touching pool with colored carp, look up the wall behind the basin. A small opening gives you a glimpse into the crocodile hall basin above you, where the crocs usually doze. If they ever fight, their strong tails splashing the water can be an alarming sight.

The extremely humid crocodile hall is in the **Reptilienabteilung** (reptile section), on the second floor, where you can stroll across a wooden walkway just a few feet above the ominous-looking crocodiles. They are fed fresh meat every Monday at 3:30. Other second-floor inhabitants include the world's largest lizards, from Indonesia—komodo dragons—as well as giant and poisonous snakes from around the world and a variety of turtles and tortoises.

The **Amphibienabteilung** (amphibian section), on the third floor, is no place for arachnophobics—it's filled not only with amphibians but also spiders and all kinds of other beasts that crawl on six legs, or eight, or more. In small boxes behind thick glass walls, you'll see scorpions and other dangerous insects, along with tarantulas as large as your fist that feed on white mice. ⊠ *Hardenbergpl. 8 and Budapester Str. 34,* ☎ *030/ 254–010,* WEB *www.zoo-berlin.de.* ⊡ *Zoo €7.50, aquarium €7.50, combined ticket to zoo and aquarium €12.* ☉ *Zoo: Nov.–Feb., daily 9–5; early Mar., daily 9–5:30; late Mar.–late Sept., daily 9–6:30; Oct., daily 9–6; aquarium: daily 9–6.*

CHARLOTTENBURG AND SPANDAU

The oldest parts of Charlottenburg are north and northwest of Kurfürstendamm. The elegant townhouses around Schloss Charlottenburg give testimony to the borough's proud heritage, first as the summer residence of the Prussian kings and later as the most prosperous Prussian city. Some of the most historic residential areas are north of the impressive streets Bismarkstrasse and Kaiserdamm and east and west of Schlosstrasse, the old path leading up to the palace. The rigid, nearly gridlike layout of many streets here dates from the 19th century, when many of the buildings served as housing for military officers and personnel. Later, shoddy tenement houses were erected in the northern parts of the borough.

West of Charlottenburg is one of Berlin's oldest and (now as ever) most independent sections of the city, the borough of Spandau. Surrounding the Spandau Citadel is a magnificent water fortification at the point where the Havel and Spree rivers meet. Spandau is also the only part of Berlin that has retained its late-medieval and early 19th-century town charm.

Numbers in the text correspond to numbers in the margin and on the Charlottenburg and Spandau map.

A Good Tour

Begin at the museums of **Schloss Charlottenburg** ①, the adjacent **Ägyptisches Museum** ②, the **Sammlung Berggruen** ③, and the **Bröhan-Museum** ④, a small museum for art nouveau design. To reach Schloss Charlottenburg, take the U-7 to Richard-Wagner-Platz, spot the palace dome, and walk northwest on Otto-Suhr-Allee (from Zoologischer Garten the total U-Bahn ride takes about 20 minutes). Once through the museums and the palace gardens, you can either walk about 30 minutes or take the S-Bahn to the next site. If walking, take Schlossstrasse south and turn right on Knobelsdorffstrasse, an old residential street. Turn left on Soorstrasse, where you'll pass an old post office and outdoor market, to Masurenallee. As you continue from the Schloss area to the west, you leave behind the old Prussian tenement houses built for officers' families and come upon the grand apartment complexes the new German bourgeoisie built itself at the turn of the 20th century. From Masurenallee you can see the **Funkturm** ⑤, Berlin's historic radio tower. For train travel here walk west on Spandauer Damm from the Bröhan-Museum to the Westend S-Bahn, and take the train one stop to Witzleben (back above ground, follow Masurenalle toward the Funkturm). The **Georg-Kolbe-Museum** ⑥ is a 25-minute walk from the radio tower (via Masurenallee and Heerstrasse). Alternatively you can take Bus 149 from the Funkturm to the stop at Mohrunger Allee. Backtrack to the Heerstrasse S-Bahn station and take the train one stop to Olympiastadion (do not attempt to walk the distance). From the station exit find Flatowallee, where the **Le-Corbusier-Haus** ⑦ is a prime example of apartment-building architecture of its time. It's only a short walk farther on Trakehnerallee to the **Olympiastadion** ⑧, the massive stadium built for the summer Olympics of 1936. Return to the S-Bahn station and take an S-Bahn to Spandau (the ride takes about eight minutes). **Spandauer Altstadt** ⑨ is one of Berlin's best-preserved and oldest neighborhoods and is dominated by the **Zitadelle Spandau** ⑩. Once you have reached the Spandau S-Bahn station, it's only a five-minute walk north on Carl-Schurz-Strasse to the Old Town area.

TIMING

A visit to the Schloss Charlottenburg area and all its museums might keep you busy for a whole day. If you only want to quickly browse the museums and skip a walk through the palace gardens, you could see most collections in four hours. Spandau is well worth half a day of sightseeing; however, the citadel and Old Town Spandau can also be inspected in about two hours. The Olympiastadion is closed until 2004, but you can still get a peek of it from the adjoining Glockenturm.

Sights to See

★ ❷ **Ägyptisches Museum** (Egyptian Museum). The exquisite 3,300-year-old portrait bust of **Queen Nefertiti** is the centerpiece of a collection that traces Egypt's history from 4000 BC and includes some of the best-preserved mummies outside Cairo. One of the world's leading museums on ancient Egyptian art and history, the Ägyptisches Museum presents more than 2,000 works of art from all major eras of ancient Egypt. A special focus is on works dating to the reign of Pharaoh Echnaton (1340 BC). Equally famous among archaeologists is the so-called **Berliner Grüne Kopf** (green-headed Berliner), a green-stone bust dating from 500 BC. It is considered one of the premier examples of that period's highly developed arts and crafts. The museum is across from Schloss Charlottenburg, in the former east guardhouse and residence of king Friedrich I's bodyguard. ✉ *Schlossstr. 70,* ☎ *030/320–911,* WEB *www.smb.spk-berlin.de.* ☞ *€4.* ◷ *Tues.–Sun. 10–6.*

❹ **Bröhan-Museum.** The forms and motifs of art nouveau, art deco, and functionalism are presented in a small museum opposite Schloss Charlottenburg. Three floors are devoted to the development and mutual influences and implications of the three art movements that dominated European arts and crafts as well as industrial design in the first half of the 20th century. The comprehensive collection includes ceramics, porce-

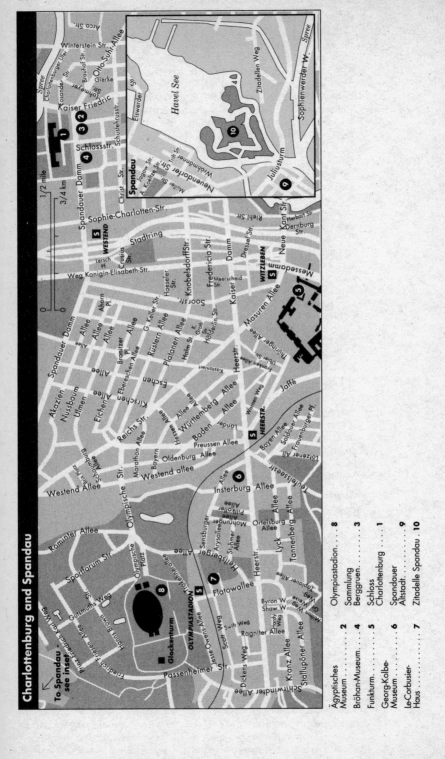

Charlottenburg and Spandau

To Spandau – see inset

Winterstein Str.

Arco Str.

Spree

Charlottenburger Ufer

Kossander Str.

Krommeyer Str.

Brauhof Str.

Gierke

Kaiser Friedric.

Schlossstr.

Schusterhausstr.

Christ. Str.

Spandauer Damm

Sophie-Charlotten-Str.

WESTEND

Stadtring

Riehl Str.

Herbert Str.

Neue Kant Str.

Dernburg Str.

Lersch Pl.

Crusius Str.

Weg Königin-Elisabeth-Str.

Knobelsdorffstr.

Fredericia Str.

Damm

Dresber Str.

Meerscheid Str.

Haseler Str.

Kaiser

Messedamm

WITZLEBEN

Masuren Allee

Ahorn Pl.

Allee

Allee

Allee

Soorstr.

G. Keller Str.

Rüstern Allee

Platanen Allee

Holm Str.

Hölderlin Str.

K. Groth Str.

Thüringer Allee

Über Str.

Spandauer Damm

Allee

Akazien

Nussbaum

Ulmen

Eichen

Allee

Bramitzer Pl.

Eberesschen Allee

Kirschen

Eschen

Allee

Allee

Allee

Heerstr.

Kastanien

Frankeh Allee

Jaffe

Reichs Str.

Hessen Allee

Württemberg Allee

Landau

Baden Allee

Warnen Weg

HEERSTR.

Marathon Allee

Boyen

Oldenburg Allee

Preussen Allee

Soldauer Allee

Boyen Allee

Frauenburger Pl.

Lötzener All

Westend allee

Westend Allee

Eingang-Sch. Allee

Str.

Box Platz

Olympische Str.

Olympische Platz

Teufelsseechaussee

Insterburg Allee

Allee

6

Sensburger

Arysallee

Mohrunger Allee

Pillkaller Allee

Ortelsburg Allee

Lyck Allee

Tannenberg Allee

Rominter Allee

Sportforum Str.

Olympische Platz

Flatowallee

Heilsberger Allee

Suhmer Allee

Heerstr.

7

8

OLYMPIASTADION

5

Jahn Str.

Glockenturm

Glockenturm

Passenheimer Str.

Gutsmuths Weg

Hanns Braun

Friedrich Friesen Allee

Platz Friesen Str.

Jesse Owens Allee

Scott Weg

Swift Weg

Ragniter Allee

Byron W

Shaw W

Milton W Weg

G. Keller Allee

Dickens Weg

Thach Weg

Kranz Allee

Stallupöner Allee

Lötzener Allee

Schfrwinder Allee

Inset: Spandau

Ziladellen Weg

Sophienwerder W.

Spree

Havel See

Eiswerder

Eiswerder Str.

Wröhmänner Str.

Neuendorfer Str.

Müller Str.

A. Kögow Str.

A. Koelze Str.

Spandau

Juliusturm

9

10

1/2 mile

3/4 km

0

0

lain, silverware, metal objects, furniture, carpet design, and paintings. Among the most famous artists showcased here are Henry van de Velde, Hector Guimard, Bruno Paul, and Peter Behrens. The museum frequently hosts special events and exhibits. ⊠ *Schlosstr. 1a,* ☎ *030/3269-0600,* WEB *www.broehan-museum.de.* 🎦 *€5.* ☉ *Tues.–Sun. 10–6.*

⑤ Funkturm (Radio Tower). One of western Berlin's landmark structures, the Funkturm was built in 1924 by Heinrich Straumer to welcome visitors to the first *"Funkausstellung"* (radio technology exhibition), held on the fairgrounds here two years later. The soaring 152-m (498-ft) tower has an observation platform and offers a splendid view of Berlin. There is also a restaurant with a panorama from its perch at 55 m (180 ft). It's best to stick to the coffee and cake.

The Funkturm is part of the **Messegelände** (fairgrounds), Europe's largest convention and fair center, where most of the city's international fairs, such as the agricultural Grüne Woche (Green Week) and the International Tourism Fair, are held each year. Right next to the Funkturm are the oldest parts of this complex, while the shiny **Internationales Congress Centrum** (International Congress Center; ICC) looks like a giant spaceship. Ironically, the ICC, heralded as a milestone in modern convention architecture in 1979, now operates with financial losses due to its now-outdated building technology. ⊠ *Hammarskjöldpl.,* ☎ *030/3038-2996.* 🎦 *€3 observation platform; €1.50 restaurant.* ☉ *Daily 10–1; restaurant: Tues.–Sun. 11:30–11.*

OFF THE BEATEN PATH

GEDENKSTÄTTE PLÖTZENSEE (Memorial Site Plötzensee) – The name *Plötzensee* has become identified with the terror the Nazis unleashed against the political opponents of the regime in Berlin. More than 2,500 people were executed here, mostly by guillotine or hanging. In 1944 and 1945 many of the leading figures involved in the attempted assassination of Hitler on July 20, 1944, were killed here. Following a direct order of Hitler, 89 of the high-ranking officers implicated (or simply suspected of being part of the conspiracy against the Führer) were slowly strangled to death by hanging from meat hooks from the ceiling. You can still see the room where this happened, as well as the hooks. Next to the building is a small exhibit about the repression during the Nazi regime, including many documents and files from the so-called *Volksgerichtshof* (people's court), whose dreaded chief judge, Roland Freisler, sentenced hundreds of people to death. To reach Plötzensee from the western downtown area, take the U-7 subway toward Rathaus Spandau and exit at the Jakob-Kaiser-Platz station. From here Bus 123 will take you directly to the memorial site. ⊠ *Huettigpfad,* ☎ *030/344-3226.* 🎦 *Free.* ☉ *Jan. and Nov., daily 9–4:30; Feb. and Oct., daily 9–5:30; Mar.–Sept., daily 9–6.*

⑥ Georg-Kolbe-Museum. Within the house and atelier of German sculptor Georg Kolbe (1877–1947), the small but intriguing art museum showcases 180 of his sculptures and more than 1,300 drawings and prints. Beginning with his bronze creation *Tänzerin (Dancer,* 1912), Kolbe gained a reputation as one of one of 20th-century Germany's most important sculptors. The museum expanded Kolbe's own art collection (including paintings by May Liebermann and Ernst Ludwig Kirchner) and also features sculptures by Ernst Barlach, Hermann Blumenthal, Max Klinger, Gerhard Marcks, and Richard Scheibe. The redbrick private home and atelier are worth a look as well; dating from 1928–29 and designed by Ernst Reutsch, they are fine examples of the period's sober, practical architecture. The grounds present some more sculptures. The museum also has a small café, an archive, a library, and a gallery for changing exhibits. ⊠ *Sensburger Allee 25,* ☎ *030/304-2144,* WEB *www.georg-kolbe-museum.de.* 🎦 *€4.* ☉ *Tues.–Sun. 10–5.*

❼ Le-Corbusier-Haus. Berlin has always attracted the leading architects of the day. The Le Corbusier Building was built by the Swiss-born architect in 1957 for the *Interbau* architectural competition. Twelve years after the war much of the residential areas were still in shambles, making the construction of inexpensive, large apartment complexes a priority. Le Corbusier, one of the 20th century's most influential architects, tackled the problem by designing this complex with 500 airy and spacious two-story apartments and shops. These days, however, the once-visionary design looks just like another of Berlin's anonymous high-rises. ⊠ *Flatowallee 16.*

❽ Olympiastadion (Olympic Stadium). A visit to the Olympiastadion inevitably triggers mixed feelings. There is undeniably a certain greatness in the visionary monumental architecture, in the grandeur of the wide-open spaces leading to the entrance, and in the sheer size of a stadium built to hold 90,000 people. The imposing structure, designed by Werner March, is on the whole reminiscent of Roman or Greek architecture. But the overwhelming aesthetic effect is hardly to be separated from the political background from which it emerged.

The Olympiastadion was conceived and built for the summer Olympic Games of 1936, held during the first years of Nazi rule in Germany. The impressive presentation of the games was carefully orchestrated by Hitler's architect Albert Speer and would later be immortalized in film by Leni Riefenstahl: one of the most famous scenes, and an ingenious idea of Speer's, was the so-called light dome around the stadium, created by pointing antiaircraft searchlights into the night sky, thus creating an artificial extension of it into a seemingly endless universe. The Olympics turned out to be a huge propaganda success for Nazi Germany, which managed to present itself convincingly to the world as a modern, energetic, and open society. But while sporting competitions were taking place here, opponents of the regime were already being tortured and killed in the Sachsenhausen concentration camp, some 35 km (22 mi) away, and in other camps and prisons. And although Berliners enthusiastically cheered for African-American athlete Jesse Owens, Hitler himself immediately left the stadium after Owens's gold-medal victory in order to avoid having to shake hands with an *"Untermensch"* ("subhuman").

Today the Olympiastadion is used mainly for the games of the city's premier soccer club, *Hertha BSC,* whose fans flood in for home games. The huge athlete statues in front were designed by Hitler's favorite sculptor, Arno Breker. The wide square in front of the stadium, the **Maifeld,** was once used as a parade ground. The 77-m (252-ft) **Glockenturm** (bell tower) offers a great panorama of Berlin and parts of Brandenburg. The stadium is closed to visitors until 2004 due to renovations and remodeling. The best way to see it is to take in a view from the Glockenturm. Right next to the stadium's cashier stand is a small exhibit about the stadium's history and the renovation. Guided tours are offered (in German) every Sunday at noon and 3 PM. ⊠ *Olympischer Platz/Am Glockenturm,* ☎ *030/305–8123.* ▣ €5. ☉ *Tours Sun. noon and 3.*

★ ❸ Sammlung Berggruen (Berggruen Collection). This small museum in the historic Stüler-Bau (once a museum of ancient art) focuses on the history of modern art, with representative work from such artists as van Gogh, Cézanne, Picasso, Giacometti, and Klee. The main focus is on Picasso. Eighty of his works, primarily from his "blue" and "pink" periods, are on display. Emphasis is also placed on paintings by Paul Klee and the artistic predecessors of Cézanne and van Gogh. Heinz Berggruen, a businessman who emigrated to the United States in the 1930s, collected the excellent paintings here and later, after he had returned to his hometown, sold them to the city of Berlin. Opened in 1996, the museum has become one of Berlin's most beloved art venues. ✉ *Schlosstr. 1,* ☎ *030/326–9580,* WEB *www.smb.spk-berlin.de.* 🎫 *€4.* ◷ *Tues.–Fri. 10–6, weekends 11–6.*

★ ❶ **Schloss Charlottenburg** (Charlottenburg Palace). This monumental reminder of imperial days served as a city residence for the Prussian rulers. The gorgeous palace started as a modest royal summer residence in 1695, built on the orders of King Friedrich I for his wife, Sophie-Charlotte. In the 18th century Frederick the Great made a number of additions, including the dome and several wings designed in the rococo style. By 1790 the complex had evolved into the massive royal domain you see today. During the war the palace was severely damaged. Unlike other ravaged buildings (such as the city palace in eastern Berlin, whose ruins were completely razed), this palace was reconstructed during the 1950s. It was rebuilt to look exactly like the original, ignoring changes made during the 19th century.

Behind heavy iron gates, the Court of Honor—the front courtyard—is dominated by the massive **Equestrian Statue of the Great Elector.** The bronze statue, considered one of Germany's finest baroque works of art, was sculpted by Andreas Schlüter and dates from 1703. It originally stood on a bridge near the front of the city palace in eastern Berlin and depicts the Great Elector Friedrich Wilhelm as a victorious monarch. The statue was lost in the deep waters of Lake Tegel after the war when it was being transported from the depot where it had been hidden to protect it from air raids. It was recovered in 1949.

The **Altes Schloss** (Old Palace; ☎ 030/3209–1275; 🎫 €4, includes tour; ◷ Tues.–Thurs. 10–5, Fri. 9–7, weekends 10–6, WEB www.spgs.de), also called the Nering-Eosander-Bau, is the main building, with the suites of Friedrich I and his wife. Paintings include royal portraits by Antoine Pesne, a noted court painter of the 18th century. On the first floor you can visit the Oak Gallery, the early 18th-century palace chapel, and the suites of Friedrich Wilhelm II and Friedrich Wilhelm III, furnished in the Biedermeier style.

The **Neuer Flügel** (New Wing; ☎ 030/3209–1202, 🎫 €2.50; ◷ Tues.–Fri. 9–6, weekends 11–6), where Frederick the Great once lived, is also called the Knobbeldorff-Flügel. Its highlight is the 138-ft-long Goldene Galerie (Golden Gallery), the palace's ballroom. West of the staircase are the rooms of Frederick, in which the king's extravagant collection of works by Watteau, Chardin, and Pesne are displayed. Visits to the royal apartments are by guided tour; palace tours leave weekdays every hour on the hour from 9 to 4, on weekends from 11 to 4

The **Neuer Pavillon** (New Pavilion), right behind the old palace, resembles an Italian country villa. During a visit to Naples, King Friedrich Wilhelm III stayed at the Villa Reale del Chiatamone and later commissioned Karl Friedrich Schinkel to build a villa right on his palace grounds. In 1825 the Neuer Pavillon (also called the Schinkel-Pavillon) became a romantic retreat for the king and his wife. Today period furnishings, accessories, and paintings are on display.

In 1697 the **palace garden** was designed and landscaped by Simon Godeau in the baroque style. It was the first garden designed in the fashion of Louis XIV in a German country, and it formed a harmonious ensemble with the palace. However, later changes and World War II greatly damaged the original design. After the war the garden was restored to what it must have looked like in the late 18th century, when it was mostly an English Garden, designed by Peter Joseph Lenné. Many parts were underdeveloped, though, and the garden was left in a rather simplified state. The old, elaborate magnificence of the baroque French Garden was lost forever. In the garden stands the Schinkel Pavilion and the **Belvedere teahouse** (☎ 030/320–911; 🎟 €2; ☉ Nov.–Mar., Tues.–Fri. noon–4, weekends noon–5; Apr.–Oct., Tues.–Fri. 10–5, weekends 11–6), overlooking the lake and the Spree River and housing a collection of Berlin porcelain. A small **mausoleum** is hidden among some trees and bushes a few hundred yards north of the palace. The somber-looking Greek building was designed by Karl Friedrich Schinkel in 1810 and holds the sarcophagi of several Prussian monarchs and their wives, including that of Emperor Wilhelm I.

In the western extension of the palace opposite Klausener Platz, the **Museum für Vor- und Frühgeschichte** (Museum of Pre- and Early History) traces the evolution of mankind from a million or so years ago through the Stone Age, the Ice Age, the Bronze Age, and the early Middle Ages. Some highlights are the jewelry, weapons, and precious accessories found by German archaeologist Heinrich Schliemann during his extensive excavations in Troy in the late 19th century. His work proved that Homer's *Iliad* was, in fact, a true story. It is hoped that the gems already on display will be supplemented by even more precious and presumably numerous pieces of the *Trojaschatz* (Trojan Treasure) still held by private collectors and Russian museums. ⊠ *Luisenpl.,* ☎ *030/2090-5555,* WEB *www.smb.spk-berlin.de.* 🎟 *Museum: €2; free 1st Sun. of every month. A Tageskarte (day card) for €7.50 covers admission for all bldgs. and exhibits.* ☉ *Museum: Tues.–Fri. 10–6, weekends 11–6.*

❾ Spandauer Altstadt (Old Town Spandau). Spandau is probably the Berlin district with the most arrogance, not only because it is the oldest settlement (dating from 1197) within Berlin's boundaries, but also because it is beyond the Havel and Spree rivers. Spandauer locals are considered a very special breed by Berliners, and Spandauers sneer on the Berliners as well. This green district is also proud of its historic Old Town, the only neighborhood in Berlin that still bears some resemblance to its original, late-medieval appearance. Cobblestone streets and small alleys comprise the district's oldest neighborhood, the **Kolk.** One of its main thoroughfares, **Breite Strasse** (Broad Street), is renowned for including Berlin's oldest private home, the **Gotisches Haus** (⊠ Breite Str. 32), which presumably dates from 1500.

St. Nikolai-Kirche (St. Nicholas Church) was the starting point of the Lutheran Reformation in the region, initiated here by the elector Joachim II in 1539. The church (built between 1410 and 1450) is one of the few redbrick Gothic churches remaining, and stands on the site of a church that dated from the 12th century. ⊠ *Reformationspl.,* ☎ *030/330–8054.* 🎟 *Free.* ☉ *Mon.–Thurs. noon–4, Sat. 11–3, Sun. 2–4.*

❿ Zitadelle Spandau (Spandau Citadel). Berlin's last remaining medieval fortification lies at the confluence of the Havel and Spree rivers. Its strategic location made the fort a prime target for all the armies that tried to conquer Berlin and the area around it through the centuries. The fort you see today is largely as it first appeared in 1560, when it was constructed by the famous Italian fortification architect Francesco Chiaramella da Gandino. The complex has four massive corner towers—known individually as Bastion Brandenburg, Bastion König, Bastion Königin, and Bastion Kronprinz—and counts among the great moated forts of Germany, typical of northern European castle architecture from the 16th and 17th centuries. You can learn about the citadel's history at the **Stadtgeschichtliches Museum Spandau** (Spandau Municipal History Museum), at the entrance to the Bastion Königin, on the southwest corner. Guided tours are available in English, but printed materials are in German.

The only remnants of the first castle built here in the 12th century are the soaring **Juliusturm** (Julius tower) and the **Palas** (main living room), in the southwest corner of the fort. Nineteen Jewish gravestones were incorporated in the masonry of the Palas, a bizarre fact that sheds light on the difficult relationship between Jews and Germans in the Middle Ages. Recovered in a careful excavation in 1950, some of these gravestones are now on display in the museum at the Bastion Königin. One dates from 1244, making it the oldest Jewish gravestone in the region.

Throughout most of its later history the citadel was used as a prison, both civilian and military. In the early 19th century it even entered Berlin jargon in the phrase *"Ab in den Julio"* ("Off to Julius with you"), used when someone was arrested. In March 1848 some 500 leaders of the failed liberal revolution were incarcerated here. In the late 19th century, prisoners of war from France and elsewhere were held captive here. This is also where the imperial war treasury was stored, containing the reparation monies France had been required to pay the Reich after the former's defeat in the Franco-German War of 1870–71. Ironically, in 1919, after the German defeat in World War I and the dissolution of the Reich, the money had to be handed back to France. During World War II the fort was used by the German army's top-secret laboratory for gas weaponry.

The citadel is not to be confused with **Spandau Prison,** where the surviving seven of the major Nazi war criminals—among them Speer, Dönitz, and Hess—were imprisoned in 1946. It was one of the last functioning joint institutions of Allied control in Germany. British, French, American, and Soviet troops guarded the last prisoner, former Hitler deputy Rudolf Hess, until his mysterious death in 1987. Having thus lost its function, the prison was then completely destroyed to prevent it from becoming a symbol or shrine for neo-Nazi movements. The small **Britain Center** shopping mall stands where the Nazi war criminals were once held. ⊠ *Am Juliusturm,* ☎ *030/3549–44200.* ▣ *€2.* ⊙ *Tues.– Fri. 9–5, weekends 10–5.*

TIERGARTEN AND THE GOVERNMENT DISTRICT

Tiergarten, once an independent district, is now a part of Mitte (a fact many people living in old West Berlin's easternmost district don't like at all). But Tiergarten is nevertheless among the winners in Berlin's reunification. After the erection of the Wall, it was largely known for the vast green park and garden that gave the district its name; these days, however, it presents itself as the new federal government district, claiming landmarks like the Reichstag, the new chancellery, and the Schloss Bellevue.

The second center of Tiergarten is rejuvenated Potsdamer Platz. World War II and the division of Berlin reduced once-bustling Potsdamer Platz to a sprawling, empty lot at the southeastern end of Tiergarten. In the mid-1990s it became Europe's largest construction site, with corporate giants such as Sony and debis, the former software subsidiary of DaimlerChrysler, erecting headquarters next to malls devoted to shopping and entertainment. Today the square and its surrounding narrow streets are a modern version of prewar Potsdamer Platz, then the epitome of the urbane Berlin of the Roaring '20s.

Numbers in the text correspond to numbers in the margin and on the Tiergarten and the Government District map.

A Good Walk

If you are up for an initial 20-minute walk, take the narrow path right next to the elevated railway tracks you'll see when turning right from the Zoologischer Garten entrance. Follow the path through the idyllic **Tiergarten** ① across two romantic bridges, passing a café and antique lamps until you hit Strasse des 17. Juni. Just turn right here. If you prefer to save your feet some walking, take Bus 100 from outside the Zoologischer Garten train station to the Siegessäule. At the center of the park is the traffic intersection known as the Grosser Stern (Big Star), so called because five roads meet here. The **Siegessäule** ② column provides a lookout from the center of the rotary. Follow Spreeweg from the Grosser Stern to **Schloss Bellevue** ③, the residence of Germany's head of state, its federal president. Next head east along John-Foster-Dulles-Allee, keeping the Spree River in sight on your left. You'll soon pass the **Haus der Kulturen der Welt** ④, which stages cultural exhibitions and concerts. Take Scheidemannstrasse, which branches off on the left, and cross Heinrich-von-Gagern-Strasse. To the north you'll see the gigantic **Bundeskanzleramt** ⑤, the official seat of the German chancellor and the main new building in the federal government district you've just entered. You'll get a fine view of the Bundeskanzleramt from atop the monumental **Reichstag** ⑥, just ahead on Scheidemannstrasse. If you turn right onto Heinrich-von-Gagern-Strasse you'll reach Strasse des 17. Juni—a name that commemorates the 1953 uprising of East Berlin workers that was quashed by Soviet tanks. Here, to the east is the **Sowjetisches Ehrenmal** ⑦, in memorial to the Soviet soldiers that took Berlin in 1945.

South of the Reichstag, where Strasse des 17. Juni meets Unter den Linden, is the mighty **Brandenburger Tor** ⑧, the most significant icon of German triumph and defeat. Only a few steps to the south of the gate off Ebertstrasse is the **Denkmal für die ermordeten Juden Europas** ⑨, Germany's national Holocaust memorial, which is still under construction.

Follow Ebertstrasse south toward the gleaming high-rises just a few hundred yards away: this is **Potsdamer Platz** ⑩, a seemingly miniature city with the finest new architecture in Berlin. Walk down Potsdamer Strasse and enter the circular ring of the **Sony Center** ⑪, which houses the **Filmmuseum Berlin** ⑫. Right behind the Potsdamer Platz neighborhood is yet another gem of modern architecture, the Kulturforum (Cultural Forum), a cluster of museums and concert halls around Kemperplatz. Taking Potsdamer Strasse, the first of the modern buildings you'll pass is the **Staatsbibliothek** ⑬, Berlin's fine state library. The adjacent **Philharmonie** ⑭ is Berlin's prime concert hall, with the adjoining **Musikinstrumentenmuseum** ⑮ giving you an earful about the history of musical instruments. Behind the two concert halls, via Scharounstrasse, is the **Gemäldegalerie** ⑯, one Germany's best art museums, and the adjoining **Kunstgewerbemuseum** ⑰, which exhibits historic European arts and crafts. In the same complex the smaller **Kupferstichkabinett** ⑱ holds a collection of historic and modern graphic art. The neoromantic **St. Matthäuskirche** ⑲ is the only historic building left standing in this area. South of it is the glass-enclosed **Neue Nationalgalerie** ⑳, designed by Mies van der Rohe. Once you've passed the Neue Nationalgalerie, turn right on Reichpietschufer and walk along the canal for about 10 minutes. On your right you'll see the Bendlerblock, Germany's former war department, which also holds the **Gedenkstätte Deutscher Widerstand** ㉑, a memorial and exhibit about the German officers who tried to assassinate Adolf Hitler in July 1944. You can reach the memorial site by turning right into Stauffenbergstrasse. Once back on Reichpietschufer, continue west and pass **Shell-Haus** ㉒, one of Berlin's first high-rises.

North of here is the old Diplomatenviertel, the capital's revived embassy district. You can explore the new and restored architecture of the area by walking north on Hiroshimastrasse and then turning left on Tiergartenstrasse. If you want to skip the diplomatic quarter and proceed to the next attraction, simply walk straight on Reichpietschufer until you hit Klingelhöferstrasse. Turn left onto that street and walk south a few yards to reach the walk's final stop, the **bauhaus archiv. museum für gestaltung** ㉓, a modern museum devoted to the design and architecture of the Bauhaus school.

TIMING

You can do the whole tour in a day, provided you take Berlin's least expensive public transportation, Bus 100 or 200, between some of the sights. They both start at the U-Bahn station Zoologischer Garten and make several stops in the western downtown and Tiergarten area. All buildings in the Tiergarten, with the exception of the Haus der Kulturen der Welt, are closed to the public, so you can explore the park in less than two hours, even if you walk. To avoid long lines for entrance to the Reichstag, arrive before 9 AM. Its cupola also provides a beautiful nighttime view of the city. Potsdamer Platz is a good place to break for lunch, and any of the museums of the Kulturforum require more than an hour each to tour.

Sights to See

★ ㉓ **bauhaus-archiv. museum für gestaltung** (Bauhaus Archive. Museum for Design). The museum here features displays of everything the artists of the Bauhaus movement ever conceived or produced between 1919 and 1933, including furniture, appliances, porcelain objects, carpets, billboards, works of graphic design, and architectural plans. The Bauhaus Archive is the world's leading research institution on the movement and holds an extensive document and photo archive in addition to a large library.

The Bauhaus school of design was founded in in Dessau, where teachers included Walter Gropius, Ludwig Mies van der Rohe, Lyonel Feininger, Wassily Kandinsky, and Paul Klee. In its last two years the Bauhaus moved to Berlin, only to be closed down in 1933 by the Nazi regime, which considered its modernist aesthetic to be "un-German." Largely in reaction to the chronic discomforts that plagued working-class city dwellers, the movement devoted itself to the overall improvement of contemporary living by rethinking and redesigning everything—from simple home appliances to the construction of whole buildings. Guided by this very modern and democratic ideal, it became one of the most influential architectural and industrial design movements of the 20th century. The Bauhaus also introduced mass production into industrial design and architecture in the 1920s, when designers were forced by an overall lack of resources and capital to come up with more standardized, easy-to-manufacture products.

The building itself was designed in 1964 by the Bauhaus's first director, Walter Gropius; it was originally planned for Darmstadt but was built here instead in 1971. It is a good, albeit modernized, example of the clear and direct Bauhaus style. Hundreds of high-quality original products sold at the museum shop, mainly useful items for the kitchen, office, or living room. A selection of articles can be bought online as well. ⊠ *Klingelhöferstr. 14*, ☎ *030/254–0020*, ⓦⓔⓑ *www.bauhaus.de.* ⊠ *€3.90.* ☉ *Mon. and Wed.–Sun. 10–5.*

★ ❽ **Brandenburger Tor** (Brandenburg Gate). Once the pride of imperial Berlin and the city's premier landmark, the Brandenburger Tor was left in a desolate no-man's-land when the Wall was built. In 1989 the gate has

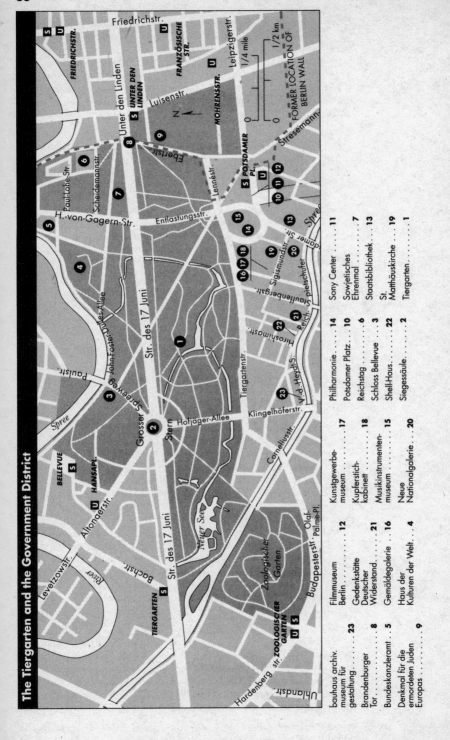

The Tiergarten and the Government District

bauhaus archiv. museum für gestaltung **23**

Brandenburger Tor **8**

Bundeskanzleramt . . **5**

Denkmal für die ermordeten Juden Europas **9**

Filmmuseum Berlin **12**

Gedenkstätte Deutscher Widerstand . . **21**

Gemäldegalerie . . **16**

Haus der Kulturen der Welt . . . **4**

Kunstgewerbe-museum **17**

Kupferstich-kabinett **18**

Musikinstrumenten-museum **15**

Neue Nationalgalerie . . . **20**

Philharmonie . . **14**

Potsdamer Platz . . **10**

Reichstag **6**

Schloss Bellevue . . **3**

Shell-Haus **22**

Siegessäule **2**

Sony Center **11**

Sowjetisches Ehrenmal **7**

Staatsbibliothek . . **13**

St. Matthäuskirche . . **19**

Tiergarten **1**

FORMER LOCATION OF BERLIN WALL

1/2 km

1/4 mile

become the focal point of celebrating the Wall's demise and is the nation's central party venue for New Year's Eve. This is the sole remaining gate of 14 built by Carl Langhans in 1788–91, designed as a triumphal arch for King Frederick Wilhelm II. Its virile classical style pays tribute to Athens's Acropolis. The quadriga, a chariot drawn by four horses and driven by the Goddess of Peace, was added in 1794. When Napoléon and his victorious troops marched into Berlin in 1806, the French emperor took the quadriga with him to Paris. It was only after Napoléon's defeat in 1814 that Prussian general Blücher would be able to retrieve it from Paris.

Just as Napoléon's troops had paraded through the gate after their successful campaigns, armies in modern times, too, used the gate as a backdrop, the last time in 1945, when victorious Red Army troops took Berlin. The upper part of the gate and quadriga were destroyed in the war. In 1957 the original molds were discovered in West Berlin, and a new quadriga was cast in copper and presented as a gift to the people of East Berlin. The East German government changed one small detail of the quadriga: the little Prussian iron cross you can see today right beneath the eagle, on top of the lance the Goddess of Peace holds, was removed because it was seen as a symbol of German militarism. A replica of the original cross was added during the quadriga's first major restoration in 1990.

The square next to the gate, **Pariser Platz,** has regained its traditional prewar design and is the beginning of Berlin's historic eastern boulevard, Unter den Linden.

❺ **Bundeskanzleramt** (Federal Chancellery). The huge white-and-gray-alabaster cube that could be mistaken for an alien space station is the ultramodern complex of the German Federal Chancellery. Completed in 2000, the chancellery is one of the very few new buildings in the government district built by a Berlin architect, Axel Schulte.

The chancellery is at the **Spreebogen,** a wide-open area defined by a curve of the Spree River, just a few hundred yards northwest of the Reichstag. This location was more than suitable because it had been left untouched since World War II. Buildings in this area had already been demolished by Nazi architect Albert Speer some 60 years ago during the redesign of Berlin.

The 118-ft-high main cube in the middle of the building holds the offices of the chancellor, while the area in front, protected by two parallel, wall-like office complexes, surrounds a ceremonial courtyard. Behind the cube and extending across the Spree River is the **Kanzlergarten** (Chancellor Garden). Former chancellor Helmut Kohl supported the chancellery's design and had expected to be the first occupant, but elections brought his political opponent, Gerhard Schröder, into office. While still a young man and on a night when he was slightly inebriated, Schröder is said to have shaken the gates of the old chancellery in Bonn, shouting, "Let me in, let me in!" He has finally been let in.

Opposite the chancellery is the new **Paul-Löbe-Haus,** which holds some offices of the representatives of the German federal parliament and extends across the Spree River to the east. Both the chancellery and the Paul-Löbe-Haus form the so-called *Band des Bundes* (Federal Ribbon), as the complex symbolically connects the former East and West Berlins.

The chancellery is not open to the public. To take in the whole layout of the building, ride any of the S-Bahn trains operating between Zoologischer Garten and Friedrichstrasse. While riding along on the

S-Bahn viaduct, you'll pass the chancellery a few hundred yards away. ⊠ *Willy-Brandt-Str. 1.*

❾ **Denkmal für die ermordeten Juden Europas** (Memorial for the Murdered Jews of Europe). Germany is commemorating the Jewish victims of Nazism just south of the Brandenburg Gate and the government district, and a few hundred yards west of the center of Nazi power on Wilhelmstrasse. The country's new national Holocaust memorial honors the more than 6 million Jewish victims killed in the concentration camps. The memorial is under construction and is projected to be finished by 2003. Designed by American architect Peter Eisenman, it consists of 2,700 concrete pillars with varied measurements that cover a total area of 7,600 square yards. This field of tomblike pillars was chosen from more than 500 submitted proposals—it was the only one that seemed to have sufficiently solved the delicate issue of how to adequately express the horrors of the Holocaust.

The first plan to build a memorial goes back to a private citizens' initiative led by German-Jewish journalist Lea Rosh and other prominent public figures, who since 1988 had campaigned fervently for a Holocaust memorial. In the following years a fierce debate about the dedication of the monument and its attendant political questions arose. One of the main issues was whether the memorial should only commemorate Jewish victims of fascism, or whether it should honor all victims of the Nazis. In the end it was decided officially to devote the memorial to Jewish victims only, though most Germans refer to it as the *Holocaust-Denkmal* (Holocaust Memorial).

The information center to be built beneath the memorial reflects a compromise, because at first the memorial was to have to none. The information center's exhibit is expected to present the history of the Holocaust. ⊠ *Between Ebert-, Wilhelm-, and Behrenstr,* WEB *www. holocaust-mahnmal.de.*

OFF THE BEATEN PATH | **DIPLOMATENVIERTEL** (Embassy District) – For almost half a century Berlin's old embassy row along Tiergartenstrasse was uninhabited. Most of the 60 embassies and consulates were destroyed in World War II and its former occupants relocated to Bonn. The area was originally known as the *Geheimratsviertel* (Privy Council District), a historically affluent area where villas and mansions of Jewish businessmen and industrialists dated to the 19th century. In the late 1930s most Jews were expelled, and their properties were sold or demolished to make way for the new embassies of the Third Reich's allies and those of other countries. During Bonn's tenure as capital the few remaining buildings here were left to decay, and some were squatted. Over the years nature reclaimed the area, and the craters left from the bombs became overgrown with bushes. Because most countries never gave up their territorial claim to their former embassies, most of these properties were off-limits to the German police. In the 1980s prostitution and heavy drug trafficking moved into the area.

Since reunification the neighborhood has changed dramatically. Old embassies were modernized and new ones built. On Tiergartenstrasse, the monumental **Italienische Botschaft** (Italian embassy), an example of fascist architecture, had been in use as a consulate and has since resumed its embassy role. Also revealing its totalitarian origins is the **Japanische Botschaft** (Japanese embassy), which had been turned into a cultural center but has now returned to its diplomatic function. Some of the largest buildings along Tiergartenstrasse and Hiroshimastrasse are the German state representative offices. A true architectural highlight in this area are the **Nordische Botschaften** (Nordic Embassies), the five connected embassies of Denmark, Norway, Sweden, Finland, and Iceland, off Klingelhöferstrasse. Built in 1997–99, the complex is shielded from the sun (and the public, for that matter) by turquoise metal blinds that cover the whole building. They can be adjusted according to the intensity and direction of the sunlight. From atop Bus 200 you can get a fairly good view of the embassies as it rolls down Tiergartenstrasse. ⊠ *Klingelhöferstr. and corner of Tiergartenstr.*

⑫ Filmmuseum Berlin. At the front of the Sony Center, Berlin's new film museum presents the early development of filmmaking and German movie history, with a particular focus on expressionist films such as those directed by Friedrich Wilhelm Murnau (*The Cabinet of Dr. Caligari*) and Fritz Lang (*M, Metropolis*). It is a definite must-see for aficionados of German movie and television stars like Heinz Rühmann, Hans Albers, Götz George, or Romy Schneider; it also features much, though, to interest visitors for whom none of these are household names. The highlights include three rooms filled with memorabilia from several renowned German-born actors and actresses—most notably, a selection of dresses, letters, and more from Marlene Dietrich. Even her complete luggage set is on display here, inspiring pity for the poor bellboys who had to carry them. A small but telling item is a cigarette case, a gift to her from director Josef von Sternberg, with the inscription "To Marlene Dietrich—woman, mother, and actress as never before there was one." ⊠ *Potsdamer Str. 2,* ☎ *030/300–9030,* WEB *www.filmmuseum-berlin.de.* 🎫 €6. ☽ *Tues.–Sun. 10–6, Thurs. 10–8.*

㉑ Gedenkstätte Deutscher Widerstand (German Resistance Memorial). One of the few landmarks in Berlin recognizing German resistance against Hitler is at the Bendlerblock in Tiergarten. It was at this location (formerly the German Military High Command Post) that the four highest-ranking officers who tried to assassinate Hitler on July 20, 1944, were arrested and shot the same day. An extensive exhibition with some 5,000 documents, photos, and other items tells the story of the officers who tried to kill Hitler and his paladins in hopes of stopping the war and ending the Holocaust.

Between the years of 1933 and 1945 there were about 40 unsuccessful attempts on Hitler's life, including this 1944 assassination attempt. After Colonel Claus Graf Schenk von Stauffenberg planted a bomb at the Führer's headquarters in East Prussia, the officer flew back to Berlin, where his fellow conspirators, waiting at the Benderblock, ordered regular troops to disarm the SS and arrest leading Nazi figures. Although "the men of July the 20th" (as they were later to be called) did not manage to take control of the German capital, the other conspirators in Vienna, Prague, and Paris were able to seize control of those cities for a few hours. In the early evening the few officers involved were implicated at the Bendlerblock and later arrested. The leading figures of the revolt, including von Stauffenberg, were then executed that same night in the courtyard. Today you will find a plaque there (and usually some wreaths) commemorating the officers.

The Bendlerblock itself is used by the German Ministry of Defense and is not open to the public. The neoclassic building dates from 1911–14 and first served as the headquarters for the imperial German navy. Later it was the seat of the German army headquarters until 1945. ⊠ *Stauffenbergstr. 13–14,* ☎ *030/269–9500,* WEB *www.gdw-berlin.de.* 🎫 €2. ☽ *Mon.–Wed. and Fri. 9–6, Thurs. 9–8, weekends 10–6.*

★ ⑯ Gemäldegalerie (Painting Gallery). Opened in 1997, the Gemäldegalerie reunites formerly separated collections from East and West Berlin. It is one of Germany's finest art galleries and houses an extensive selection of European paintings from the 13th to the 18th centuries, mostly portraiture and religious and mythical representations. The single-floor museum enjoys natural light from carefully arranged skylights. Specially designed walls with light-absorbing material let the colors of the paintings glow.

The museum's collections focus mainly on Italian and French paintings from the 14th to 19th centuries, though the first seven exhibition rooms showcase German painters from the 14th to 19th centuries, among them Dürer, Cranach the Elder, and Holbein. Ten figures pray beneath the mantel of the *Schutzmantel-Maria* (1480), an unusual and colorful carving from Ravensburg in Room I. Another collection has works of the Italian masters—Botticelli, Titian, Giotto, Lippi, and Raphael—as well as paintings by Dutch and Flemish masters of the 15th and 16th centuries: Van Eyck, Bosch, Brueghel the Elder, and van der Weyden. The museum also holds the world's second-largest Rembrandt collection, the most important works being *The Man with the Golden Helmet* and *The Mennonite pastor Conreils Claesy Ansio and his wife.*

The gallery is the most important part of a unique ensemble of museums, galleries, and concert halls known as **Kulturforum** (Cultural Forum) and is considered one of Germany's cultural jewels. The forum was conceived as a second and modern *Museumsinsel* in the West Berlin, since the historic Museum Island was behind the Wall in East Berlin. ⊠ *Matthäikirchpl. 8,* ☎ *030/2660; 030/2090–5555 for all state museums in Berlin,* WEB *www.smb.spk-berlin.de.* ⊠ *€2; free 1st Sun. of every month.* ☉ *Tues.–Sun. 10–6, Thurs. 10–10.*

Steps from the Gemäldegalerie is yet another example of ultramodern architecture. The **Kunstbibliothek** (Art Library; ☎ 030/2090–5555 or 030/2660; ☉ Mon. 2–8, Tues.–Fri. 9–8) contains art posters, a costume library, ornamental engravings, and a commercial art collection.

❹ Haus der Kulturen der Welt (House of World Cultures). A daringly curved roof is the eye-catching feature of this inspiring building in the Tiergarten park. It serves as an exhibition hall and cultural venue, presenting a changing program of exhibits, lectures, art, and music from Africa, South America, and Asia. Set behind two long water basins and adorned by modern sculptures, it was built in 1957–58 by architect Hugh Stubbins. The building was the official U.S. contribution to the 1957 architectural competition "Interbau." It first served as Berlin's congress hall and quickly became a beloved landmark of a new and modern West Berlin. However, in 1980 the roof collapsed, killing one journalist and injuring many others. After its careful (and this time, more stable) reconstruction, the congress hall reopened as the House of World Cultures in 1989.

Behind the building is the dock of Berlin's **Weisse Flotte** (White Fleet), which tours the canals. To the left of the complex, right off John-Foster-Dulles-Allee, stands a solemn, dark bell tower called the **Carillon.** It was built in 1987 in honor of Berlin's 750th anniversary. The tower's 68 automated bells make it one of the world's largest bell instruments. They can usually be heard daily at noon and 6 PM. ⊠ *John-Foster-Dulles-Allee 10,* ☎ *030/397–870.* ⊠ *Depends on events.* ☉ *Depends on events.*

☺ ⓯ Musikinstrumentenmuseum (Musical Instruments Museum). This collection of some 750 keyboard, string, wind, and percussion instruments includes exquisite violins made by Stradivari and Amati, as well as a harpsichord that once was owned by Prussian king Frederick the Great. The museum is part of one of the world's leading institutions on music research. ⊠ *Tiergartenstr. 1,* ☎ *030/2548–1129,* WEB *www.sim.*

spk-berlin.de. ✉ €2; *free 1st Sun. of every month; tour* €1.50. ☉ *Tues.–Fri. 9–5, weekends 10–5; tour Sat. at 11; presentation of Wurlitzer organ 1st Sat. of month at noon.*

⑰ Kunstgewerbemuseum (Museum of Decorative Arts). One of the world's oldest museums for decorative art and arts and crafts, the museum was founded in 1867 and has incorporated many royal and church collections. The exhibits of European arts and crafts from the Middle Ages to the present cover four floors and chronicle the historic development of furniture, fashion, jewelry, and accessories, as well as porcelain, carpets, and home furnishings. A real treat is a look at the bright ornamental wall carpets and furnishings from Italian Renaissance courts. Among other notable exhibits are the Welfenschatz (Welfen Treasure), a collection of 16th-century gold and silver plates from Nürnberg, as well as ceramics and porcelains. The 20th century is primarily represented by art nouveau and art deco objects and some modern industrial design. ✉ *Matthäikirchpl. 8,* ☎ 030/266–2902, WEB *www.smb.spk-berlin.de.* ✉ €2; *free 1st Sun. of every month.* ☉ *Tues.–Fri. 10–6, weekends 11–6.*

⑱ Kupferstichkabinett (Drawing and Print Collection). This museum at the Kulturforum contains one of the world's largest collections of graphic art, and includes European woodcuts, engravings, and illustrated books from the 15th century to the present. The museum holds more than 80,000 drawings and more than half a million prints. On display are several pen-and-ink drawings by Dürer and 150 drawings by Rembrandt. Modern examples of graphic art by Pablo Picasso and German artist Joseph Beuys are also part of the exhibits. Another building displays paintings dating from the late Middle Ages to 1800. ✉ *Matthäikirchpl. 6,* ☎ *030/2090–5555 or 030/2660,* WEB *www.smb.spk-berlin.de.* ✉ €2. ☉ *Tues.–Fri. 10–6, weekends 11–6.*

⑳ Neue Nationalgalerie (New National Gallery). This glass-and-steel art gallery designed by Mies van der Rohe and built in the mid-1960s houses all of its exhibits on underground floors. The collection comprises paintings, sculptures, and drawings from the 19th and 20th centuries, with an emphasis on works by such impressionists as Manet, Monet, Renoir, and Pissarro. Other schools represented are the German romantics, realists, expressionists, and surrealists, also German political art of the 1920s (represented by the paintings of Otto Dix and George Grosz) and the artists of the *Brücke* movement (Ernst Ludwig Kirchner and Karl Schmidt-Rottluff). The gallery frequently presents outstanding international art exhibitions. ✉ *Potsdamer Str. 50,* ☎ 030/266–2662, WEB *www.smb.spk-berlin.de.* ✉ €4. ☉ *Tues.–Fri. 10–6, Thurs. 10–10, weekends 11–6.*

⑭ Philharmonie (Philharmonic Hall). The roof that resembles a great tent belongs to Berlin's Philharmonic Hall, home since 1963 to the world-renowned Berlin Philharmonic Orchestra. The golden-yellow building was designed by Hans Scharoun and is famous for its splendid acoustics. Screens hanging from the ceiling control the flow of sound. At the time of its construction, the architectural layout represented an avant-garde version of the traditional concert hall. Berliners used to call the Philharmonic Hall *"Zirkus Karajani"* ("Karajan's Circus") in mockery of the late star conductor, a vain and eccentric man who controlled his musicians with a firm but loving hand. The Berlin Philharmonic Orchestra was founded in 1882 and elects its chief conductor. Karajan's successor was Italian maestro Claudio Abbado, who will be followed by Sir Simon Rattle in 2002. The smaller **Kammermusiksaal** (Chamber Music Hall) adjoining the Philharmonic was completed in 1988 by Edgar Wiesniewski in accordance with plans by Hans Scharoun.

✉ *Matthäikircherstr. 1,* ☎ *030/254–880 or 030/2548–8132,* [WEB] *www.berlin-philharmonic.com.*

❿ Potsdamer Platz (Potsdam Square). East and West are rejoined on this square, which was Berlin's inner-city center and Europe's busiest plaza before World War II. Today's buildings of steel, glass, and concrete make it hard to imagine that the square was once a no-man's-land divided by the infamous Wall. Amid the new buildings, whose construction costs came to a whopping $92 billion, only a red line on the streets traces the old border. Where the British, American, and Russian sectors once met, Sony, debis, DaimlerChrysler, Asea Brown Boveri, and other companies have built their new headquarters. Only one historic building has been left standing (and has been integrated into the debis complex), the **Weinhaus Huth.** The former wine restaurant now houses a coffee shop and an upscale wine merchant.

The two high-rise towers dominating the square are part of the headquarters of debis, the former software subsidiary of DaimlerChrysler, and other companies. The debis center was designed by star architect Renzo Piano. One of the towers (to your right when you stand on Potsdamer Platz) offers rides in an express elevator to the spectacular **Panorama** observation platform 315 ft above the ground. ✉ *Potsdamer Pl. 1,* ☎ *030/2529–4372.* €3. ☉ *Tues.–Sun. 11–8, last admission at 7:30.*

The shopping and entertainment mecca **Potsdamer Platz Arkaden** covers 40,000 square yards and houses 140 shops and restaurants on three levels. Right next to it are the Grand Hyatt Berlin, the movie complex Cinemaxx, and a 3-D IMAX cinema, as well as the new Berlin casino and Germany's largest musical theater. ✉ *Alte Potsdamer Str. 7,* ☎ *030/2559–2766.* ☉ *Weekdays 9:30–8, Sat. 9:30–4.*

Among the ultramodern constructions are reminders of the area's historic past. In front of the left debis tower, you can see an antique-looking green traffic light and clock, a replica of Europe's first automatic traffic light, which stood here in 1928. Street names in this neighborhood honor prominent figures who fought against Hitler. **Marlene-Dietrich-Platz,** in front of the **Stella Musical Theater,** commemorates the actress and singer who who fled the Nazis and performed for Allied soldiers. **Varian-Fry-Strasse** is named for the American activist Varian Fry, who smuggled refugees from Nazi-occupied France, and **Ludwig-Beck-Strasse** is a reminder of German general Beck, who who plotted against Hitler in 1944.

❻ Reichstag (Parliament Building). For more than a century the staid gray Reichstag has been a symbol of modern German history. The neo-Renaissance building, one of Berlin's premier landmarks, was erected between 1884 and 1894 by Paul Wallot to house the imperial German parliament, and later served as such during the ill-fated Weimar Republic. On the night of February 28, 1933, the Reichstag burned under mysterious circumstances. Dutch Communist Marius van der Lubbe was tried and sentenced for arson the next day, and the National Socialists used the fire as an excuse to present strict laws nullifying most civil rights in Germany (which makes it likely that the Nazis themselves started the fire). The laws marked the beginning of Nazi persecution and increasingly totalitarian rule in Germany. Because of the fire, the parliament had to convene in the Kroll opera house next door. This made the Reichstag the only major building in Berlin that was never associated with National Socialism.

The Reichstag was heavily damaged during the war and almost completely destroyed during the last days of fighting in April 1945 (the Red Army focused on conquering the Reichstag first, and only then attacked the now-destroyed chancellery, where Hitler and many leading Nazi generals were hiding). The graffiti of the victorious Russian soldiers (and visiting American GIs in the last months of 1945 and 1946) can still be seen on some of the walls in the hallways. In September 1948, during the Soviet blockade of West Berlin and the ensuing airlift, the square in front of the Reichstag, **Platz der Republik** (Square of the Republic), witnessed one of West Berlin's most important political events. In a now-famous speech former mayor Ernst Reuter called on the Western world to remember the suffering of West Berliners and shouted, *"Ihr Völker der Welt, schaut auf diese Stadt!"*—"Peoples of the world, look upon this city!"

For decades during Berlin's division the Reichstag only occasionally served parliamentary committees and the political parties, as the Bundestag was not officially allowed to be in session in West Berlin. Because of Allied laws, West Berlin was not a sovereign part of the Federal Republic of Germany. Therefore, the Reichstag was usually crowded with school classes from West Germany on their compulsory excursions to West Berlin.

The events of November 1989 suddenly brought the almost-forgotten Reichstag to the forefront of worldwide attention. On June 20, 1991, it was decided the German federal government and parliament would eventually relocate to the old German capital and the Reichstag. In 1995, after a heated debate and with only a slim majority, the parliament gave the American artists Christo and Jeanne-Claude a go ahead to wrap the newly celebrated symbol of German unification. In a two-week process in June and July, the Reichstag was wrapped in shiny silver high-tech polypropylene tied with blue rope—and remained so for weeks. Millions of visitors came to see it, enjoying parties and picnics on the Platz der Republik.

Beginning in 1997, the radical redesign of the Reichstag under British architect Sir Norman Foster started at a price tag of roughly €300 million. The process of reconstructing the Reichstag entailed extensive remodeling and even the cool, Bauhaus-like interior, designed by Paul Baumgarten from 1961 to 1969, was removed. The debris was processed into street gravel, just like the remains of the infamous Berlin Wall. Only the facade was left standing as an empty hull, and behind it one of the most advanced parliamentary buildings in the world was slowly taking shape. The building process was accompanied by tiresome discussions about details. One of the more amusing debates focused on the official *Bundesadler,* the "federal eagle" that was mounted in the parliament's main chamber. The new design of the bird resulted in an eagle that somehow didn't look as lean or as elegant as the old one, so it had to be changed again. You can judge the eagle for yourself on a Reichstag tour.

The most striking new feature of the Reichstag is the glass cupola that has been compared to the one that topped the Reichstag before the fire of 1934. The heavily criticized 131-ft-high cupola became a top attraction for both Berliners and tourists once it opened in 1999. At its base is a pictorial history of the Reichstag (with translations in English), and a gently spiraling ramp allows visitors a spectacular panorama of Berlin. The design of the cupola is practical as well. Its 360 mirrors deflect the sunlight into the parliamentary chamber beneath it, thus avoiding the need for electric lighting during the day. In addition, the cylinder serves as a ventilation system for the parliamentary chamber. Air drifts upward and passes out through an opening in the cupola's top.

Since the German parliament resumed its work at the Reichstag in April 1999, yet another controversial piece of art sparked discussions in the fall of 2000. This contentious piece, designed by Berlin conceptual artist Hans Haacke is in the Reichstag's north courtyard, visible from the top of the Reichstag, but outside the cupola. Within a trough filled with earth from German counties and are the words DER BEVÖLKERUNG ("To the Population") amid sprouting plants. It is a critical reinterpretation of the inscription DEM DEUTSCHEN VOLKE ("To the German people") on the Reichstag's portico. The new sign's message and presentation caused a great division of opinion among representatives and the public. Haacke's message specifically includes all foreigners living in Germany—a new and liberal interpretation of the German people, which usually is defined by German "blood." But in the end, after a vote in parliament, the work was left in place (though most representatives refrained from submitting earth from their respective home counties as requested).

Visit either in the early morning or in the evening to avoid the longest lines. For a short tour that includes a view of the chambers before you ascend the dome, use the south entrance of the Reichstag. Several crosses (most of them decorated with flowers) hanging on a fence just a few steps from the south entrance sadly remind you that the Berlin Wall stood just a few yards away. Each of the white wooden crosses bears the name of one of the East Germans killed by East German border guards while trying to cross the Wall. ✉ *Reichstagsgebäude, Platz der Republik 1,* ☎ *030/2270,* WEB *www.bundestag.de.* ⌨ *Free.* ☺ *Daily 8 AM–10 PM.*

❸ **Schloss Bellevue** (Bellevue Palace). This small palace has served as the official residence of Germany's federal president since 1959. It was built on the Spree River in 1785 for Frederick the Great's youngest brother, Prince August Ferdinand. In 1994 then-president Richard von Weizsäcker made it his main residence. Since then it has been closed to the public. To the left of the palace is the new egg-shape executive building—all marble, glass, and steel. Erected in 1998, it was the first new building built by the federal government in Berlin. It's powered by solar-energy panels on the roof. ✉ *Schloss Bellevue Park.*

㉒ **Shell-Haus** (Shell House). The Shell-Haus was designed by Emil Fahrenkamp in 1930–31 and served as the branch offices of Shell Corporation in Berlin. It was not only a fine example of Berlin's *Neue Sachlichkeit* (new objectivity) style but was also one of the city's first "high-rises" to be erected with a steel skeleton, in this case hidden behind a zigzagging facade. For its time it was a very avant-garde building: the windows were extremely large, allowing more sunlight in and giving the offices an airy atmosphere. The general floor plan and layout are based on a series of rounded corners extending toward the street, giving the building a very organic look. After the war the building (which is now used by Berlin's largest gas utility company) was left abandoned, despite protests from the public. In 1997 the building was restored. ✉ *Reichpietschufer at corner of Stauffenbergstr.*

❷ **Siegessäule** (Victory Column). The 227-ft-high granite, sandstone, and bronze column has a splendid view. It was erected in front of the Reichstag in 1873 to commemorate the German Empire's and Prussia's military victories over Denmark, Austria, and France, which are depicted in the relief on the granite platform. On top of the column is a golden Goddess of Victory designed by Friedrich Drake. Berliners like to simply call the statue *"Goldelse"* ("Golden Else"). As part of the redesign of Berlin as the *Welthauptstadt Germania* (Germania World Capital) that the Nazis envisioned after their planned victory, the column was moved to the Tiergarten in 1938–39 and put on an additional platform to make it look larger and more majestic. The 285-step climb up the column to the observation platform can be tiring, but the view is rewarding. ⊠ *Am Grossen Stern,* ☎ *030/391–2961.* 🎟 *€1.* ☉ *Nov.–Mar., daily 9:30–5:30; Apr.–Oct., weekdays 9:30–7, weekends 9:30–6:30 (last admission 1 hr before closing).*

★ ⑪ **Sony Center** (Sony Center). The light glass-and-steel construction of the Sony Center, encircling a spectacular 4,800-square-yard forum, is an architectural jewel designed by German-American architect Helmut Jahn. Since its opening on Potsdamer Platz in 2000, the ultramodern building has become a prime attraction, with the piazza under the tent-like roof bustling with crowds in summer. In addition to Sony's European headquarters, there are apartments and offices here, along with several restaurants, an eight-screen Sony Cineplex movie theater, and a Sony "style store," where you can buy the latest sleek Sony entertainment equipment.

Of particular interest, though, is the distinctive **Kaisersaal** (Emperor's Hall)—a complex of several historic rooms and halls meticulously restored from the Grand Hotel Esplanade, which stood on this spot until World War II. Well, not exactly this spot—its original location was actually some 50 yards away, and it was carefully moved inch by inch on air cushions in 1996 in order to integrate it into the new center. It now houses the restaurant and café Josty, an homage to the legendary Café Josty, a fixture on the square before the war. Along with the **Weinhaus Huth,** the remaining halls of the Kaisersaal are some of the very few pieces of architecture from the old Potsdamer Platz to have survived the heavy bombings of World War II. ⊠ *Potsdamer Str. 2,* ☎ *030/2575–5700,* 🌐 *www.sony-center.de.* ☉ *Open 24 hrs.*

❼ **Sowjetisches Ehrenmal** (Soviet Memorial). Built directly after World War II, this semicircular monument stands as a reminder of the bloody Soviet victory over the shattered German army in Berlin in May 1945. It features a bronze statue of a soldier atop a marble plinth taken from Hitler's former *Reichkanzlei* (headquarters). The memorial is flanked by what are said to be the first two T-34 tanks to have fought their way into the city in the last days of the war. ⊠ *Str. des 17. Juni.*

⑬ **Staatsbibliothek** (State Library). Generations of students have labored in the state library of Berlin, one of the largest libraries in Germany, currently holding more than 9 million items. The modern building is a part of the **Kulturforum** and was built in 1967–76 by Hans Scharoun and Edgar Wisnieswki in the same style as the two concert halls just across the street. After reunification, the library was reunited with its eastern counterpart. Today the state library of Berlin thus has two main locations: one on Potsdamer Strasse in the west and another on Unter den Linden in the east.

Called the *"Stabi"* by students, the institution is not only known for its good research facilities and changing exhibits in the foyer, but thanks to its highly flirtatious atmosphere, it's also known as the "marriage market for academics." ⊠ *Potsdamer Str. 33,* ☎ *030/266–2303,* 🌐 *www.sbb.spk-berlin.de.* 🎟 *€0.50.* ☉ *Weekdays 9–9, Sat. 9–7.*

⑲ **St. Matthäuskirche** (St. Matthew's Church). Surrounded by some of the most modern architecture Berlin has to offer, this church dating from 1844–46 seems strangely out of place. Designed by Friedrich August Stüler, the Protestant church was destroyed during the war and later carefully reconstructed. The yellow and red ribbonlike pattern of its bricks gives the church a friendly and almost playful appearance. The inside, however, is somewhat disappointing, since a simple and sober interior design was chosen over a historically accurate renovation. The church also serves as a prime venue for modern classical concerts. ⊠ *Matthäikirchplatz,* ☎ *030/262–1202.* ⊟ *Free.* ☉ *Tues.–Sun. noon–6.*

❶ **Tiergarten** (Animal Garden). The Tiergarten, a beautifully laid-out 630-acre park, is Berlin's "green lung." In the 17th century it served as the hunting grounds of the Great Elector. Its eastern end, between the grandiose landmarks of the Reichstag and the Brandenburger Tor, is being developed into the new seat of the federal government. For Berliners the quiet greenery of the Tiergarten is a beloved oasis in the heart of urban turmoil. In summer the park, with some 14 mi of footpaths, playgrounds, and white-marble sculptures, becomes the embodiment of multicultural Berlin: Turkish families gather in the green meadows for spicy barbecues, children play soccer, and gay couples sunbathe. The inner park's 6½ acres of lakes and ponds were landscaped by garden architect Joseph Peter Lenné in the mid-1800s. On the shore of the lake in the southwestern part of the park you can relax at the **Café am Neuen See,** a café and beer garden.

In the past few years the tranquillity of the Tiergarten has been disturbed by the construction of a huge highway, railway, and metro tunnel, the multibillion-dollar **Nord-Süd-Tunnel.** It will redirect downtown traffic when all branches of the federal government have finally moved into the new government quarter and the new central train station at **Lehrter Stadtbahnhof** is finished.

MITTE: FROM UNTER DEN LINDEN TO ALEXANDERPLATZ

The district of Mitte (Middle) was the center of old Berlin and proudly rolls out landmarks, museums, and upscale malls along the thoroughfares of Unter den Linden and Friedrichstrasse, streets that once languished in the shadow of the Wall. Some rather unattractive office buildings along Unter den Linden, hastily erected in the 1970s, are reminders that the boulevard was remodeled by Communist East Germany. At the end of Unter den Linden, around vast Alexanderplatz, eastern Berlin's handful of high rises cluster beneath one of the city's premier silhouettes, the Berliner Fernsehturm.

Unter den Linden served as the government district during the era of the Prussian kings, the German emperors, and, later, the German Democratic Republic governments. In 1999 Mitte resumed its role of yore when the German government relocated here from Bonn.

Numbers in the text correspond to numbers in the margin and on the Mitte map.

A Good Walk

Begin your walk at **Pariser Platz** ①, right behind the Brandenburger Tor (the restaurant there, Theodor Tucher, may make a goldmine off its location, but it's best avoided.) Berlin's historic landmarks extend eastward along **Unter den Linden** ②, an older, more elegant counterpart to Kurfürstendamm. A few steps south of Unter den Linden on Wilhelmstrasse is the British embassy. One of the United Kingdom's largest and most important new government buildings opened with a dignified ceremony hosted by Queen Elizabeth II in 2000. Designed by British architect Michael Wilford with a facade that includes decidedly un-British splashes of lilac and aqua, it is on the site of the 1872–1945 British embassy. Return to Unter den Linden, and as you make your way east you'll pass parliamentary offices and consulates, among them the huge **Russische Botschaft** (Russian embassy), and souvenir shops. From the turn of the 20th century until the beginning of World War II, the intersection of Unter den Linden and Friedrichstrasse was the busiest in all Berlin. Turn right here, passing both quaint and fancy shops, then left at Französische Strasse to reach **Gendarmenmarkt** ③, one of Europe's finest early 19th-century plazas, with the twin towers of the **Französischer Dom** ④ and the adjacent **Deutscher Dom** ⑤. Walk back on Charlottenstrasse to Unter den Linden and pay a visit to the gallery at the **Deutsche Guggenheim Berlin** ⑥. On both sides of the boulevard are dark gray buildings. On the north side is a branch of the Staatsbibliothek (State Library), a classical edifice with a column-decorated facade dating from 1903–14. The building has a particularly nice inner courtyard with a fountain. On the south side is the Altes Palais (Old Palace), a small classical palace built in 1834–1837 by Carl Ferdinand Langhans, which served as city palace for the young Prince Wilhelm I.

Next to the palace, facing Bebelplatz, is the baroque 1775 Alte Bibliothek, the city's old central public library. Thanks to its three-part, curved facade, Berliners call the odd-looking building *"die Kommode,"* or "chest of drawers." Also off Bebelplatz are **St. Hedwigskathedrale** ⑦ and the **Staatsoper Unter den Linden** ⑧, the city's premier opera house. These buildings, along with the **Kronprinzenpalais** ⑨ and the Opernpalais—which adjoins the opera house, and the **Humboldt-Universität** ⑩, on the north side of Unter den Linden, form the Forum Fridericianum, the model of Prussian glory, designed by Frederick the Great himself. Just south of the Kronprinzenpalais is the **Friedrichswerdersche Kirche** ⑪, a redbrick church presenting the best of Prussian classical sculptures.

Back on Unter den Linden, opposite the Kronprinzenpalais and next to the university, is the **Neue Wache** ⑫ memorial and the **Deutsches Historisches Museum** ⑬. Hidden behind these buildings is the **Palais am Festungsgraben** ⑭, one of the few remaining historic city villas in Berlin. Turn left at the Spree Canal, which is lined with craft and souvenir stalls, and cross the second bridge to the **Museumsinsel** ⑮, the site of one of Berlin's original medieval settlements and home to staggering museums. From the museum complex follow Am Zeughaus back to Unter den Linden for the best views of what comes next. As the Schlossbrücke (Palace Bridge) crosses the Spree River it leaves you on the multilane Karl-Liebknecht-Strasse. From here you have the most impressive view of the **Altes Museum** ⑯, one of the world's most beautiful museums, and the Lustgarten meadow spread out before it. The city palace once stood on the wide open square to your right, the **Schlossplatz** ⑰, now occupied by the former parliament building of East Germany. South of Schlossplatz is Germany's new and ultramodern Ministry for Foreign Relations, the **Auswärtiges Amt** ⑱. After the Lustgarten turn left to reach the enormous cathedral **Berliner Dom** ⑲.

The Karl-Liebknecht-Strasse approach toward Alexanderplatz used to be the urban showcase of East Berlin. The high-rises on the north side of the street make for a dull walk after the parade of architecture that preceeded it. More pleasant to stroll are the public areas south of the busy street. Statues of Marx and Engels mark the **Marx-Engels-Forum** ⑳, and a few hundred yards east is the 13th-century **St. Marienkirche** ㉑. Look up to spot the **Berliner Fernsehturm** ㉒, which is separated from **Alexanderplatz** ㉓ by the S-Bahn station and tracks. Walk through the station to view the vast square. Head back westward via Rathausstrasse to the **Berliner Rathaus** ㉔, the city's town hall, and the **Nikolaiviertel** ㉕, Berlin's ancient quarter with the medieval St. Nikolaikirche (St. Nicolas Church) and plenty of gift shops. Wander down Spreeufer to Mühlendamm, turn left onto this boulevard, and cross the Spree River to

Fischerinsel ㉖. Turn left onto the street Fisher Insel and cross another bridge to Wallstrasse, where you should turn left to reach the **Märkisches Museum** ㉗, which displays the history of Berlin. From here continue east to the Märkisches Ufer with its **Historischer Hafen Berlin** ㉘, an open-air ship museum.

TIMING

The walk down Unter den Linden to Alexanderplatz and then to the Nikolaiviertel and beyond takes at least three hours if you don't look closely at any museums or highlights. Allow at least the same amount of time for each of the museums on Museumsinsel. You won't regret one minute. Most of the other sights can be seen in less than one hour each. The Museumsinsel is crowded on weekends, so try to visit there early or during the week.

Sights to see

㉓ **Alexanderplatz.** German writer Alfred Döblin (1878–1957) christened the square the "heart of a world metropolis" before it became merely the hub of East Berlin. It's a bleak sort of place even today, open and windswept and surrounded by grim modern buildings, with no hint of its prewar activity—a reminder not just of the results of Allied bombing but of the ruthlessness practiced by the East Germans when demolishing the remains of old buildings. Gone is the legendary and lively atmosphere, which once served as a literary backdrop for Döblin's famous portrait of prewar Berlin in his novel *Berlin Alexanderplatz*. Except for the two gray office buildings next to the S-Bahn station, the **Berolinahaus,** and the railway station itself, all the original buildings on the square were leveled during the war. The Socialist regime tried to revitalize the square by building a department store, the Forum Hotel, and the **Weltzeituhr** (World Time Clock). But the square has remained listless and unoccupied, which is fine with the teenagers skateboarding and inline skating around it. Otherwise a few street vendors and homeless populate the area.

⑯ **Altes Museum** (Old Museum). With its facade of columns striping a bright red wall, the austere, neoclassical Altes Museum, designed by Karl Friedrich Schinkel in 1830, is undoubtedly one of most elegant museums in the world. At the time of its opening it was also the world's first building specifically built as a museum complex. Today it features antique sculptures, clay figurines, and bronze art, which constitute part of the **Antikensammlung** (Antiquities Collection). It is also home to vases and everyday utensils from ancient Greece and Rome. Another division of the Antikensammlung is housed in the Pergamonmuseum. The Altes Museum is part of Museumsinsel but is best accessed from Unter den Linden.

Adjacent to the Altes Museum is the **Lustgarten** (Pleasure Garden), which—despite its promising name—is simply the green square between the museum and Unter den Linden. Originally the spice and herb garden for the royal palace, the Lustgarten dates fromo the 16th century and was first turned into a park by the Great Elector in 1646. Later on it became a parade ground until Schinkel built the Altes Museum and transformed it into an open square modeled on the ancient Roman citizens' forums. During the political turmoil following World War I, the Communists and other parties held rallies here, as did the Nazis in 1932–33, who furthermore went on to redesign it as a parade ground. The Lustgarten has now regained its classical appearance and is one of the loveliest areas for taking a nap or relaxing in the historic downtown area. ⊠ *Lustgarten,* ☎ *030/2090–5555,* WEB *www.smb. spk-berlin.de.* ☑ *€4; free 1st Sun. of every month.* ☉ *Fri.–Wed. 10–6.*

Mitte

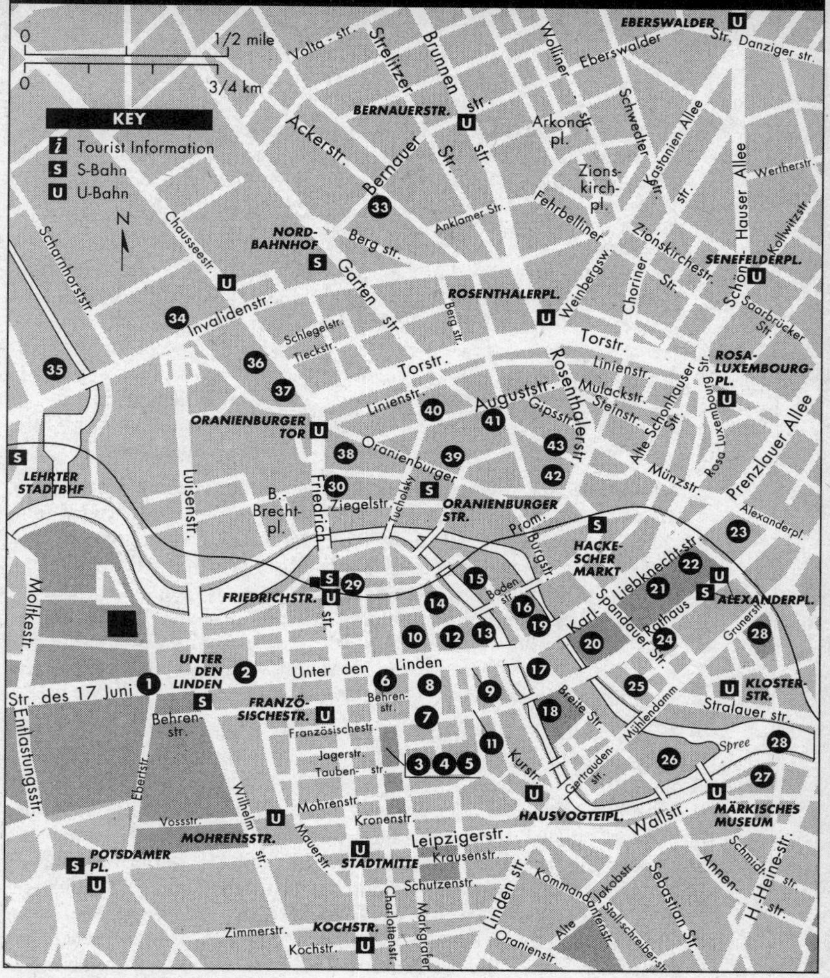
0
1/2 mile
0
3/4 km
KEY
Tourist Information
S-Bahn
U-Bahn
N
Volta - str.
Strelitzer
Brunnen str.
Wolliner str.
EBERSWALDER
Eberswalder Str.
Danziger str.
BERNAUERSTR.
Ackerstr.
Bernauer Str.
Arkona pl.
Schwedter Str.
Kastanien Allee
Zions-kirch-pl.
Schön-Hauser Allee
Wertherstr.
Kollwitzstr.
Chausseestr.
Scharnhorststr.
NORD-BAHNHOF
Berg str.
Anklamer Str.
Fehrbelliner
Zionskirchestr.
SENEFELDERPL.
Garten str.
ROSENTHALERPL.
Weinbergsw.
Choriner Str.
Saarbrücker Str.
Invalidenstr.
Schlegelstr.
Tieckstr.
Berg str.
Torstr.
Linienstr.
ROSA-LUXEMBOURG-PL.
Mulackstr.
Steinstr.
Alte Schönhauser Str.
Rosa Luxembourg Str.
Prenzlauer Allee
Augustsstr.
Gipsstr.
Rosenthalerstr.
ORANIENBURGER TOR
Oranienburger
LEHRTER STADTBHF
Luisenstr.
B.-Brecht-pl.
Friedrich
Ziegelstr.
Tucholsky
ORANIENBURGER STR.
Münzstr.
Alexanderpl.
Prom.
Burgstr.
HACKE-SCHER MARKT
Karl-Liebknecht-str.
Moltkestr.
FRIEDRICHSTR.
str.
Boden str.
Spandauer Str.
Rathaus str.
ALEXANDERPL.
Grunerstr.
UNTER DEN LINDEN
Unter den Linden
Str. des 17 Juni
Behrenstr.
FRANZÖ-SISCHESTR.
Behren-str.
Französischestr.
Breite Str.
KLOSTER-STR.
Stralauer str.
Mühlendamm
Spree
Entlastungsstr.
Ebertstr.
Jagerstr.
Tauben- str.
Kurstr.
Gertrauden-str.
Wilhelm str.
Mohrenstr.
Vossstr.
Mauerstr.
Kronenstr.
HAUSVOGTEIPL.
Wallstr.
MÄRKISCHES MUSEUM
MOHRENSSTR.
Leipzigerstr.
Krausenstr.
POTSDAMER PL.
STADTMITTE
Schutzenstr.
Linden str.
Kommandantenstr.
Jakobstr.
Sebastian Str.
Annen-str.
Schmidstr.
H.-Heine-str.
Charlottenstr.
Markgrafen
Zimmerstr.
KOCHSTR.
Kochstr.
Alte
Stall-schreiber-str.
Oranienstr.

From Unter der Linden to Alexanderplatz

- Alexanderplatz 23
- Altes Museum 16
- Auswärtiges Amt . . . 18
- Berliner Dom 19
- Berliner Fernsehturm 22
- Berliner Rathaus . . . 24
- Deutsche Guggenheim Berlin 6
- Deutscher Dom 5
- Deutsches Historisches Museum 13
- Fischerinsel 26
- Französischer Dom 4
- Friedrichswerdersche Kirche 11
- Gendarmenmarkt . . . 3
- Historischer Hafen Berlin 28
- Humboldt-Universität 10
- Kronprinzenpalais . . . 9
- Märkisches Museum 27
- Marx-Engels-Forum 20
- Museumsinsel 15
- Neue Wache 12
- Nikolaiviertel 25
- Palais am Festungsgraben 14
- Pariser Platz 1
- Schlossplatz 17
- Staatsoper Unter der Linden 8
- St. Hedwigskathedrale . . 7
- St. Marienkirche 21
- Unter der Linden 2

Friedrichstrasse

- Admiralpalast 29
- Friedrichstadtpalast . .30
- Friedrichstadt-passagen 32
- Lindencorso 31

Scheunenviertel

- Augustrasse 40
- Brecht-Weigel-Gedenkstätte 36
- Dorotheenstädtischer Friedhof 37
- Gedenkstätte Berliner Mauer 33
- Grosse Hamburger Strasse 41
- Hackesche Höfe 42
- Hamburger Bahnhof 35
- Museum für Naturkunde 34
- Neue Synagoge 39
- Sophienstrasse 43
- Tacheles 38

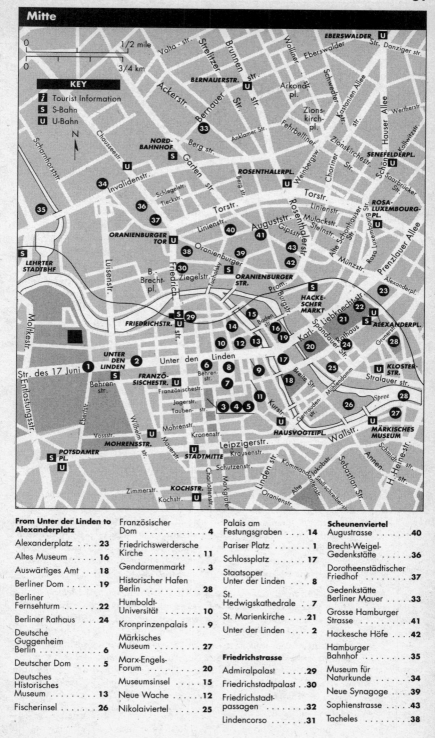

⓮ **Auswärtiges Amt** (Ministry of Foreign Affairs). One of the most notable new federal buildings in Mitte is the Auswärtiges Amt, a fine example of how to combine the old and the new. After years of debating where to locate, the ministry moved into the prewar **Reichsbank** in 1996. The gray and rather monumental Reichsbank (Germany's old National Bank) was created between 1934 and 1940 but lacks the strict Nazi style in architecture. In fact, when the competition for this building began shortly after Hitler had come to power, even architects known for their modern visions such as Mies van der Rohe and Hans Poelzig submitted their designs.

In front of the original building, looking toward Schlossplatz (where the ministry first hoped to gain pride of place), stands the new extension, designed by Berlin architects Thomas Müller and Ivan Reimann between 1997 and 1999. The building is made of glass and stone and features an open entrance area and two courtyards. Except for this lobby area and a café, called the Coffeeshop, the building is closed to the public. The Staatsratsgebäude (State Council Building) is next door. ⊠ *Werderscher Markt 1,* ☎ *030/01888170,* WEB *www.auswaertiges-amt. de* ⊙ *Weekdays 8–5; café: weekdays 8–7, weekends 10–6.*

Bebelplatz. This square serves as the center for the **Forum Fridericianum,** an architecturally unique ensemble of baroque and classical buildings that was envisioned by Prussian king Frederick the Great in the 1740s. They include the **St. Hedwigs-Kathedrale**, the **Staatsoper Unter den Linden,** the **Opernpalais,** the **Kronprinzenpalais,** and **Humboldt-Universität.** The king himself is immortalized on horseback at the heart of his creation. The majestic bronze statue was cast by Christian Daniel Rauch in 1839–51. The relief on the statue's plinth depicts famous generals and other notable contemporaries of the king.

It was on this square that on the evening of May 10, 1933, Nazi students burned more than 25,000 books by Jewish and politically undesirable writers such as Thomas Mann, Heinrich Mann, Klaus Mann, Lion Feuchtwanger, Robert Musil, Kurt Tucholsky, and Erich Kästner (who happened to come by and watch in disgust)—in short, the elite of contemporary German literature. The public book burning marked the beginning of Nazi suppression of free thought and publishing and prompted another wave of emigration. A subtle memorial, *Empty Library,* designed by Micha Ullmann in 1995, commemorates what happened here in the shadow of the old library. In the middle of the square is a box set into the cobblestone and covered with glass. Beneath it is a small subterranean room with empty bookshelves. The inscription in the ground, WHERE BOOKS ARE BURNT, PEOPLE WILL EVENTUALLY BE BURNT TOO, is a quote from Heinrich Heine, who wrote this sentence 120 years before the Holocaust. ⊠ *Unter den Linden.*

★ ⓯ **Berliner Dom** (Berlin Cathedral). The 19th-century cathedral, with its enormous green copper dome, is one of the great ecclesiastical buildings in Germany. Its main nave was reopened in June 1993 after a 20-year renovation. Apart from the breathtaking cupola, one of the most beautiful and ornate parts of the cathedral is the **Kaiserliches Treppenhaus,** the Emperor's Staircase. Another staircase leads to the observation balcony, which allows a view of the cathedral's ceiling and interior. More than 80 sarcophagi of Prussian royals are on display in the cathedral's catacombs.

The hard-hit cathedral, which was almost completely burned by an Allied phosphorous bomb on May 24, 1944, could very well have shared the fate of the royal palace that once stood opposite it: both buildings were considered symbols of Germany's imperialist and militaristic past, which had no place in the Germany that the Socialist Unity Party planned to build after the war. The cathedral was not demolished but restored, thanks to the stubborn and persistent East German Protestant church, art historians, and the city's policy regarding preservation of historical monuments. The restorations between 1975 and 1983 were done as historically accurately as possible. ⊠ *Am Lustgarten,* ☎ *030/2026–9136,* WEB *www.berlinerdom.de.* ▣ *€4 (combined ticket for church, crypt, and imperial staircase); with balcony €5.* ⊘ *Church and crypt: Mon.–Sat. 9–7, Sun. noon–7; balcony: Mon.–Sat. 9–7, Sun. noon–7 (last admission at 6); imperial staircase: Mon.–Sat. 10–6, Sun. noon–6.*

㉔ Berliner Rathaus (Berlin City Hall). A redbrick design and friezes depicting Berlin's history are the distinguishing features of city hall, which is known by its popular name: "Rotes Rathaus" (Red City Hall). This name and the building's color don't have anything to do with the Socialist, "red" past of the city hall, which served as the seat of East Berlin's magistrate until 1990. The name has been around since the city hall was built (1861–69); it describes the famous red bricks from Brandenburg used in its construction. To satisfy the city's aspiration of becoming one of Germany's leading metropolises, architect Hermann F. Waesemann modeled the facade after Italian Renaissance palazzi and used the bell tower of the cathedral in Laon, France, as a model for the hall's tower. The result is an oversize building whose outside fresco from 1879 adds that touch of self-importance that Berlin has been known for ever since. ⊠ *Jüdenstr. at Rathausstr.,* ☎ *030/90290.* ▣ *Free.* ⊘ *Weekdays 9–6.*

❻ Deutsche Guggenheim Berlin (German Guggenheim Berlin). The top-shelf names of international finance and art, Deutsche Bank and the Solomon R. Guggenheim Foundation, have joined forces to present changing conceptual art and installation exhibits. In a Deutsche Bank sandstone building dating from 1920, it is the Guggenheim's fifth location worldwide. Among past shows were those of internationally acclaimed artists such as Dan Flavin, James Rosenquist, and Robert Delaunay. The Deutsche Guggenheim also presents works of art from the extensive collection the Deutsche Bank has assembled in the past 130 years, most of it contemporary art. ⊠ *Unter den Linden 13–15,* ☎ *030/202–0930,* WEB *www.deutsche-guggenheim-berlin.de* ▣ *Free 1st 2 weeks of exhibition, €2.50 thereafter.* ⊘ *Fri.–Wed. 11–8, Thurs. 11–10.*

❺ Deutscher Dom (German Cathedral). The German Cathedral, opposite its identical twin, the French Cathedral, is a fine baroque building dating from 1781–85. It's especially worth a visit if you're interested in an official view of German history with a particular accent on the cold war and the division of Germany. The multifloor exhibit was originally presented at the Reichstag and is an obligatory stop for any school class visiting Berlin. It is being revised and updated and will reopen some time in 2002. A small café and a bookstore with attractive books on Berlin are on the top floor. ⊠ *Gendarmenmarkt 1,* ☎ *030/2273–0431.* ▣ *Free.* ⊘ *Sept.–May, Tues.–Sun. 10–6; June–Aug., Tues–Sun. 10–7.*

⓭ Deutsches Historisches Museum (German History Museum). This magnificent baroque building, constructed between 1695 and 1730, was once the Prussian arsenal (Zeughaus) and normally houses Germany's National History Museum. After two years of renovation and the addition of a wing designed by I. M. Pei, the museum, called DHM, will reopen in early in 2002. Until then, its exhibits are in the Kronprinzenpalais across the street.

The museum is one of Berlin's finest combinations of ultramodern and historic architecture. The baroque Zeughaus, the oldest building along

Unter den Linden, is acclaimed for its delicately sculptured facade and central courtyard. The 22 masks in the courtyard above the windows, *Sterbende Krieger* (*Dying Warriors*), by Andreas Schlüter, are of particular interest, as are the sculpted faces that clearly show the realistic horrors of war and death—something highly unusual for the time of their creation. They are considered some of the world's best baroque sculptures. The airy glass complex by I. M. Pei (it is the star architect's first project in Germany) behind the northern facade of the Zeughaus will house changing exhibitions. The most striking feature of the wing is a large spiral staircase visible behind glass at the corner of the building. Part of the museum's face-lift will be a glass roof covering the historic courtyard, thus adding new exhibition space for the (notoriously largely endowed) collections of the DHM.

The Zeughaus once housed East Germany's national history museum, which showcased the development of socialism virtually from the Stone Age to Erich Honecker's rule in the 1980s. In the first years of its present incarnation it was regarded highly skeptically by many who feared that the museum, a special pet project of then-chancellor Helmut Kohl, would present a politically streamlined, conservative, and biased interpretation of German history. But the museum director, Christoph Stölzl, who in 2000 went on to become Berlin's minister for cultural affairs, proved critics wrong. Since the opening of the DHM at the Zeughaus in 1991, the museum has created several widely acclaimed exhibitions, mostly dealing with contemporary German history. Many shows featured subjects on East-West German relations and will certainly continue to do so. A permanent exhibition will cover two floors and feature 12 crucial historic "stations" illustrating the country's national history as a part of larger European and global movements. ⊠ *Unter den Linden 2,* ☎ *030/203–040,* WEB *www.dhm.de.* ⊠ *Permanent exhibit: free.* ☉ *Fri.–Wed. 10–6, Thurs. 10–10.*

㉖ **Fischerinsel** (Fisher Island). Fisher Island encompasses a densely built peninsula southwest of the Nikolaiviertel and was the core of Berlin 750 years ago. Modern life goes on here, and the area is filled with stores and restaurants. It retains some of its medieval character, primarily at **Brüderstrasse**, where two small museums occupy restored Renaissance houses. The **Museum Nicolaihaus** was the home of one of Berlin's great enlightenment thinkers, Christoph Friedrich Nicolai (1733-1811), and dates from the late 17th century. A museum, planned to open in 2002, will chronicle the life and work of the publisher, writer, and book dealer. His house was an intellectual center, a salon for Prussia's leading minds in the 18th century, including Hegel, Schadow, and Schinkel. ⊠ *Brüderstr. 13,* ☎ *030/2400–2162.* ⊠ *€3.* ☉ *Tues.–Sun. 10–6.*

Museum Galgenhaus (Museum at the House of the Gallows), dating from the 17th century, was occupied by a high-ranking city official. The very name of his mansion, however, is the result of a tragic event: in 1735 one of his female servants was accused of having stolen a silver spoon and was publicly hanged. A few days later the spoon was found again. The museum will document how Berliners lived in the 18th century. ⊠ *Brüderstr. 10,* ☎ *030/201–1208,* WEB *www.stadtmuseum.com.* ☉ *Tues.–Sun. 10–6.*

At Breite Strasse you'll find two of Berlin's oldest buildings: No. 35 is the **Ribbeckhaus**, the city's only surviving late Renaissance structure, dating from 1624. It once served as the royal office for the control of the treasury and, some 200 years later as the office supervising Berlin's unsuccessful bid for the summer Olympics 2000—one of Berlin's darkest financial scandals. At neighboring No. 36 is the early baroque **Marstall**, built by Michael Matthais between 1666 and 1669.

❹ Französischer Dom (French Cathedral). The French cathedral's tower is the highest historic viewing platform (216 ft) in all of Berlin. An ascent to the platform gives you a spectacular panoramic view of the city and a magnificent glimpse of Pariser and Potsdamer squares as well as Alexanderplatz.

The Französischer Dom was built in 1781–85 by Karl von Gontard and is simply a showy front for the **Französische Friedrichstadtkirche** (French Friedrichstadt Church) behind it. The tower was inspired by that of the Pantheon in Paris and the churches on the Piazza del Popolo in Rome. The church itself, designed by French architect Jean Cayart in 1701–05, is a circular structure in which Huguenot services continue to be held today. It also contains the **Hugenottenmuseum** (☎ 030/229–1760, 🎟 €1.50, ⏰ Tues.–Sat. noon–5, Sun. 11–5), with exhibits charting the history and art of these Protestant refugees, expelled from France at the end of the 17th century by King Louis XIV. The admittance of these refugees was one of history's first examples of religious tolerance as well as a symbol of enlightened absolutism typical of Prussia. The Huguenots' energy and commercial expertise did much to boost life in Berlin during the 18th century. ✉ *Gendarmenmarkt 5,* ☎ *030/2016–6883.* 🎟 *€1.50.* ⏰ *Daily 10–8.*

⓫ Friedrichswerdersche Kirche (Friedrichwerder Church). This dark red-brick church off Unter den Linden was designed after plans by Karl Friedrich Schinkel, many of whose sculptures have now found a new home here. Built in 1824–30 for both a German and a French congregation, the neo-Gothic church was demolished during World War II but was reconstructed for the city's 750th anniversary in 1987. The small museum in the empty nave includes many sculptures and figures by such premier German artists as Gottfried Schadow, Christian Daniel Rauch, and Christian Friedrich Tieck, but above all by Schinkel himself. The highlight of this collection is his famous *Double Statues of Prussian Princesses Luise and Friederike,* from 1795. Its elegant, curving, and playful-looking forms influenced classical sculpturing in Europe for almost a century. An exhibition on the gallery chronicles the life and works of Schadow. ✉ *Werderscher Markt,* ☎ *030/208–1323,* 🌐 *www.smb.spk-berlin.de* 🎟 *€2.* ⏰ *Tues.–Sun. 10–6.*

★ ❸ Gendarmenmarkt. Anchoring this large classic square are the beautifully reconstructed **Schauspielhaus** (✉ Gendarmenmarkt 2, ☎ 030/2030–92101, 🌐 www.konzerthaus.de), one of Berlin's main concert halls, and the German and French cathedrals to its left and right. Berliners usually don't hesitate to boast that this is one of Europe's most beautiful squares. It first developed in the 1770s, when Frederick the Great had the whole area redesigned. The square's name is derived from the French *Gens d'Armes* (men at arms), after a military regiment that was quartered not far away. Frederick had a theater built on the spot of today's Schauspielhaus, and in 1780–85 the twin cathedrals followed. In 1818–21 Schinkel designed the Schauspielhaus, which remained one of Germany's premier drama theaters until 1945. Heavily damaged in World War II, the edifice was reconstructed from scratch in 1984 and now houses the Konzerthaus Berlin, a renowned concert hall for classical performances.

In the square's center stands the **Schiller-Denkmal** (Schiller Monument), from 1871, whose restoration in the 1980s was a rare example of East–West cooperation. After the war the marble statue had been removed to West Berlin, while the plinth and the fountain basin remained in East Berlin. In 1986 the authorities decided to join forces to rebuild the unique memorial, and the West transferred the statue.

In summer Gendarmenmarkt is particularly attractive, with street cafés putting out tables and chairs and tourists covering the steps of the Schauspielhaus. In June and July monumental open-air classical concerts are held here. In the 1990s the area around Gendarmenmarkt evolved into one of Berlin's most exclusive and popular areas for nightlife, with some of the city's best (and most expensive) restaurants and bars opening in the neighborhood. The clientele ranges from established artists to businesspeople and German federal chancellor Gerhard Schröder.

㉘ Historischer Hafen Berlin (Historic Harbor Berlin). Although far from being a maritime city, Berlin nevertheless sees busy water traffic on its more than 62 km (100 mi) of waterways. Thanks to an extensive canal system, the city has direct links to sea harbors like Rotterdam, in the west, and Stettin, in the east, and the rivers and canals in and around Berlin provide a perfect means of transporting goods on barges. Twenty-one historic ships, some dating from the 19th century, can be viewed at the historic harbor, which is the largest of its kind in Germany. Most ships are long boats from the early 20th century, moored at the docks. Others are historic passenger boats that you can board in summer for a canal trip, complete with an old-style Berlin buffet and nostalgic entertainment. A small exhibit on one of the boats tells the history of seafaring in Berlin. ⊠ *Märkisches Ufer at Jannowitzbrücke,* ☎ *030/2147–3257,* WEB *www. historischer-hafen-berlin.de.* 🎟 *€2.* ☉ *Tues.–Fri 2–6, weekends 11–6.*

Hotel Adlon Berlin. The luxury Hotel Adlon towers high above Pariser Platz. Completed in 1997, it was the first new building erected in the neighborhood and is a near replica of the famous old Hotel Adlon, which opened in 1907. The Adlon was one of the Western world's leading hotels, widely known for its plush elegance and for welcoming guests like Charlie Chaplin, Greta Garbo, Thomas Mann, and the like. Bombarded during the war and then transformed into a field hospital during the Battle of Berlin, the ruin was demolished after the war. The new hotel, designed by two Berlin architects, was first heavily criticized for its attempt to re-create a historic piece of architecture with a style that has long since vanished, and many doubted it could live up to its former reputation. But the Adlon, run by the Kempinski hotel group, has proven its critics wrong. The Adlon has not only managed to become the unofficial guest house for heads of state and royals but has also won the hearts of Berliners, who visit the lobby for tea or champagne. If you're by yourself or with a companion, take a peek at the marvelous lobby; larger groups will be turned away by the security personnel. ⊠ *Unter den Linden 77,* ☎ *030/22610,* WEB *www.hotel-adlon.de.*

➓ Humboldt-Universität (Humboldt University). Berlin's grand old university has lived through equally glorious and depressing times. Founded in 1810 as the city's first university, it quickly evolved into one of Europe's important scientific and intellectual centers. Considered the "mother of all modern universities," the Humboldt-Universität followed the innovative and progressive educational principles of the famous Humboldt brothers, who advocated *Studium Generale,* a solid general knowledge of science, law, philosophy, and history, as well as medicine. Among the first professors were such intellectual heavyweights as Hegel, Fichte, and von Savigny. In the course of the next 120 years, the university generated 29 Nobel Prizes in various fields and attracted the best scientists of its time: professors like Albert Einstein, Max Planck, Fritz Haber, and Robert Koch did their research here and pushed ahead the frontiers of physics, nuclear science, and medicine. Among its notable students were Heinrich Heine, Otto von Bismarck, Karl Liebknecht, Karl Marx, and Kurt Tucholsky. The university's years of disgrace began in 1933, when some of its students participated in the book burnings led by the

Nazis. Between 1933 and 1945, Jewish and politically undesirable professors and students were expelled, and with most of the best and brightest emigrating to the United States, the university—and indeed Germany on the whole—suffered a brain-drain from which it would never fully recover. After the war the university quickly came under Communist control, and free speech and academic freedom were dramatically reduced again. In December 1948 frustrated students and professors, with funding from American foundations, finally established the Free University in West Berlin. The Humboldt-Universität subsequently lost much of its international reputation.

Since German reunification the university has successfully reconnected with its proud heritage from the years before 1933, and today is attended by 34,000 students. The process of getting rid of Communist professors and Stasi-infected departments, however, proved not to be easy. You can visit the lobby of the main building, a 1766 palace built for the brother of Friedrich II of Prussia. The entrance gate is flanked by seated statues of Alexander and Wilhelm von Humboldt, and a used-book market usually sprawls in front of the gate. ⊠ *Unter den Linden 6,* ☎ *030/20930,* WEB *www.hu-berlin.de.* ☉ *Weekdays 6 AM–10 PM.*

❾ Kronprinzenpalais (Crown Prince's Palace). A temporary exhibition hall for the Deutsches Historisches Museum until spring 2002, this magnificent baroque building was constructed in 1732 by Philippe Gerlach for Crown Prince Friedrich (later Frederick the Great). The inscription on the facade, PALAIS DU PRINCE ROYAL DE PRUSSE, mirrors the era's affinity for French elegance, which is perfectly expressed in the grandiose architecture. A driveway passes beneath the balcony of the richly decorated front, and to the left of the building is a playful series of Corinthian columns added in the mid-1900s. When the Hohenzollern monarchy was thrown out of Germany, the building served as a museum for avant-garde art, exhibiting mostly French and German impressionist painters. The Nazis closed the museum in 1937 and used many of its paintings for their infamous exhibition "Entartete Kunst" ("Degenerate Art"), a show of the art of "Jews" and other "subhumans" the Nazis made so much political bluster about. During World War II the building was destroyed and the ruins completely demolished. It was only in 1968 that the Kronprinzenpalais was reconstructed as a replica of the original. In East Berlin the building was never called by its historic name because it included a reference to the despised imperialist German Reich. It was first called Palais Unter den Linden and then Berlin Palais. The dislike for its former name, however, didn't prevent the city of East Berlin from using it as its official state guest house. ⊠ *Unter den Linden 3,* ☎ *030/203–040,* WEB *www.dhm.de.* ✉ *Varies with exhibit. English-speaking guide €30.* ☉ *Thurs.–Tues. 10–6.*

Opernpalais (Opera Palace). Today's Opera Palace originally served as the city palace for the Hohenzollern princesses. This Prinzessinnenpalais was not far from the corresponding Kronprinzenpalais for the princes of the kaiser (who lived farther up the boulevard, in the city palace). The building later adopted its current name because it stands right next to the State Opera Unter den Linden. The Opernpalais is a more or less accurate replica of the original edifice, constructed in 1733–37. When the monarchy was abolished in Germany, the palace served as a museum, and it later became home to various cafés and restaurants. ⊠ *Unter den Linden 3–5.*

NEED A
BREAK?

The **Operncafé** (⊠ Unter den Linden 5, ☎ 030/202–683), right next to the opera house, is home to four restaurants and cafés, all famous for their rich German cakes, pastries, and original Berlin dishes.

㉗ Märkisches Museum (Brandenburg Museum). This chronicler of Berlin's history is the main local history museum. Completed in 1908, the red-brick complex combines historic styles from Berlin and Brandenburg buildings, creating the look of a medieval church or fortification. The Middle Ages is covered in the basement with correspondences, wax seals, coins, and weaponry. The upper floors include Bronze Age artifacts, religious icons, and paintings depicting the grandeur of Berlin before it crumbled under World War II. Themed rooms cover guilds, the March Revolution of 1848, the numerous newspapers of the 1950s, and even mechanical musical instruments (which are demonstrated on Sunday at 11 and Wednesday at 3). A few placards are translated into English; a thorough bilingual guide to the exhibits is for sale. The closest U-bahn stations to this out-of-the-way museum are Märkisches Museum and Jannowitzbrücke. ⊠ *Am Köllnischen Park 5,* ☎ *030/308–660,* WEB *www.stadtmuseum.de* ▣ *€4, instrument demonstration €2.* ⊙ *Tues.–Sun. 10–6.*

⑳ Marx-Engels-Forum. A lovely green spot in the summer and an unpleasant windy expanse in the winter, the Marx-Engels-Forum is one of the last reminders that East Berlin was once the capital of Eastern Europe's most radical Socialist state. In an effort to give East Berlin a face-lift for the city's 750th anniversary, the barren area was outfitted in 1986 with trees and benches, and a memorial was placed in its center. The **Marx-Engels-Denkmal,** created by East German sculptor Ludwig Engelhardt, shows the two great theorists and intellectual founders of Marxism. In a brotherly pose Friederich Engels stands and Karl Marx sits. With the collapse of real socialism in East Berlin, the memorial quickly became the target of all sorts of protests, usually expressed on its backside with very funny slogans. The days of graffiti like *"Wir sind unschuldig"* ("We are innocent") or *"Beim nächsten Mal wird alles besser"* ("Next time everything will turn out better") are over, as dissatisfaction with socialism and disappointment over the practical shortcomings of the two men's theories have largely been forgotten.

Just a few hundred yards to the east stands the **Neptunbrunnen** (Neptune Fountain), a richly sculpted fountain within view of the redbrick Berliner Rathaus. The fountain dates from 1886 and was originally near the Berlin city palace. The commanding Greek god of the seas is surrounded by women symbolizing the four great (then-German) rivers Rhein, Weichsel, Elbe, and Oder.

★ **⑮ Museumsinsel** (Museum Island). Like a Greek acropolis of art and culture or a Roman pantheon of design and religion, the classical Museumsinsel is one of the world's largest and best museum complexes. On the site of one of Berlin's two original settlements, this collection of five state museums is an absolute must. The majestic buildings, adorned with classical porticoes and columns, are among the finest of Germany's cultural heritage. But the tides of time, lack of money, two world wars, and Socialist mismanagement have taken their toll on the 19th-century buildings. For years the museums have been undergoing renovations, and over the next decade the Museumsinsel, which has been declared a UNESCO World Heritage Site, will receive a comprehensive face-lift.

Most of its museums will be closed at some point between 2001 and 2010. The **Alte Nationalgalerie** (Old National Gallery, entrance on Bodestrasse), one of the first buildings to have been completely restored, is also one of the most elegant. Built in 1866–76 after designs by Friedrich August Stüler, the building, set high on an elevated foundation, was inspired by the temples of Corinth. In front of it stands the 1886 equestrian statue of Frederick Wilhelm IV, a bronze symbol of Prus-

HOW TO
USE THIS GUIDE

Great trips begin with great planning, and this guide makes planning easy. It's packed with everything you need—insider advice on hotels and restaurants, cool tools, practical tips, essential maps, and much more.

COOL TOOLS

Fodor's Choice Top picks are marked throughout with a star.

Great Itineraries These tours, planned by Fodor's experts, give you the skinny on what you can see and do in the time you have.

Smart Travel Tips A to Z This special section is packed with important contacts and advice on everything from how to get around to what to pack.

Good Walks You won't miss a thing if you follow the numbered bullets on our maps.

Need a Break? Looking for a quick bite to eat or a spot to rest? These sure bets are along the way.

Off the Beaten Path Some lesser-known sights are worth a detour. We've marked those you should make time for.

POST-IT® FLAGS

Dog-ear no more!

"Post-it" is a registered trademark of 3M.

Favorite restaurants • Essential maps • Frequently used numbers • Walking tours • Can't-miss sights • Smart Travel Tips • Web sites • Top shops • Hot nightclubs • Addresses • Smart contacts • Events • Off-the-beaten-path spots • Favorite restaurants • Essential maps • Frequently used numbers • Walking tours • Can't-miss sights • Smart Travel Tips • Web sites • Top shops • Hot nightclubs • Addresses • Smart contacts • Events • Off-the-beaten-path spots • Favorite restaurants • Essential maps • Frequently used numbers • Walking tours •

ICONS AND SYMBOLS

Watch for these symbols throughout:

★   Our special recommendations

✕   Restaurant

☷   Lodging establishment

✕☷   Lodging establishment whose restaurant warrants a special trip

☝   Good for kids

☞   Sends you to another section of the guide for more information

✉   Address

☎   Telephone number

FAX   Fax number

WEB   Web site

💷   Admission price

☉   Opening hours

$-$$$$ Lodging and dining price categories, keyed to strategically sited price charts. Check the index for locations.

①❶   Numbers in white and black circles on the maps, in the margins, and within tours correspond to one another.

ON THE WEB

Continue your planning with these useful tools found at **www.fodors.com**, the Web's best source for travel information.

"Rich with resources." —*New York Times*

"Navigation is a cinch." —*Forbes* "Best of the Web" list

"Put together by people bursting with know-how."
                 —*Sunday Times* (London)

Create a Miniguide Pinpoint hotels, restaurants, and attractions that have what you want at the price you want to pay.

Rants and Raves Find out what readers say about Fodor's picks—or write your own reviews of hotels and restaurants you've just visited.

Travel Talk Post your questions and get answers from fellow travelers, or share your own experiences.

On-Line Booking Find the best prices on airline tickets, rental cars, cruises, or vacations, and book them on the spot.

About our Books Learn about other Fodor's guides to your destination and many others.

Expert Advice and Trip Ideas From what to tip to how to take great photos, from the national parks to Nepal, Fodors.com has suggestions that'll make your trip a breeze. Log on and get informed and inspired.

Smart Resources Check the weather in your destination or convert your currency. Learn the local language or link to the latest event listings. Or consult hundreds of detailed maps—all in one place.

sian glory. The gallery now houses an outstanding collection of 18th-, 19th-, and early 20th-century paintings and sculptures. Works by Cézanne, Rodin, Degas, and Germany's famous portrait artist Max Liebermann make up part of the permanent exhibition. The **Galerie der Romantik** (Gallery of Romanticism) includes masterpieces from such 19th-century German painters as Karl Friedrich Schinkel and Caspar David Friedrich, the leading figures of the German romantic school.

The ruins of the **Neues Museum** (New Museum), originally built between 1841 and 1855 and the second-oldest structure in the ensemble, are still undergoing a massive restoration that began in 1986. It will be home to parts of the Egyptian and other early collections of the state museums but will not open until 2008. Many sections and details of the interior survived the war, so restorers are integrating these into the newly built parts.

★ The standout of Museumsinsel is the magnificent **Pergamonmuseum** (entrance on Am Kupfergraben). The youngest building on Museumsinsel (built 1912–30), it is also the most impressive in terms of sheer size. The soaring halls accommodate original ancient temples and gateways, floor mosaics, sarcophagi, Islamic art and much more. Its name is derived from its principal display, the Pergamon Altar, a monumental Greek temple discovered in what is now Turkey and dating from 180 BC. The altar was shipped to Berlin in the late 19th century. Equally impressive are the Babylonian processional path in the Asia Minor section, and the market gate of Miletus (which still bears the carved advertisement of a barber on the right side). The inscription "V.Chr." on placards is the equivalent of BC. The English-language audio tour (€4) will greatly aid your appreciation of the museum. Adjoining the Pergamon Museum on its northern side is the **Bodemuseum**. When completed in 2004, it will house Renaissance sculptures and Byzantine art. ⊠ *Entrances to Museumsinsel: Am Kupfergraben,* ☎ *030/209–5577 or 030/2090–5560 for Museumsinsel,* WEB *www.smb.spk-berlin.de.* ⊠ *Each museum €4; free 1st Sun. of every month; Tageskarte applicable.* ⊘ *Mon.–Wed. and Fri.–Sun. 10–6, Thurs. 10–10.*

⑫ **Neue Wache** (New Guardhouse). Constructed in 1818, this served as the Royal Prussian War Memorial until the declaration of the Weimar Republic in 1918. Badly damaged in World War II, it was restored by the East German state and rededicated in 1960 as a memorial for the victims of militarism and fascism. In November 1993 it was inaugurated as Germany's central war memorial. Inside the otherwise empty space, beneath an open portal to the skies, is a copy of Berlin sculptor Käthe Kollwitz's *Pietà*, which shows a mother enveloping her dead son on the battlefield. A new inscription reads, TO THE VICTIMS OF WAR AND TYRANNY. ⊠ *Unter den Linden, east of Deutsches Historisches Museum.*

㉕ **Nikolaiviertel** (Nicholas Quarter). This tiny quarter of mostly traffic-free, cobblestone streets grew up around Berlin's oldest parish church, the medieval twin-spire **St. Nikolaikirche** (St. Nicholas Church), dating from 1230. The St. Nikolaikirche houses a small museum concerning the church's and city quarter's history. The quaintness of this quarter belies the fact that most of its buildings were erected between 1981 and 1987 as part of the face-lift East Berlin underwent for the 750th anniversary of the city. Even the church itself is a replica—only the foundation remains from the original structure, which was destroyed along with the original Nikolaiviertel during the war. The architects took care during the restoration, however, to preserve the medieval layout of the streets and the original building dimensions. ⊠ *Church: Nikolaikirchpl.,* ☎ *030/240–020, www.stadtmuseum.com* ⊠ *€1.50.* ⊘ *Tues.–Sun. 10–6.*

You can easily stroll through the whole quarter in less than 30 minutes. The most charming little alley is **Poststrasse.** At No. 28 you'll find the **Gerichtslaube,** a perfect replica of the late-13th-century court pavilion that once stood nearby. The white building with its arches and old-style windows, now housing a restaurant and beer garden, was built in 1987. It doesn't have any of the original parts from the first building; they can all be found at Babelsberg Park, in Potsdam. The Gerichtslaube served as the city's main court, which was manned by the city magistrate, not the ruler. Therefore it was a proud symbol of Berlin's early independence, despite being the resident city of the Hohenzollern family.

Poststrasse also has the only completely unharmed historic building, the pink **Knoblauch-Haus,** whose small museum provides a glimpse into bourgeois life in the early 19th century. The 1759 house is named after its owners, one of whom, architect Eduard Knoblauch, built the Neue Synagoge. ✉ *Poststr. 23,* ☎ *030/2400–2195, www.stadtmuseum.com.* 🎫 *€1.50.* ⊙ *Tues.–Sun. 10–6.*

When walking back from the Knoblauch-Haus on Poststrasse, make a left turn toward the greenish bronze statue of St. George fighting the dragon, which once stood in a palace courtyard. Behind it is the River Spree, lined by two narrow streets, the Spreeufer and the Rolandufer. The restaurants and cafés here mostly cater to tour groups. Walking south along the riverbanks you'll hit Mühlendamm and the **Museum Ephraim-Palais** on your left, and the adjacent **Palais Schwerin,** at Molkenmarkt 1–3. The latter was built in 1704 and is one of Berlin's few remaining grand baroque mansions. It was later used as Berlin's mint, which is now adjoining the old Palais. The rococo Ephraim-Palais was built in 1762–66 and later owned by the wealthy court jeweler Veitel Heine Ephraim. The ornamental curved facade with its golden balconies and elegant, slender columns was once praised as Berlin's most beautiful corner. The front, some of whose sections are actually original, is a perfect replica of how the palace first looked. Inside, a three-floor museum stages changing exhibits about Berlin's history and culture. ✉ *Poststr. 16, at Mühlendamm,* ☎ *030/240–020,* 🔲 *www.stadtmuseum.com* 🎫 *€2.* ⊙ *Tues.–Sun. 10–6.*

★ ⑭ **Palais am Festungsgraben** (Palace at the Fortress Moat). Behind the old buildings off Unter den Linden, this small palace is a fine example of mixed baroque and classical architecture. One of Berlin's few intact grand government buildings from the early 19th century, it has an elegant facade, with an entrance portico and columns as well as a small balcony—all of which are very clear-cut and straightforward in their layout yet richly decorated. Originally the building served as Prussia's treasury, but a ballroom was added in 1934 and it has since served as one of Berlin's most sophisticated cultural venues. Today it is not only home to the borough's museum, the **Stadtmuseum Mitte,** and its changing exhibits about local history, but is also a hall for chamber music concerts, lectures, and other cultural events. ✉ *Am Festungsgraben 1,* ☎ *030/208–4000.* 🎫 *Free.* ⊙ *Mon. 1–5, Thurs. 1–6, Fri. 1–8, Sat. 11–8, Sun. 11–5.*

❶ **Pariser Platz** (Paris Square). Berlin's most famous square, in front of the Brandenburg Gate, has regained its traditional prewar design, yet is the setting of some of the capital's most modern architecture. Pariser Platz has always been a showcase. Created in 1734 as a baroque square, it later received a classical refit that turned it into an elegant 19th-century space where high society and sometimes even the emperor himself showed off on horseback. Naturally it became one of the city's most desirable addresses. The square's name was derived from the victory of Prussian armies over Napoléon in 1814. Ironically, the French general had marched in triumph on this square just seven years earlier. During the Battle of Berlin the square was the center of fighting (it lies between the Reichstag and Hitler's chancellery). Only the Brandenburg Gate and some ruins of the Akademie der Künste were still standing when the Wall was built directly in front of the gate. Pariser Platz, then in East German territory, became a high-security zone and an off-limits space.

After reunification, the redesigned Pariser Platz quickly became one of the hottest architectural spots of the new capital, as the open spaces surrounding the gate were quickly developed by some of the world's most renowned architects. With the Brandenburg Gate in front of you, take a look at the **Haus Liebermann** and **Haus Sommer,** adjoining the gate on either side. Designed by Berlin architect Josef Paul Kleihues and built in 1996-98, they were among the first buildings on the square after the fall of the Wall. They are also the only structures that loosely resemble the original buildings that once stood here. Their somber appearance is typical of the somewhat rigid style of 19th-century Prussian architecture. The name "Haus Liebermann" is a reference to the German painter Max Liebermann, who lived in the house that once stood here. When watching the torchlit march of SA troops through the Brandenburg Gate after Hitler came to power on January 31, 1933, he remarked, *"Ich kann gar nicht so viel essen wie ich kotzen möchte"* ("I cannot eat as much as I want to throw up"). Liebermann, who was a member of the Prussian Academy of Arts, later emigrated. Turning around, now with your back to the Brandenburg Gate, you can take in the various sandstone facades on either side of the boulevard Unter den Linden, behind the two fountains balancing the square.

On the square's north side, the **Palais am Pariser Platz** and the **Eugen-Gutmann-Haus Dresdner Bank** are more modern interpretations of Prussian architecture but definitely fit the overall style of the square. They house cafés and the headquarters for one of Germany's major banks, the Dresdner Bank. Right next to the bank, the **French embassy** is under construction on the very spot where its predecessor from 1860 stood. Until the outbreak of World War II the French embassy had been a center of Berlin's high society, with lavish dinners and receptions that were famous for their exquisite food and challenging conversation. The embassy is slated to be completed in 2002 and will feature two-story-high windows as well as an elegant driveway, reminders of the former palacelike structure. The new embassy is flanked by two rather dull-looking offices. One of them is called **Europäisches Haus** (European House), which houses the Berlin office of the European Commission.

On the south side of the square are the esteemed Hotel Adlon and, next to it, the **Akademie der Künste Berlin-Brandenburg,** the region's prestigious Academy of Arts. The ruin of the old academy was the only edifice left on Pariser Platz in the postwar years. The new academy will be finished in 2002, and architect Günter Behnisch has cleverly put the historic facade behind a glass wall. The work of American architect Frank O. Gehry is most recognizable from within the **DG Bank** headquarters, not from the outside of the tawny building with oversize windows. Completed in 2000, the best feature of the bank can be viewed from the foyer: a giant podlike structure projects into the atrium. It nearly resembles an oversize insect that has burst in from the back of the building.

The final cornerstone of Pariser Platz will be built to the right of the DG Bank, the **American embassy.** It's long delayed construction has been a local farce. Because of heightened concerns about the safety of the U.S. State Department, the Clinton administration wanted Berlin to relocate two streets, Eberstrasse and Behrenstrasse, so that the embassy would have extra space for security. The Senate of Berlin, no longer the magistrate of an Allied-occupied city, flexed its newly grown political muscles and refused this request on the grounds of historic preservation. For years there were minor as well as major clashes between the then-mayor of Berlin, Eberhard Diepgen, and U.S. ambassador John Kornblum. German chancellor Gerhard Schröder eventually resolved the problems with the Bush administration.

Russische Botschaft (Russian Embassy). The massive Russian embassy runs a full 262 ft on the south side of Unter den Linden. Behind an iron fence with gilt finials, the elegant Stalinist building was erected in 1950–53 on the site of the Russian embassy that stood here until the 1940s. The sheer size of the embassy, which was the first one established in the young GDR after its founding in 1949, was not only a triumphant symbol of victory over Nazi Germany but also a reminder of the Soviet Union's watchful eye on the GDR, its small, but crucial ally. Each detail—such as the four statues representing working Soviet men and women—is a celebration of Communist ideology. The gold bust of Lenin, which once stood in front of the entrance, has been removed, however. The interior is adorned with red marble taken from Hitler's New Chancellery, which was around the corner. ✉ *Unter den Linden 63–65.*

⓱ Schlossplatz (Palace Square). Nothing about this vast square suggests that this was where the Hohenzollern city palace once stood. The palace, comparable in size and importance to Buckingham Palace in London or the Louvre in Paris, dated from the 15th century, and for more than 500 years the Hohenzollern dynasty enlarged and improved it according to changing style and taste. In the late 19th century the hybrid complex had a total of 1,200 rooms, several courtyards, and measured a full 630 ft by 380 ft. One of the more famous rooms was the royal reception room, the *Weisser Saal,* clad in magnificent white marble. When the Hohenzollern were thrown out of the country in 1918, the palace was left standing empty and then housed Berlin's arts and crafts museum. In 1944 it was damaged by Allied bombs but not as severely as other buildings lining Unter den Linden. The main reason for outcry when the Communist regime dynamited its remains in 1950–51 was the relatively good condition of the palace. A renovation was well within the financial and architectural grasp of the time, but Communist leader Walter Ulbricht wanted to erase any memory of Germany's feudal and imperialist past. He built a tribune in its place.

With the redevelopment of Berlin, the Schlossplatz has sparked one of the most intense architectural and political discussions in town: should the palace be rebuilt, or should the square house something new? The issue continues to be hotly debated, as the Schlossplatz is Berlin's last open space. A private initiative to rebuild at least the facade seems to have the upper hand. In addition, old statues, wall and ceiling sections, and other architectural features from the palace have been located throughout the city (many of which were reused in the 1950s to construct other buildings). The question of how this building should be used is still open.

The eastern side of the square holds the brassy **Palast der Republik** (Palace of the Republic), where East Germany's so-called People's Chamber (parliament) met. The colossal building dating from 1973–76 was closed in 1991, and the future use of the unappealing leftover is undecided. To the great discomfort of the Communist rulers (and Schadenfreude on the part of those they governed), the glass material covering the building was the ideal mirror for the Berliner Dom, just opposite it. The attempt by the regime to outshine the politically rebellious Protestant church in the heart of its own capital backfired miserably.

The smaller building at the southern end of Schlossplatz used to house East Germany's **Staatsrat** (State Senate), the GDR's executive institution and offices of GDR leader Erich Honecker. It also served as the federal chancellor's provisional Berlin office until the chancellery, next to the Reichstag, was completed in 2001. The Staatsrat's entrance actually contains an original gate section of the palace, complete with windows and ornamental balcony. It was preserved by the Communists because it was purportedly the very window from which Karl Liebknecht proclaimed the "Free Socialist German Republic" in November 1918. That republic never materialized, as only a few hundred yards away, at the Reichstag, social democrat Philip Scheidemann had proclaimed the "German Republic" two hours earlier. The latter marked the birth of the ill-fated Weimar Republic. In the near future, the Staatsrat is likely to serve as an exhibition hall for architectural shows.

The **Schlossbrücke** (Palace Bridge) is the only reminder of the architectural splendor the city palace must have exhibited. The bridge is adorned by eight marble ensembles designed by Karl Friedrich Schinkel in 1842–57. They depict the path of an ancient warrior from his first fight to his death and his subsequent ascent to the gods.

❽ **Staatsoper Unter den Linden** (State Opera). Berlin's lavish top opera house lies at the heart of the Forum Fridericianum. It is not only one of the world's most beautiful classical opera houses but also the city's oldest stage. Built in 1741–43 by Georg Wenzeslaus von Knobelsdorff, under direct supervision by Frederick the Great himself, the opera house gained an international reputation in the 19th and 20th centuries for its innovative and daring performances. In 1941 the building was hit by a bomb; it was reconstructed only to be completely destroyed in troop fighting in 1945. The opera was quickly restored and reopened in 1955. Though a proud cultural institution of East Berlin, it lagged behind West Berlin's opera in the quality and selection of performances. After reunification, in 1992, Daniel Barenboim became the maestro of the house and turned it into one of Europe's grand operas, with an emphasis on pre-Mozart operas, modern dance, and Wagner interpretations.

The opera's orchestra, the **Staatskapelle Berlin,** is the city's oldest classical orchestra, founded in 1570 by order of Elector Joachim II. In 1742 Frederick the Great made the orchestra Berlin's official Prussian Royal Orchestra. Among its many noted conductors-in-residence have been two famous composers, Giacomo Meyerbeer and Felix Mendelssohn Bartholdy. In modern times such luminaries as Richard Strauss, Leo Blech, Wilhelm Furtwängler, Otto Klemperer, and Herbert von Karajan have conducted it. ✉ *Unter den Linden 7,* ☎ *030/2035–4555,* WEB *www. staatsoper-berlin.de* ☯ *Box office: weekdays 10–6, weekends 2–6.*

OFF THE
BEATEN PATH

STADTGERICHT (Municipal Court) – Extraordinary architecture makes this the only court you'd want to enter voluntarily. Built in 1896–1905, when legal institutions in Germany were the most visible branch of imperial wisdom and mercy, the Stadtgericht is a giant neobaroque edifice with a breathtaking entrance hall. At the time of its construction, only the city palace was larger. The curving galleries and staircases and the delicate Gothic columns and ornamental balustrades exude elegance. The court is off Gruner Strasse, south and slightly west of Alexanderplatz. ✉ *Littenstr. 13–17.* ☯ *Weekdays 8–6.*

㉑ **St. Marienkirche** (St. Mary's Church). This medieval church, one of Berlin's finest, is worth a visit for its many pieces of art. The church's construction began in 1270 and ended only in the 14th century. The interior is particularly notable for the late-Gothic, macabre fresco *Der Totentanz (Dance of Death)*. The massive 1762 baroque altar, designed by Andreas Krüger, shows scenes from the life of Christ. Equally impressive is the pulpit by sculptor Andreas Schlüter. The cross on top of the church tower was an everlasting annoyance to Communist rulers, as its gilding was always mirrored in the windows of the Fernsehturm TV tower, the pride of Socialist construction genius. ⊠ *Karl-Liebknecht-Str. 8,* ☎ *030/242–4467.* ⌑ *Free.* ☉ *Mon.–Thurs. 10–4, weekends noon–4; tour: Mon.–Tues. 1, Sun. noon.*

❼ **St. Hedwigs-Kathedrale** (St. Hedwig's Cathedral). This large circular building, which resembles the Pantheon in Rome, is Berlin's chief Catholic church and the official seat of the city's bishop. When the cathedral was erected in 1747 it was the first Catholic church built in resolutely Protestant Berlin since the Reformation. It was a product of Frederick the Great's effort to appease Prussia's Catholic population after his invasion of Catholic Silesia. The king himself allegedly chose the odd architecture by simply turning over a coffee cup and saying, "This is what it's supposed to look like." Designed by Jean Legeay, the church has a roof that gives it an egglike appearance, with a classical facade and a plain interior. In 1930–32 the church was finally completed according to Legeay's original drafts and was officially named a cathedral. However, on March 2, 1943, it received a direct hit by a bomb and burned to a shell. In 1950 it was reconstructed, but the interior (because of lack of funds and surviving historic elements) was given a minimalist design. Among the few historic features are several wooden religious figures, including a statue of St. Peter dating from the 14th century. In 2001 the old **Domschatz** (cathedral treasury) returned to the church's basement. ⊠ *Bebelpl.,* ☎ *030/203–4823,* WEB *www.hedwigs-kathedrale.de.* ☉ *Weekdays 10–5, Sun. 1–5.*

❷ **Unter den Linden.** As Marlene Dietrich once sang, "As long as the old linden trees still bloom, Berlin is still Berlin." Once the most prestigious address in Berlin, the grand boulevard is slowly regaining its old glamour. Lined by grand hotels, an opera house, some cafés and shops, parliamentary buildings, embassies, and consulates, the avenue reminds you that Berlin was once the capital of the German Empire.

The boulevard was originally laid out in 1573 as a riding path between the Hohenzollern city palace and the Tiergarten, the hunting ground of the royals. In the mid-17th century the Great Elector had the linden trees planted along a now-paved path, but it was Frederick the Great who in 1740, with the erection of an ensemble of fine cultural buildings called the Forum Fridericianum, gave the boulevard its majestic look. After Prussia's victory over Napoléon, Prussian king Friedrich Wilhelm III tried to transform the avenue into a pompous showpiece.

Unter den Linden begins behind the Brandenburg Gate, at Pariser Platz, and extends almost a mile eastward, toward Alexanderplatz. The western part, once the wealthy center of downtown Berlin (hence the label "New West" for the Charlottenburg and Wilmersdorf areas around Kurfürstendamm), was completely destroyed in World War II. The buildings on this stretch are a rather dull mix of old-time GDR design dating from the 1960s along with some recently built office buildings. The intersection with Friedrichstrasse has lost its historic appeal altogether, and the densest and most interesting part of Unter den Linden begins just east of it.

WILHELMSTRASSE

IMPERIAL AND NAZI BERLIN'S OLD center of power, the once elegant Wilhelmstrasse, was utterly destroyed during World War II. Apart from the new British embassy, the Department of the Treasury (Bundesfinanzministerium), and some government offices on its northernmost end, Wilhelmstrasse is now mostly residential. Most traces of the palaces, offices, and ministries south of Behrenstrasse have vanished. Lying nearly cheek by jowl were the magnificent city villa occupied by the president of the Weimar Republic (who lived here from 1919 to 1934) at No. 73; the ministry of foreign affairs at No. 76; and the imperial Reichskanzlei (chancellor's office) at No. 77. In the late 19th century the Reichskanzlei served as an office and apartment complex for Count Bismarck, who virtually orchestrated Continental power politics between 1876 and 1890 from Wilhelmstrasse. In those days Wilhelmstrasse was the German Empire's equivalent to the French Quai d'Orsay (the Foreign Office) and Britain's No. 10 Downing Street (home of the British prime minister). Adjacent to the Reichskanzlei was the Nazi Ministry for Propaganda, where Joseph Goebbels unleashed his media blitzkrieg against political enemies at home and abroad. The area under development behind the buildings along the western side of Wilhelmstrasse was once the the Minister's Gardens, a series of lovely interconnected green parks behind grandiose villas.

With the rise of Adolf Hitler to German Chancellor in 1933, the old center of power at Wilhelmstrasse slowly shifted. First the Nazis built their Air Force Ministry, now housing the Bundesfinanzministerium at No. 97, and then the Neue Reichskanzlei, on the corner of Vossstrasse. This new chancellery satisfied the dictator's taste for monumental and vain self-presentation. In 1939 the building was heralded by Nazi Germany as the first landmark of a new architectural style. However, the building, designed by the young Albert Speer, was ridiculously out of scale. A 146-m-long (480-ft-long) mirrored gallery leading to Hitler's personal office surpassed the similar gallery

at the Palace of Versailles by 50 m (165 ft). It was here that the German attack on Europe and the Holocaust were decided. The new chancellery was destroyed in the last days of the war. Parts of the interior, particularly the valuable red marble, were used in other buildings (such as the U-Bahn station Mohrenstrasse and the Soviet war memorials at Treptower Park and in the Tiergarten).

Beneath the chancellery's gardens was a bunker system that included the infamous *Führerbunker* (Führer's Bunker). Hitler spent his last weeks underground while the Soviet Army slowly approached the chancellery. On the afternoon of April 30, 1945, less than 48 hours before Soviet soldiers stormed the bunker, Hitler and his wife, Eva Braun, committed suicide. Their bodies were then burned by SS soldiers in the garden. The bunker was blown up several times, but its concrete foundation resisted all destructive efforts and is still in the ground today. For decades after the war a sandy hill on the western side of the Wall (where Vossstrasse meets Ebertstrasse) was often erroneously presented to tourists as the last remains of the bunker. However, the bunker is on the eastern side of what was the Wall: today it's covered by a playground off Vossstrasse, right next to a parking lot.

Farther west down Vossstrasse, another bunker was found in the mid-1990s, when the whole area was probed for bombs and ammunition. The concrete complex was almost completely intact, stocked with bunks, helmets, ammunition, and other equipment. The most striking feature was the homemade Nazi propaganda art on the walls. It turned out to be the bunker of the chancellery's drivers' unit. Once the bunker was examined, it was decided to keep its location a secret, lest it become a shrine for neo-Nazis.

Wilhelmstrasse ends in Kreuzberg. Governmental building remains include the Prinz-Albrecht-Palais (formerly No. 102) and others that were occupied by Nazi institutions, including the secret police and the SS.

FRIEDRICHSTRASSE

No other street in eastern Germany has changed so dramatically as Friedrichstrasse. The once-bustling 5th Avenue of prewar Berlin has risen from the rubble of war and Communist neglect to recover its glamour of old, although it still doesn't offer the sheer number of establishments found on its western competitor, the Kurfürstendamm. Historically, the corner where Friedrichstrasse, one of the most important north–south traffic arteries in Berlin, crosses elegant Unter den Linden was one of the city's busiest areas. Berlin's culinary landmark, the Café Kranzler, had resided on this intersection since 1825. Along with other famous cafés and restaurants nearby, it was destroyed in World War II.

Unter den Linden divides 3-km (2-mi) Friedrichstrasse into two distinct sections. To the north is the historic theater district, an area still under development. The livelier southern section of Friedrichstrasse is chockablock with modern architecture and design and mostly has shopping centers.

Numbers in the text correspond to numbers in the margin and on the Mitte map.

A Good Walk

The intersection of Unter den Linden and Friedrichstrasse is dominated on the north by rather unattractive buildings constructed in the 1960s GDR architectural style. The Hotel Unter den Linden is likely to be demolished. Walking north, you'll come across the modern **Kulturkaufhaus Dussmann** store after Mittelstrasse. In the rear of the glass building is a mesmerizing cascade of water from several floors above. Two blocks farther is the Bahnhof Friedrichstrasse. Next to the railway tracks is the Internationale Handelszentrum, a white-and-black "skyscraper" that was built in 1978 by a Japanese firm, and became, along with branches of many Western companies, a Western enclave in Socialist East Germany. Hidden beneath the redbrick S-Bahn-Viadukt are many small antiques shops, bookstores, cafés, and restaurants. Directly behind the railway station is a reminder of the bitter past of Friedrichstrasse—the so-called Tränenpalast (Palace of Tears). It was under its curved roof that West Berliners and West Germans entered and left East Berlin, and where many heartbreaking scenes took place as East Berliners saw their relatives, friends, and lovers depart again. Today the Tränenpalast has been transformed into a trendy venue for pop music and other performances.

On the east side of the street is one of the few historic buildings left standing here, the old **Admiralspalast** ㉙, now occupied by the Metropoltheater. Across the Spree Canal is yet another symbol of the glorious old days of entertainment on Friedrichstrasse, the famed **Friedrichstadtpalast** ㉚. Friedrichstrasse ends at the Oranienburger Tor, once the site of a city gate and now the beginning of Oranienburger Strasse.

Return to the south side of the Friedrichstrasse and Unter den Linden intersection. On the east corner is the **Lindencorso** ㉛, a business and office center built in 1993–96 that heralded Friedrichstrasse's new chic era. On the west side, the enormous Westin Grand Hotel was built in 1987 as part of the street's redesign into a Socialist Kurfürstendamm. The first-class hotel was meant to attract Western guests and hard currency. Now run by the American Westin chain, the hotel's main feature is a soaring atrium hall surrounded by galleries that try to exude a late-19th-century elegance. As you head south on Friedrichstrasse, the first of several modern shopping and business arcades awaits, the Rosmarin-Karree, built in 1995–98. The series continues with the Hofgarten am Gendarmenmarkt, which integrates two historic buildings. Opposite the Hofgarten stands the Haus der Demokratie (House of Democracy). It gained its portentous name during the 1989–90 political upheavals in East Germany, when the building was headquarters for the country's emerging political parties as well as for citizens' protest and alternative groups. It has become part of Germany's federation of state employees' office, built here in 2001.

The jewel of Friedrichstrasse is the **Friedrichstadtpassagen** ③, a gigantic complex of three buildings praised for their completely different designs. The department stores Quartier 205, 206, and 207 within are connected by an underground passageway. Once you've emerged from the seductive layout of merchandise, continue south. You'll pass more new buildings—though not as spectacular as those you've already seen—until you reach the end of the street at Checkpoint Charlie.

Timing

The southern part of Friedrichstrasse and particularly the Galeries Lafayette are crowded on weekends, so try to visit there early or during the week. You could walk down Friedrichstrasse from north to south in about an hour, but if you want to do some shopping or simply indulge in the sights along the way, plan for at least two hours.

Sights to See

② **Admiralspalast** (Admiral Palace). This historic theater, now occupied by the **Metropoltheater,** once marked the beginning of Berlin's nightlife and theater district. The bombs of World War II completely silenced the happy-go-lucky variety shows and *Operettenhäuser* (theaters featuring a light form of opera, comparable to a musical). The Admiralspalast, once a competitor of the famous Wintergarten on Potsdamer Strasse, was built in 1910 and originally served as a bathhouse after a hot water source was found on the site. In the 1920s the bath was transformed into the theater you see today. The Admiralspalast was home to the famous Haller-Revue, which featured the Comedian Harmonists ensemble and other acclaimed artists. In April 1946 the richly ornamented building served as a venue for the party and congress celebrating the unification of East Germany's Social Democratic Party with the Communist Party, forming the SED, which was to rule East Germany for 43 years.

The theater will reopen as a musical stage, owned and funded by Dutch investors, who will have to undertake an enormous amount of restoration. ✉ *Friedrichstr. 102/102*

③ **Friedrichstadtpalast.** This ode to a famous theater is a rather gaudy building (built in 1981–84) that holds the world's largest variety revue. The original Friedrichstadtpalast, built in 1865–67, served several functions, including that of a dramatic theater run by Max Reinhardt and a magnificent variety show produced by Eric Charell. Socialist-era shows of topless dancing girls, circuslike extravagance, and some singing never reached the standard of similar revues in Paris or Las Vegas. It was demolished in 1980. Today the ensemble and the legendary female dancers of the Friedrichstadtpalast have succeeded in making the revue more international, daring, and artistic. ✉ *Friedrichstr. 107.*

③ **Friedrichstadtpassagen.** This elegant underground mall connects scores of shops. At the corner of Französische Strasse is a daring, sleek building, the **Quartier 207,** designed by French architect Jean Nouvel, which houses the French department store **Galeries Lafayette** (✉ Französische Str. 23, ☎ 030/209–480; ⊘ weekdays 9:30–8, Sat. 9–4). Its interior is dominated by a huge steel-and-glass funnel surrounded by six floors of merchandise. Even if you don't have a lot of time, take the escalators to the top floor and walk around the funnel. Also not to be missed is the seductive French gourmet food section in the basement, where you can enjoy breakfast, lunch, coffee and cake, or dinner.

From the gourmet section you can cross the complete length of the Friedrichstadtpassagen in the underground mall. At night the adjoining **Quartier 206** (☎ 030/2094–6815), designed by Pei, Cobb, Freed & Partners, is undoubtedly the most spectacular sight on Friedrichstrasse. The building's facade is covered by rows of illuminated glass fixtures, which turn the complex into a sea of light. The interior is equally impressive, with an atrium at its center and a marble floor whose white-and-black squares inspired the Quartier 206's official symbol, which can also be found throughout the small but very exquisite department store, which sells designer fashion and accessories. Right next to this building is the rather sober **Quartier 205,** built by German architect Oswald Mathias Ungers.

The Friedrichstadtpassagen were a long time coming. The GDR government had begun a similar project that languished unfinished once the Socialist regime was swept away in November 1989. In 1993 international investors brought in to rejuvenate Friedrichstrasse decided to demolish the late 1980s complex and start from scratch. But the first years of construction and the opening of the Friedrichstadtpassagen were accompanied by ill feelings among the merchants and frustration among prospective customers. Because of the enormous task of establishing a modern infrastructure (water, gas, telecommunications, U-Bahn) along Friedrichstrasse, the street remained a construction site well into 1999. Some shops couldn't lure shoppers away from Kurfürstendamm, and the street's commercial heavyweights, such as the Galeries Lafayette department store, reportedly lost so much money they threatened to close. The situation has improved, though many former main attractions here—for example, Planet Hollywood and the huge Karstadt.sports department store—closed because people didn't flock to the area in the numbers expected. ✉ *Friedrichstr. 71.* ☺ *Weekdays 10–2, Sat. 10–4.*

NEED A BREAK?   The airy **Café 206** (✉ Friedrichstr. 71, ☎ 030/2094–6045; ☺ weekdays 5–7, weekends 2–4), in the basement level of Quartier 206, is the perfect place to sit back in a heavy leather chair and enjoy a crisp, cool glass of chardonnay or an espresso after a shopping spree in the Friedrichstadtpassagen. On afternoons a pianist entertains with jazz and swing tunes.

Kulturkaufhaus Dussmann (Culture Department Store Dussmann). This combination bookstore, CD shop, and video outlet within a glass building is Germany's only business of this size that stays open until 10 PM—a rare exception in a country with rigidly enforced closing hours. The owner, Mr. Dussmann, is one of Germany's most controversial businessmen. His core business is cleaning (you may have seen Dussmann employees cleaning in an airport somewhere in the world), and the Kulturkaufhaus was an old dream of the flamboyant entrepreneur. In order to keep late hours, he cleverly used a loophole in German law that stipulates that only senior managers or family members are allowed to work past official closing times. He quickly promoted 25 employees to senior managers (and gave them a share of the revenue) and then extended the hours. That the store can remain open that long in the first place is the result of yet another German legal exception: any store in the direct vicinity of a railway station can stay open longer. ✉

Friedrichstr. 90, ☏ 030/20250, WEB *www.kulturkaufhaus.de* ☉ *Mon.– Sat. 10–10.*

③① **Lindencorso.** The strikingly elegant yet simple limestone facade and the soaring, three-story-high entrance exudes the metropolitan grandeur eastern Berlin has cultivated since 1990. Within the Lindencorso, automobile buffs can check out the **Automobilforum Unter den Linden,** a commercial car showroom and official corporate representation of the Volkswagen company. Apart from the latest models from Audi and other sports-car manufacturers, the forum also has some fine old-timers by Audi, Bugatti, Opel, Porsche, and others. It also frequently stages art and photo exhibits. ⊠ *Unter den Linden 21,* ☏ *030/2092–1200,* WEB *www.volkswagen.de/automobilforum;* ▨ *free;* ☉ *weekdays 9–8, weekends 10–6.*

MITTE'S SCHEUNENVIERTEL

The atmosphere of the smallest of all Berlin districts is best experienced in the alleyways of the Spandauer Vorstadt—Berlin's old Jewish quarter—and of the now-fashionable and hip Scheunenviertel (Barn Quarter), north of Unter den Linden. Both areas are among Mitte's oldest and most intriguing sections.

During the second half of the 17th century the Great Elector invited artisans, small businessmen, and Jews into the country to improve his financial situation; most of them moved into the Scheunenviertel. As industrialization intensified, the Scheunenviertel became poorer, and in the 1880s many Eastern European Jews escaping pogroms settled in the neighborhood to the west of it, the Spandauer Vorstadt. By the 20th century the Scheunenviertel had a number of bars, stores, and small businesses frequented by gamblers, prostitutes, and the poor, while the Spandauer Vorstadt remained a lower-middle-class residential area for Jews.

The two distinct areas are often confused as one today. The streets around and west of Oranienburger Strasse were the original Jewish quarter, Spandauer Vorstadt, while the old red-light Scheunenviertel lay to the east. All of this area is now called Scheunenviertel—a late victory of Nazi propaganda: in the 1930s the Nazis deliberately used the presence of the Scheunenviertel undesirables to stigmatize the Jewish families living west of there. In 1938 the first Jews, numbering 10,000, were forced to leave Spandauer Vorstadt. Most of those who stayed were later killed in concentration camps.

Numbers in the text correspond to numbers in the margin and on the Mitte map.

A Good Walk

After exiting the Nordbahnhof S-Bahn station, turn left on Invalidenstrasse, pass the old Reichsbahnämter at No. 130/131—a former office building of Germany's national railway company—and make your next left at Gartenstrasse, home to a flea market. Take the next right onto Bernauer Strasse, which is still lined by an original section of the Berlin Wall. In 1964, 57 East Berliners escaped through a tunnel that led to a bakery on Bernauer Strasse. Friends and family in West Berlin spent a year digging the escape route. An artistic representation of the Wall system is part of the **Gedenkstätte Berliner Mauer-Dokumentationszentrum** ③③. Return to Invalidenstrasse and walk westward until you see the huge gray **Museum für Naturkunde** ③④, a fascinating museum of natural history. From here, either walk further westward or take a bus to the **Hamburger Bahnhof** ③⑤, Berlin's museum for contemporary art, located just across the Spree Canal. Backtrack on In-validenstrasse and turn right on Chausseestrasse to reach the **Brecht-Weigel-Gedenkstätte** ㊱, a museum in the living quarters of playwright Bertolt Brecht, and the bordering **Dorotheenstädtischer Friedhof** ㊲, a graveyard where many famous figures are buried. From here continue south on Chausseestrasse and make a left onto Oranienburger Strasse to reach the heart of the Mitte district. This is also the center of the old Jewish quarter, spread around **Tacheles** ㊳, an alternative art cen-ter, and the massive **Neue Synagoge** ㊴. Detour to **Auguststrasse** ㊵, one of the district's most intriguing side streets. Walk northeast on that street and make a right turn onto **Grosse Hamburger Strasse** ㊶, yet another significant street of Jewish history, and then right on Rosenthaler Strasse to reach the Hackescher Markt and the **Hackesche Höfe** ㊷, an art deco warehouse complex. Follow the crowds through the various courtyards and exit at the entrance to the **Sophienstrasse** ㊸, a quaint little alley typical of the district.

TIMING

Both the Museum für Naturkunde and the Hamburger Bahnhof are closed on Monday, and the Gedenkstätte Berliner Mauer-Dokumen-tationszentrum is closed Monday and Tuesday. The courtyards, art gal-leries, and shops of the Scheunenviertel invite spontaneous breaks and wandering, so to truly get into the spirit of the neighborhood, don't schedule your time too tightly. The area is relatively compact, and can be seen at a relaxed pace in three hours, without visiting any of the museums. If you plan on visiting the museums, plan to spend up to six hours in the area.

Sights to See

㊵ **Auguststrasse.** Long and narrow Auguststrasse, together with Oranien-burger Strasse, forms the heart and soul of the Spandauer Vorstadt. Con-necting Rosenthaler Strasse in the east and Oranienburger Strasse in the west, the street has some airy courtyards as well as many bars and restau-rants. Beginning a walk at its west end, you first pass the entrance to a restored complex, the three **Heckmann's Höfe** (⊠ Auguststr. 9), which extend through to Oranienburger Strasse. A mix of restaurants, art gal-leries, workshops, and the Berliner Bonbonmacherei (where you can buy homemade candy) occupies the meticulously restored buildings that date back to the 1850s through 1870s. Farther up Auguststrasse, on the other side, are the **Kunst-Werke** (⊠ Auguststr. 69), run by an artist commu-nity that organizes performances and other art events in the court. A nice café set in an ultramodern cubicle extends from the historic facade. A few steps east of the Kunst-Werke is an old school (⊠ Auguststr. 21) built in 1894–95. The beautiful redbrick structure now houses the dis-trict cultural services, galleries, and a café.

㊱ **Brecht-Weigel-Gedenkstätte** (Brecht Weigel-Memorial). After years of exile in Denmark, Sweden, Finland, and the United States, Bertolt Brecht (1898–1956), one of this century's greatest German playwrights, and his wife, Helene Weigel (1900–71), moved into this old tenement house (dat-ing from 1840), establishing themselves anew in Berlin. Brecht himself moved into a rented apartment on the first floor in 1953; Weigel moved into her own apartment on the second floor in January of the following year. The couple quickly regained their international reputations by run-ning the **Berliner Ensemble** Theater, their drama laboratory for modern "epic" theater. They both lived here until their deaths and were buried in neighboring Dorotheenstädtischer Friedhof. Today you can visit the former working and living quarters of the playwright, and scholars can browse the Brecht library. The artists' spartan apartments, which look as if their inhabitants were expected to return any minute, exude a distinctly utilitarian atmosphere. However, despite this austere living environment and its working-class appearance, Brecht cherished a good meal and elegant women and knew how to make money. The downstairs restaurant serves Viennese cuisine using Weigel's recipes. ⊠ *Chausseestr. 125,* ☎ *030/28305–7044,* WEB *www.adk.de.* 🖃 *Apartment €3, library free.* ⊙ *Apartment: Tues.–Wed. and Fri. 10–noon, Thurs. 10–noon and 5–7, Sat. 9:30–noon and 12:30–2, Sun. 11–6; tours: Mon.–Sat. every ½ hr, Sun. every hr; library: by appointment only.*

㊲ Dorotheenstädtischer Friedhof (Dorotheenstadt Cemetery). The most romantic of Berlin's cemeteries also assembles some of Germany's greatest minds and most famous figures. Established in 1762 and named after the historic designation for this quarter of the city, the small cemetery is laid out around two paths. Once you have entered, turn onto the first path to your left to see the graves of playwright Bertolt Brecht, who lived right next to the cemetery, and his wife, Helene Weigel. To the left of the couple rests Heinrich Mann (1871–1950), brother of Thomas Mann and one of the country's leading essayists and intellectuals, as well as the last president of the Prussian Academy of Arts before it was taken over by the Nazis. Walk back to the main path and then make another left turn into a smaller path. Two plain columns mark the gravesites of philosopher Georg Wilhelm Friedrich Hegel (1770–1831) and Johann Gottlieb Fichte (1762–1814). Both men lectured at Berlin's Humboldt-Universität, and both established their own systems of philosophy. The next path (parallel to the one you just left) is called Birkenallee and leads to the north end of the cemetery. Among the many richly decorated monuments, many built in the form of sarcophagi or obelisks or surrounded by low fences, are the final resting places of three famous Berlin architects: Karl Friedrich Schinkel (1781–1841), who built many of Berlin's classic palaces and buildings (and, as a matter of fact, designed many gravestones in this cemetery); Johann Gottfried Schadow (1764–1850), who designed the quadriga on the Brandenburg Gate; and Friedrich August Stüler (1800–65). ⊠ *Chausseestr. 126,* ☎ *030/461–7279.* ⊙ *Apr.–Oct., daily 8–8; Nov.– Mar., daily 8–4.*

★ ㉝ Gedenkstätte Berliner Mauer-Dokumentationszentrum (Berlin Wall Memorial Site). This is the only almost-original piece of the Berlin Wall border system left in the city. The memorial took almost seven years to realize, as most former East Berliners living nearby didn't want a reminder of German separation right in front of their homes. Others who had suffered under the oppression of the Socialist regime criticized the memorial's official plaque, which simply read, IN COMMEMORATION OF THE CITY'S SEPARATION. It was later changed with the addition of AND IN COMMEMORATION OF THE VICTIMS OF THE COMMUNIST TERROR DICTATORSHIP.

East Germany erected the Berlin Wall on August 13, 1961 to block the stream of people (mostly young and well-educated) leaving the country for the West. It measured a total of 154 km (96 mi) and essentially also walled West Berliners in, turning the city into an island amid Socialist East Germany. In the late 1960s the first Wall was improved and made higher (in its final stage, the Wall was as high as 4 m (13 ft), crowned by a round concrete pipe and protected at its foot by a 40-m-wide (131-ft-wide) grass or sand strip as well as a deep ditch. Between 1961 and 1989 at between 80 and 120 people were killed, either by accident or by the East German border guards, when they attempted to cross the Wall. A few months before it came down altogether 20-year-old Chris Gueffroy was shot dead trying to escape. On the night of November 9, 1989, the Wall was opened to East Berliners for the first time, and the very first border station to let people leave East Berlin was right here, on Bernauer Strasse. Some time later—also on Bernauer Strasse—the first sections of the Wall were demolished. In the ensuing process the Wall was almost completely demolished and processed into street gravel, except for the sections at Bernauer Strasse, at the East Side Gallery in Friedrichshain, and behind the Martin-Gropius-Bau on Niederkirchnerstrasse in Kreuzberg.

The memorial includes a 70-m-long (230-ft-long) piece of the whole Wall system, which consisted of two walls separated by a control path, which border guards patrolled with their German shepherds or army jeeps. Contrary to public belief, the inner-city wall system was never mined. Standing behind the thinner eastern wall, you can look through narrow gaps to the much thicker wall bordering the west. With its photos, televison and radio excerpts, and documents, the documentation center chronicles the building of the Wall and life on both of its sides during the nearly 30 years of its existence. Not to be missed is a superb home movie dating from 1965, made by a couple that lived on the western side of the Bernauer Strasse, that simply recorded life in the shadow of the Wall.

In 2000 the modern and spare **Kapelle der Versöhnung** (Chapel of Reconciliation) was was added to the memorial ensemble. The chapel of wood and earth stands directly on the location of an historic Protestant church that was blown up by the East German regime in 1985 so as to erase any visible reminder of its community that had become separated by the Wall. ⊠ *Bernauer Str. 111, at Ackerstr.,* ☎ *030/464–1030,* WEB *www.berliner-mauer-dokumentationszentrum.de.* ⌑ *Free.* ☉ *Wed.–Sun. 10–5.*

㊶ Grosse Hamburger Strasse (Big Hamburg Street). Once a hub of Jewish life in Berlin, the street was home to the city's oldest Jewish cemetery (dating from 1672), as well as schools, a hospital, and a home for the elderly. However, the Nazis turned lively Grosse Hamburger Strasse into surely the most somber street in Berlin. In 1941–42 the Nazis transformed the home at Nos. 25–26 into the central assembly site for the last 50,000 Berlin Jews who were transported from here to the gas chambers. The cemetery and its 3,000 tombs, including that of Prussia's great Enlightenment thinker Moses Mendelssohn, were completely destroyed by the Nazis. Only a few old gravestones can be seen as part of the low wall surrounding the little green lawn. A memorial marks the spot where Mendelssohn was thought to be buried.

The horrible past of this street is commemorated by a memorial designed by Wil Lammert. The memorial consists of a plaque, often covered with wreaths and flowers, and a group of bronze statues showing simply clothed Jewish men, women, and children awaiting the gas chamber. The Jewish high school next to the memorial is protected today by high gates, fences, security cameras, and a police presence.

★ **㊷ Hackesche Höfe** (Hacke Warehouses). Built in 1905–07, the completely restored Hackesche Höfe are the finest example of *Jugendstil* (art nouveau) industrial architecture in Berlin. The huge complex is comprised of nine courtyards connected by narrow passageways. Most buildings are covered with glazed white tiles and blue-and-gray mosaics. Today the courtyards draw crowds with their several style-conscious bars and pubs, the restaurant Hackescher Hof, the variety theater Chamäleon Varieté, a drama stage, and a movie theater. ⊠ *Rosenthaler Str. 40–41,* WEB *www.hackeschehoefe.de.*

㉟ Hamburger Bahnhof, Museum für Gegenwart–Berlin (Museum of Contemporary Art). The best place in Berlin to get a survey of Western art after 1960 is in this former train station. When the early 19th-century structure was remodeled, a huge and spectacular new wing was added, designed by Berlin architect J. P. Kleihues. The addition is a stunning interplay of glass, steel, neon lighting fixtures, and sunlight coming through skylights. The extensive collections belong to art buff and renowned German collector Erich Marx, and include many large-scale installations by Anselm Kiefer, as well as paintings by Richard Long and Mario Merz, and works by Joseph Beuys, as well as Damien Hirst, Andy Warhol, Cy Twombly, Robert Rauschenberg, and Robert Morris. Two fathers of modernism, Marcel Duchamp and Marcel Broodthaers, are exhibited on the second floor. Shooting stars of the international arts scene are presented in the changing exhibitions. The closest S-Bahn stop is Lehrter Bahnhof. ✉ *Invalidenstr. 50–51,* ☎ *030/397–8340,* WEB *www.smb.spk-berlin.de.* 🎫 *€6.* ⊙ *Tues., Wed., and Fri 10–6, Thurs. 10–10, weekends 11–6.*

OFF THE BEATEN PATH

LABYRINTH-KINDERMUSEUM BERLIN (Labyrinth-Children's Museum Berlin) – This place is a dream for children and adolescents who too often have to endure the wagging finger at grown-up museums. Fun is for the having (and touching), as kids explore the small museum and world following their own curiosity. The 13 exhibits include the senses, music and noise, painter Marc Chagall, dreams and visions in a big city, LegoWorld, and *Spies, Sniffers, and Private Eyes: Following the Traces of Sherlock Holmes.* The exhibits are interactive (without using a great many high-tech toys or computers), letting kids play out roles, dress up in costumes, or solve riddles. Call ahead for information on exhibits and opening hours; the museum may be closed for some weeks during summer. ✉ *Fabrik Osloer Str., outside the U-9 Osloer Strasse station terminus,* ☎ *030/4930–8901,* WEB *www.kindermuseum-labyrinth.de.* 🎫 *€3; children €2.50.* ⊙ *Tues.–Fri. 9–1 and 2–6, Sat. 1–6, Sun. 11–6.*

Museum für Naturkunde (Natural History Museum). The more than 60 million items on display make this a thrilling and educational Jurassic Park for all ages. Built in 1883–89, the museum was one of many in imperial Germany proudly showcasing the leading position Germany held at the time in scientific endeavors. One of these was paleontology, and indeed, the collection of fossils and dinosaur skeletons is one of the finest to be found anywhere. Most visitors are drawn into the soaring and brightly lighted main hall, which was built to house the world's largest dinosaur skeleton, a 75-ft-long and 40-ft-high *Brachiosaurus brancai* that lived 150 million years ago. Other exhibits include insightful collections of stuffed mammals organized into groups that show the natural interdependencies among species. Most of these animals stand in skillfully arranged dioramas.

Among the deceased propped up here are some of the Berlin zoo's late darlings such as the gorilla Bobby, who lived at the Zoologischer Garten and later become the zoo's official mascot, and Kiri, a baby African elephant who died in 2000. A special exhibit at the museum is devoted to minerals, rocks, gems, and meteorites—including a little stone found in 1789, in which uranium was identified for the first time ever. ✉ *Invalidenstr. 43,* ☎ *030/2093–8591,* WEB *www.museum.hu-berlin.de.* 🎫 *€2.50.* ⊙ *Tues.–Sun. 9:30–5.*

Neue Synagoge (New Synagogue). This meticulously restored landmark, built between 1859 and 1866, is an exotic amalgam of styles with a faintly Middle Eastern impression, thanks to is bulbous, richly decorated dome, glittering in a gold and blue design. Berlin architect Eduard Knobloch took his inspiration from the Alhambra in Grenada. At the time the synagogue's doors opened, it was—with 3,200 seats—the largest in Europe. The Jewish congregation that flocked to the new synagogue was mostly an assimilated and not strictly Orthodox community. Their new synagogue had a magnificent organ, which was typical for "modern" Jewish services. The very building testified to the rapid growth of the Jewish community in Berlin, whose old synagogue on Heidereutergasse had become too small. The influx of Jews was largely the result of a Prussian law from the early 19th century that gave Jews living in the state the same legal rights as Germans.

That the Neue Synagoge wasn't completely demolished on "Kristall-nacht" was the result of the courageous action of Wilhelm Krützfeld, the chief police officer for the district: he confronted the SA mob that had set fire to the synagogue's anteroom and convinced it to stop the burning in deference to an old German law concerning the protection of historic buildings. A small plaque today commemorates his act—that night police officers throughout the rest of Germany simply stood back and watched the destruction. Further demolished in 1943 by Allied bombing and in 1958, when the decaying main synagogue hall was blown up, its ruins remained untouched until restoration began under the East German government in the mid-1980s. The gigantic main hall has not been rebuilt, but some ruins and markings behind the breathtaking, richly decorated facade give you an idea of its former dimensions. The building is connected to the modern **Centrum Judaicum,** a center for Jewish culture and learning that sponsors exhibitions and other cultural events. A small exhibit tells the story of the synagogue and Jewish life in Germany. ✉ *Oranienburger Str. 28–30,* ☎ *030/2840–1316,* WEB *www.cjudaicum.de* ✎ *€2.50.* ☽ *Sun.–Thurs. 10–6, Fri. 10–2.*

㊸ Sophienstrasse. Carefully reconstructed or renovated late-17th-century buildings line this narrow and quaint alley. Typical of the Spandauer Vorstadt were the interconnected commercial *Höfe,* or courtyards, where craftsmen and small shop owners both worked and lived. That tradition has been revived today, as you can see when walking up Sophienstrasse from its beginning, at Rosenthaler Strasse next to Hackesche Höfe. One of the nicest of the smaller courtyards is the **Sophiensäle** (✉ Sophienstr. 17–18), which dates from the early 19th century. The still unrenovated buildings are decorated with redbrick ornaments and have traditionally been a center of political activity. In 1849, for example, the German craftsmen's association resided here—associations of this sort were the precursors of today's political parties. The complex also served as a stage for music and drama performances. Equally charming are the **Sophie-Gips-Höfe** (named after the two streets they connect), at Sophienstrasse 21–22. The red-and-yellow brick complex is partly owned by an art dealer, Rolf Hoffmann, and has been lovingly renovated.

Near the end of the street stands the **Sophienkirche,** named after its patron and donor, Queen Sophie Luise of Prussia, who funded the neobaroque building in 1712. The first Protestant church in the Spandauer Vorstadt, it later received a round bell tower and has a well-preserved 18th-century interior design. Next to the church is a small cemetery with the grave of the German historian Leopold von Ranke. ✉ *Grosse Hamburger Str. 29 (entrance),* ☎ *030/308–7920.* ☽ *During service, Sun. 10.*

㊳ Tacheles. The heyday of this alternative, now-well-known art project is over. The scene that occupied this decaying ruin of an old department store has been diluted by the stream of tourists that came to gawk after reading about it in travel magazines and international art journals. The avant-garde-like role Tacheles played between 1991 and 1998 came to the end when the property's rightful owner began building an office and apartment complex right behind it, to be called Johannisviertel. The Tacheles building is the last remnant of the historic **Friedrichstrassepassage,** built in 1909 by Franz Ahrens. It was one of Berlin's most luxurious shopping malls and extended all way to Friedrichstrasse.

In the past, Tacheles and the large courtyard (which, for the most part, looked like desert scrub) was one of Berlin's hottest art scenes and nightspots. The square was filled with hundreds of mostly young people every night, drifting in and out of the building where music, performances, dancing, and exhibits took place on various floors. These days, despite its uncertain funding, Tacheles tries to concentrate on its original mission: to provide an inexpensive and pressure-free working environment for young artists. Public pressure forced the landlord to back down on his plan to demolish the building, and the artists will pay a nominal rent of €50. The restoration and other improvements needed to make the Tacheles a permanent institution must be paid for by the artists. ⊠ *Oranienburger Str. 54–56a,* ☎ *030/2809–6835 for taped recording or 030/282–6185,* WEB *www.tacheles.de.* ☉ *Hrs depend on event.*

PRENZLAUER BERG

The old working-class district of Prenzlauer Berg used to be one of the poorest sections of Berlin. In Socialist East Germany the tenement housing here attracted the artistic avant-garde, which transformed the area into a refuge for alternative lifestyles. Like Mitte, Prenzlauer Berg charms with its blend of worn-down, turn-of-the-20th-century architecture and an active nightlife.

Numbers in the text correspond to numbers in the margin and on the Prenzlauer Berg map.

A Good Walk

Begin your tour of Prenzlauer Berg at the **Pfefferberg** ①, an alternative music and cultural center on Senefelderplatz. Just north on Schönhauser Allee is the cemetery **Jüdischer Friedhof Schönhauser Allee** ②. Within a 10-minute walk of Senefelderplatz (walk up Schwedter Strasse and turn left on Kastanienallee) is the historic **Zionskirche** ③, at the center of a quiet square, surrounded by late-19th-century tenement houses. From here head back to Kastanienallee and walk north. If you're thirsty, you can stop for a beer or coffee and cake at the **Prater** ④. At the Eberswalder Strasse intersection, turn left to reach **Mauerpark** ⑤, an expansive sports and activities center. From the same intersection follow the district's grand old boulevard, Schönhauser Allee, until you hit Kopenhagener Strasse on your left. Turn here to pay a visit to the ultramodern **Vitra Design Museum Berlin** ⑥. Head back south on Schönhauser Allee and take a left on Danziger Strasse. After passing several cross streets you'll see the fringe art center **Kulturbrauerei** ⑦, which was an old brewery and is a typical example of late-19th-century industrial architecture. A section of it houses the **Sammlung Industrielle Gestaltung** ⑧, a small museum about East German design. Backtrack on Danziger Strasse and turn south onto Husemannstrasse, a restored 19th-century street, now, like many streets in the area, marked by graffiti scrawls. Its wrought-iron parapets on balconies and stucco decoration are typical of a time when handicrafts and small shops flourished amid the large tenements built for the working class. The East German government began renovating the street in 1987, and others in Prenzlauer Berg have followed suit since reunification. Follow Husemannstrasse to the center of Berlin's old working-class district, **Kollwitzplatz** ⑨, a good place to find a bar or restaurant. South of it is the

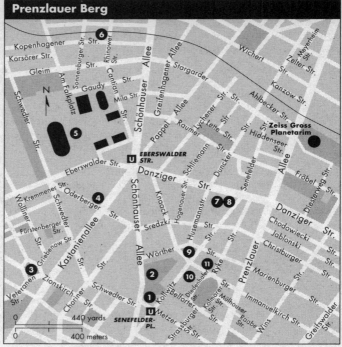

Prenzlauer Berg

Wasserturm ⑩, the old water tower on the hill that gave the district its name. At the southern tip of Kollwitzplatz turn right on Knaack Strasse for a short walk to the **Synagoge Rykestrasse** ⑪, which survived both World War II and the Nazis.

TIMING

If you want to indulge in the street life of this bustling district and relax at any of the many cafés along the way, reserve at least half a day for Prenzlauer Berg. It's also possible to take in all the sights within four hours.

Sights to See

② **Jüdischer Friedhof Schönhauser Allee** (Schönhauser Allee Jewish Cemetery). Hidden behind a brick wall, the small Jewish cemetery off Schönhauser Allee is rarely visited. It was laid out in 1827, and after the cemetery on Grosse Hamburger Strasse closed in the 19th century it served as the city's second main Jewish burial ground. Unlike the larger cemetery in Weissensee, it contains few prominent figures. Two are the painter Max Liebermann (1847–1935), in the back section of the cemetery (from the entrance, walk to the last crossing path and make a left), and the composer Giacomo Meyerbeer (1791–1864), lying just a few yards from Liebermann's grave. ⌧ *Schönhauser Allee 23–25.*

★ ⑨ **Kollwitzplatz.** Named for painter, sculptor, and political activist Käthe Kollwitz (1867–1945), this beautiful square is the center of the old working-class district. The sculpture of Kollwitz cast by Gustav Seit is based on her self-portrait. Kollwitz lived in a now-destroyed building at Kollwitzstrasse 25, and many of her works portray the hard times of the area residents. An enlarged copy of one of her Pietà sculptures, popularly known as *Trauernde Mutter mit totem Sohn* (*Grieving Mother with Dead Son*), stands at the Neue Wache on Unter den Linden. Since reunification, hip bars, restaurants, and shops have moved into Kollwitzplatz and the surrounding streets—much to the dismay of the established residents, most of whom are senior citizens. Young and ultracool students from the West, and a fair share of yuppies and dinks (double income, no kids couples) are moving in, pushing up the rents, and slowly but surely changing the face of the neighborhood.

NEED A BREAK?

For coffee and cake or a good German beer, stop by at the **Restauration 1900** (✉ Husemannstr. 1, ☎ 030/442-2494), one of the few popular cafés and restaurants from Socialist times still in business today.

❼ **Kulturbrauerei** (Culture Brewery). The red-and-yellow-brick Schultheiss brewery, designed by Franz Schwechten, now houses a fringe arts and entertainment center, containing galleries, pubs, a movie center, and a concert hall. Parts of the brewery were built as early as 1842. Around the turn of the 20th century the complex was expanded to include the main brewery of Berlin's famous Schultheiss beer, then the largest beer-producing center in the world. Because of the hilly countryside in Prenzlauer Berg, many breweries found it a perfect location for constructing underground, and therefore cool, warehouses. The Kulturbrauerei was completely restored in 1997–99, though beer is no longer brewed here. ✉ *Schönhauser Allee 36–39,* ☎ *030/441-9269,* WEB *www.kulturbrauerei.de.*

❺ **Mauerpark** (Wall Park). Where there once was a wall is now an extensive green sports and activities center, originally intended to serve the 2000 summer Olympics. To support city's Olympic bid, the Berlin Senate decided to build new arenas suitable for international contests. The bid failed miserably but the complex was finished nonetheless—much to the delight of Berlin's sports community.

The **Velodrom,** a huge silver UFO-like bicycle-racing arena, can hold more than 11,000 spectators. Designed by French architect Dominique Perrault, it opened in 1997 and is a sleek reinterpretation of the former cycling arena in the Deutschlandhalle, where the legendary *Sechstagerennen* (Six-Day Races), one the circuit's most important races, took place. The Velodrom now hosts these races every January, continuing a more than 80-year-old tradition. Next to the Velodrom is a new swimming hall.

The **Friedrich-Ludwig-Jahn-Stadion,** a stadium for soccer and track-and-field events built in 1951, has undergone considerable modernization. North of it is the ultramodern **Max-Schmeling-Halle,** named for the famous world boxing champion. Although the hall is Berlin's largest multifunctional sports complex, it is set largely below ground level and thus keeps a low profile when seen from the outside. ✉ *Am Falkplatz,* ☎ *030/443-045,* WEB *www.velomax.de.*

❶ **Pfefferberg** (Pepper Mountain). One of Prenzlauer Berg's old breweries, dating from the 1840s, Pfefferberg has been converted into one of eastern Berlin's best alternative cultural institutions for rock, pop, and folk concerts, as well as parties, comedy shows, cafés, and restaurants. It's down-market compared to the Kulturbrauerei and caters to a younger, more politically left-wing crowd. ✉ *Schönhauser Allee 176,* ☎ *030/4438-3112.* ◷ *Weekdays 9 PM–end of event; weekends 10 PM–end of event.*

❹ **Prater.** More than Berlin's largest beer garden, Prater is also one of the city's liveliest entertainment spots. The name *"Prater"* is an ironic reference to the world-famous Prater amusement park in Vienna. Built in the 1840s, this former inn and brewery evolved as a beer garden that can accommodate up to 2,000 thirsty throats. In days of yore it was also a cultural venue featuring mostly folk music. Prater has undergone a complete renovation and now accommodates parties, tango nights, pop and rock music performances, and, of course, beer drinking. It is frequented mostly by a younger crowd, but a cross section of Prenzlauer Berg residents mingles in the buzzing garden. ⊠ *Kastanienallee 7–9,* ☎ *030/247–6772.* ☉ *Events vary. Beer garden: weekdays 4 PM–1 AM, Sat. noon–1 AM, Sun. 10–1 AM.*

⑧ Sammlung Industrielle Gestaltung. (Industrial Design Collection). This small museum within the Kulturbrauerei highlights the developments and trends of design in the former East Germany. Its changing exhibits are a journey through a world that has very much vanished from everyday life since 1990, when West German products began to flood the former East. The museum's large collection starts in the 1950s with former Bauhaus member Maart Stam's Institut für Industrielle Gestaltung (Institute for Industrial Design), which was an early attempt to establish a distinctive approach to industrial design for the GDR based on functionality. In the course of the cold war, though faced with increasing ideological constraint and political repression, the East German aesthetic would become ever more antimodern and anti-Western. The lack of real competition, together with a dramatic shortage of resources, led to peculiar design concepts in, for example, product packaging, as well as in everyday items such as furniture, electronic devices, appliances, and clothing. The museum hopes to provoke serious discussion regarding an aesthetic that has until now served as little more than the butt of jokes in unified Germany, as GDR memorabilia such as clothes or even foodstuffs are dug out for "*Ostalgie*" (a combination of the words for "east" and "nostalgia") theme parties. As the museum is in the process of reorganizing, call ahead to be sure an exhibition is up for viewing. ⊠ *Knaackstr. 97,* ☎ *030/443–9382.* ▦ €2. ☉ *Hrs vary depending on exhibition.*

⑪ Synagoge Rykestrasse (Ryke Street Synagogue). Despite the synagogue's sheer size (it has seats for 700 worshipers) and its original interior, the synagogue is rarely visited by tourists. Part of the reason is its remote location, in the courtyard of a tenement house, along with the fact that there are more visible Jewish institutions such as the Jüdisches Gemeindehaus, in Charlottenburg, and the Neue Synagoge, on Oranienburger Strasse. Completed in 1904, it features a basilica-like nave with three aisles and a redbrick design almost reminiscent of a Protestant church. The interior survived the terror of Kristallnacht only because it was directly in an apartment complex, so that the SA didn't dare loot it. During the war no bombs hit the synagogue, but the main halls were nevertheless demolished when the German army used it as a warehouse for weapons and as a horse stable. The restored synagogue looks exactly as it did nearly 100 years ago. ⊠ *Rykestr. 53,* ☎ *030/442–5931 or 030/880–280.* ☉ *Tours by appointment only.*

⑥ Vitra Design Museum Berlin. The chair you've always dreamed of— and the love seat you would never have imagined—are typical pieces at Berlin's design museum, the first branch to sprout from the institution's base in Weil am Rhein and the first venue exclusively devoted to the art of furniture design, product design, and architecture in Berlin. The museum itself is housed in a gem of German architecture— a redbrick industrial building designed by Hans Heinrich Müller in 1925 that originally served as a power station. The opening shows, a retrospective of Danish-born designer Verner Panton and an exhibit called "Blow Up," about inflatable furniture, smartly capitalized on the 1970s style revival. The museum also aspires to build bridges between eastern European and western European design but has yet to fully prove

JOINING THE TWO HALVES

IN 1989 THE TELEVISED IMAGES OF jubilant Berliners dancing atop the Wall stunned the world. Once the parties were over, two city administrations managed to integrate without stirring any uproar, but in the decade since, interpersonal relationships have soured. After initially embracing one another with mutual bewilderment and curiosity, East and West Berliners have gradually returned to their respective circles.

People no longer even discuss the *Mauer in den Köpfen* (the Wall in the minds), a once hot psycho-political issue in past years. Instead, a sort of post-reunification hangover lingers throughout the city. In the mid-1990s close to 50,000 Berliners moved between the east and west halves of the city, a number slowly declining. The rate of intermarriages among East and West Berliners has continuously dropped since 1991, and now averages a mere 500 per year—not even 2.5 percent of all marriages in Berlin. Old neighborhood turfs are not immune to intrusion: Prenzlauer Berg and Mitte, two historic and proud East Berlin districts, are now flooded by transplanted yuppies and dinks (double-income, no kids couples). It would be traumatic enough if those moving in were West Berliners, but these new transplants are often West Germans who herald the arrival of chic eateries and bars that push the traditional *Kiez* (local neighborhood) to the side.

The extensive city reorganization of January 2001 reduced the number of city districts in Berlin from 23 to 12, and has only deepened resentments. Suddenly, Kreuzberg and Friedrichshain are one district; the same holds true for Mitte and Tiergarten, as well as for Prenzlauer Berg, Pankow, and Weissensee. In this last case, the adminsitrative reform turned into a hilarious *Provinzposse* (local farce) when 10,000 people, mostly westerners living in Prenzlauer Berg, protested adopting the former Socialist district name of Pankow because of its connotations within the East German regime. A compromise was reached, and the district's title now consists of three names and a number instead of the simple "Pankow."

Living conditions East and West are increasingly meeting the same levels, but external appearances and manners of speaking often give away a person's origin. East Berliners, for example, are still teased for carrying around a cheaply made shopping bag when running errands. East Berliners speak with a more pronounced Berlin accent, and each half of the city has its own lingo. Some East Berliners tend to speak softly, West Berliners loudly and self-assuredly. Even uniformed civil servants within the same organization manage to distinguish themselves. Police officers from West Berlin push down their soft uniform hat in order to make it look more casual, whereas those from the East prefer it crisply formal.

In the civic arena, the two worlds have a hard time reconciling and Western conventions are often chosen over Eastern ones. An East Berlin design that *has* gained wide appreciation are the figures that appear on the crosswalk traffic lights. The little green man ("walk signal") on the traffic lights from West Berlin is a stick-figure representation, but the East Berlin equivalent wears a hat and walks with an animated, cheerful gait. He has won over all Berliners and thus has held his ground in most of East Berlin.

The days of *Ostalgie* (nostalgia for the East) memorabilia parties—enjoyed by both East and West Berliners—that affectionately poked fun at the symbols of the Eastern regime are long over, and GDR-leader Erich Honecker impersonators are no longer being booked. Overall, East and West are getting along fairly well, precisely because both sides often stay within their former boundaries: that's not a pretty truth, but a truth that works.

itself in this respect. ⊠ *Kopenhagener Str. 58,* ☏ *030/473–7770,* WEB *www.design-museum-berlin.de* 🖼 *€5.* ⊙ *Tues.–Sun. 11–8; tours: Thurs. and weekends at 4.*

❿ Wasserturm (Water Tower). High above the sea of tenements, the water tower on the former "mill hill" is the unofficial landmark of Prenzlauer Berg. Built between 1852 and 1875, it provided pressure for Germany's first running water system. In the 20th century, after the water tower was put out of service, several floors of apartments were added to the building and the old tanks around the tower were filled with earth, allowing a small park to be laid out above it. The hill on which the tower stands was once the district's major source of income. Thanks to it and other hills in an otherwise completely flat landscape, Prenzlauer Berg made an ideal spot for windmills in the early 19th century. In the mid-1900s some 30 mills produced flour for the bakeries of Berlin here. Not a single windmill has survived the winds of time. ⊠ *Knaackstr. at Belforter Str.*

OFF THE BEATEN PATH 🖐	**ZEISS-GROSSPLANETARIUM BERLIN** (ZEISS-Large Planetarium Berlin) – One of Europe's largest and most advanced planetariums, the ZEISS-Grossplanetarium is a popular destination for stargazers and amateur astronomers frustrated by the bright lights of the big city. The 9,000 artificial stars and planets the high-tech ZEISS projector flashes onto the domed theater screen are clearer than what the naked eye could actually see. The shows vary and also include live music accompaniment. Exhibitions about astronomical subjects or space travel are staged in the foyer. If you still want to take a look at Berlin's real sky (and its few faint stars in the rare event of good weather), you can try your luck at the affiliated Archenhold-Sternwarte at Treptower Park. ⊠ *Prenzlauer Allee 80 in Ernst-Thälmann-Park,* ☏ *030/4218–4512,* WEB *www.astw.de.* 🖼 *€4.* ⊙ *Mon., Tues., and Thurs. 9–11, Wed. 9–12:30 and 1:30–9, Fri. 9–1:30 and 7:30–9, Sat. 1:30–9, Sun. 1:30–5; shows usually start at 6 and 8.*

❸ Zionskirche (Church of Zion). Once a cell of political opposition against the Nazis, the Zionskirche later continued its activist tradition as a home to church groups fighting the East German regime. In 1986 it became legendary with the founding of the Umweltbibliothek (Environmental Library), which was an unofficial, that is, not state-controlled, information resource (covering more than simply ecology issues). The church stands on an old vineyard hill now called **Zionskirchplatz,** a quaint little square that has become one the hottest pieces of real estate in eastern Berlin. The redbrick church dates from 1866–73 and is richly decorated. It's also a popular venue for classical concerts. ⊠ *Zionskirchpl.,* ☏ *030/449–2191.* 🖼 *Free.* ⊙ *Sun. noon–4, Wed. noon–7, Thurs. 5–7.*

FRIEDRICHSHAIN AND LICHTENBERG

Many run-down and somewhat seedy streets in these eastern working-class districts are still awaiting renovation. Even though both Friedrichshain and Lichtenberg have a somewhat bad reputation—the latter for frequent right-wing attacks on foreigners, the former as one of the city's poorer districts—Friedrichshain is beginning to gain new appeal as an avant-garde area in the spirit of artsy Kreuzberg. At night parts of the districts, such as Boxhagener Platz, are buzzing with some nightlife. Treptower Park (in the district of Treptow) and Volkspark Friedrichshain provide leafy green relief.

Numbers in the text correspond to numbers in the margin and on the Friedrichshain, Lichtenberg, and Köpenick map.

A Good Tour

Stretching east off Alexanderplatz, **Karl-Marx-Allee** ① is a Socialist-style grand avenue built in the 1950s. Stroll down the boulevard until Strausberger Platz, where you can detour north on Lichtberger Strasse to the **Volkspark Friedrichshain** ②, a lovely public park with a memorial, or take the subway to **Forschungs- und Gedenkstätte Normannenstrasse** ③, a memorial and museum in East Germany's former secret security police headquarters. Take the U-5 train from Strausberger Platz to Magdalenenstrasse and use the Ruschestrasse exit when leaving the station. A small sign with a red arrow points the way to the museum. From the Magdalenenstrasse station continue three subway stops to Tierpark station for a visit to Berlin's second zoo, **Tierpark Friedrichsfelde** ④. From the Tierpark station it's a 15-minute ride on Bus 396 south to the **Deutsch-Russisches Museum** ⑤, at the site of Germany's final surrender in May 1945. From the museum take Rheinsteinstrasse and then Trewkowallee and Stolzenfelsstrasse to the S-Bahn station Karlshorst. Board the S-3 (going in the direction of Westkreuz) and change at Ostkreuz for one of the several lines going one stop farther, to Warschauer Strasse, for the **East Side Gallery** ⑥ Wall remains. Walk downhill on Warschauer Strasse and turn right at the river to reach it. At Ostkreuz you could also change to the S-8 to **Treptower Park** ⑦ (in the direction of Günau). The station is just a few steps from the extensive landscaped garden whose many attractions include an observatory and an impressive Soviet military memorial.

TIMING

Touring the sights in Lichtenberg and Friedrichshain can take up a full day if you want to enjoy the Treptower Park and the Tierpark Friedrichsfelde. Each museum can be explored in less than an hour. Even when using public transportation, allow some extra time for moving across districts.

Sights to See

⑤ **Deutsch-Russisches Museum.** On May 8, 1945, Nazi Germany finally signed its unconditional surrender in this mansion, which today chronicles German-Soviet relations in the 20th century. The building once served as a German army officers' casino. After the war the Red Army occupied the property for the Soviet Military Government. In 1967 it was turned into a museum featuring the capitulation ceremony. In 1994 the museum was reestablished to commemorate the often difficult relations between Germany and the Soviet Union. In addition to the Kapitulationssaal (Capitulation Room), where the German military command signed the surrender in front of four Allied officers (including the famous Soviet marshal Shukov), you can inspect 13 rooms. They contain uniforms, written and photographic documents, flags, military objects, and other materials primarily covering World War II, with a special emphasis on Germany's attack on the Soviet Union in June 1941. All tables, figures, and printed materials are written in both German and Russian. ✉ *Zwieseler Str. 4,* ☎ *030/5015–0810,* WEB *www.museum-karlshorst.de.* ✇ *Free.* ☉ *Tues.–Sun. 10–6.*

⑥ **East Side Gallery.** In 1990, just months after the Berlin Wall was rendered obsolete, 118 artists from around the globe painted the longest remaining section of it. The 1.2-km (.8-mi) stretch has been declared a historic monument. The Wall stands in an industrial area parallel to Mühlenstrasse and the Spree River. The heavily trafficked road makes for an unidyllic walk, but it's a fitting reminder that the Wall was a grim borderland before becoming a tourist attraction. Unlike the spray-painted graffiti on the west side of the Wall, the works hand-painted on the east side have deteriorated, though some artists return to ren-

Friedrichshain, Lichtenberg, and Köpenick

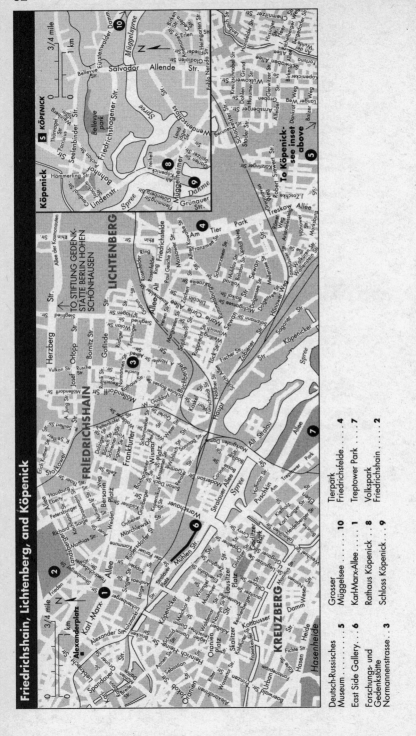

ovate occasionally. The painting of a Star of David superimposed over a German flag is a turf continually fought over by the artist and neo-Nazis spraypainters. A charismatic English-speaking Berliner sells souvenirs at a stand. ✉ *Mühlenstr. at Oberbaumbrücke.*

3 **Forschungs- und Gedenkstätte Normannenstrasse** (Normannenstrasse Research and Memorial Site). Normannenstrasse was the address of the notorious East German secret service, the Staatssicherheitsdienst (State Security Service), simply called *"Stasi"* by East Germans. The Stasi ministry, which was responsible for intelligence abroad and in East Germany, occupied this gray and anonymous-looking concrete high-rise. It was the nerve center of the *"Krake Stasi"* (Stasi octopus)—as it was disdainfully referred to by its victims—which controlled more than 90,000 employees and at least 174,200 informants and collaborators. At one point during the 1980s, 2% of the general population directly or indirectly spied on their fellow citizens for the powerful Stasi.

The ministry was raided and then ransacked by demonstrators on January 15, 1990. They not only demolished some of the equipment and offices but also destroyed many files, hated symbols of the Stasi's surveillance of their society. Back then the day was celebrated as a citizens' victory over an institution straight out of Orwell's *1984.* However, in the years since it has been revealed that many demonstrators were actually Stasi agents who rushed into their own offices to destroy implicating evidence.

Today the small museum includes several exhibits about the history and organization of the Stasi, its crimes, and the resistance of many East German citizens. The office complex of Stasi minister Erich Mielke has been kept in its original condition. His personal office includes his desk, a death mask of Lenin, and a black phone (a connection to the top-secret Warsaw Pact communications system). One of the few funny items on display is in the kitchen (Room 5): a drawing and instructions describe how the minister's breakfast had to be prepared. The egg, jelly, salt, knife, and plate had to be arranged the same way every morning.

You can view a documentary on Mielke while taking a coffee break in the same cafeteria Stasi generals used. Mielke, a devoted Communist and Hitler opponent, was probably the GDR's most powerful minister, running the Stasi for 32 years. On the video you can witness his famous response to allegations that he spied on his own people—*"Aber ich liebe Euch doch alle!"* ("But I love all of you")—which elicited chuckles in a tumultuous parliament session in 1989 shortly before the fall of the SED regime. After the demise of the GDR, the then 86-year-old Erich Mielke was tried, not for his responsibilities as a Stasi minister, but for the murder of two police officers in 1931. Because of his age and poor physical condition, he was sentenced to only six years in prison but was released after two years and died in 2000.

The museum is run by a citizens' committee that established and organized the memorial site some 10 years ago, a time when no state institution was interested in or capable of doing it. ✉ *Ruschestr. 103, Haus 1,* ☎ *030/5515–4757,* WEB *www.stasimuseum.de.* 🎫 *€2.50.* ☉ *Weekdays 11–6, weekends 2–6.*

1 **Karl-Marx-Allee** (Karl Marx Avenue). Once the proudest avenue in Socialist East Berlin, the wide and long (2.5 km/1.6 mi) east–west axis is a showcase of Stalinist architecture and is still the main thoroughfare of Friedrichshain. The palacelike apartment and business complexes you see today date from the 1950s. Their distinctly ornamental yet somehow totalitarian look, called *"Zuckerbäckerstil"* (sugar baker style) by Germans, is a remnant of Stalinist design. In fact, the avenue was once called Stalinallee, before being renamed for Karl Marx. As it continues eastward into Friedrichshain, it takes on its original name again: Frankfurter Allee (the road once led all the way to Frankfurt an der Oder, now on the Polish border).

The rebuilding of the area around Karl-Marx-Allee was one of the largest projects of East Germany's first economic five-year plan and provided work for thousands. But it was here on June 17, 1953, that frustrated construction workers first demonstrated against the regime, sparking a public uprising throughout East Germany. Wages were the reason for the strike. The uprising was mistakenly celebrated in West Germany as a demand for German reunification, and thus immortalized in the street name "Strasse des 17. Juni" in Tiergarten. West Germany even made June 17 a national holiday, which was only dropped after reunification. In 1953 the protests were crushed by Soviet tanks, but the workers of Stalinallee are still remembered throughout Germany.

The somewhat dilapidated appearance of the gigantic apartment complexes along Karl-Marx-Allee and Frankfurter Allee—especially the 14-story-high buildings surrounding **Strausberger Platz**—are a bit deceptive, for on the inside these apartments offered East Berliners what were relatively modern living standards for the 1950's. At a time when most of the city was still in ruins, its residents had amenities such as large bathrooms, elevators, and central heating systems. The apartments are still quite popular among tenants today.

OFF THE
BEATEN PATH
STIFTUNG GEDENKSTÄTTE BERLIN-HOHENSCHÖNHAUSEN – Among the many memorials in Berlin, this one is a notable exception: it's not only one of the few sites left in its original state, but it's also one of the few that relates to the postwar era. The memorial encompasses the central holding prison of the East German Stasi, the regime's security police. Until early 1990 the complex served as a prison, mostly for political inmates. The property has been well preserved, and cell blocks can be seen on a guided tour. Before the Stasi took over the prison in 1951 it had been used between May 1945 and October 1946 as a transit prison and temporary internment camp of the Soviet Army. From here an estimated 10,000–20,000 German inmates were sent to Siberia. Many of those destined to be sent away died at Hohenschönhausen due to malnutrition and the poor hygienic conditions. An especially gruesome punishment of those days was to be assigned to the U-Boot-Zellen (submarine cells), windowless cells where inmates were tortured. To reach the memorial, take the S–8 train to the Landsberger Allee station and then board a tram (5, 6, 7, 15, or 17). ⊠ *Genslerstr. 66, ☎ 030/9860–8236,* WEB *www.gedenkstaette-hohenschoenhausen.de.* ⊐ *Free.* ۞ *Tours: Mon.–Sat. 11 and 1; English-language tours by appointment.*

☺ ❹ **Tierpark Friedrichsfelde** (Friedrichsfelde Zoo). Founded in 1955 to give East Berliners the same pleasures West Berliners continued to enjoy, the Tierpark Friedrichsfelde makes Berlin one of the world's few cities with two zoos. Berlin's second zoo is much smaller and younger than the Zoologischer Garten, in the west, but it, too, is devoted to the breeding and protection of endangered animals. Among the 950 species living here are rare wild cats such as Amur leopards and Corbett tigers, as well as nearly extinct animals like the Persian fallow deer and the African wild ass. A special resident is Matibi, a young African elephant born here in 1999. The two *Felsinnenhallen,* artificial rock landscapes in two huge halls, are home to several lions and Siberian tigers. The equally impressive *Dickhäuterhaus* has 14 elephants and eight rhinos. Camels and zebras roam in vast enclosures. The Tierpark is within a landscaped park that includes **Schloss Friedrichsfelde,** once the GDR's official state guest house. ✉ *Am Tierpark 125,* ☎ *030/515–310,* WEB *www.tierpark-berlin.de.* 🎫 *€7.50.* ☉ *Apr.–Oct., daily 9–7; Nov.–Mar., daily 9–dusk.*

❼ **Treptower Park.** Generously laid out at the banks of the Spree River, this rolling park with clumps of forest was landscaped as an English garden in the late 19th century. Just like the Volkspark Friedrichshain, Treptower Park was conceived as a park for the public, and thus even featured—quite modern for its time—a soccer field, that is, a meadow that was not meant to be simply scenic. The park was a budget-friendly way to spend a weekend: here and elsewhere in Berlin, throughout the late 19th and 20th centuries, special cafés attracted low-income families with the advertisement *"Hier können Familien Kaffee kochen"* (families can brew their own coffee here). Guests brought their own coffee (and cake, for that matter) and paid only for additional food and for seats. The only one of these cafés remaining is the **Haus Zenner** (✉ Alt-Treptow 14–17, ☎ 030/533–7370), at the Treptower Park waterfront.

Other attractions such as the **Archenhold-Sternwarte** (Archenhold Observatory) added to the appeal of this verdant retreat. The historic observatory (1809) once offered a glimpse of the stars through the world's largest lens telescope. With a focal length of 69 ft, it still is the world's longest traditional lens telescope. ✉ *Alt-Treptow 1,* ☎ *030/534–8080,* WEB *www.astw.de.* 🎫 *€2,* ☉ *Wed.–Sun. 2–4:30 for exhibits; call for observation hrs.*

A very terrestrial matter, however, is commemorated at the center of the park, with the graves of 5,000 Soviet soldiers killed during the Battle of Berlin. The **Sowjetisches Ehrenmal** (Soviet Honorary Memorial) was built in 1947–49 and covers an extensive area. It is dominated by a 39-ft-high bronze statue of a heroic Soviet soldier holding a child in one arm while smashing the Nazi swastika with his sword. Beneath is a traditional Russian crypt hidden in a hill-like construction. Here, as elsewhere in the memorial, the red-color marble used was taken from Hitler's destroyed New Chancellery. ✉ *Alt-Treptow.*

❷ **Volkspark Friedrichshain** (People's Park Friedrichshain). Berlin's second-largest public park is also the city's oldest landscaped green space, dating from 1840. Garden architect Joseph Peter Lenné designed the 130 acres of hills, meadows, woods, and a lake to be an eastern counterpart to the Tiergarten. The park was intended to serve as a retreat for all social classes. Despite the park's destruction in World War II, it still serves its original purpose. Its two defining features now are two artificial hills called the **Kleiner und Grosser Bunkerberg** (Smaller and Larger Bunker Mountain). Completely covered by natural greenery, they were originally two huge piles of rubble taken from the ruins of the city after World War II. The larger hill, which rises to a height of 220 ft, is nicknamed **"Mont Klamott,"** after the German slang term *"Klamotten,"* which translates as "cheap clothes," and something just hastily thrown together.

The reminders of war, however, are quickly forgotten in the serene setting, which also has the **Märchenbrunnen** (Fairy-Tale Fountain) on the western side of the park. Built by Ludwig Hoffmann in 1903, the neobaroque fountain is graced by more than 106 delicately sculpted figures from the most popular German fairy tales. The park also contains important memorials and grave sites, most significantly the **Friedhof der Märzgefallenen** (Cemetery of Those Killed in March). It holds the graves of 183 Berlin revolutionaries, all of whom were killed by the

Prussian army in March 1848 in the course of Germany's failed liberal revolution. ⊠ *Am Friedrichshain and Friedenstr.*

KÖPENICK

The green and very inviting southeast, traditionally a weekend destination for urbanites, offers vast spaces of parks, gardens, and lakes. Köpenick is Berlin's largest district and has preserved the spirit of the independent town it once was. Köpenick's small, 18th-century Altstadt (Old Town) has been incompletely and not quite harmoniously restored, but looks more like a provincial village than the administrative and cultural center of Berlin's largest district. Köpenick only became part of Berlin in 1920 and first emerged as a small settlement north of a castle on today's Schlossinsel (Castle Island). Most of the houses date from the 18th century, especially those in the Kiez, a small fishing settlement in the center of town. The cobblestone streets today remain quaint—with nothing geared toward tourism.

Numbers in the text correspond to numbers in the margin and on the Friedrichshain, Lichtenberg, and Köpenick map.

A Good Tour

From the Köpenick S-Bahn station take Bus 169 three stops to the **Rathaus Köpenick** ⑧ in the heart of the Alt-Köpenick, off Alt-Köpenick-Strasse. **Schloss Köpenick** ⑨, with its arts and crafts museum, is at the end of Alt-Köpenick, facing the Dahme River. Reach this palace by carefully crossing busy Müggelheimer Strasse. Before you head back to the S-Bahn station to set out into the surrounding greenery, take in some more of the historic town. From the palace, take a right onto Müggelheimer Strasse and then turn right into a tiny street called Kietz. The cobblestone street is lined with old fishermen's houses that once formed their own fishing village. Walk straight back (north) on the same street, which eventually becomes Kirchstrasse, and take a right onto Jägerstrasse to reach historic Schüsslerplatz. It's the town's central market square, where a colorful market is held Tuesday and Thursday, against the backdrop of a few nicely restored townhouses Walk up Lüdersstrasse a few hundred yards to the bus stop; bus No. 169 will take you back to the S-Bahn station. Next up is Berlin's largest lake, the **Grosser Müggelsee** ⑩, where you can sunbathe or swim. Take the S-3 two stops from Köpenick to the Friedrichshagen station, then switch to Tram 61.

TIMING

The old town center of Köpenick and the museum at the palace can be toured in half a day. You could, however, spend several days in the greater Müggelsee area, relaxing at the lakes, hiking, or taking boat trips. Afternoon boat trips leave for one of the restaurants along the lake shores—a 4- to 5-hour excursion with Stern- und Kreisschiffahrt. In summer try to avoid going to the lake on Sunday afternoon, when it's most crowded.

Sights to See

⑩ **Grosser Müggelsee** (Great Müggelsee). Despite its remote and peaceful setting, its clear water, and some nice restaurants, Berlin's largest lake has never become as popular as its smaller counterparts in the west. One reason is the relatively long travel time from the center of Berlin, even from the eastern outskirts of Köpenick. Having been part of East Berlin, the area is still less commercially developed than Wannsee or the Grunewald region, which were favorite destinations for West Berliners. Nonetheless, the lake is a perfect retreat for a relaxed day on a boat (whether a canoe, a paddleboat, or a steamer), for hiking and walking, or for climbing up the **Müggelturm** (Müggel Tower), a

Close-Up

CAPTAIN OF KÖPENICK

WILHELMINE GERMANY WAS A RIGID SOCIETY dominated by the Prussian military spirit and absolute obedience to the state. That mentality, however, was challenged in 1906 by a poor homeless Berliner by the name of Wilhelm Voigt. A former shoemaker and ex-convict, Voigt hatched a plan to change his fortunes and began studying the harsh regulations of the German army. Outfitted in a army captain's uniform he bought at a secondhand thrift shop in Potsdam, he commandeered a small platoon of soldiers in the streets of Berlin; rode the train to the town hall of Köpenick; arrested the mayor and the treasurer, whom he sent to a prison in Berlin; seized the city's cash; and left. All this was achieved with no resistance, since a captain of the Reichswehr was a figure of unquestionable authority. City officials didn't dare protest or even ask for the reason for their sudden arrest. Voigt eventually turned himself in (with only some of the cash missing), served his prison time, and later became Germany's most popular gangster, writing memoirs and touring the country. Even the kaiser himself, the very personification of the cult of authority that Voigt had debunked, is said to have laughed. Voigt actually had lesser aspirations when he pulled the stunt: he wanted only to steal an identity card so he could get a job. As a convicted criminal, he couldn't obtain one without a job contract. His effort to escape this vicious circle was in vain: the Rathaus Köpenick did not have a *Meldebehörde,* the agency authorized to issue identity cards.

95-ft observation tower that provides a splendid view of the lake and the hilly landscape of the **Müggelberge** (Müggel Mountains).

In summer many of the most loyal visitors hang loose on the waterfront, sunbathing, swimming, and walking around—in the nude. This is called *Freikörperkultur* (free body culture), or FKK for short, and it has always been more popular in eastern than in western Germany, but the practice shares a long tradition in both parts of the country. The **Strandbad Rahnsdorf,** a stretch of sandy or grassy beach, used to be the GDR's only official, state-run nude-only swimming area. ⊠ *Friedrichshagen,* ☎ *030/651–6512.* ☒ €1.20. ☺ *Apr.–mid-Nov., daily 10–7; mid-Nov.–Mar., weekends 10–7.*

❽ Rathaus Köpenick (Köpenick Town Hall). If not for a desperate homeless man who once invaded the town hall, this small redbrick building, a replica of the original from 1904, would have remained in obscurity. But the now-famous Captain from Köpenick, who is immortalized in bronze in front of the building, successfully made the town hall and its mayor the laughingstock of the entire nation. You can enter the building, but there's nothing in particular to see inside. ⊠ *Alt-Köpenick 21,* ☎ *030/656–840.* ☒ *Free.* ☺ *Weekdays 9–6.*

❾ Schloss Köpenick (Köpenick Palace). The plain white palace on the Schlossinsel at the confluence of the Dahme and Spree rivers is one of Berlin's lesser-known Hohenzollern palaces. The baroque palace was erected in 1677–81 as a residence for Prince Frederick but was later used as "simple" living quarters for family members of the Hohenzollern dynasty. Today the palace houses sections of the Tiergarten's **Kunstgewerbemuseum** (Arts and Crafts Museum) and is undergoing a costly renovation. The palace and the museum are scheduled to reopen in 2002. ✉ *Schlossinsel,* ☎ *030/2090–5566,* 🕸 *www.smb.spk-berlin.de.*

KREUZBERG

When Kreuzberg literally had its back against the wall, West German social outcasts, punks, artists, and the radical left made this old working-class district their own private hideout. Since the 1970s the population has been largely Turkish, and today many of yesterday's outsiders have turned into successful owners of trendy shops and restaurants. However, since the *"Wende"* (the fall of the Wall), Kreuzberg has lost its edginess. Young artists and style mongers who enjoyed the cheap rents of the location are moving on to populate the eastern districts of Prenzlauer Berg and Friedrichshain. Remaining in Kreuzberg is a largely Turkish population that lives cheek by jowl with a variegated assortment of New Agers, down-at-heel artists real and fake, and bohemians of all nationalities.

Historically, the district has always been separated into two distinct areas: SO 36 (an old, prewar zip code) around Oranienstrasse and the region east of it, and Kreuzberg 61 (a postwar zip code) around Mehringdamm and Gneisenaustrasse. While SO 36 has working-class tenement houses now occupied by students, Turkish families, and many poorer people, the more chic Kreuzberg 61, southwest of it, is an increasingly affluent area. Also well developed is Paul-Lincke-Ufer, along the Landwehr Canal. Still, Kreuzberg is western Berlin's poorest and most troubled district.

Numbers in the text correspond to numbers in the margin and on the Kreuzberg map.

A Good Tour

Begin at Potsdamer Platz U- or S-Bahn station, which is in Mitte, but is just north of Kreuzberg. Above ground you'll see the construction area of Leipziger Platz, soon to be home of the Canadian embassy, banks, and more corporate headquarters. Head east on Leipziger Strasse and on the right is the Preussisches Herrenhaus (Prussian Privy Council), where the federal Bundesrat (Germany's upper legislative chamber) meets, comparable to the U.S. Senate. The neoclassical building dates from 1899–1904. At the corner of Wilhelmstrasse is one of the few Nazi-era buildings still standing, the former air force ministry, now home to the **Bundesfinanzministerium** ①. Just ahead on Leipziger Strasse is the **Museum für Kommunikation** ②. Follow Wilhelmstrasse south and turn right at Niederkirchnerstrasse, where the mammoth Bundesfinanzministerium finally ends, and Kreuzberg proper begins. A stretch of the badly damaged Berlin Wall is on the left: much of the concrete has been wrenched out by people claiming their personal piece. Also on the left is the barely noticeable **Prinz-Albrecht-Gelände** ③, which contains the underground ruins of Nazi SS headquarters. Next door is the ornate **Martin-Gropius-Bau** ③, and directly across from it, the old **Preussischer Landtag** ⑤, the seat of Berlin's parliament.

At the end of the street, turn left onto Stresemannstrasse and walk one long block to the impressive ruin of the **Anhalter Bahnhof** ⑥, once Berlin's largest railway station. (From here you could continue south on Stresemannstrasse and then right on Möckernstrasse if you were eager to get to the Deutsches Technikmuseum Berlin.) Head east on Anhalter Strasse, turn left on Wilhelmstrasse and then east on Kochstrasse, the media drag of the 1920s. At the corner of Friedrichstrasse, gripping stories of the Wall, refugees, and spies are told in the museum at the former **Checkpoint Charlie** ⑦. Continue east on Kochstrasse and turn right onto Markgrafenstrasse, which leads straight to the **Jüdisches Museum** ⑧, whose entrance is in the yellow baroque building, not the silver modern extension. Check the bus schedule across the street from the museum for when to catch a bus to Hallesches Tor, or be prepared to walk about 12 minutes to this U-bahn station. Across from the museum, take E.T.A. Hoffmann to Friedrichstrasse, and turn south. From Hallesches Tor, either take a bus or the U-Bahn to Möckernbrücke U-Bahn station. A bit further west on the south side of the canal is one of Germany's finest technology museums, the **Deutsches Technikmuseum Berlin** ⑨.

After the museum hop on the U–7 at the Möckernbrücke U-Bahn station and ride one stop to Mehringdamm. Head south and turn right at Hagelberger Strasse to find **Riehmers Hofgarten** ⑩, one of Kreuzberg's finest 19th-century housing complexes. Take Grossbeerenstrasse south to reach the district's loveliest park, **Viktoriapark** ⑪. After a stroll through the greenery, make your way to the shops of nearby Bergmannstrasse, or to move on the SO 36 neighborhood of Kreuzberg, board the U–6 at either the Platz der Luftbrücke or Merhringdamm U-Bahn stations. Change at Hallesches Tor for a train to Kottbusser Tor. Above ground, take Adalbertstrasse away from the station to **Oranienstrasse** ⑫, a street known for its progressive, hip cafés and nearby markets. Turn right on Oranienstrasse and then left on Mariannenstrasse to reach **Mariannenplatz** ⑬, a quaint square. From here it's a 15-minute walk through the poorer but picturesque part of Kreuzberg, down Muskauer Strasse and then east on Skalitzer Strasse. You'll eventually reach **Oberbaumbrücke** ⑭, a historic, richly decorated bridge connecting Kreuzberg and the district of Friedrichshain.

TIMING

You can cover this tour in less than a day if you don't spend too much time at the museums. You should, however, reserve at least an hour for any of the museums you visit and take in some of the street life in Kreuzberg. Oranienstrasse and its neighboring side streets are filled with cafés that are perfect places to unwind at the end of the day.

Sights to See

❻ **Anhalter Bahnhof** (Anhalt Train Station). Within a large field, the ruined remains of this train station constitute one of the most memorable sights in western Berlin. The Anhalter Bahnhof was once a magnificent 557-ft-long glass-covered structure, built in 1876–80 by Franz Schwechten. As one of the largest train stations of its time, it served as the imperial capital's main long-distance station. During World War II it was heavily damaged but not completely destroyed. In the first post-war years trains still operated here. It was not until 1960 that the entire building was condemned. For decades West Berliners discussed what they should do with the grassy area behind the ruins; proposals included an open-air movie theater and a park. It wasn't until 2001 that the music venue Tempodrom moved into a newly constructed building here. ⊠ *Askanischer Pl. 6–7, off Stresemannstr.*

❶ **Bundesfinanzministerium** (Ministry of Finance). You might wonder what's worth seeing at the official site of any country's most boring ministry, but Germany's Federal Ministry of Finance is an exception. The extensive building once served as Nazi Germany's air force ministry and thus displays distinctively Nazi architecture, with a monotone limestone facade, small windows, and square columns. Built between 1934 and 1936 by Ernst Sagebiehl, who also designed the Tempelhof Airport, the complex was one of the largest and most modern office buildings of its time, based on an ingenious steel-skeleton construction. Its sheer size reflects the attitude of its first proprietor, Her-

Kreuzberg

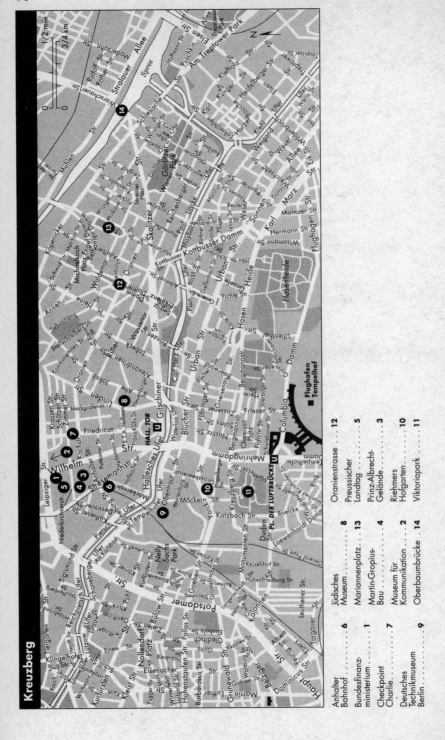

Anhalter Bahnhof 6
Bundesfinanzministerium 1
Checkpoint Charlie 7
Deutsches Technikmuseum Berlin . . 9

Jüdisches Museum 8
Mariannenplatz . . 13
Martin-Gropius-Bau 4
Museum für Kommunikation . . 2
Oberbaumbrücke . . 14

Oranienstrasse . . . 12
Preussischer Landtag 5
Prinz-Albrecht-Gelände 3
Riehmers Hofgarten 10
Viktoriapark 11

mann Göring, who was known for his grotesque egomania. Historically, Wilhelmstrasse was the site of the most important German ministries, and Hitler's New Chancellery at Vossstrasse was only a few steps around the corner.

The building survived the war mostly unharmed because it had been constructed to withstand heavy bombardments. A colorful wall mural, created in 1952 by Max Lingner, at the corner of Wilhelmstrasse and Leipziger Strasse, is a reminder that the East German ministries occupied the building next. It shows a simplistic and idealized series of "happy" socialist men and women going about their work.

After German reunification, this building, at least for East Germans, became the despised symbol of a West German takeover of the East. The **Treuhand-Anstalt,** the federal administration to organize the transition of East Germany's bankrupt Socialist economy into a Western-style capitalist market economy, was housed here from 1991 to 1997. In fact, the very name of the building now, the **Detlev-Rohwedder-Haus,** is a reminder of Mr. Rohwedder, an industrialist who headed this office until his 1992 assassination by the German terrorist organization RAF (which hoped to gain the approval of East Germany, an attempt that failed completely). This building is not open to the public. ⊠ *Wilhelmstr. 97.*

★ **❼ Checkpoint Charlie.** This famous crossing point between the two Berlins is where American and Soviet tanks faced off in the tense months of the Berlin blockade (1948–49). All evidence of the crossing point has disappeared along with the Wall, but the **Haus am Checkpoint Charlie** (House at Checkpoint Charlie—the Wall Museum) is still here to tell the the Wall's fascinating stories. The museum reviews the events leading up to its construction and displays actual tools and equipment, records, and photographs documenting methods used by East Germans to cross over to the West (one of the most ingenious instruments of escape was a miniature submarine). The new building close to the museum, the **American Business Center,** was erected on the eastern side of the former Iron Curtain.

Checkpoint Charlie was originally an American border station established in September 1961. This was the only border crossing point in the city that Allied soldiers and citizens from foreign countries could use. West Germans or West Berliners were not allowed to use this crossing. In the middle of Friedrichstrasse stands a pole with blown-up portraits of Allied soldiers who worked here. ⊠ *Friedrichstr. 43–45,* ☎ *030/ 253–7250,* WEB *www.mauer-museum.com.* ⌷ *€4.* ☉ *Daily 9 AM–10 PM.*

NEED A BREAK? Try your best to conjure up an image of the Wall from a window seat at **Café Adler** (⊠ Friedrichstr. 206, ☎ 030/251–8965), which once bumped right up against it. The soups and salads are all tasty and cheap.

🍴 **❾ Deutsches Technikmuseum Berlin** (German Technology Museum Berlin). One of Europe's largest museums for technology, the Deutsches Technikmuseum constantly adapts its presentations to the fast-changing high-tech world and gives nontechies a chance to grasp what the whirlwind is all about. It's one of the few German museums that emphasizes a clear and easy-to-grasp display of its 30,000 items (of which only 25% are exhibited at any given time). At the historic Anhalter freight depot station, the museum holds the collections of several earlier museums destroyed in World War II. Today it comprises seven buildings, each with a focus on a special subject.

In the main building the first floor is devoted to historic arts and crafts such as jewelry and textile production, while the second floor spans from the first simple calculators to superconductors and computers. On the third floor, the technology of paper production and the printing industry is explained.

A new building adjoining the historic museum has exhibits detailing the thrilling story of air and space transportation as well as that of shipbuilding and sea transportation. The highlights of these collections are 40 planes, including the German Junkers Ju 52, which was Lufthansa's first commercial airplane as well as the backbone of the German air force during World War II. Dangling high above your head is an original *"Rosinenbomber"* ("raisin bomber"), a shining silver C-47 sky train. It was one of the planes that transported goods and food to West Berlin during the heroic 1948–49 airlift conducted by the United States and Great Britain. The area of the museum that focuses on shipping has two original tugboats, one of which dates from 1840 and the other from 1901. You can even see (and smell) an old engine from the tugboat *Jean Cousin* in action.

Two 19th-century buildings hold a variety of historic engines and locomotives and several vintage railway stations. Tucked between these two large buildings is the *Beamtenhaus,* which features, among other subjects, the development of movie and photography technology and scientific instruments. Opposite it, in a small historic brewery, visitors can see how beer was brewed in 1910. A park on the site of the former freight station has two old windmills and a modern solar voltaic system, and leads to the Oldtimer-Depot, with its more than 70 historic carriages, cars, and motorcycles. Right next to the depot is a special exhibit called "Spectrum," with 250 experiments and presentations about optics, acoustics, electricity, and radio activity.

In addition to its permanent collection, the museum presents special exhibits and always offers demonstrations. There's a special guidance system for visitors who are blind or visually impaired. ⊠ *Trebbiner Str. 9,* ☎ *030/254–840,* WEB *www.dtmb.de.* ⊡ *€2.50.* ☉ *Tues.–Fri. 9–5:30, weekends 10–6.*

OFF THE
BEATEN PATH

FLUGHAFEN TEMPELHOF (Tempelhof Airport) – Tempelhof is one of the few completed buildings from the Nazis' "grand design" plan for Berlin—and gives you a pretty good impression of what the city would have looked like had Germany won World War II. Designed by Ernst Sagebiel in 1936–39, Tempelhof was one the most advanced airports of its time. Historically, the wide-open field had been used as a parade route for the Prussian army, and as early as 1923 it became Berlin's first central airport.

Tempelhof became world famous not because of its bombastic Nazi architecture but for the daring feats of American and British forces during the 1948–49 Berlin airlift. The Soviets had sealed off West Berlin in an effort to break the city's ties to Western Allies. No ground transportation was possible, so starving West Berliners could only be supplied by air. American and British *"Rosinenbombers"* ("raisin bombers") touched down to unload a total of 1.831 million tons of coal, food, clothes, and technical equipment (even a complete coal power plant was brought to the city). Many German civilians and airmen from the Allied forces died during the missions. **Platz der Luftbrücke** (Airlift Square) and the arcing, 65-ft-high **Denkmal der Luftbrücke** (Airlift Memorial) in front of the airport commemorates these pilots and crews. Frankfurt am Main Airport has a copy of the monument, and a smaller version can also be found at Celle Airport, in northern Germany. Both airfields served as starting points for the planes.

Tempelhof is due to close but will probably operate its domestic flights for another dozen years. Proposals for the future use of the huge complex are nevertheless thriving; the most original idea has come from conductor Daniel Barenboim of the Staatsoper Unter den Linden, who envisions using the soaring main arrival and departure hall as a concert venue—it supposedly has superb acoustics. ⊠ *Columbiadamm and Tempelhofer Damm, U-Bahn Platz der Luftbrücke,* ☎ *0180/500–0186,* WEB *www.airport-berlin.de.*

8 **Jüdisches Museum** (Jewish Museum). Berlin's newest museum showcases the complete history of German Jews, with an emphasis on Jewish life in Berlin. Germany's Jewish community was one of the world's largest prior to the Holocaust. The museum's very creation and striking architecture make it the most talked-about museum in the city. The lightning-bolt appearance of the building, designed by architect Daniel Libeskind, draws frequent comparisons to a broken Star of David. Libeskind has interpreted the building's zigzagging floor plan as ribbons connecting the Jewish past with its present. Five rooms in the museum will be left empty to symbolize the loss of culture, traditions, and heritage as a result of the Holocaust. The entrance to the modern wing is through the old Berlin-Museum, West Berlin's former city history museum. The yellow, baroque building whose portico has the Prussian coat of arms dates back to 1734–35 and once housed a higher Berlin court. Outside the museum is a small garden called **E. T. A. Hoffmann-Garten** (named for the German-Jewish romantic poet).

The museum was built between 1993 and 1999 but didn't open until September 2001. The long delay was a result of extensive debates among historians, politicians, and curators over how to present the Holocaust and centuries of Jewish–German relations in the proper context. Some wanted to make the museum similar to the Holocaust museum in Washington, D.C. (which was a strong case since Germany doesn't have a similar institution). Others felt that the Holocaust, horrible as it was, should not overshadow the much longer and mostly peaceful coexistence of Jews and Germans in Germany. They also believed that focusing on the Holocaust would present a belated victory for the Nazis, and the true Jewish heritage would be underemphasized in comparison to Nazi atrocities. ⊠ *Lindenstr. 9–14,* ☎ *030/2599–3300,* WEB *www.jmberlin.de.* 🎟 *€5.* ☼ *Daily 10–8.*

Kochstrasse. In the 1920s Kochstrasse was Berlin's newspaper and media district, where most of the city's 120 newspapers and journals were produced. The war and the subsequent division of the city changed all that. Only two newspapers still have their offices here; they are the voices of the most conservative and the most left-wing public opinion leaders in Germany. The extensive complex of the **Axel-Springer-Verlag,** which publishes one of the world's largest street papers, *Bild-Zeitung,* is within view of the small (and notoriously underfinanced), alternative *Tageszeitung.*

13 **Mariannenplatz.** Restored 19th-century tenement houses surround this square, the highlight of which is the **Künstlerhaus Bethanien,** a former hospital where artists from around the world are given studio space. A gallery presents works of artists in residence. ⊠ *Mariannenpl. 2,* ☎ *030/616–9030,* WEB *www.bethanien.de.* ☼ *Wed.–Sun. 2–7 (hrs vary depending on exhibition).*

3 **Martin-Gropius-Bau.** This renowned, magnificent exhibition hall once housed Berlin's Arts and Crafts Museum and dates from 1877–81. It was one of the first major buildings designed by architect Walter Gropius, who later became famous for his Bauhaus style. Over the past 20 years many of Berlin's most spectacular art and history exhibits have been staged here. It stands opposite the Preussischer Landtag. ✉ *Niederkirchnerstr. 7,* ☏ *030/2548–6101,* WEB *www.berlinerfestspiele.de.* ⊙ *Weekdays 10–8 (hrs vary depending on exhibit).*

② Museum für Kommunikation (Museum of Communications). A treasure trove for philatelists, the museum pours out the surprisingly thrilling story of communication, from the first drum signals to high-speed broadband connections. Housed in a lavish neobaroque building dating from 1893–97, it is the world's oldest mail service museum. After reunification this museum and West Berlin's mail service museum were reunited, and it reopened in March 2000. The four floors of exhibitions organized around a central atrium go far beyond what you might expect from an institution run by the rather dull Deutsche Post.

The most valuable items are in the basement exhibit. Included are both a red and a blue Mauritius, the world's most valuable stamps; the world's first telephone system (dating from 1863); and the world's first postcard (sent from Austria in 1869). A largely interactive exhibit on the ground level lets you explore the world of communications firsthand, while three talking robots (unfortunately, they only speak German) entertain visitors.

The two top floors are filled with memorabilia—old mailboxes, one of the first functioning telephones designed by Bell, a Thomas Edison phonograph (the technical precursor of the gramophone), and the first television set, from 1938. The exhibits are organized around six main subjects, including the accelerating speed of communication, the coding and decoding of messages, the evolution of stamps, and mass media. A favorite among children is the **Computergalerie,** on the top floor, where you can play computer games, interact, learn, and paint with PCs. ✉ *Leipziger Str. 16,* ☏ *030/202–940,* WEB *www.museumsstiftung.de* ☙ *Free.* ⊙ *Tues.–Fri. 9–5, weekends 11–7.*

⑭ Oberbaumbrücke (Oberbaum Bridge). This lavishly decorated red-brick bridge with its turrets and round arches looks like something straight out of Moscow's Red Square. The bridge, which spans the Spree River, served local trains heading to the eastern district of Friedrichshain. During World War II the old bridge (built from 1894 to 1896) suffered major damage and was only used as a pedestrian border crossing during Berlin's division. After reunification the bridge was restored to its old glamour and is used by pedestrians, U-Bahn Lines 1 and 15, and cars. Heading east, you can see the start of the East Side Gallery on the left. ✉ *Skalitzer Str. and Warschauer Str.*

⑫ Oranienstrasse. The core of life in Kreuzberg, Oranienstrasse has tempered somewhat since reunification. You'll find a lively and curious mixture of Muslim culture and alternative lifestyles—the contrasts in the streets of this neighborhood couldn't be starker.

To the south of Oranienstrasse is the depressing and seedy Kottbusser Platz. Its public housing projects date from the 1970s. Drug dealing goes on here, but it's still a safe area. Just stay away from both the dealers and drug addicts and do not give them any money.

⑤ Preussischer Landtag (Prussian State Legislature). The monumental parliament building on the north side of Niederkirchnerstrasse now houses Berlin's House of Deputies and is one of Germany's most impressive 19th-century administration buildings. Take a look inside and admire the huge entrance hall. ✉ *Niederkirchnerstr. 3–5,* ☏ *030/23250,* WEB *www.parlament-berlin.de.* ⊙ *Weekdays 9–6.*

③ Prinz-Albrecht-Gelände (Prince Albrecht Grounds). The headquarters of the SS, the Main Reich Security Office, and other Nazi security or-

COMMUNAL LIVING

A **SUPPORTIVE SPOUSE, TWO** freckly kids, and a dachshund isn't everyone's idea of home. In Berlin a group of seven thirtysomething apartment sharers gathered around a pot of lentil soup is family enough. A concept on which Berlin prides itself, the *Wohngemeinschaft* (WG—pronounced "vay gay") can consist of any number of people, from students to professionals, who choose to live in a communal atmosphere. This spirit, however, is not just confined to living arrangements. Public kitchens, food cooperatives, and pay-what-you-want restaurants are all part of Berlin's alternative community. Although some of this lifestyle can be attributed to an egalitarian ethic encouraged by a Communist state, it can also be explained by a counterculture attracted to West Berlin by what the city afforded them. Today's WGs are the mere leftovers of an anarchistic ideal that's been put through the wash.

The time was the '60s. The mood was revolution. In West Berlin protests for social change erupted, and youth flirted with Communism. Activism and cross-gender cohabitation were commonplace in *Wohngemeinschaften*, communes in which the inhabitants could organize their living arrangements around cooperatives, art studios, and small shops that allowed them to support their autonomous lifestyle. Taking advantage of Berlin's unique building configurations, the WGs centered their activities in apartments that looked onto *Höfe* (courtyard gardens), where the one main door onto the street would quite often serve as the entrance to up to four interconnected courtyard complexes arranged around them.

The tax cuts, subsidies, and military service exemptions that were intended to bolster the population of the capitalist outpost that was West Berlin only succeeded in adding to the ever-growing population of artists and bohemians who gathered in the peripheral, working-class district of Kreuzberg. A 1970s Senate scheme to rejuvenate the run-down and now overpopulated city led to real-estate speculation, and when the communes caught wind of this property exploitation, shortlisted buildings were taken over by squatters who refused to leave. When the situation reached a boiling point in the early '80s, the authorities, seeing no way out, backed down and issued leases to some of the squatters. The squatting movement, however, was far from over.

The mass exodus from East to West after the Wall fell in '89 left many apartments empty. Seeing their opportunity in the central districts of Mitte and Prenzlauer Berg, squatters moved in. Because of the confusion that surrounded property ownership after more than a decade of Nazi acquisition and more than 40 years of Communist state control, the situation was allowed to smolder without any real opposition. Squats like the infamous Tacheles opened bars, clubs, and art studios that helped consolidate Berlin's reputation as the place to be. Even with rents in traditional apartments as low as €40 a month, many still considered life in communal squat conditions to be preferable. Although conventional mentality tends to condemn as ne'er-do-wells squatters and even those who live in ordinary communes, individuals who choose this lifestyle do not exempt themselves from responsibilities. Someone who participates in a proper *Besetztes Haus* (occupied, or squatted, house) must comply with house rules and attend regular meetings, called *Plena*, where tasks are set and individual contributions are assessed. Saving money, you would surely hear, is not the only point.

This form of cohabitation, however, is on the wane. Time has seen the WG evolve into a more general rent-based flat-share arrangement, and the communal pot of lentil soup is being replaced by the more convenient, individually packaged servings that ease the Berliner's ever-tightening schedule. Anarchy and protest have had to compromise with the increasingly ordered structure of a global metropolis, and the radical remnants face mounting pressure to shape up or ship out. Renting a room in a WG is now just a cheaper alternative to having your own flat.

ganizations were housed on this site from 1933 until 1945. After the war the buildings were leveled. The grounds remained untouched until 1987, when the buildings' foundations, once used as "house prisons" by the SS, were excavated and an open-air exhibit on their history and Nazi atrocities opened, called the **"Topography of Terror."**

Although the more interesting basements are hidden under the new construction, you can tour the ones north of this site (behind the Martin-Gropius-Bau). There you'll find some exhibition boards explaining the history of the buildings. Standing right behind these excavated basements is an original (though badly damaged) section of the graffiti-covered Berlin Wall. Within a humble trailer are many official documents for viewing and a free, English audio guide to the exhibition. ⊠ *Niederkirchnerstr. 8,* ☎ *030/254–5090,* WEB *www.topographie.de.* ▨ *Free.* ☉ *Oct.–Apr., daily 10–6; May–Sept., daily 10–8.*

🔟 **Riehmers Hofgarten** (Riehmer's Courtyards). When this complex of 20 apartments and office buildings was built in 1881–92 it represented a new vision for urban living. Contrary to the traditional floor plan and layout of large tenement houses in Berlin, the complex (named for its architect and founder Wilhelm Riehmer) consists of several fairly spacious courtyards and small streets interconnecting them. The surrounding buildings, designed in neoclassical and Renaissance style, are standing far enough from each other to avoid the dreadful, dark sense of confinement typical of urban architecture of that time. Thanks to two careful restorations since World War II, the ornamental facades, decorated with elaborate stone statues, look wonderful, and the buildings have become one of Kreuzberg's most upscale residential areas. ⊠ *Yorkstr. 83–86, Grossbeerenstr. 56–57, Hagelberger Str. 9–12.*

OFF THE
BEATEN PATH

TÜRKENMARKT (Turkish Market) – On Tuesday and Friday from noon to 6:30 you can find the country's best selection of Arab and Turkish foods along the Landwehr Canal. Vendors line the bank roads of Maybachufer and Paul-Lincke-Ufer. You can walk here from Kreuzberg's Kottbusser Tor U-Bahn station via Kottbusser Damm. The cafés and restaurants on Paul-Lincke-Ufer are great places for a cup of coffee.

⓫ **Viktoriapark** (Victoria Park). The park was designed to be a green retreat for the overworked proletarian classes living in the cheap tenement housing of Kreuzberg. Today it is still a green oasis amid a sea of gray concrete, but the crowd of people bathing in the sun, picnicking, and playing soccer here has drastically changed (as has Kreuzberg). Yuppies, Turkish families, and young kids with radios peacefully mingle here and climb up the **Kreuzberg** in the middle of the park, primarily on weekends. The little hill, which Berliners proudly refer to as a mountain, is only about 217 ft high. Even though much of the setting around the mountain looks fairly rugged, it was carefully laid out in 1888–94. The waterfall you see running down from the Kreuzberg, for instance, is completely artificial, and the rocks that the water runs over were brought here from southeastern Germany. In the past the mountain was also used as a vineyard. These days, however, the Kreuzberg vintages are cultivated on a small piece of property off Methfesselstrasse, east of the park. The wine is not sold publicly, but that's probably just as well.

A Prussian war memorial designed by Karl Friedrich Schinkel juts out of the Kreuzberg. This towering gray monument (1821) has a somewhat awkward name, Nationaldenkmal zur Erinnerung an die Freiheitskriege (National Monument in Commemoration of the Liberation Wars), namely Prussia's victories over the armies of Napoléon in 1813–1815. It is topped with the Prussian *Eisernes Kreuz* (Iron Cross), one

MULTIKULTI BERLIN

BERLIN LIKES TO PORTRAY itself as Germany's most international city, a capital with a tolerant, worldly population that celebrates its diversity in street festivals, ethnic restaurants, and demonstrations for minority rights: "Multikulti," slang for *multikulturell* (multicultural), denotes an accepting attitude toward different cultures and religions, and by any standard Berlin is indeed international: 13% of its population has a non-German background (more than any other part in Germany); the culture, nightlife, and social scenes are a global potpourri; and representatives of more than 180 nations can quip, tongue in cheek, *"Ich bin ein Berliner!"*

But how truly multikulti is Berlin as a society? A good indicator of what life is like for foreigners in Berlin is the situation of the 132,000 Turks living here, mostly in Kreuzberg and Neukölln (making Berlin the largest Turkish community outside Turkey). In early 2001 the city's office for the affairs of foreigners published an eye-opening report that revealed that 42% of Turks were registered as unemployed. The surprised amazement of the German public indicated the distant spheres Germans and Turks occupy, other than when the two cross paths at restaurants and stands serving *Döner Kebab*. Turks are not an integral part of Berlin state politics, culture, sports, or social life. In fact, none of the larger ethnic minorities in the city, whether Russian, Greek, or immigrants from the former Yugoslavia, are visible except in ethnic restaurants, schools, and certain neighborhoods. Slowly, however, the third generation of Turkish immigrants is breaking from this isolation. A growing number are applying for German citizenship, young and polished Turkish businessmen are shaping parts of the city's economy, and Turkish rock, pop, and rap groups are proudly performing their own songs in Turkish, showing the German public that this generation has a new Turkish self-awareness worlds apart from an underdog image.

A worse fate was shared by former East Berlin *Gastarbeiter* (guest workers) from other Socialist countries, most notably Vietnamese residents. In the first years after reunification many of them tried to survive by selling smuggled cigarettes; others desperately tried to marry a German or apply for citizenship. But the majority of the 30,000 foreigners were sent home. Those who stayed—particularly blacks from Angola and Mozambique—are afraid to ride certain S-Bahn lines in such eastern districts as Friedrichshain, Lichtenberg, and Marzahn because they might be targets of right-wing violence. It is only now that former East Germans are openly displaying their dislike of their erstwhile comrades, as if to distance themselves from their shared past. But even during GDR times, foreigners were isolated in special apartment complexes, and apart from officially arranged party meetings, Germans and their Communist guests didn't mix. The xenophobic violence of the 1990s is largely a result of ignorance and economic insecurity.

Historically, Berlin has always attracted foreigners, and at times, as in the 17th century, the tolerant Prussian royals actively sought them out. About 20,000 Huguenots, persecuted in France as Protestants, emigrated to Prussia, bringing with them not only exquisite craftsmanship, but also enlightened science, and cuisine. In 1671 the first Jews fleeing Vienna arrived in Berlin and were granted special protection by the Great Elector. Later, thousands of Jews from Eastern Europe and Russia immigrated to Prussia (and Berlin), as they continued to gain full German citizen rights until 1919.

Berlin's solid middle-class, well-educated, Jewish citizenry shaped the city's history for centuries, and the loss of this population, which numbered more than 150,000, can still be felt today. The Jewish community has grown rapidly since 1990, as many Jewish immigrants from the former Soviet Union have settled in Berlin.

of the important military medals in German military history. This cross is said to have inspired the naming of the "mountain," and ultimately the whole district. One of *the* things for young lovers to do is grab a bottle of red wine, a blanket, some food, and a tea light and walk up to the memorial at night to toast the splendid panorama. Once the bright spotlights illuminating the memorial are switched off at midnight, it's one of the most romantic places Berlin has to offer. On the back of the hill is the dance club and beer garden **Golgatha**, an establishment that has attracted a mostly student crowd for decades. ⊠ *Between Katzbachstr. and Kreuzbergstr.*

ZEHLENDORF

Palaces, museums, and lakes are set in lush greenery in the city's outlying southwest areas. Zehlendorf is privileged to share with neighboring district Wilmersdorf the vast Grunewald (forest), which covers most of southwestern Berlin. It's an ideal spot for walking or for relaxing on one of the lake's islands. Some of the city's most intriguing museums are in the well-to-do neighborhood of Dahlem. The most serene greenery can be found in yet another Zehlendorf neighborhood, the Wannsee lake area, which has some of the most elegant villas in town. Since Grunewald and Wannsee are close to Potsdam, you might want to consider visiting the area directly before or after a trip to Potsdam and Sanssouci.

Numbers in the text correspond to numbers in the margin and on the Zehlendorf map.

Dahlem

Dahlem once was a small village outside Berlin but ultimately was swallowed up by its large neighbor in 1920. Today the wealthy neighborhood is known for its many old mansions and villas.

A Good Tour

To begin, take U-Bahn Line 1 to Dahlem-Dorf to visit two museums. The open-air farm-life museum at the **Freilichtmuseum Domäne Dahlem** ① is next to the station on Königin-Luise-Strasse. From here it's only a short walk back via Fabeckstrasse to the four **Dahlemer Museen** ②, with their collections of antique African, Asian, and Islamic arts and crafts. From here you can take a leisurely five-minute walk via Königin-Luise-Strasse to the **Botanischer Garten und Botanisches Museum Berlin-Dahlem** ③, the city's botanical gardens, in the Steglitz district. Leave the gardens at the Unter den Eichen exit and walk to the S-Bahn station Botanischer Garten. Take the S-1 toward Wannsee and get off at **Mexikoplatz** ④, a beautiful early 20th-century square. From here make your way to the **Museumsdorf Düppel** ⑤, a medieval open-air crafts museum. You can either take a leisurely 15-minute walk down Lindenthaler Allee or take a bus (No. 211 or No. 629) from Mexikoplatz.

TIMING

Depending on how much time you spend at the Dahlem museums and at the gardens, this tour can easily last a full day. If you take in only one of the Dahlem museums and skip one of the open-air museums, you will have enough time to have a look at Mexikoplatz and still be back in central Berlin in about four hours.

Sights to See

☙ ❸ **Botanischer Garten und Botanisches Museum Berlin-Dahlem** (Botanical Garden and Botanical Museum Berlin-Dahlem). Plants and flowers from the world over enliven the grounds of Berlin's botanical gardens, which were one of the many initiatives of the Great Elector Friedrich Wilhelm. In 1679 he enlarged his herb garden into a model garden for the scientific study of plants. The gardens have since moved to Dahlem and still function as one of the largest scientific research centers of its kind.

Covering more than 43 hectares (106 acres), the gardens are home to 20,000 species, which grow either in the meticulously arranged outdoor beds or in the various greenhouses. The garden's highlight is the **Grosses Tropenhaus** (Large Tropical House), which is one of the world's largest greenhouses, measuring 196 ft in length and 75 ft in height. The 15 annex greenhouses (most of them interconnected) recreate the climatic environments of the Sahara, the South African bush, the Australian desert, various tropical rain forests, and the North American plains. A favorite among Berliners is the Victoria greenhouse, where the huge tropical water plant Victoria, with leaves up to nearly 7 ft in diameter, can be seen in summertime. A small museum in the gardens reveals different elements of plant life usually hidden from the human eye—for example, microbes, the stinging hairs of the nettle, and a plant's internal vital functions are examined here. ⊠ *Entrances at Unterden Eichen and Königin-Luise-Pl.,* ☎ *030/8385–0100,* WEB *www.bgbm.fu-berlin.de/bgbm.* ▤ *€1* ⊙ *Nov.–Jan., daily 9–4; Feb., daily 9–5; Mar. and Oct., daily 9–6; Sept., daily 9–7; April and Aug., daily 9–8; May–July, daily 9–9.*

② **Dahlemer Museen** (Dahlem Museums). This complex of four museums is one of Europe's finest assemblies of ancient history and art. The complex includes the museums of Indian, East Asian, and early European art and is near the campus of the Freie Universität Berlin (Free University of Berlin) in Dahlem.

★ The **Ethnologisches Museum** (Ethnographic Museum) is a treasure for those interested in ancient societies. The extensive collections give testimony to the *Sammelleidenschaft* (passion for collecting) of Germany's 19th-century archaeologists, who found and retrieved half a million items from all over the world and brought them back to Berlin to add exotic flair to the capital. The gentle smells of old wood, feathers, and textiles take you back to mostly lost worlds. Thanks to some reorganization within Berlin's state museums, the museum is able to show a large portion of its collection permanently for the first time since it opened in 1976. Among these collections are African art and the culture and art of Native Americans. Highlights, especially for children, are the main hall's original houses and boats from southern Pacific cultures. You can even walk through some of them. Equally impressive is the large collection of Mayan, Aztec, and Incan ceramics and stone sculptures. These archaeological treasures should not be missed.

The **Museum für Ostasiatische Kunst** (Museum of East Asian Art) covers the art of East Asia from the early Stone Age forward. The collections are mostly made up of porcelain, lacquer ware, and calligraphy from Korea, China, and Japan. Some of the most beautiful items on display here are the ancient Chinese jades and bronzes.

An often-overlooked museum in this complex is the **Museum für Indische Kunst** (Museum of Indian Art). It holds mostly religious sculptures from both India and Central Asia, spanning a time period from 200 BC to the present. The museum contains the country's most extensive collection of Indian artifacts, and also houses the Turfan Collection of Central Asian art, collected from monasteries and temples along the Silk Route. Included here are textiles and paintings, as well as statues made of wood and clay that are world-famous for their delicate style. Elaborate craftsmanship is evident in these works of art, which date from the 2nd to the 12th centuries. Also on display are manuscripts from these same centuries, made of palm leaves and birch bark and written in the region's many languages.

The **Museum Europäischer Kulturen** (Museum of European Cultures; ✉ Im Winkel 6–8), one of the smaller museums in the Dahlem complex, presents arts and crafts from all over Europe from the 16th century onward. The emphasis is on common objects used by ordinary people, thus providing a glimpse into something Germans love to call *Alltagskultur* (everyday culture). ✉ *Lansstr. 8,* ☎ *030/83011,* WEB *www.smb.spk-berlin.de.* ✉ *€2; free 1st Sun. of month.* ☉ *Tues.–Fri. 10–6, weekends 11–6.*

🐾 ❶ **Freilichtmuseum Domäne Dahlem** (Open-Air Dahlem Museum). The Domäne Dahlem, formerly one of a number of large city-owned farms in Berlin, is today both a museum and a modern and ecologically friendly working farm. The farm dates from 1560, and the main building, the *Herrenhaus* (manor house), is one of Berlin's oldest buildings. Inside are exhibits on the history of agriculture in Berlin. The real attraction, though, is observing how a farm functions by strolling the grounds, talking to the farmers, viewing the farm animals—pigs, cows, chicken, sheep, horses, ponies, and even bees, and admiring the gardens and crops. At the small store (closed Sunday), you can buy some of the Domäne's fresh produce. A market is held each Saturday from 8 to 1. Special exhibits and cultural events are also staged periodically in the museum or on the farm. ✉ *Königin-Luise-Str. 49,* ☎ *030/832–5000,* WEB *www.domaene-dahlem.de.* ✉ *€2.* ☉ *Wed.–Mon. 10–6.*

❹ **Mexikoplatz** (Mexico Square). One of the most architecturally harmonious squares in Berlin, Mexikoplatz is rarely if ever seen by tourists because it lies in a far-off, upscale residential area. But if you plan to visit the Zehlendorf or Wannsee, you should stop here to admire the art nouveau setting. Two symmetrical buildings follow the curves of landscaped lawns. The squat and bulbous S-Bahn railway station here is in itself a gem, as it is the only surviving art nouveau railway station in Berlin. Historic photos of the square are on a plaque across from the station, next to the bus stop. To the south is **Lindenthaler Allee,** one of the few streets in Berlin that was rechristened Adolf-Hitler-Strasse during the Nazi reign. It serves as the main thoroughfare to Zehlendorf's poshest side streets. A few grand historic villas line the partly cobblestone streets in the area.

🐾 ❺ **Museumsdorf Düppel** (Düppel Museum Village). The neighborhood of Düppel lies on Berlin's border and was founded some time in the early 13th century. Its medieval village was first detected in 1940 and was later excavated and transformed into a open-air museum during the 1970s. Most of the 30 buildings you can visit today amid the greenery are reconstructions based on the original floor plans. The volunteers, who "live" in the museum and dress in medieval costume, demonstrate handicrafts like wool making, woodworking, firing ceramics, and basket weaving. There are several historic (as well as modern) beehives and a small *Backhaus* (village oven) for baking bread. The museum also researches medieval agricultural techniques and works to protect endangered animals (such as certain pigs) and plants that once thrived throughout medieval Europe. ✉ *Clauerstr. 11,* ☎ *030/ 802–6671,* WEB *www.dueppel.de.* ✉ *€2.* ☉ *Apr.–Oct., Sun. 10–5, Thurs. 3–7 (last admission is 1 hr before closing).*

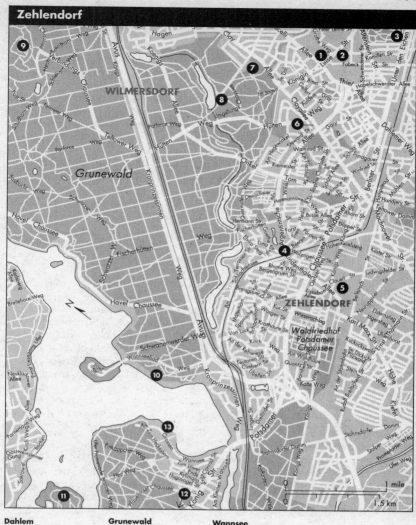

Zehlendorf

Dahlem

Botanischer
Garten und
Botanisches Museum
Berlin-Dahlem **3**

Dahlemer
Museen **2**

Freilichtmuseum
Domäne Dahlem **1**

Mexikoplatz **4**

Museumsdorf
Düppel **5**

Grunewald

Alliiertenmuseum **6**

Brücke-Museum **7**

Jagdschloss
Grunewald **8**

Teufelsberg **9**

Wannsee

Bildungs- und
Gedenkstätte
Haus der
Wannsee-
Konferenz **13**

Pfaueninsel **11**

Schloss Klein-
Glienicke **12**

Strandbad
Wannsee **10**

Grunewald

Together with the lakes that make up the Wannsee, this splendid forest is the most popular retreat for Berliners. In good weather people come out in force, swimming, sailing their boats, tramping through the woods, and riding horseback. In winter a downhill ski run and even a ski jump operate on the modest slopes of the Teufelsberg. Originally a royal hunting ground, the Grunewald was reserved for the pleasure of the imperial family until 1903. Since then it has evolved as the most natural landscape Berlin has to offer. However, the Grunewald has suffered ecologically in the past decades. Allied troops used the remote areas as grounds for military maneuvers and ammunitions testing, and today the police bomb squad operates a testing range for explosives in the forest. Making the headlines every summer are the forest's infamous wild boars, notorious for attacking dogs and raiding the manicured gardens of nearby Zehlendorf villas.

A Good Walk

If you are picking up this walk after having visited the Mexikoplatz area, ride Bus 211 up Argentinische Allee, a grand tree-lined boulevard, to the the U-1 Oskar-Helene-Heim station. One block north on Clayallee is the old Outpost movie theater, which now houses the **Alliiertenmuseum** ⑥ and its exhibits on the role Allied forces played in Berlin. Continue on Clayallee to narrow Käuzchensteig, where you can turn left for the **Brücke-Museum** ⑦, which holds paintings by the artist group of the same name. The walk from the Alliiertenmuseum takes 15 minutes, or you can take Bus 115. It's now time for the great outdoors. From the Brücke-Museum walk west on Pücklerstrasse through the greenbelt of the Grunewald directly to **Jagdschloss Grunewald** ⑧, an old hunting palace with a small art exhibition. The Grunewald's hill, the **Teufelsberg** ⑨, is one of the few in Berlin, but cannot be reached by public transportation: from the palace it can take one hour to walk there. Take Hüttenweg to Teltower Weg and enjoy the forest greenery.

TIMING

If you plan to rely on public transportation to visit Grunewald, bear in mind that the area is quite extensive and the Teufelsberg is not served by bus, so set aside more time than usual for getting around. The S-Bahn Line 7 stops close by the forest and relatively close to the Teufelsberg at Grunewald station.

Sights to See

⑥ **Alliiertenmuseum** (Allied Museum). OUTPOST, spelled out in huge letters on the facade, is the name of this former movie theater, which was just what its name says—part of a U.S. army base in southwestern Berlin, on quiet Clayallee. When the Federal Republic of Germany finally achieved complete sovereignty in 1994, the forces of the former Allies left Berlin. The Deutsches Historisches Museum then opened a branch here to document 50 years of Allied–German relations.

A visit here is like a voyage back to the era of the cold war, which more than once threatened to become a hot one in Berlin. Among the many objects on display are uniforms, weapons, military equipment, and loads of documents from the three Western Allied forces. Special sections focus on the Berlin airlift of 1948–49, Western propaganda, and the cultural efforts the Western Allies, primarily the United States through its Amerikahaus, undertook to "reeducate" West Germans. Two of the larger highlights are the control booth from Checkpoint Charlie on Friedrichstrasse and the Hastings TG 503, a vintage British transport plane that delivered lifesaving supplies during the Berlin airlift. ⊠

Clayallee 135, ☎ *030/818–1990,* WEB *www.dhm.de.* 🎟 *Free.* ☉ *Thurs.–Tues. 10–6.*

❼ Brücke-Museum (Brücke Museum). With the brightest and most intense colors imaginable, the 400 works of art here herald the birth of expressionism in Europe. Artists in Dresden founded the Brücke association in 1905 as a reaction against the conservative art style of the time. The Brücke group valued palette and artistic expression over realism. The four founders—Ernst Ludwig Kirchner, Fritz Blyl, Erich Heckel, and Karl Schmidt-Rottluff—are represented here. Most of their motifs are inspired by nature, and canvases were used to reflect the artists' inner emotions. In addition to the original Brücke painters, the museum also holds works by Max Pechstein, Emil Nolde, Otto Mueller, and others. The small museum opened in 1967 after Karl Schmidt-Rottluff donated 74 of his paintings to the city of Berlin for exhibition. Tours take place Monday and Thursday at 3. ✉ *Bussardsteig 9,* ☎ *030/831–2029,* WEB *www.bruecke-museum.de.* 🎟 *€4.* ☉ *Wed.–Mon. 11–5.*

❽ Jagdschloss Grunewald (Grunewald Hunting Palace). Deep in the forest and close to the shore of the Grunewaldsee is a small hunting palace that served as a retreat for the Prussian royals until the early 20th century. Built in 1542, the simple white palace was later transformed into the Renaissance and baroque showpiece it is today. It houses a small collection of paintings, mostly works by Dutch and German painters from the 14th to 19th centuries. ✉ *Hüttenweg am Grunewaldsee,* ☎ *030/813–3597,* WEB *www.spsg.de.* 🎟 *€2.* ☉ *May–Oct., weekends 10–5; Nov.–Apr., weekends 10–4.*

❾ Teufelsberg (Devil's Mountain). To Soviet and East German intelligence, this little mountain in the middle of the dense Grunewald had indeed been a devil's mountain. During the cold war U.S. intelligence had its headquarters on the hilltop and installed high-tech listening devices to scan, tap, or tape the "enemy's" radio transmissions and telephone conversations. The 380-ft-high mountain itself is a reminder of World War II. It is the city's highest and most famous *Trümmerberg* (rubble hill), and was created between 1950 and 1972 with the debris of buildings destroyed in the war.

Parts of the mountain were off-limits, but every West Berliner knew that top-secret activities were taking place in its huge white and egg-shaped buildings. Not far away, kids flew their model planes, Alpine hikers practiced at an artificial climbing wall, and, in winter, sledders rushed down Berlin's best hill. This odd yet peaceful coexistence of military operations and everyday leisure-time activities was typical of West Berlin during the cold war. The installations have been demolished since then, but the Berliners have stayed, making the Teufelsberg one of the city's most popular weekend destinations.

At the foot of the hill, primarily around the cool, green waters of the **Teufelssee,** a very mixed crowd of young Berliners congregates. The disappearance of the former military presence has made this area increasingly appealing for all, and the lake is also very popular among gays. The lakefront and the forest around the hill provide Berliners with some of the best jogging, biking, and hiking areas. The whole area is a protected nature reserve and offers some of the most unspoiled nature Berlin has to offer. *Closest S-Bahn stations: Grunewald and Eichkamp.*

Wannsee

The Wannsee is Berlin's most popular weekend retreat. The lake actually consists of two lakes (covering about 642 acres), called Grosser Wannsee and Kleiner Wannsee, which receive fresh water from the Havel

River. Perfect wind and water conditions attract many windsurfers and sailors. But as you can see from the numerous sunbathers crowding the artificial Strandbad Wannsee, the hikers exploring the forests and outskirts of the lake, and the picnickers in the meadows, the Wannsee offers something for everyone. Since the mid-1900s the Wannsee area has developed into one of Berlin's most affluent residential areas, home to many successful artists and industrialists. Eventually the street addresses here became a who's who of German capitalism, especially when Arnold Siemens, Eduard von Heydt, and the like moved in. Many of the big-business elite make their home on the street Am Sandweder.

The seemingly lovely island of Schwanenwerder, was, during the Third Reich, very popular among Nazi leaders like Joseph Goebbels and Albert Speer, who lived here in grand old villas that had been taken away from their legal Jewish owners in the 1930s. The SS had some of its offices in the area as well. Now Schwanenwerder is again the peaceful and upscale area it was before 1933—and has literally become a center for the promotion of democracy and liberty: one of the most distinguished private policy institutions of the United States, the Aspen Institute, has its European branch here.

A Good Tour

To escape to the shores of the Wannsee, the city's second-largest lake, get off at either the Nikolassee or Wannsee S-Bahn station. The huge artificial beach, the **Strandbad Wannsee** ⑩, can be reached quickest by taking Bus 513 from the Nikolassee station. From the Wannsee station you can catch Buses A-16 or 316 to the **Pfaueninsel** ⑪, an island with a small, romantic palace, and farther on (take Bus 116), the **Schloss Klein-Glienicke** ⑫, a lovely palace and park. A grim reminder of the area's past is the **Bildungs- und Gedenkstätte Haus der Wannsee-Konferenz** ⑬, an old villa in which the Holocaust was agreed upon. Board Bus 114 across the street from the Wannsee station to get to the villa.

TIMING

Depending on how much time you spend at the lake, this tour is manageable in a day. Reserve at least two hours each for the Pfaueninsel and the Schloss Klein-Glienicke, as the transportation to get there will take some time. You'll need at least 2½ hours to view the exhibits and property of the Bildungs- und Gedenkstätte Haus der Wannsee-Konferenz.

Sights to See

⑬ **Bildungs- und Gedenkstätte Haus der Wannsee-Konferenz** (Wannsee Conference Memorial Site). The tranquil setting of this typical Berlin villa belies the unimaginable Holocaust atrocities planned here. This elegant edifice hosted the fateful conference held on January, 20, 1942, at which Nazi leaders and German bureaucrats under SS leader Reinhard Heydrich planned the systematic deportation and mass extinction of Europe's Jewish population. This so-called *"Endlösung der Judenfrage"* (final solution of the Jewish question) is illustrated in an exhibition that documents the conference, and more extensively, the escalation of persecution against Jews, and the Holocaust itself. Upstairs is a research center, with over 1,500 source materials in English. ✉ *Am Grossen Wannsee 56–58,* ☎ *030/805–0010,* WEB *www.ghwk.de.* 🎫 *Free.* ☉ *Daily 10–6.*

★ ⑪ **Pfaueninsel** (Peacock Island). The Pfaueninsel is a small oasis in the Great Wannsee that served as a romantic hideaway for Prussian king Friedrich Wilhelm II and his mistresses. **Schloss Pfaueninsel,** the small palace on the island, was erected in 1794 according to the ruler's plans and—in accordance with the taste of his era—was built as a fake ruin. In the early 19th century, garden architect Joseph Peter Lenné designed an English garden on the island, which ultimately became western Berlin's favorite summer getaway. ✉ *Pfaueninselchaussee,* ☎ *0331/969–4202,* WEB *www.spsg.de.* ✆ *€1.* ⊙ *Ferry to Pfaueninsel: Nov.–Feb., daily 10–4; Mar. and Oct., daily 9–5; Apr. and Sept., daily 8–6; May–Aug., daily 8–8; palace: Apr.–Oct., Tues.–Sun. 10–5.*

⑫ **Schloss Klein-Glienicke** (Klein-Glienicke Palace). No other palace or garden in former Prussia testifies better to the deep love and admiration the royals and their architects shared for antique Roman and Greek design and Italian Renaissance style. Prinz Carl von Preussen's summer palace, built in 1826 by Karl-Friedrich Schinkel, is set amid the remote greenery of the southern Grunewald area, on the banks of the Havel River and Glienicker Lake.

The garden was designed by Peter Joseph Lenné, one of the most prominent landscape gardeners of his time. It was his 1816 design of this park that first revealed his mastery of landscaping. The plan allows wonderful sightlines between the ground's highlights. Thanks to extensive and careful restoration based on historic notes, both the palace and the park look almost exactly as they did some 200 years ago. On the other side of the river you can see the palace buildings of Babelsberg and the **Sacrower Heilandskirche** (Sacrow Church of the Savior).

For the best view of the palace and its fountain, go around to the back, which is guarded by two golden lions modeled after statues at the Villa Medici in Rome. Another attraction is the odd-looking building right next to Königsstrasse, called **Grosse Neugierde** (Big Curiosity), a circular garden house. There you will also find the **Kleine Neugierde** (Little Curiosity), a small teahouse with ancient reliefs carved between 300 and 500 BC. Other buildings on the grounds include the **Kasino** (casino), right on the waterfront (once used as a guest house); the **Orangerie**; a greenhouse; and the **Klosterhof** (Cloister Court), a fake monasterylike building characteristic of the era's romanticism.

West of the palace and the garden house is the **Glienicker Brücke** (Glienicke Bridge), which became famous during the cold war because captured spies from both East and West were frequently exchanged here. In November 1989 the bridge that was formerly part of East Germany and ironically called Brücke der Einheit (Bridge of Unity) turned out to be just that. West Berliners greeted their East German counterparts here with champagne. ✉ *Königsstr. 36,* ☎ *030/805–3041,* WEB *www.spsg.de.* ✆ *€2.* ⊙ *Mid-May–mid-Oct., weekends 10–5.*

⑩ **Strandbad Wannsee** (Wannsee Beach). The vast Strandbad Wannsee, Europe's largest artificial white-sand beach resort, has always had a reputation for being Berlin's Riviera, or so the Berliners like to think. Even today, when it's possible to travel to many sunnier destinations around the world, you'll find 40,000–50,000 sun worshipers, including families, punks, and gays, peacefully crowding the narrow beach on any given summer weekend.

Strandbad Wannsee was established in 1929–30 at the site of an even older public bath as an attempt to provide a healthy and enjoyable environment for the poor working-class people of Berlin. But over the years, primarily in the 1950s, it began to attract Berliners from all walks of life and quickly evolved into the city's prime outdoor recreation destination. The bath itself is nothing more than a two-story, 550-m-long (1,600-ft-long) building with changing rooms, bathrooms, and showers. In front of it is the sandy beach, which is up to 262 ft wide and more than half a mile long. If you plan to visit on a sunny day, try to get here early (it doesn't work to show up late in the afternoon, as Germans like to stay at the beach until well beyond dinnertime) and—by any means—avoid weekends (unless, of course, you enjoy people-watching at extremely close quarters.) ⊠ *Wannseebadweg 25,* ☎ *030/ 803–5612.* ⌨ *€3.* ⊙ *Apr.–Oct., daily 8–8.*

3 DINING

Berlin's restaurants are as creative and fast-changing as the city itself. Diversity defines the scene, with a few top dining rooms, many good ethnic eateries, and ever-opening hot spots where trends are launched. Most any restaurant–café you find will provide very decent meals.

By Jürgen
Scheunemann

ONCE MOCKED AS A GASTRONOMIC DESERT, Berlin's culinary scene has improved dramatically over the past 10 years. The transformation is still taking place at an unbelievable pace, and seven restaurants currently hold one Michelin star. While international and chic restaurants open almost every week, others close their doors just as quickly, as the clientele finds a better place around the corner. Today some 10,000 restaurants, eateries, cafés, and pubs compete for Berliners' attention.

Characteristic of Berlin is the abundance of ethnic eateries, including even those that serve regional Brandenburg cuisine, which for Westerners disappeared behind the Wall for 30 years. Chefs are again turning to traditional fresh produce from Brandenburg (the state surrounding Berlin) and preparing old recipes such as *Eisbein* (knuckle of pork) with sauerkraut, *Rouladen* (rolled stuffed beef), *Spanferkel* (suckling pig), *Berliner Schüsselsülze* (potted meat in aspic), *Hackepeter* (ground beef), and *Kartoffelpuffer* (fried potato cakes). Spicy *Currywurst*, a chubby frankfurter that's served with thick tomato sauce, curry, and pepper, remains popular. It's sold at *Bockwurst* (a steamed pork sausage) stands all over the city. Turkish specialties are also an integral part of the Berlin diet. And on almost every street you'll find snack stands selling *Döner kebab* (roasted, pressed lamb in pita bread).

Prices

CATEGORY	COST*
$$$$	over €21
$$$	€16–€20
$$	€11–€15
$	under €10

per person for a main course at dinner, excluding drinks, tip, and 16% sales tax

Western Downtown and Charlottenburg

Downtown western Berlin once prided itself on its lively restaurant scene on Kurfürstendamm and its side streets. That scene has moved east, but top-quality restaurants remain around Savignyplatz.

Austrian

$$–$$$ ✕ **Ottenthal.** With its low vaultlike ceiling and thick walls, black-and-★ white-tile floor, and white linen–covered tables, the Ottenthal makes for an evening of fine dining. Its authentic Austrian cooking is considered some of the best in Germany. The Wiener schnitzel and the *Zwiebelrostbraten* (a roast in an onion sauce) are among the favorites and should be accompanied by an Austrian wine—try the *Gewürztraminer* or a *Grauburgunder*—both are light white wines with a slight sulfur taste. ⊠ *Kantstr. 153,* ☎ *030/3133–162. AE, V. No lunch.*

Chinese

$$ ✕ **Good Friends.** Opinions about this Chinese restaurant diverge ★ sharply. The regulars assert it's the best Chinese restaurant in Berlin, preparing fare with Chinese spices not watered down to typical German taste and with the best roasted Peking duck west of Beijing. Those loathing the joint point to the unfriendly service and the completely unimaginative interior. A good deal for budget travelers is the lunch menu (daily between noon and 3), when the generally low prices are even cheaper. ⊠ *Kantstr. 30,* ☎ *030/3132–659. AE, MC, V.*

Contemporary

$$$$ ✕ **Die Quadriga.** This low-profile restaurant is one of the city's most
★ successful hotel restaurants. The many awards chef Wolfgang Nagler
earns—he was twice voted Berlin Master Cook and has a Michelin star—
is always met with a mixture of surprise and envy by the rest of Berlin's
top cuisine gurus. A typical Nagler menu includes dishes such as *Kotelett
von der Miral Taube mit Schmorgemüse und Kartoffelkrapfen* (Miral
dove fillet with braised vegetables and potato doughnuts). Reservations
are advised. ✉ *Hotel Brandenburger Hof, Eislebener Str. 14,* ☎ *030/
2140–5650. AE, DC, MC, V. No Lunch. Closed weekends.*

$$$ ✕ **Stil.** Contrary to geographic trends, this is one the few new restau-
rants to open in the western part of town, and it is smartly ensconced
in the fashionable Stilwerk mall. The emphasis is on light fish, beef,
and veal dishes such as the unbelievably pliant *Havelzander* (Havel River
perch) served with noodles and cherry tomatoes. Service is outstand-
ing and yet casual, something previously unheard of in Berlin's some-
what stiff and unfriendly service landscape. ✉ *Kantstr. 17,* ☎ *030/315–
1860. AE, DC, MC, V.* •

French

$$$$ ✕ **Heising.** Conveniently located off Ku'damm, the Heising is one the
★ few restaurants that has survived the boulevard's demise as a dining
mecca. Its single four-course French menu, which is often just a shade
shy of genuine French cuisine, is delicious. Dinner is served in an ele-
gant 19th-century-like living room, complete with heavy carpets, cur-
tains, and fine porcelain. ✉ *Rankestr. 32,* ☎ *030/302–5515. Reservations
essential. No credit cards. Closed Sun. No lunch.*

$$$–$$$$ ✕ **Paris Bar.** This trendy restaurant off Ku'damm attracts a polyglot
clientele of film stars, artists, entrepreneurs, and executives who care
more for glamour than the gourmet food on their plates. The cuisine,
including such delights as Jacques oysters and lamb chops with Provençal
herbs, is reliable French cooking. ✉ *Kantstr. 152,* ☎ *030/313–8052.
Reservations essential. AE.*

$$$ ✕ **Bovril.** A Kurfürstendamm fixture for almost 20 years, the Bovril
has outlasted most of the boulevard's other restaurants. The small French
brasserie has a following of artists and intellectuals and recognizes the
regulars with brass name tags at some of the tables. As in most real
French restaurants, a sure bet is the three-course menu, which is less
than €14 during lunch hours and up to €44 for dinner. Not to be missed
are some of the seasonal and often exotic dishes such as a curry of Brazilian grouper fillet served with sweet potatoes. Even standard French fare
like crème brûlée is a real treat here. ✉ *Kurfürstendamm 184,* ☎ *030/
8818–461. Reservations essential. AE, MC. Closed Sun.*

$$$ ✕ **Lubitsch.** The small Lubitsch was a buzzing place 10 years ago—
then with a different name—when the Savignyplatz area was the
hippest district in West Berlin. These days the restaurant seems to be
forgotten, to the delight of the *Stammgäste* (regulars) here. The cui-
sine is a mix of light German and traditional French brasserie cook-
ing, with an emphasis on fish and game dishes. The three-course lunch
menus for less than €11 are a good deal. ✉ *Bleibtreustr. 47,* ☎ *030/
8823–756. AE, MC, V. No lunch Sun.*

$$–$$$ ✕ **Manzini.** Manzini has safely guarded its reputation for daring French
★ and Italian cuisine in spite of the ups and downs typical of hip restau-
rants. One of the reasons for its continuing success (it even opened a
subsidiary in the Mitte district on Reinhardtstrasse) is the jovial atmo-
sphere, where businessmen, local artists, and some tourists all happily
enjoy light salads with chicken, or goat or sheep cheese, or one of the
delicious risotto recipes. ✉ *Ludwigkirchstr. 11,* ☎ *030/8857–820; Rein-
hardtstr. 14,* ☎ *030/2804–5510. AE, DC, MC, V.*

Western Downtown, Charlottenburg, Schöneberg, Tiergarten,

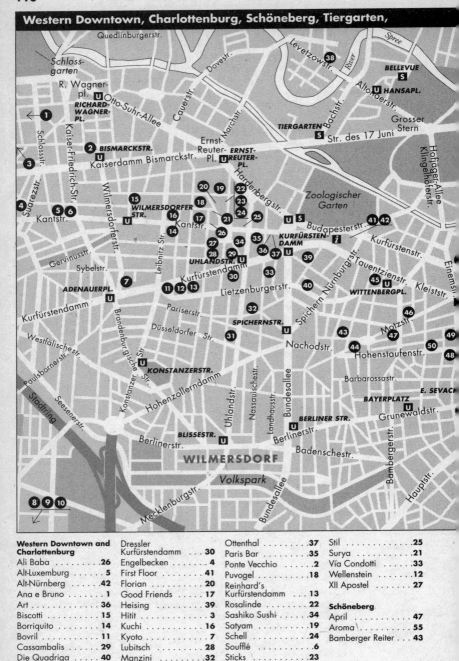

Kreuzberg and Zehlendorf Dining

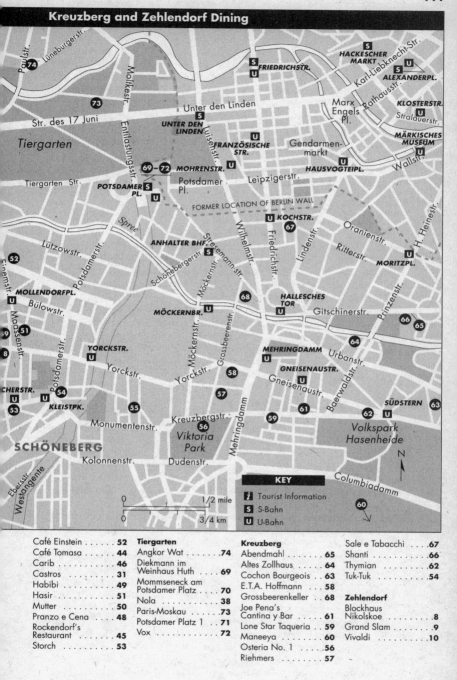

KEY

- **i** Tourist Information
- **S** S-Bahn
- **U** U-Bahn

0 — 1/2 mile
0 — 3/4 km

German

$$$$ ✕ Alt-Luxemburg. This popular restaurant's warm and intimate setting is enhanced with dark, 19th-century-style furniture, wrought-iron lamps, and antique kitchen sideboards. Chef Karl Wannemacher uses only the freshest ingredients for his nouvelle German dishes, including his divine lobster lasagna. As you might expect from a restaurant of this caliber, service is attentive and knowledgeable. ⊠ *Windscheidstr. 31,* ☎ *030/323–8730. AE, DC, V. No lunch. Closed Sun.*

$$$$ ✕ First Floor. Few hotel-restaurants are so outstanding that they be-
★ come a sensation, but this Michelin star–holder is unique. It's even more unusual that Chef Matthias Buchholz succeeds with traditional German fare, and not with the typically favored spread of light nouvelle cuisine. The menu changes according to the season and the chef's moods, but most dishes are new interpretations of heavy German dishes such as *Müritzlammrücken in Olivenkruste mit Bohnenmelange* (Müritz lamb back in olive crust, served with green beans). ⊠ *Hotel Palace, Budapester Str. 42,* ☎ *030/2502–1020. Reservations essential. AE, DC, MC, V. No lunch Sat.*

$$–$$$ ✕ Dressler. Its cuisine and service are each mixtures of French brasserie culture and German down-to-earth reliability. Accordingly, the seasonal menus are conceived for a wide range of palates: duck with red cabbage, or cod with Pommery mustard sauce, for example. Compared to other French restaurants, the Dressler's *plateaux de fruits de mer,* with oysters, lobster, and clams, is a good value and beautiful to behold as well. ⊠ *Kurfürstendamm 207–208,* ☎ *030/883–3530;* ⊠ *Unter den Linden 39,* ☎ *030/204–4422. AE, DC, MC, V.*

$$–$$$ ✕ Florian. In a big city like Berlin, the idea of creating a series of dishes
★ based on down-home Franconian cuisine might seem like a joke were there not so many successful Swabians in Berlin. Yet this intimate little place turned out to be one of the most popular restaurants in town. The food is a dashing combination of Swabian cuisine with a slight French accent. Featured prominently are game dishes, pasta, and ingredients such as mushrooms, asparagus, and sausages. But the food is only one of the draws: most people come for the warm, relaxed atmosphere and to watch the writers, artists, and film people who congregate here. Florian is famous for its *Nürnberger Rostbratwürstchen,* deliciously pan-fried, spicy sausages served until the wee hours of the morning—they're best enjoyed with a glass of beer. ⊠ *Grolmanstr. 52,* ☎ *030/313–9184. Reservations essential. MC, V.*

$$–$$$ ✕ Reinhard's. Smaller than the Reinhard's in Mitte, this one resembles an artsy theater pub. The high, mustard-colored walls with deep blue trim are covered with prints of famous paintings and photos of movie stars of yesteryear. Tables are set very closely (when making a reservation, ask for the table in the curved part of the plush bench running along the back wall). There's also sidewalk seating. Both the menu and prices are the same as at the Mitte Reinhard's. Reservations are advised. ⊠ *Kurfürstendamm 190,* ☎ *030/881–1621. AE, DC, MC, V.*

$$ ✕ Engelbecken. A friendly and brightly lighted place, the Engelbecken
★ welcomes its guests with relaxed Bavarian hospitality. Tables are filled by young artists and actors and by teachers who live around the corner. The Bavarian food, such as *Linsenpflanzerl mit Schafkäsefüllung* (lentil burger filled with sheep's cheese) or, in winter, the various game and wild poultry dishes, are top quality at very reasonable prices. In summer make sure to reserve a sidewalk table: it's one of the loveliest open-air dining spots in town. ⊠ *Witzlebenstr. 31,* ☎ *030/6152–810. MC, V. No lunch Mon.–Sat.*

$$ ✕ Puvogel. A cozy little restaurant away from the bustle of Savigny-platz, the Puvogel has a loyal fan base of mostly middle-aged intellectuals. The black-clad patrons drink a lot of red wine while sitting in old, squeaking chairs and having good conversations over candlelight. The food is superb and tastes like good home cooking. The eclectic mixture includes many German standards. ✉ *Pestalozzistr. 8,* ☏ *030/ 313–4364. MC, V. No lunch.*

$$ ✕ **Soufflé.** A charming little restaurant, the Soufflé won over snobbish Charlottenburgers, who now try to keep it one of their district's best-kept secrets. Dimmed light, candles, and the warm colors of the interior make this the perfect setting for a romantic dinner. Dishes such as orange gnocchi pasta or coq au vin won't leave you uncomfortably stuffed. The Soufflé also has an extensive vegetarian menu. ✉ *Kantstr. 70,* ☏ *030/3240–155. AE, V. Closed Sun.*

$–$$ ✕ **Art.** It bills itself as a gay bar and restaurant, but the Art is not strictly gay, and the atmosphere is very relaxed. The Art used fresh and controlled organic beef from selected *Ökobauern* (chemical-free farms) years before anyone in Germany worried about mad cow disease. Even the German wines on the menu are from organic wineries. The restaurant is tucked away under the S-Bahn viaduct. ✉ *Fasanenstr. 81a, Bogen 559,* ☏ *030/3132–625. AE, MC, V.*

$–$$ ✕ **Wellenstein.** The Wellenstein started as a bar and café some years ago and has desperately tried to become the old-fashioned and even more elegant version of Café Einstein on the Ku'damm. Instead, it attracts an odd mixture of teenagers, tourists, Russian immigrants, and old West Berlin entertainment tycoons such as Berlin's playboy, forever-blond Rolf Eden. In winter traditional German dishes such as duck with red cabbage and potatoes are a sure bet, as are pork with pasta or the salad dishes in summer. In the spring you can enjoy a selection of very good (white) asparagus dishes on the terrace. ✉ *Kurfürsten-damm 190,* ☏ *030/881–7850. AE, DC, MC, V.*

$ ✕ **Alt-Nürnberg.** You won't find any Berliners in this restaurant in the basement of the Europa-Center, but you will find many Japanese and American tourists sampling the delicious and original Franconian cuisine. Hearty dishes such as *Schweinshaxe* (pork knuckle) and *Nürn-berger Würstchen* (pan-fried pork sausages), are hard to come by in Berlin, and enjoying them in the replicated interior of a historic Nürn-berg half-timber house is another rare opportunity. ✉ *Europa-Center, Breitscheidpl.,* ☏ *030/261–4397. AE, DC, MC, V.*

$ ✕ **Rosalinde.** The Rosalinde has been around for so long that the Savignyplatz area wouldn't be the same without it. Never mind that her heydays are over, Rosalinde still clings to her past as a favorite hang-out of West Berlin's literary circles. The food is not particularly exciting, but the kitchen serves up solid cooking, with a heavy touch of Swabian cuisine such as *Maultaschen,* hearty pasta pockets filled with meat loaf or vegetables. In summer, the sidewalk tables are the perfect spot for drinking and people-watching on a lazy afternoon, while enjoying one of the delicious asparagus meals: a good choice is white asparagus with parslied potatoes, a buttery sauce hollandaise, and fried pork chops. ✉ *Knesebeckstr. 16,* ☏ *030/3135– 996. AE, MC, V.*

Greek

$$–$$$ ✕ **Cassambalis.** On entering you might wonder if this is an Italian trattoria, a Greek taverna, a Spanish bodega, or an upscale Turkish kebab joint: the deliberately casual yet shiny interior design tries unsuccessfully to evoke a Mediterranean country cottage, with a huge buffet table and wooden bar dominating the large dining room. Cassambalis does serve dishes from all the countries mentioned above, and is frequented by chic, liberal *Multikulti*-aficionados who love to dine on freshly grilled fish, meat with a lot of garlic, and simple red country wine. ✉ *Grolmannstr. 35,* ☏ *030/885–4747. MC, V. Closed Sun.*

Indian

$ ✕ **Satyam.** It's easy to overlook this small and strictly vegetarian
★ restaurant nestled between boutiques and shops. But those in the know
and from the neighborhood love "their" Indian restaurant, which pre-
pares inexpensive northern Indian fare, some using cheese made from
soybeans. The best chance to grab a table here is during lunch and during late afternoon hours. Unusual for Berlin is that the small Satyam
has a no-smoking area in the back. ✉ *Goethestr. 5,* ☎ *030/312–9079.*
No credit cards.

$ ✕ **Surya.** Of the many Indian restaurants in the Savignyplatz area, the
★ Surya is not the most popular, but it is the best. The wide variety of
mostly northern Indian food more than makes up for the uninspired
atmosphere in the large dining room. Flip through the menu right to
the last page, where a dozen or so spicy, pan-fried chicken, beef, fish,
and lamb dishes are listed. These are the best choices and will be
served sizzling hot at your table. ✉ *Grolmanstr. 22,* ☎ *030/312–
9123. No credit cards. No lunch Fri.–Sun.*

Italian

$$$$ ✕ **Ana e Bruno.** A Berlin classic with consistently well-prepared dishes,
★ this restaurant is expensive but has a warm and homey atmosphere
thanks to the heartfelt hospitality of the owners, Bruno and Ana.
Don't expect hearty Italian home cooking, though: the chef presents
a low-calorie reinterpretation of Mediterranean cuisine and prefers fresh
vegetables and salads over pasta. The four-course meals and daily specials are a good value.✉ *Sophie-Charlotten-Str. 101,* ☎ *030/325–
7110. Reservations essential. AE. Closed Sun. and Mon.*

$$$–$$$$ ✕ **Via Condotti.** This tiny Italian restaurant is hidden between the chic
boutiques on Fasanenstrasse, just opposite the Literaturhaus. The
clientele like to show off the goods they just purchased, but more im-
portant than the cooing and bag ruffling, the Via Condotti delivers solid
Italian home cooking. If you want to stroke the pride of chefs Lucca
and Rosario, order their heavenly *tagliolini al tartufo* (pasta with truf-
fles), which arrives flaming at your table. ✉ *Fasanenstr. 73,* ☎ *030/
8867–7897. AE, DC, MC, V.*

$$$ ✕ **Schell.** This upscale and chic restaurant in an old Shell gas station
has seen so many owners that no one quite knows who is running the
place. But despite its frequent changes of management, the Schell has
always appealed to Charlottenburg's nouveau-riche crowd, those folks
who love to show off their new convertible on a sunny Saturday morning. The menu has great breakfast and brunch choices, with many light,
Italian-style salads and fish dishes. Reservations are advised. ✉ *Knesebeckstr. 22,* ☎ *030/312–8310. V.*

$$–$$$ ✕ **Biscotti.** When the Biscotti opened some years ago, most residents
thought it wouldn't survive more than a few months, as it seemed like
yet another Italian restaurant in a quarter already bored by its many
Italian eateries. But the neighborhood was wrong, and the Biscotti is
thriving, with many guests flocking hither from other districts as well.
The country cooking stresses homemade pasta, which really is made
by the owners, and fresh-fish recipes. ✉ *Pestalozzistr. 88,* ☎ *030/3123–
937. AE, MC. Closed Sun. No lunch.*

$$–$$$ ✕ **Ponte Vecchio.** It's slightly off the beaten path, but Ponte Vecchio
has attracted devoted aficionados of good old Italian home cooking
for more than 10 years. It's one of those places where you can actually discuss with the knowledgeable and amiable waiters and even the
owner the pros and cons of a specific wine, dish, or ingredient. The
best bets here include braised sweet-sour wild boar, or kid, baked with
milk and spices. Reservations are advised. ✉ *Spielhagenstr. 3,* ☎ *030/
342–1999. DC. Closed Tues. No lunch Mon.–Sat.*

\$\$ ✕ **XII Apostel.** One of the city's nicest and liveliest Italian restaurants, the XII Apostel isn't for the pious. The restaurant made its debut with 12 pizzas, one for each apostle of Jesus Christ—the biggest (and tastiest) is called the Judas. These and other pizzas are outstanding for their thin and crunchy crust; most people flock to this place, however, simply because it's hip. ⊠ *Bleibtreustr. 49,* ☎ *030/312–1433. Reservations essential. No credit cards.*

\$ ✕ **Ali Baba.** The German version of a college hangout, this simple pizze-
★ ria just around the corner from Savignyplatz has served each and every student generation of West Berlin. The always-packed Ali Baba definitely makes the best pizza north of Italy, and has numerous toppings to choose from. Order a slice to go up front, or take a seat at the one of the large round tables in the back (you don't have to share your pie, but you may have to share a table with another party). In season (usually every month except June, July, and August), the Ali Baba also serves steamed clams in a sauce of white wine and lemon. You can do it as the Belgians do, and order them as *moules et frites,* with french fries. ⊠ *Bleibtreustr. 45,* ☎ *030/881–1350. AE, DC, MC, V.*

Japanese

\$\$–\$\$\$ ✕ **Kyoto.** Measure the quality of a Japanese restaurant by looking around
★ you: the more Japanese patrons, the better the food. And as the clien-
tele will attest, the Kyoto is one of Berlin's most authentic Japanese restaurants, where guests gladly sit cross-legged at low tables (west-ern-style tables are in the front). The interior and the clientele are worlds apart from the new and sleek sushi bars around Kurfürstendamm, but food is the most important draw. If you can't decide which of the many sushi items to choose, go for the *Kyoto Bento,* a sampler selection for €20. Reservations are advised. ⊠ *Wilmersdorfer Str. 94,* ☎ *030/883–2733. AE, DC, MC, V. Closed Mon. No lunch.*

\$\$ ✕ **Kuchi.** A Japanese restaurant serving Japanese, Thai, Chinese, and
★ Malaysian food? Kuchi is doing just that, and all dishes are delicious. Apart from the sushi (you might find some combinations here you've never sampled before), Kuchi also serves grilled, broiled, or seared fish and poultry dishes. And if you're in a hurry, walk a few yards down the street to the Kuchi Imbiss, where sushi and appetizers are sold to go or for enjoyment at a stand-up table. ⊠ *Kantstr. 30,* ☎ *030/3150–7815. AE, MC, V.*

\$\$ ✕ **Sashiko Sushi.** An ultracool sushi bar under the S-Bahn viaduct,
★ Sashiko Sushi has many features hard to find in Germany. It's a smoke-free restaurant; the chef will try to satisfy your extra sushi, *nigiri,* or *maki* requests; and the food is presented on little wooden boats that pass by on the semicircular bar. The special €7.50 lunch menu makes for a cheap place to break after a tour of the Kurfürstendamm area. ⊠ *Savignypassage, Grolmanstr. 47,* ☎ *030/313–2282. AE, MC, V.*

Spanish

\$–\$\$ ✕ **Borriquito.** At first sight this small Spanish restaurant off Ku'damm
★ may look like your average local Mediterranean eatery. After your first visit, however, you'll be planning your next thanks to the authentic and lively atmosphere. Flamenco singers and guitarists perform their melancholy but passionate songs most evenings, while diners dig into their hearty food. Surprisingly, the paella is not that recommendable, but all meat dishes, foremost the roasted lamb neck or *Keule* (lamb haunch), are superb (and often sold out). ⊠ *Wielandstr. 6,* ☎ *030/312–9929. Reservations essential. No credit cards.*

Thai

\$ ✕ **Sticks.** A friendly restaurant in the Charlottenburger Kiez, Sticks serves
★ traditional Thai and Vietnamese dishes (any kind of meat prepared with

coconut milk, sweet-and-sour sauce, or bell peppers) in a bright, modest, and tasteful setting. You won't find fake Asian artifacts or kitsch decorations here. Food is king at Sticks, where the fairly large portions on your dish—not common in Thai restaurants—are a big plus. It's also one of the few Asian restaurants in Berlin where you can eat your meal alfresco in summer at sidewalk tables. ⊠ *Knesebeckstr. 15,* ☎ *030/3129–042. AE, MC, V.*

Turkish

$$ ✕ **Hitit.** Not one of the coziest but definitely one of the best Turkish
★ restaurants in town, Hitit has a dining area that draws comparison to a modern version of a temple: bright-white walls with abstract, somehow Babylonian-looking reliefs, a tile floor, and heavy wooden chairs. The wide selection of grilled meat dishes and vegetarian meals (there are a total of 90 items to choose from on a menu written in German and English) at very reasonable prices, and the friendly service make Hitit an unbeatable choice in the western downtown area. A real insider's choice here is the flat Arabian bread baked with seven different vegetables and served with wheat grits: it's light, healthy, and mildly spicy. ⊠ *Knobelsdorffstr. 35,* ☎ *030/322–4557. V. No lunch Mon.–Sat.*

Schöneberg

Not as fancy as Charlottenburg, Schöneberg is primarily a place to do some pub- and barhopping. Hidden among the many (mostly gay) watering holes of Motzstrasse, within the district's two great squares, Nollendorfplatz and Winterfeldplatz, and all the way down to Hohenstaufenstrasse are some intriguingly creative restaurants.

Austrian

$$$ ✕ **Café Einstein.** A mixture of German stiffness and Viennese elegance
★ with attitude, Café Einstein, in the former villa of German silent movie star Henny Porten, is still a welcome relief from the basic and quick satisfaction found in other restaurants. Here waiters dressed in black suits with bow ties glide across the parquet floor, and a busy maître d' chases out rowdy teenagers and tourists dressed too casually, while intellectuals read newspapers and indulge in dishes like Wiener schnitzel or goulash. During the summer you shouldn't miss the garden, and be sure to try the strawberry cake with whipped cream. Reservations are advised. ⊠ *Kurfürstenstr. 58,* ☎ *030/261–5096. AE, DC, MC, V.*

Caribbean

$$ ✕ **Carib.** Welcome to Berlin's only true Caribbean restaurant, the laidback Carib. With its colorful interior and constant music, it's easy to dream of the islands. To make your fantasy complete, munch on some barbecue pork and sip inexpensive cocktails, which start at €5. ⊠ *Motzstr. 30,* ☎ *030/213–5381. MC, V. No lunch.*

$$ ✕ **Castros.** Germans have a love affair with Cuba and its girls and boys, cigars, drinks, music, and sun. All of this explains the success of Castros, one of Berlin's few Cuban restaurants and one that's always packed. Besides the superb drinks and appetizers, choices from the changing menu, like salmon in coconut sauce, are always good. ⊠ *Pfalzburger Str. 72a,* ☎ *030/882–1808. MC, V. No lunch.*

Contemporary

$ ✕ **Mutter.** When Schöneberg nighthawks get hungry in the middle of the night, they flock to "mother" (the name of this restaurant), where Asian food is served in the crowded main *Kneipenraum* (pub room) or, in summer, at tables on the sidewalk. The opulent breakfasts, healthy green salads served with barbecued spicy chicken, and cold Thai glass-noodle salads are great pluses. ⊠ *Hohenstaufenstr. 4,* ☎ *030/216–4990. V.*

German

$$$$ ✕ **Bamberger Reiter.** One of the city's leading restaurants, the Bamberger Reiter is presided over by chef Christoph Fischer from Freiburg. Like his famous predecessor, Franz Raneburger, he relies on fresh market produce for his *Neue Deutsche Küche* (new German cuisine), but adds a more international touch. The menu changes daily, and the Bamberger Reiter is famous for the freshest top-quality fish in town. ⊠ *Regensburgerstr. 7,* ☎ *030/218–4282. Reservations essential. AE, MC, V. Closed Sun.–Mon. No lunch.*

$$$$ ✕ **Rockendorf's Restaurant.** For almost 20 years Rockendorf's has been the city's top restaurant. With the sudden death of Mr. Rockendorf, the chef who once spearheaded the revolution of German nouvelle cuisine, it remains to be seen whether his successor can live up to his predecessor's standard. Right next to the gourmet restaurant is its upscale bistro where the three-course lunch menus are a good deal. The restaurant itself has only prix-fixe menus, some with up to nine courses. The outstanding wine list—with 800 choices—has the appropriate accompaniment to any menu. ⊠ *Passauer Str. 5–7,* ☎ *030/402–3099. Reservations essential. AE, DC, MC, V.*

$$$ ✕ **Storch.** For more than a decade the Storch has upheld its reputation
★ as Berlin's premier *Gasthaus* with Alsatian cuisine, that odd but sumptuous mixture of French ingeniousness and German quality. The rustic interior—simple, dark furniture and sober-looking, cream-color walls sparsely decorated with antique enamel advertising signs fits the meals. Chef Hannes Behrmann once cooked his hearty dishes such as *Wildschweinragout mit Speck und Gemüse* (ragout of boar with bacon and vegetables) for the German navy. The menu changes daily. Reservations are advised. ⊠ *Wartburgstr. 57,* ☎ *030/784–2059. AE, MC, V. No lunch.*

$ ✕ **April.** In an old city mansion, April is far away from the hustle and
★ bustle of Schöneberg's restaurant and bar scene. It has established itself as a restaurant Germans like to call *unaufgeregt* (unpretentious), and that holds true for the cuisine—a mixture of Italian, Turkish, French, and German cooking—the clientele, and the service. The cost of the consistently delicious meals is amazingly reasonable. One of the best deals is the *Vorspeisenteller* (selection of appetizers) for two, which is a full meal in itself, and includes couscous, marinated tomatoes, and other spicy finger foods from Mediterranean countries. Reservations are advised. ⊠ *Winterfeldstr. 56,* ☎ *030/216–8869. No credit cards.*

$ ✕ **Café Tomasa.** For years, Café Tomasa has been one of the top places to breakfast, with a wide selection of healthy food from around the world served from 8 to 1:30. Salads, baguettes, and some hot dishes are available for lunch and dinner. The casual and friendly service makes eating here not only nutritious but relaxing as well. ⊠ *Motzstr. 60,* ☎ *030/213–2345. AE, MC, V.*

Italian

$$ ✕ **Aroma.** Aroma is neither your typical neighborhood Italian tratto-
★ ria nor an exquisite or stylish restaurant. Slightly off the beaten track, Aroma serves excellent pizza and pasta to a mostly young crowd. The thin-crust white pizza (without tomato sauce) is very recommendable. As the place is rather small, expect to share one of those huge round tables with other guests. ⊠ *Hochkirchstr. 8,* ☎ *030/7825–821. Reservations essential. V. No lunch weekdays.*

$–$$ ✕ **Pranzo e Cena.** One of the few good restaurants in the Winterfeld-
★ platz neighborhood, otherwise known for its bars, the Pranzo e Cena is your average Italian pizza parlor turned trendy and young. With its

faded wood panels and simple wooden floor and tables, this popular eatery exudes the forlorn but deliberately designed interior of a 1960s restaurant. Musts are the thin-crust pizzas, which come in all imaginable varieties. Reservations are advised. ⊠ *Goltzstr. 32,* ☎ *030/216–3514. MC, V.*

Middle Eastern

$ ✕ **Habibi.** One of Berlin's most beloved Arabic *Stehimbisse* (stand-up
★ cafés), Habibi carries a wide variety of finger foods. On weekend nights it stays open until 5 AM. You can consume a huge falafel or baklava at one of the tables, or grab a bite to go. ⊠ *Goltzstr. 24,* ☎ *030/215–3332. No credit cards.*

$ ✕ **Hasir.** The Hasir is a growing chain of (now) five small fast-food
★ restaurants, with two in Schöneberg and in Mitte that are nicely decorated in bright Middle Eastern colors and motifs. In both places you can eat Döner kebab, falafel, *schawarma,* and other Arabic snacks, as well as salads and full dinner plates. Both Hasir locations are open until 4 AM daily. ⊠ *Maassenstr. 10, Schöneberg,* ☎ *030/215–6060;* ⊠ *Oranienburger Str. 4, Mitte,* ☎ *030/2804–1616. AE, MC, V.*

Tiergarten

The area known as Tiergarten gets its name from the beautiful and extensive Tiergarten park. Since Tiergarten has become home to the federal government district, some good restaurants have sprung up around the Reichstag.

American

$–$$ ✕ **Nola.** If you're a homesick American, get your fix at Nola. Of the
★ many attempts by German restaurants to re-create the food and atmosphere of an American restaurant and bar, this one ranks among the best. The food is a wild stampede of American classics (buffalo wings, to name just one) and Mexican standards (the fajitas are excellent). While waiting for a meal, you can doodle on the paper tablecloth, and if it's good enough, the Nola team might hang it on the walls. ⊠ *Dortmunder Str. 9,* ☎ *030/399–6969. AE, MC, V. No lunch Mon.–Sat.*

Cambodian

$$–$$$ ✕ **Angkor Wat.** Once an insider's secret, the Angkor Wat is on the verge
★ of becoming a star among the city's Asian restaurants. It's not only the slightly different cooking—this is neither standard Thai, Chinese, nor Vietnamese—but also the genuinely warm service that wins back guests. Here you get the feeling that your host is genuinely overjoyed when you enter his restaurant. A must is the Cambodian fondue with all sorts of meat and spices for €21. ⊠ *Paulstr. 22,* ☎ *030/393–3922. No credit cards. No lunch Mon.*

Contemporary

$$$$ ✕ **Vox.** The restaurant's name pays homage to the famous Vox entertainment and dining complex of the Roaring '20s that once stood nearby. But the new Vox is a cool Asian-style restaurant with a high-tech show kitchen preparing inventive Asian and Mediterranean fish dishes. Here even your ordinary tuna gets spiced up and suddenly turns out to be a superb fillet with citrus pepper and cucumbers—served as sushi. Reservations are advised. ⊠ *Grand Hyatt Hotel Berlin, Marlene-Dietrich-Pl. 2,* ☎ *030/2553–1234. AE, DC, MC, V.*

$$–$$$ ✕ **Potsdamer Platz 1.** Squeezed into a narrow triangle-shape dining room, Potsdamer Platz 1 is a minimalist, ultrachic restaurant in DaimlerChrysler city. Despite its aspiring name, the restaurant is still struggling to establish itself as hip place (compared to Stil, Margaux, and the like). The French-German food, however, is very imaginative,

cooked with many healthy ingredients (using pumpkin, and pumpkinseed oil). ⊠ *Potsdamer Pl. 1,* ☎ *030/2537–8945. AE, MC, V.*

French

$$ ✕ **Diekmann im Weinhaus Huth.** The new Dieckmann is a fascinating place to eat, not so much for the ordinary French cooking but for its location. The old Weinhaus Huth was once the last building standing in the no-man's-land of Potsdamer Platz. The service is smooth and friendly. The interior tries to imitate a Paris bistro but lacks some warmth. It's a less expensive, more casual alternative to Borchardt. One stand-out on the reliable menu is the fresh oysters, which are less expensive than elsewhere in Berlin. ⊠ *Alte Potsdamer Str. 5,* ☎ *030/2529–7524. MC, V.*

German

$$–$$$ ✕ **Paris-Moskau.** The name of this upscale restaurant is a reminder of Berlin's old position as a railway hub between these two cities. Paris-Moskau is appropriately located in a stand-alone half-timber house right next to the railway tracks. In the days of old West Berlin, Paris-Moskau was one of the most popular restaurants; however, these days it looks somewhat forlorn in the swirl of time. But the high-energy food, mostly made with fish and accompanied by a great selection of wine, is still revered by the gourmands of the west. ⊠ *Alt-Moabit 141,* ☎ *030/394– 2081. No credit cards. No lunch.*

$–$$ ✕ **Mommseneck am Potsdamer Platz.** Among the few restaurants on Potsdamer Platz, the Mommseneck is the only traditional restaurant serving Berlin classics and hearty meat dishes. Ordering any of the *Pfannengerichte* (pan-fried and roasted meats) is a quick and inexpensive way to fill your belly. Barring the many worthwhile aspara-gus meals (in April and May only), the food here is generally reliable but not exceptional. A great plus is the quiet terrace in the half-open courtyard, which has a great view of a playful, neon bicycle sculpture in a small fountain. ⊠ *Alte Potsdamer Str. 1,* ☎ *030/2529–6615. AE, MC, V.*

Mitte

Berlin's most historic and smallest district has the greatest number and variety of cafés and restaurants. The streets around magnificent Gendarmenmarkt have become home to some of the city's classiest restaurants, while a hip and inexpensive scene with many ethnic eateries has emerged along Oranienburger Strasse, in the Spandauer Vorstadt. The district's great boulevard, Unter den Linden, has only a handful of places to eat, while the medieval Nikolaiviertel (Nikolai Quarter) features some good old Berlin restaurants and pubs.

Austrian

$$$ ✕ **Aigner.** One of the first arrivals around the Gendarmenmarkt, the
★ Aigner, with its Austrian cuisine, quickly became one of the area's top restaurants. In fact, the Aigner was a Vienna-based restaurant that was moved lock, stock, and barrel to Berlin. It is more elegant than Lutter & Wegner, the service swifter and more knowledgeable, and the food generally of a higher quality. Typical of Austrian cooking (and celebrated to perfection here) is the mixture of warm and hot food served in one dish, such as perch from the local Havel River with lukewarm potato salad and cool sliced cucumbers. If you've ever wanted to try one of those rich Austrian deserts, indulge in the *Kaiserschmarrn,* a hearty diced-up pancake, baked with raisins and served hot with vanilla powdered sugar. Reservations are advised. ⊠ *Französische Str. 25,* ☎ *030/20375–1850. AE, DC, MC, V.*

Mitte and Prenzlauer Berg Dining

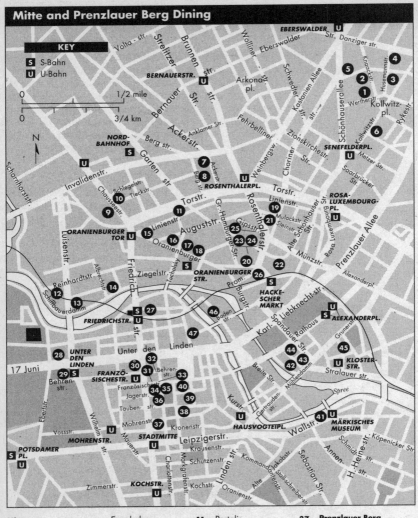

$$ ✕ **Barist.** The long bar, gilt-framed mirrors, and arched ceiling beneath the railroad viaducts make this stylish bar-restaurant a magnet for those taking in the hip Mitte nightlife scene. A piano player and a jazz singer perform on weekend nights. Most dishes—an assortment of some Italian and French, but mostly Austrian recipes—are delicious. The gnocchi are homemade and served with Parma bacon and wild mushrooms. Outdoor tables are beneath the trees across the street. ✉ *Am Zwirngraben, S-Bahnbögen 13–14,* ☎ *030/2472–2613. AE, MC, V.*

$ ✕ **Kellerrestaurant im Brecht-Haus.** In the Brecht-Haus, where playwright Bertolt Brecht once lived and worked, the cellar kitchen still prepares the master's favorite dishes. Some of them were once cooked here by his Vienna-born wife, Helene Weigel, most notably the *Tafelspitz* (boiled, marinated rump steak). ✉ *Chausseestr. 125,* ☎ *030/282–3843. AE, MC. No lunch.*

Contemporary

$$$$ ✕ **Guy.** In summer Guy's quiet courtyard is one of the nicest places to dine. Hidden behind a narrow entrance is the plain courtyard, surrounded by three-story walls and topped by a patch of the dark blue Berlin sky. Tables are nicely decorated with white linen, and the elaborate menus are a mixture of Mediterranean and regional fare—the atmosphere recalls Rome or Barcelona. Guy is frequently mostly by business and media people, the men often accompanied by the notorious Berlin blonde girls (thin, but hungry). The clientele, attractive staff, and polished design of the restaurant are the pinnacle of hip. Reservations are advised. ✉ *Jägerstr. 59–60,* ☎ *030/2094–2600. AE, MC, V. Closed Sun. No lunch Sat.*

$$$$ ✕ **Margaux.** Small Margaux has quickly risen to the heights of gourmet
★ heaven in Berlin, not only because of its exquisite, eclectic cuisine with a nice touch of French but also because of the imaginative way in which ingredients are treated. Here asparagus is not steamed but fried; chicken breast is not broiled but cooked in an aspic jelly, placed in a puff pastry, and topped with baked fresh fruits. Any dinner should be complemented with a wine—the experienced sommelier is happy to help you choose from a list of almost 750 vintages. The interior design is urban in its stylishness and minimalism. ✉ *Unter den Linden 78,* ☎ *030/2265–2611. Reservations essential. AE, DC, MC, V. Closed Sun.*

$$$$ ✕ **Maxwell.** The wonderfully ornate facade and courtyard tables of Maxwell aren't visible from the street entrance. This fine restaurant first opened in Kreuzberg, where it was hounded by militant anarchists who resented the gentrification Maxwell signaled. The cuisine combines French, German, and Asian touches in a Berlin interpretation of fusion cooking. The restaurant has a loft-like tier, and the decor is kept serene with cream-colored walls and artwork here and there. Reservations are advised. ✉ *Bergstr. 22,* ☎ *030/2807–121. AE, DC, MC, V. No lunch.*

$$$$ ✕ **Portalis.** This is the latest arrival to Berlin's small gourmet clique.
★ Munich-based entrepreneur Fritz Eichbauer (who made Tantris, in Munich, one of Germany's best restaurants) and his chef, Volker Drkosch, try to educate the unsophisticated Berliner on how to appreciate contemporary food—much to the liking of the Michelin Guide, which awarded Portalis one star. The cuisine consists of fresh and light fish, veal, and hard-to-come-by vegetables. Reservations are advised. ✉ *Kronenstr. 55–58,* ☎ *030/2045–5496. AE, MC, V. Closed Sun.–Mon.*

$$$$ ✕ **VAU.** Trendsetter VAU ushered in the movement of restaurants to
★ the Mitte district a couple of years ago. The excellent German fish and game dishes prepared by Chef Kolja Kleeberg might earn him a second Michelin star. Daring combinations include *Ente mit gezupftem Rotkohl, Quitten, und Maronen* (duck with red cabbage, quinces, and sweet chestnuts) and *Steinbutt mit Kalbbries auf Rotweinschalotten* (tur-

bot with veal sweetbreads on shallots in red wine). The VAU's cool interior is all style and modern art: it was designed by Wolfgang Schmidt, one of Germany's leading industrial designers. ⊠ *Jägerstr. 54/55,* ☎ *030/202–9730. Reservations essential. AE, DC, MC, V. Closed Sun.*

$$$ ✕ **Die Weltbühne.** For German intellectuals, the very name of this
★   stylish restaurant evokes the Roaring '20s, as the cultural magazine *Die Weltbühne* published the best and brightest writers of its time. The famous Kurt Tucholsky and the like undoubtedly would have frequented this shiny place, bemoaning writer's block while seated at a green-leather banquette and checking who else was in the room via the many wall mirrors. All in all, the room's design is an appealing mixture of art deco, Bauhaus, and a touch of good old Berlin wood paneling. The menu features many fish dishes. Close to perfection is the red snapper served with a sour green-herb sauce and saffron potatoes. If you want to stay after dinner—there's always a free spot at the 90-ft-long bar. Reservations are advised. ⊠ *Gormannstr. 14,* ☎ *030/2800–940. AE, DC, MC, V. Closed Sun.*

$$–$$$ ✕ **Langhans.** German, Italian, and Japanese ingredients are the key play-
★   ers at Langhans, a creative restaurant that is more than your average East-meets-West venue. The cuisine, envisioned and prepared by chef Holger Zurbrüggen, is a daring triad of tastes and is a must for connoisseurs on a quest for novelty. His creative dish of young chicken stuffed with ginger risotto and sukiyaki sauce was the talk of the gourmet purists, who quickly warmed up to such offbeat combinations. Reservations are advised. ⊠ *Charlottenstr. 59,* ☎ *030/2094–5070. AE, MC, V.*

$$–$$$ ✕ **Viehauser im Presseclub.** If you want to observe how Germany's political journalists wine and dine, this is the place to spy. Power brokers and headline hacks mingle here, where the food is superb, naturally, thanks to the tutelage of chef Josef Viehauser. The recipes are a veritable journey through European cooking, including *Zander, Kalbshaxe, Hummer,* and *Kalbrücken* (pike perch, veal hocks, lobster, and saddle of veal). Many dishes surprise with unusual variations of old recipes: veal is served stuffed in ravioli, and the perch is fried with risotto. ⊠ *Schiffbauerdamm 40,* ☎ *030/2061–670. AE, DC, MC, V.*

$$ ✕ **Hackescher Hof.** The restaurant's setting in the hopping Hackesche Höfe makes it without question one of the most *in* restaurants in the Mitte district and a great place to experience the upswing in the old East. With oversize industrial lamps, the large, high-ceiling rooms have an urban and breathless atmosphere. The food is a mixture of international nouvelle cuisine and beefy German cooking—there is also a special dinner menu with more refined dishes. ⊠ *Rosenthaler Str. 40–41,* ☎ *030/283–5293. AE, MC, V.*

$$ ✕ **McBride's.** The English name of this new eatery, in the former barn of the Heckmann Höfe, was created to attract the fashionable crowd of the Mitte district—and it worked. Thanks to the bistrolike, casual atmosphere, McBride's is perfect for both a lunch break or a quick dinner, with dishes such as lamb neck with whipped potatoes and rosemary sauce—one of the meatier choices on a menu where salads and appetizers dominate. ⊠ *Oranienburger Str. 32,* ☎ *030/2838–6461. MC, V.*

$$ ✕ **Sion am Reichstag.** Within the hotel Künstlerheim Luise and in two
★   rooms under an S-Bahn viaduct, this restaurant and bistro is mostly patronized by those working in the new federal district and the many business offices nearby. The Sion, run by chef Jürgen Fehrenbach, a well-known Michelin chef, puts several completely different cuisines on his menu: choose from Spanish tapas, or robust Rheinland or delicate French entrées. Wines can be sampled in the basement Weinstube; the sommelier will guide you through all the vintage regions of the world. ⊠ *Luisenstr. 19,* ☎ *030/2854–5491. DC, MC, V.*

$ ✕ **Goa.** Goa is Berlin multikulti at its best, serving Asian, Indian, and even some Australian food. Its specialties are the wok dishes, such as the tasty *Safrancurry mit Hühnerfilet in Blätterteigpastetchen* (chicken fillet with saffron and curry, baked in puff pastry). A great idea for dinner is the "Reise durch Asien" (journey across Asia), a special three-course menu that includes a a changing variety of Indian and Asian specialties. If you're going for a traditional experience, try to grab one of the low tables with Thai sitting cushions. ⊠ *Oranienburger Str. 50,* ☎ *030/2859–8451. AE, MC, V.*

Eastern European

$ ✕ **Beth-Café.** Gefilte fish, bagels, hummus, baba ghanouj, and tabbouleh make this kosher restaurant run by eastern Berlin's Jewish congregation, Adass Jisroel, a first choice among Berlin's Israeli eateries. It's the ideal vantage point from which to check into the Jewish community and its current upswing, a result of the influx of Russian immigrants. ⊠ *Tucholskystr. 40,* ☎ *030/281–3135. AE, DC, MC, V. Closed Fri.–Sat.*

$ ✕ **Café Oren.** Traditional Jewish cooking, long absent from the old Jewish quarter of Berlin, is now thriving again at this popular vegetarian eatery next to the Neue Synagoge on Oranienburger Strasse. The room buzzes with loud chatter all evening, and the atmosphere and service are friendly. Try the gefilte fish, a tasty (and very salty) German-Jewish dish, or *Bachsaibling in schäumender Butter* (red-meat trout in hot butter). ⊠ *Oranienburger Str. 28,* ☎ *030/282–8228. AE, V.*

French

$$$$ ✕ **Adermann.** In an old city mansion in the Scheunenviertel, the Ader-
★ mann brings some glamour to a district that still bears the peculiar charm of decay. The restaurant is on the second floor, the so-called *bel étage.* It is an elegant space, with doors covered with leaf gold and a wooden parquet floor so precious it is protected under glass. This is the ideal setting for a delicious dinner, and the menu prepared by chef Wolfgang Müller changes daily, but the emphasis is on French fish and game dishes. ⊠ *Oranienburger Str. 27,* ☎ *030/2838–7371. Reservations essential. AE, DC, MC, V. Closed Mon. No lunch.*

$$$$ ✕ **Borchardt.** This is one of the most fashionable of the celebrity meet-
★ ing points that have sprung up in Mitte. The high ceiling, columns, red-plush benches, and art nouveau mosaic (discovered during renovations) create the impression of a 1920s café. The cuisine is high-quality French-Mediterranean, including several dishes with fresh fish and veal, such as *Praline vom Steinbutt und Hummer im grünen Reismantel* (fillet of stone flounder and lobster with green rice). ⊠ *Französische Str. 47,* ☎ *030/2038–7110. Reservations essential. AE, V.*

$$$$ ✕ **Lorenz Adlon.** What would an international first-class luxury hotel
★ be without a star-struck gourmet restaurant? Not much. And so the Hotel Adlon opened this fine restaurant, whose chef, Karl-Heinz Hauser, is on the way to being knighted by the order of Michelin. The classic French dishes are prepared to utmost perfection, even though the selection is not very imaginative. A good deal in this pricey establishment are the menus for €92–€140. A very knowledgeable sommelier (surprisingly, without any attitude) will help you with the wine selection. ⊠ *Hotel Adlon, Unter den Linden 77,* ☎ *030/2261–1960. Reservations essential. AE, DC, MC, V. Closed Sun.–Mon. No lunch.*

$$$ ✕ **Refugium.** Nestled in the basement of the French church on Gendarmenmarkt, this restaurant first looks like the dining hall of a monastery. But the gentle modernization of the historic building, replete with new frescos and wall and ceiling paintings, has effectively softened the sober environment. Among the mostly light and small-portioned French bistro-type dishes, the plat du jour or the "quick lunch" at €12 is a very good deal. They include a main dish and a dessert. In

summer the restaurant sets out tables on the northern end of the Gendarmenmarkt. ⊠ *Gendarmenmarkt 5,* ☎ *030/229– 1661. V.*

$$–$$$ ★ ✕ **Brasserie am Gendarmenmarkt.** Almost everything in this perfectly replicated brasserie from the 1920s looks, smells, and feels French. The lively art deco restaurant shows its true colors on its menu, where a great many German and international dishes compete with French country-style cooking, such as salmon fillet baked in a potato crust with a leek-and-nut sauce. Surprisingly, for a Gallic brasserie, you'll most likely say *à votre santé* with a Californian wine. ⊠ *Taubenstr. 30,* ☎ *030/ 2045–3501. AE, MC, V.*

$$ ✕ **Ganymed.** Ganymed has reappeared at its original location, right next to the Brecht Ensemble theater, once again providing an upscale place to meet after the theater. The food, served on elegantly decorated tables, is by and large French, with a smattering of regional fare such as spicy *Berliner Kartoffelsuppe* (potato soup). ⊠ *Schiffbauerdamm 5,* ☎ *030/2859–9046. AE, MC, V.*

German

$$$$ ★ ✕ **Kaiserstuben.** Next to the Pergamonmuseum, soft candlelight spills onto the cobblestone street, inviting gourmands to make their way down into the Kaiserstuben's half-basement. The restaurant (German for "emperor's parlor") serves ingeniously prepared cuisine that carefully balances regional heritage with influences from all over the world. Chef Christian Ramlau surprises guests with constantly changing combinations such as *Zweierlei vom Lammcarré auf Balsamicolinsen* (variation of rack of lamb on balsamic lentils). ⊠ *Am Kupfergraben 6a,* ☎ *030/ 2045–2980. AE, MC, V. Closed Sun.–Mon.*

$$$ ✕ **Die Möwe.** The Seagull's name refers to East Berlin's famous artists' club, which is housed in the same building. The restaurant has quite an affiliation with the arts: on Friday and Saturday nights there's a piano player—rather unusual even for the best German restaurants—and a special *Kunstgenuss* (art enjoyment) dinner on Monday night, a two-course dinner created along an artistic theme. The light German nouvelle cooking is delicious, with a tendency toward fish such as *Dialog von Meeresfrüchten auf Wildreis,* a combination of perch, salmon, and loup de mer (a white Mediterranean fish) on wild rice. ⊠ *Am Festungsgraben 1, at Palais am Festungsgraben,* ☎ *030/2061–0540. AE, DC, MC, V. Closed Sun.*

$$$ ★ ✕ **Lutter & Wegner.** One of the city's oldest vintners (it began producing *Sekt,* German champagne, in 1811) has returned to its original salesroom across from Gendarmenmarkt. It must take acres of crisp white linen to fill the huge space, where dark-wood paneling, an equally elegant parquet floor, and charming service evoke a 19th-century Viennese restaurant. In fact, the menu does consist mostly of Austrian cuisine, with superb game dishes in winter (the lamb neck with a crust of fresh cheese is unbeatable) and, of course, a perfect Wiener schnitzel with appropriately lukewarm potato salad. Reservations are advised, particularly in summer, when the alfresco tables quickly fill up. ⊠ *Charlottenstr. 56,* ☎ *030/2029–540. AE, MC, V.*

$$–$$$ ✕ **Reinhard's.** Friends meet here in the Nikolaiviertel to socialize over the carefully prepared entrées, tongues loosened by spirits from the amply stocked bar. Reinhard's has several dining rooms (a quiet spot is just to your right upon entering), and its walls are packed with modern art reproductions and black-and-white photos of movie stars. In summer you can dine in the open courtyard. The honey-glazed breast of duck, *Adlon,* is a specialty, and, during fall and winter months this is the place to try Germany's favorite Christmas dinner, a sizzling hot and crispy duck breast or leg, served with a heavy brown sauce, red cabbage, and potatoes. A fine wine to complement this meal is the heavy Spanish

Rioja. Reservations are advised. ✉ *Poststr. 28,* ☎ *030/242–5295. AE, DC, MC, V.*

$$ ✕ **Oxymoron.** Within the first courtyard of the Hackesche Höfe, Oxy-
★ moron is quieter and not so geared to out-of-towners as the bustling
Hackerscher Hof. The plush red sofas, heavy curtains, and antique chan-
deliers make for a café-like setting. The kitchen serves delicious salads
and light meals such as veal steak with green asparagus (rare in Ger-
many) and potatoes—more intriguing than the typical German creations
at the other nearby restaurants. The best time to visit is when the ter-
race is open: you can quietly enjoy your dinner while watching the crowds
pass by at a distance. ✉ *Hackesche Höfe, Rosenthaler Str. 40–41,* ☎
030/2839–1886. AE, MC, V.

$ ✕ **Brauhaus Georgbräu.** In general, jovial Bavarians are in a difficult
★ position when they try to make it in this stiff Prussian capital—not so
at the Georgbräu, one of the most popular breweries in town with a
great location on the Spree Canal. The kitchen peacefully unites the
cooking of northern and southern Germany and meals such as *Eisbein
mit Erbpüree* (pork hock with mashed peas) and *Harzer Platte mit
Schmalztopf* (a selection of cheese with schmaltz—a pork fat substi-
tute for butter) are worth the indulgence. ✉ *Spreeufer 4,* ☎ *030/242–
4244. AE, DC, MC, V.*

$ ✕ **Sieke's Weinhaus.** Originally nothing more than a well-selected
wineshop, Sieke's is now a restaurant, bistro, and café serving German
dishes at incredibly low prices. The emphasis is still on wine, mostly
from the German Baden region. With popularity gaining by the day,
it's doubtful the prices will remain this low. Until the markup you can
indulge in southern German specialties from the Baden region, such
as *Flammkuchen,* a hearty pie made of cheese, beacon, onions, and mush-
rooms that has a delicious smoky flavor. The region also produces the
right wine for this dish—a *Weissburgunder,* a slightly sulfuric white
wine with a spicy taste reminiscent of nuts and pepper. ✉ *Chausseestr.
15,* ☎ *030/3087–2980. AE, DC, MC, V. Closed Sun.*

$ ✕ **Zur Letzten Instanz.** Established in 1621, Berlin's oldest restaurant
★ combines the charming atmosphere of Old Berlin with a limited but
very appealing menu. Napoléon is said to have sat alongside the tile
stove in the front room, and Mikhail Gorbachev quaffed a beer here
during a visit in 1989. The emphasis is on beer, both in the recipes and
in the mugs. Service can be erratic, though it's always engagingly
friendly. ✉ *Waisenstr. 14–16,* ☎ *030/242–5528. AE, DC, MC, V.*

$ ✕ **Zur Nolle.** One of the many new restaurants built under the reno-
vated S-Bahn viaducts in Mitte, the Zur Nolle is immensely popular
among young tourists and students. It's near the Antik- und Flohmarkt
(antiques and flea market) and thus has tried to create an interior both
art nouveau and art deco, with dark antique furniture, many mirrors,
palm trees, and vintage billboards. It's a great place to take in some
old-style atmosphere typical of the Berlin *Eckkneipe,* the pub around
the corner (though the Nolle is somewhat more upscale). Not surprisingly,
Zur Nolle serves fairly large portions of standard Berlin food. ✉ *Geor-
genstr., S-Bahnbogen Nr. 203,* ☎ *030/208–2655. AE, MC, V.*

$ ✕ **Zur Rippe.** This small old-style Berlin place is popular for its authentic
dishes and Nikolaiviertel location. Wholesome food is served in an in-
timate setting with oak paneling and ceramic tiles. Specialties include
the herring casserole and the cheese platter with Camembert, Dutch
Blumaster, and a small variety of German *Schnittkäse,* which is like
Edam or Gouda. ✉ *Poststr. 17,* ☎ *030/242–4248. AE, DC, MC, V.*

Italian

$$$ ✕ **Ermelerhaus.** The Ermelerhaus, within the art'otel Berlin, offers
two restaurants under one roof. The more traditional Raabediele and

its Tabaklounge serve traditional German dishes. The Ermelerhaus à la carte restaurant relies on exceptional Mediterranean preparations (with an accent on seafood) to attract old and new patrons. Of the four rococo dining rooms, the lavishly decorated Rosenzimmer is one of the most romantic historic dinner settings in Berlin. ⊠ *Märkisches Ufer 10*, ☎ *030/2406–2904. AE, DC, MC, V.*

$$$ ✕ **Trenta Sei.** The Trenta Sei is very modern, very elegant, and very sophisticated in its style, food, and service. In a nutshell, it's a very good but not excellent Italian restaurant. The small, somewhat overpriced menu is reduced to all-too-familiar Italian dishes, with only a hint of a difference. The Trenta Sei also charges you for the prime location: a panoramic view of the Gendarmenmarkt. In summer the restaurant is one of only two that puts its tables and chairs on the square's south end. ⊠ *Markgrafenstr. 36*, ☎ *030/2045–2630. AE, MC, V.*

$ ✕ **Rosmini Pastamanufaktur.** Eating lunch at the Pastamanufaktur
★ tells you a lot about the people who live and work in the Mitte district. You'll see freelancers and media or Internet entrepreneurs in sneakers along with some stiff-suit types from the government. The daily pasta menu has a special lunch price until 5. All the sauces are homemade. ⊠ *Invalidenstr. 151*, ☎ *030/2809–6844. No credit cards. No lunch weekends.*

Spanish

$ ✕ **Yosoy.** The ideal nightspot for the party crowd, this Spanish restau-
★ rant serves a vast variety of tapas for €2.50 each or as a medley for just €10. The atmosphere of this popular place near the Hackesche Höfe is always lively and, thanks to the Spanish men circling the blond German Juanitas, always flirtatious. ⊠ *Rosenthaler Str. 37*, ☎ *030/ 2839–1213. AE, DC, MC, V.*

South American

$$ ✕ **Brazil.** One of the Mitte scene's darlings, this restaurant is more about what Germans imagine Brazil to be like than about the real thing. Exceptions are the tequila and *caipirinha* cocktails and some of the dishes, such as the black-bean chowder or the fish and *gambas* (prawns) fried in chili sauce. The food is generally standard-quality fare. The real draw here are the gregarious twenty-somethings. ⊠ *Gormannstr. 22*, ☎ *030/ 2859–9026. DC, V. No lunch.*

Prenzlauer Berg

Berlin's northeastern district had a special reputation for its freewheeling restaurant scene even in Socialist times. Today tourists from around the world find their way to thriving Kollwitzplatz.

Chinese

$ ✕ **Ostwind.** "East Wind," as the basement restaurant's name translates,
★ definitely carries you away to Beijing. The standard and good Chinese food attracts a young crowd. A new experience for many might be the Chinese dim-sum brunch on Sunday. The Ostwind doesn't use any MSG in its meals—something rare in Berlin's Chinese restaurants. ⊠ *Husemannstr. 13*, ☎ *030/441–5951. No credit cards. No lunch Mon.–Sat.*

Eastern European and Russian

$$ ✕ **Pasternak.** If you planned to travel on to Moscow after your stay in Berlin, do some prep work here. When the Pasternak opened, shortly after German reunification, its very modest rooms, looking rather like a dusty pub, quickly became a safe haven for Russian intellectuals, while East Berlin's art scene (Russian-speaking thanks to the GDR school system) quickly followed and mingled. Those days might be over, but you still can enjoy borscht or a hearty beef Stroganoff here while listening to Russian music—it's often live, played by traveling Russian musicians. ⊠ *Knaackstr. 22–24,* ☎ *030/4413–399. No credit cards.*

French

$$
★ ✕ **Gugelhof.** Since former president Bill Clinton was pampered here, the Gugelhof has changed dramatically: tourists flood the small restaurant and sample its French, Swiss, and southern German cuisine. Long-time guests claim that the Gugelhof has lost its charm, but if you show up for lunch you can still experience that special mixture of Alsatian hospitality and the Prenzlauer Berg's alternative attitude. Specialties include self-made dishes cooked in a personal *Raclette,* swiss cheese fondue, and *Flammekuchen* (a kind of pizza). Bill Clinton, by the way, refrained from eating the blood sausage, potatoes, and pork that are part of the *choucroute.* Reservations are advised. ⊠ *Knaackstr. 37,* ☎ *030/442–9229. AE, MC, V.*

German

$–$$ ✕ **Soda.** After a tour of Prenzlauer Berg, Soda is a good place to stop and have lunch or an early dinner. The restaurant is always crowded and very noisy, but does capture the district's trendy culture scene. The chefs don't really have a mission statement, so the resulting meals are an adventurous mixture of German, Italian, Spanish, and French recipes. ⊠ *Schönhauser Allee 36,* ☎ *030/4405–8708. MC, V.*

$$ ✕ **Zander.** One of the few upscale restaurants in the Kollwitzplatz neighborhood, newcomer Zander is trying to put regional Berlin-Brandenburg cuisine back on the map. The kitchen is committed to using only the freshest produce brought in from Brandenburg. A good way to sample dishes is the *Kiez-Menü* (neighborhood menu), two courses for only €7.50, or the three-course *Tagesmenü* (menu of the day), for around €26, which includes a glass of wine and mineral water. ⊠ *Kollwitzstr. 50,* ☎ *030/4405–7679. MC, V.*

Italian

$$$ ✕ **Schwarzenraben.** No other restaurant in Berlin exemplifies the arrival of the New East better than Schwarzenraben. At its white-clothed
★ tables, uncomfortably squeezed together in a long, narrow room, the rich and beautiful of the new metropolis gather to toast their rise. The atmosphere is noisy and not very elegant. The cooking lets you discover new Italian recipes such as Milanese veal hocks. ⊠ *Neue Schönhauser Str. 13,* ☎ *030/2839–1698. Reservations essential. AE, DC, MC, V.*

$$ ✕ **Trattoria Paparazzi.** There aren't any real members of the paparazzi here, even though the former cultural and political elite of East Germany like to dine on the superb pasta here. The chef, Doris Burneleit, was once famous for running East Berlin's only Italian restaurant. After moving west and then returning east, she has found her way back to her roots, continuously inventing new pasta dishes. ⊠ *Husemannstr. 35,* ☎ *030/440–7333. No credit cards. No lunch.*

Kreuzberg

Turkish and Middle Eastern food is king in Kreuzberg, Berlin's most diverse district. Most eateries can be found on Oranienstrasse and in the Kottbusser Tor neighborhood. A few restaurants that are more upscale are scattered through the district, and mostly offer vegetarian or jazzed-up traditional German cuisine.

Austrian

$$ ✕ **Thymian.** The city's best mostly vegetarian restaurant has a plain
★ setting where guests can concentrate on superb dishes. Fish such as perch, grouper, salmon, tuna, and trout is offered in various styles and is often pan-fried. The atmosphere is rather relaxed, thanks to the fascinating

mix of Kreuzberg patrons. The restaurant's name alludes to thyme, one of the cook's favorite spices, though plenty of other fresh herbs are used here. A German specialty here are *Bioweine,* mostly crisp white wines from ecologically sound wineries. Reservations are advised. ⊠ *Gneisenaustr. 57,* ☎ *030/6981–5206. MC. No lunch. Closed Mon.*

French

$$$ ✕ **Cochon Bourgeois.** Virtually unknown even among many Francophiles because of its location, the small Cochon Bourgeois prepares top-quality French cuisine. Chef Günter Behrmann prefers to cook the heavier and heartier French recipes, including many beef dishes and seafood soups. The restaurant is far from elegant; it's really more down to earth, with its bistro tables, bare wooden floor, and nonexistent decor. The Südstern U-Bahn station is a five-minute walk away. ⊠ *Fichtestr. 24,* ☎ *030/693–0101. No credit cards. Closed Sun.–Mon. No lunch.*

German

$$$$ ✕ **Altes Zollhaus.** In a historic farmhouse in the middle of Kreuzberg, ★   Altes Zollhaus is the place to find excellent German country cooking in Berlin's Turkish district. It's an island of tranquillity, where you'll be pampered with good old German hospitality under a soaring roof and wooden beams. You won't find à la carte options, but two- to five-course meals here. The classic entrée is the *Brandenburger Bauernente mit Wirsing und Kartoffelpuffern* (Brandenburg farm duck, with savoy cabbage and potato fritters), baked crisp and spicy. ⊠ *Carl-Herz-Ufer 30,* ☎ *030/692–3300. Reservations essential. AE, DC, MC, V. Closed Sun.– Mon. No lunch.*

$$$$ ✕ **E. T. A. Hoffmann.** Don't expect any traditional homages to tradi-★   tional German cooking, as the name of this fine restaurant implies (Hoffmann is a renowned German romantic poet). Chef Tim Raue, after an odyssey through several of Berlin's best restaurants, has finally found his home. Here he dares to cook his own way through tastes and styles of the world, creating a true fusion of foods, with a heavy dose of Asian-German combinations. ⊠ *Hotel Riehmers Hofgarten, Yorckstr. 83,* ☎ *030/7809–8800. AE, MC, V. Closed Sun.–Mon.*

$$–$$$$ ✕ **Abendmahl.** The exquisite vegetarian cuisine here proves that a meatless meal doesn't have to leave you hungry. Chef Udo Einenkel gives his hearty creations playful names such as "Flammendes Inferno" (flaming inferno), a fish curry whose spiciness means business, or "The Day I Shot Andy Warhol" (an ice-cream sampler). Healthy eaters such as Wim Wenders and Nina Hagen are among the artsy crowd frequenting the small restaurant. ⊠ *Muskauer Str. 9,* ☎ *030/612–5170. No credit cards.*

$$ ✕ **Riehmers.** A charming German restaurant with a lovely courtyard, Riehmers is an inviting escape from the gritty street scene of Kreuzberg. The menu changes often, according to season and to which fresh produce is available, but generally leans toward meat dishes dishes like *Poulardenbrust auf Balsamicosauce* (barbecued chicken with balsamic sauce), served with vegetables and potato gratin. ⊠ *Hagelberger Str. 9,* ☎ *030/786–8608. MC, V. Closed Mon. No lunch Tues.–Sat.*

$–$$ ✕ **Grossbeerenkeller.** This meat-and-potatoes cellar restaurant, with ★   massive dark-oak furniture and decorative antlers, is undoubtedly one of the most atmospheric dining spots in town. Owner and bartender Ingeborg Zinn-Baier presents such dishes as *Sülze vom Schweinekopf mit Bratkartoffeln und Remoulade* (diced pork with home fries and herb sauce) or *Kasseler Nacken mit Grünkohl* (boiled salt-pork with green cabbage). Her fried potatoes, flecked with bacon, onions, and spices are excellent. There's outdoor seating too. ⊠ *Grossbeerenstr. 90,* ☎ *030/251–3064. No credit cards. Closed Sun.*

Indian

$ ✕ **Shanti.** A longtime Kreuzberg *Kiezgrösse* (resident), the Shanti
★ brings northern Indian food, music, and style to wild Oranienstrasse.
All the people at the restaurant, from punks with red hair to local In-
dians, get along just fine. This is probably due to a mutual love and
respect of inexpensive soup and vitamin-packed fruit salads (often
made with a shot of rum), which are a perfect finish to a spicy meal.
⊠ *Oranienstr. 6,* ☎ *030/6128–1733. AE, DC, MC, V.*

Indonesian

$-$$ ✕ **Tuk-Tuk.** This small Indonesian restaurant at the border of Schöneberg
★ and Kreuzberg hosts a German just-turned-40 backpacker crowd that
loves to indulge in memories of trips taken to Bali more than a few
years ago. The atmosphere is genuine, the menu makes note of all of
the spicy dishes, and vegetarian options are abundant. ⊠ *Gross-
görschenstr. 2,* ☎ *030/781–1588. MC, V. No lunch.*

Italian

$$-$$$ ✕ **Sale e Tabacchi.** Dark woods, seemingly endless leather benches, crisp
linens, and a small courtyard in the back make this a prime setting (not
to mention the good-looking waiters). But the buzzing atmosphere is often
filled with the annoying *grandezza* of excited shouting, running, and bluster of the personnel. Admittedly, the authentic Italian country cooking
is very good, but it's not very imaginative and a bit overpriced. Reservations are advised. ⊠ *Kochstr. 18,* ☎ *030/252–1155. AE, MC, V.*

$$ ✕ **Osteria No. 1.** The staff at this buzzing restaurant is certainly as proud
as its name, and most guests feel it is indeed the best Italian osteria in
town. But since reunification, a lot of the dining-out crowd has flocked
east, and the old cutting-edge feel to this eatery has been blunted. The
food, primarily the pizzas, is still good. A big plus is the Osteria's loca-
tion, close to the Kreuzberg's Viktoriapark: after dinner you can walk
over to the Golgatha beer garden and club and dance the night away. Reser-
vations are advised. ⊠ *Kreuzbergstr. 71,* ☎ *030/786–9162. AE, V.*

Mexican

$$ ✕ **Joe Pena's Cantina y Bar.** Joe Pena's, whose clientele is a typical
Kreuzberg mixture of students and wanna-be media stars, has the
atmosphere of a never-ending house party. It's not too crowded
though—you can pretty much get a table right away. The food includes
spicy Mexican standards. ⊠ *Marheinikepl. 3–4,* ☎ *030/693–6044. AE,
DC, MC, V. No lunch.*

$-$$ ✕ **Lone Star Taqueria.** With its faded yellow paint on plain walls,
Lone Star Taqueria, despite its name, mostly serves Mexican food; not
Tex-Mex fusion. In summer you can enjoy quesadillas and baked tor-
tilla-chips dishes along with good (and cheap) wines at the long wooden
tables outdoors. It seems like all of Bergtmannstrasse, including many
students and shop owners, comes over to mingle in the early evening,
trying to forget that Kreuzberg is not some romantic Mexican town.
⊠ *Bergmannstr. 11,* ☎ *030/692–7182. AE, V.*

Thai

$-$$ ✕ **Maneeya.** People with sensitive lips and tongues claim that Maneeya
★ is the spiciest Thai restaurant around—but even with a burning mouth,
every one of them would return. To get here, you do have to travel to
the seedy area of Neukölln, but you'll be rewarded with a friendly and
authentic Thai atmosphere and dishes such as *Gebratene Meeres-
früchte in Currysauce und Kokosnussmilch* (fried seafood with curry
sauce and coconut milk) or *Knusprige Ente mit Knoblauchchilisauce
und Gemüse* (crisp duck with garlic and chili sauce and vegetables).
⊠ *Kienitzer Str. 22,* ☎ *030/681–8233. AE, MC, V. Closed Thurs. No
lunch.*

Zehlendorf

Within the vast forests, parks, and lake landscapes of southwestern Berlin, in the district of Zehlendorf, the typical eatery is an *Ausflugslokale,* a simple restaurant in a great location.

Contemporary

$$$$ ✕ **Vivaldi.** The formal wood-paneled dining room offers the epitome
★ of fine dining, and if you are not familiar with extraordinarily elegant settings, exceptional service, and the nuances of flawless cuisine, you might be intimidated at first. But once you've sampled the appetizers of a six-course meal prepared by Swiss newcomer Paul Urchs, tasted the well-chosen vintages, and started your entrée (mostly game or fish), you'll get used to the euphoric satisfaction. ⌧ *Ritz-Carlton Schlosshotel, Brahmsstr. 10,* ☎ *030/895–840. Reservations essential. AE, DC, MC, V. Closed Sun. No lunch.*

French

$$$ ✕ **Grand Slam.** The Grand Slam continues to live up to its legendary
★ reputation as one of Berlin's most reliable restaurants for fine dining. Chef Jürgen Fehrenbach puts a German spin on classic French cuisine, which is particularly successful when it comes to à la carte seafood dishes. ⌧ *Gottfried-von-Cramm-Weg 47–55,* ☎ *030/825-3810. AE, DC, MC, V. Closed Sun.–Mon. No lunch.*

German

$ ✕ **Blockhaus Nikolskoe.** Prussian king Frederick Wilhelm III built this Russian-style wooden lodge for his daughter Charlotte, wife of Russian czar Nicholas I. South of the city, in Glienecker Park, it offers open-air riverside dining in summer. Game dishes are prominently featured. Wannsee is the closest S-Bahn station. ⌧ *Nikolskoer Weg 15,* ☎ *030/ 805-2914. DC, MC, V. Closed Thurs.*

4 · LODGING

No other European city is experiencing
a construction boom of new hotels like
Berlin's. Appropriate for a capital with
some downtime to make up for, most new
lodgings are ultramodern first-class luxury
accommodations, often behind historic
facades. Old-style, charming little boutique
hotels and private, intimate pensions
are also a city trademark, and offer a
considerable variety of choice.

By Jürgen
Scheunemann

A**S A EUROPEAN METROPOLIS DEMANDS,** all major international first-class hotel chains are represented in Berlin. Even the luxurious ones are but a faint reminder of the prewar era, when Berlin was considered Europe's hospitality capital. Elegance and style were bombed to rubble during World War II, and only a few native havens were rebuilt. Moderately priced pensions and small hotels offering good value are common in western districts like Charlottenburg, Schöneberg, and Wilmersdorf; many of these date from the turn of the 20th century and preserve some traditional character.

Year-round business conventions and the influx of summer tourists mean you should make reservations well in advance. If you arrive without reservations, consult hotel boards at airports and train stations, which show hotels with vacancies; or go to the tourist offices at Tegel Airport, at the Ostbahnhof or Zoologischer Garten train stations, or in the Europa-Center for help.

Prices

CATEGORY	COST*
$$$$	over €250
$$$	€150–€250
$$	€75–€150
$	under €75

All prices are for a standard double room, including tax and service

Western Downtown

$$$$ 🏨 **Inter-Continental Berlin.** Popular with American business travelers, the rooms and suites here show exquisite taste. The more recently renovated east wing has views of the vast Tiergarten park. Service is efficient and smooth, but compared to hotels of similar quality the atmosphere here is bland. ⊠ *Budapester Str. 2, D–10787,* ☎ *030/26020,* FAX *030/2602–2600,* WEB *www.berlin.interconti.com. 510 rooms, 67 suites. 3 restaurants, bar, in-room data ports, minibars, no-smoking floor, room service, pool, hot tub, sauna, exercise room, baby-sitting, dry cleaning, laundry service, concierge, business services, convention center, meeting room, parking (fee). AE, DC, MC, V.* ·

$$$–$$$$ 🏨 **Hotel Palace.** This is the only first-class hotel directly in the heart
★   of the western downtown area, and probably the only hotel of its caliber in which each guest room is individually decorated. The interior is mostly done in dark blues or reds and dark-color woods. The spacious business and corner suites are a good deal; you might also want to ask for the special Panda Suite or the Zackebarsch Suite, both personally designed by the hotel's directors. Because of its low profile, the hotel is a favorite among the international film stars who attend the Berlin Film Festival in February. ⊠ *Europa-Center, Budapester Str. 26, D–10789,* ☎ *030/25020,* FAX *030/2502–1161,* WEB *www.palace.de. 239 rooms, 43 suites. 3 restaurants, 2 bars, in-room data ports, in-room safes, minibars, no-smoking floor, room service, pool, barbershop, hot tub, massage, sauna, steam room, health club, shops, baby-sitting, dry cleaning, laundry service, concierge, business services, convention center, meeting room, parking (fee). AE, DC, MC, V.*

$$$–$$$$ 🏨 **Kempinski Hotel Bristol Berlin.** Rebuilt in 1952, the "Kempi" is a renowned Berlin classic, yet its age makes it hard to compete with the many new first-class hotels opening up around town. All rooms and suites are luxurious, if somewhat small, and have marble bathrooms and cable TV. Reserve a room in the "superior" category and you'll get all the elegance and space you'll need at a fair rate. Children under

12 stay free if they share their parents' room. The best shopping is at your doorstep, and there are some fine boutiques within the hotel as well. ⊠ *Kurfürstendamm 27, D–10719,* ☎ *030/884–340,* FAX *030/883–6075,* WEB *www.kempinski-berlin.de. 301 rooms, 52 suites. 2 restaurants, bar, lobby lounge, in-room data ports, minibars, no-smoking rooms, room service, pool, hair salon, massage, sauna, gym, shops, babysitting, dry cleaning, laundry service, concierge, business services, meeting room, parking (fee). AE, DC, MC, V.*

$$$–$$$$ 🏨 **Crowne Plaza Berlin City Centre.** Hardly a minute goes by without a busfull of American tourists pulling up in front. Nonetheless, this is a charming and personal hotel right off Tauentzien Strasse and just a few steps from the KaDeWe emporium. The guest rooms and the service are upscale although not particularly special. If you don't mind the crowds, this is a desirable option. ⊠ *Nürnbergerstr. 65, D–10787,* ☎ *030/210–070,* FAX *030/213–2009,* WEB *www.cp-berlin.com. 415 rooms, 10 suites. Restaurant, bar, minibars, in-room data ports, no-smoking rooms, room service, massage, sauna, exercise room, babysitting, dry cleaning, laundry service, concierge, business services, meeting rooms, parking (fee). AE, DC, MC, V.*

$$$–$$$$ 🏨 **Dorint Schweizerhof Berlin.** The once ailing Schweizerhof has reopened
★ under the management of the aspiring Dorint-Gruppe and has thus transformed completely, emerging stylish to the last detail. The new Schweizerhof is a fine example of a practical yet luxurious business hotel, with an extensive wellness center and pool area (complete with real palm trees), a hip restaurant called Xxenia (serving a mix of hearty Brandenburg fare and international fish creations), as well many artworks by Scandinavian painter Ter Hell. All in all, it is the best choice in its class in the western downtown area. ⊠ *Budapester Str. 25, D–10787,* ☎ *030/26960,* FAX *030/2696–1000,* WEB *www.dorint.de. 384 rooms, 22 suites. 2 restaurants, bar, minibars, in-room data ports, no-smoking rooms, room service, indoor pool, steam room, massage, sauna, health club, baby-sitting, dry cleaning, laundry service, concierge, business services, meeting rooms, parking (fee). AE, DC, MC, V.*

$$$–$$$$ 🏨 **Steigenberger Berlin.** Of all the traditional first-class hotels in what was West Berlin, the Steigenberger has probably suffered most from the rise of new competitors in the former East Berlin. These days, however, the hotel is on the upswing, thanks to its central location (just off Ku'damm) and consistently high standard in service, food, and rooms. A good deal is a deluxe room, with elegant maple-wood furniture, marbled wallpaper, and heavy rugs covering carpeted floors. The rate includes amenities such as a private lounge, daily newspapers, beverages, late checkout, and more. ⊠ *Los-Angeles-Pl. 1, D–10789,* ☎ *030/21270,* FAX *030/212–7799,* WEB *www.steigenberger.de. 397 rooms, 11 suites. 2 restaurants, café, piano bar, in-room data ports, in-room safes, minibars, no-smoking floor, room service, pool, massage, sauna, baby-sitting, dry cleaning, laundry service, concierge, meeting room, parking (fee). AE, DC, MC, V.*

$$$–$$$$ 🏨 **Swissôtel Berlin.** The ultramodern Swissôtel opened in mid-2001 and tries to make a special point of providing better service, larger rooms, and better (Swiss) food than comparable hotels. Its biggest advantage, however, may be its location at the corner of Ku'damm and Joachimsthaler Strasse. Don't worry about the traffic noise: all rooms have soundproof windows, and the the nighttime view of the high-rises and bright city lights is fantastic. ⊠ *Kurfürstendamm 227, D–10719,* ☎ *030/8540–9268,* FAX *030/8540–9269,* WEB *www.swissotel.com. 315 rooms, 31 suites. Restaurants, bar, in-room data ports, minibars, no-smoking rooms, room service, concierge, massage, sauna, health club, baby-sitting, dry cleaning, laundry service, concierge, business services, meeting room, parking (fee). AE, DC, MC, V.*

Western Berlin Lodging

KEY

i Tourist Information
S S-Bahn
U U-Bahn

0   1/2 mile
0   3/4 km

$$$ ⌕ **Alsterhof.** Welcome to the Alsterhof, most certainly the friendliest
★ hotel in town. The fancy rooms have a rustic look and are rather
small, but the nicely decorated bathrooms make up for that. if you want
to rest your feet after shopping at nearby KaDeWe, sit down with a
Berliner Weisse mit Schuss (a beer with green woodruff liquor) in the
hotel's open-air beer garden. ⊠ *Augsburger Str. 5, D–10789, ☎ 030/
212–420,* FAX *030/218–3949,* WEB *www.alsterhof.de. 155 rooms, 45 suites.
Restaurant, bar, café, minibars, in-room data ports, in-room safes, no-
smoking floor, room service, massage, sauna, health club, baby-sitting,
dry cleaning, laundry service, concierge, business services, meeting
rooms, parking (fee). AE, DC, MC, V.*

$$$ ⌕ **Bleibtreu Hotel Berlin.** Even residents of this fashionable street are
★ drawn to the lovely courtyard and café here. The stylish yet tranquil
hotel is owned by one of Berlin's most daring entrepreneurs and attracts
an international crowd that values the airy and bright rooms, the many
objects d'art, and the easygoing atmosphere. The rooms have neutral
tones and natural materials, but you may have to ask for an explana-
tion of the remote-controlled lights, shades, and messaging system. The
location on Bleibtreustrasse is ideal for Ku'damm shopping, and—last
but not least—this is the only hotel in Berlin where beverages from your
minibar are free—prost! ⊠ *Bleibtreustr. 31, D–10707, ☎ 030/884–740,*
FAX *030/8847–4444,* WEB *www.bleibtreu.com. 60 rooms. Restaurant, bar,
minibars, in-room data ports, no-smoking rooms, room service, massage, sauna, baby-sitting, dry cleaning, laundry service, concierge, business services, meeting room, parking (fee). AE, DC, MC, V.*

$$$ ⌕ **Brandenburger Hof Relais & Chateau.** The Brandenburger Hof is one
★ of Berlin's best-kept first-class secrets. That it inhabits a late-19th-cen-
tury Wilhelmine mansion is alluring enough. This privately owned
hotel, on a quiet side street within walking distance of Kurfürsten-
damm, has an interior design that is strictly Bauhaus, while the lobby
and the beautiful winter garden are more classical. If possible, don't miss
the candlelight dinner at the hotel's Michelin-star restaurant, Quadriga,
or the chance to visit Thaleia, where you will find an extraordinary spa
program of Shiatsu massage and Japanese facial treatments. ⊠ *Eisleben-
erstr. 14, D–10789, ☎ 030/214–050,* FAX *030/2140–5300,* WEB *www.bran-
denburger-hof.com. 78 rooms, 4 suites. Restaurant, piano bar, minibars,
in-room data ports, no-smoking rooms, room service, massage, sauna,
spa, gym, baby-sitting, dry cleaning, laundry service, concierge, busi-
ness services, meeting rooms, parking (fee). AE, DC, MC, V.*

$$$ ⌕ **Golden Tulip Residenz Hotel Berlin.** This historic art nouveau hotel
offers simple late-19th-century-style rooms with high ceilings and tall
windows, and a quiet location close to Kurfürstendamm and the transport hub of Zoo Station. The long, meandering corridors and heavy
room key (which you leave with the front desk) do make the hotel feel
pleasantly old-fashioned. Rooms on the top floor have more modern
furnishings and exude a homey atmosphere. Service is up to international standards, and the restaurant serves good German fare. ⊠
Meinekestr. 9, D–10719, ☎ 030/884–430, FAX *030/882–4726,* WEB
*www.hotel-residenz.com. 77 rooms, 4 suites. Restaurant, bar, minibars,
no-smoking floor, room service, sauna, gym, dry cleaning, laundry service, business services, meeting rooms, free parking. AE, DC, MC, V.*

$$$ ⌕ **Hecker's Hotel.** High hopes and high ambitions are the trademarks
of this ultramodern, ultrachic—and ultimately ultraboring—hotel.
The minimalist decor of the lobby and rooms may well have once been
avant-garde but now simply looks outdated. As its sleek but notori-
ously empty bar suggests, Hecker's is only a place for design buffs. The
hospitality, though, is close to perfect. When you tire of all the blacks,
grays, and browns, escape to the colorful Cassambalis restaurant, next
door, for some hearty and authentic fare. ⊠ *Grolmanstr. 35, D–10623,*

☎ *030/88900,* FAX *030/889–0260,* WEB *www.heckers-hotel.com. 71 rooms. Restaurant, bar, minibars, in-room data ports, no-smoking rooms, room service, massage, sauna, gym, baby-sitting, dry cleaning, laundry service, concierge, business services, meeting room, parking (fee). AE, DC, MC, V.*

$$$ ⊡ **Hotel am Zoo.** One of western Berlin's oldest family-owned hotels, the elegant Hotel am Zoo is centrally located and a perfect starting point for a stroll on the Ku'damm. Guest rooms are fairly large (some even feature a separate sitting area). Not all rooms face the boulevard, and thanks to soundproof windows, you won't hear any noise from the street. ⊠ *Kurfürstendamm 25, D–10719,* ☎ *030/884–370,* FAX *030/8843–7710,* WEB *www.hotel-am-zoo.de. 136 rooms. Bar, minibars, in-room data ports, in-room safes, no-smoking rooms, room service, dry cleaning, laundry service, concierge, business services, meeting rooms, parking (fee). AE, DC, MC, V.*

$$$ ⊡ **Hotel Savoy.** The grand days of the 1930s, when stars like Greta Garbo
★ checked in, are clearly over, but this old-fashioned yet classic hotel remains popular and draws a loyal clientele. Its discreet charm is understated, but it's a must if you love Old Europe design and hospitality. The decor is especially nice, as each and every room has been individually furnished using soft colors and exquisite materials. Reading a copy of the *Times* of London is a good way to enjoy part of the day, while your nights can be spent in the unique *La Casa del Habano,* a Cuban-licensed smoking club where you can puff away on real Havana cigars. ⊠ *Fasanenstr. 9–10, D–10623,* ☎ *030/311–030,* FAX *030/3110–3333,* WEB *www.hotel-savoy.com. 115 rooms, 10 suites. Restaurant, bar, minibars, in-room data ports, no-smoking rooms, room service, massage, sauna, exercise room, baby-sitting, dry cleaning, laundry service, concierge, business services, meeting room, parking (fee). AE, DC, MC, V.*

$$–$$$ ⊡ **Best Western Hotel Boulevard am Kurfürstendamm.** A longtime fixture on the Ku'damm, the Hotel Boulevard is a solid middle-range hotel offering simple, outdated-looking rooms done in dull colors and late 1980s decor. Its location is its huge plus, and the rooftop terrace has a nice panorama view. Service is reliable but not overly friendly. ⊠ *Kurfürstendamm 12, D–10719,* ☎ *030/884–250,* FAX *030/8842–5450,* WEB *www.hotel-boulevard.com. 57 rooms. Bistro, minibars, in-room data ports, in-room safes, no-smoking floor, dry cleaning, laundry service, concierge, business services, meeting rooms, parking (fee). AE, DC, MC, V.*

$$–$$$ ⊡ **Comfort Hotel Berlin Frühling am Zoo.** Right in the the midst of bustling Ku'damm and Joachimsthaler Strasse, one of Germany's busiest street corners, this mid-range hotel is all about centrality. The place tries to exude an elegant Old World atmosphere but ultimately fails because rooms lack the nice little touches that make a hotel unforgettable. Breakfast is served in a very pleasant room, though, and the staff is extremely helpful. Don't worry about the traffic outside— your windows are completely soundproof. Rates are somewhat high for what you get in rooms and service, but the location is outstanding. ⊠ *Kurfürstendamm 17 , D–10719,* ☎ *030/881–8083,* FAX *030/881– 6483,* WEB *www.hotelchoice.com. 64 rooms, 2 suites, 7 apartments. Breakfast room, bar, minibars, in-room data ports, in-room safes, kitchenettes, no-smoking floor, health club, dry cleaning, laundry service, meeting room, parking (fee). AE, DC, MC, V.*

$$–$$$ ⊡ **Concept Hotel.** The Concept is a young and innovative hotel that aims to please in every possible way. It succeeds in attention to detail and adding those special little touches, such as long beds (Germans are tall on average) and impeccable service. The fairly large rooms may be a bit too flowery, and the furnishings a bit home-office-like. Suites are a good deal as they all have a private terrace. When making a reservation, insist on a front or courtyard room (you might hear squeaking S-Bahn trains in

a back room). ⊠ *Grolmanstr. 41–43, D–10623,* ☎ *030/884–260,* FAX
030/8842–6500, WEB *www.concept-hotel.com. 139 rooms, 14 suites.*
Restaurant, bar, minibars, in-room data ports, no-smoking floors, sauna,
gym, solarium, baby-sitting, dry cleaning, laundry service, concierge, busi-
ness services, meeting rooms, parking (fee). AE, DC, MC, V.

$$–$$$ ⌂ **Hotel Avantgarde.** You'll be paying for the location and proximity
to the Kaiser-Wilhelm-Gedächniskirche here, rather than for the rooms
or the service. Behind the building's neobaroque facade is an outdated
yet nice hotel with surprisingly large rooms and a great breakfast buffet. Another advantage is the soundproof windows in the rooms. ⊠ *Kur-*
fürstendamm 15, D–10719, ☎ *030/884–8330,* FAX *030/882–4011,* WEB
www.hotel-avantgarde.com. 27 rooms. Breakfast room, bar, minibars,
in-room data ports, laundry service, meeting room. AE, DC, MC, V.

$$–$$$ ⌂ **Hotel Mondial.** No matter that the Mondial's tinted-window facade,
lobby, and restaurant look dated, the hotel is a good and affordable
choice on western Kurfürstendamm. Guest rooms have been tastefully
refurbished, and the hotel particularly excels at accommodating people with disabilities. ⊠ *Kurfürstendamm 47, D–10707,* ☎ *030/884–*
110, FAX *030/8841–1150,* WEB *www.hotel-mondial.com. 75 rooms, 1 suite.*
Restaurant, bar, minibars, in-room data ports, in-room safes, no-smok-
ing rooms, room service, indoor pool, sauna, solarium, baby-sitting,
dry cleaning, laundry service, concierge, business services, meeting
room, free parking. AE, DC, MC, V.

$$–$$$ ⌂ **Hotel Sylter Hof.** It's unfortunate that this high-end-of-middle-range
hotel hides its advantages so well. Hardly known outside Berlin, ad-
joined by a cheesy night club, and behind an unappealing facade, the
hotel, once you've entered the lavish and elegant lobby, exudes a pleasant and soothing atmosphere. You won't find the jet-set hot air you
might encounter in other hotels of this category. The rooms are adequately furnished, and the rustic restaurant, Friesenstube, serves hearty
north German fare. ⊠ *Kurfürstenstr. 114–16, D–10787,* ☎ *030/*
21200, FAX *030/214–2826,* WEB *www.sylterhof-berlin.de. 126 rooms, 40*
suites. Breakfast room, bar, café, minibars, in-room data ports, in-room
safes, no-smoking floor, room service, massage, sauna, gym, baby-sit-
ting, dry cleaning, laundry service, concierge, business services, meet-
ing room, parking (fee). AE, DC, MC, V.

$$ ⌂ **Art Nouveau Hotel.** The ride to the fourth floor, where this small hotel-
pension is located, is a thrill in itself. The antique elevator runs directly
in the middle of a winding staircase—a typical Berlin construction. Once
upstairs, you'll be captivated by the minimalist yet comfortably furnished
art nouveau rooms, even those that remind you of your dorm room (with
a bed lying directly on the parquet floor and the TV set on a small table).
Other rooms resemble those of a grand city mansion. With bare walls
(with only one original and interesting artwork featured) and high ceil-
ings, this typical Charlottenburger *Altbauwohnung* (old apartment) is
one of the nicest downtown pensions. ⊠ *Leibnitzstr. 59, D–10629,*
☎ *030/327–7440,* FAX *030/3277–4440,* WEB *www.hotelartnouveau.de.*
13 rooms, 2 suites. Breakfast room, café, no-smoking rooms, dry clean-
ing, laundry service, parking (fee). AE, MC, V.

$$ ⌂ **Hotel Astoria.** This privately owned and operated hotel-pension is
one of the most traditional in Berlin. It provides every service with a
personal touch. Rooms are spacious, though the 1980s furniture may
seem outdated. The location is good for exploring the Ku'damm area,
yet it's on a quiet side street. Weekend specials offer discounts of €10
(single) or €35 (double) per night for a two-night stay. There are also
several package deals for stays of up to six nights. ⊠ *Fasanenstr. 2,*
D–10623, ☎ *030/312–4067,* FAX *030/312–5027. 31 rooms, 1 suite. Bar,*
minibars, in-room safes, no-smoking rooms, room service, dry clean-
ing, laundry service, parking (fee). AE, DC, MC, V.

$$ ⊞ **Hotel Garni Askanischer Hof.** One of the last family-owned hotels on the Kufurürstendamm, the traditional German Askanischer Hof is also one of this area's friendliest places to stay. Mrs. Glinicke will make you feel at home, keeping herself busy in the beautiful 19th-century breakfast room. Guest rooms are lavishly furnished, with chandeliers, old-time furniture, and heavy carpets, attracting not only tourists but also prominent figures like star photographer Helmut Newton. ⊠ *Kurfürstendamm 53, D–10707,* ☎ *030/881–8033,* FAX *030/881–7206. 16 rooms. Restaurant, bar, minibars, in-room data ports, in-room safes, no-smoking rooms, bicycles, baby-sitting, dry cleaning, laundry service, business services, meeting room, fee and free parking. AE.*

$$ ⊞ **Hotel Berliner Hof.** The Berliner Hof's biggest advantage—its central location a few steps from KaDeWe—is also a serious drawback. It's in a rather seedy shopping mall next to the Europa-Center, and once you leave the hotel you are right on Tauentzien, Berlin's always-crowded and congested western boulevard. Rooms, on the other hand, are very large and well equipped with a desk, TV set, and hair dryer. All in all, given the location, the rates are unbeatable. ⊠ *Tauentzien-str. 8, D–10789,* ☎ *030/254–950,* FAX *030/262–3065,* WEB *www.berliner-hof.com. 80 rooms. Breakfast room, minibars, in-room data ports, in-room safes, no-smoking rooms. AE, DC, MC, V.*

$$ ⊞ **Hotel Garni Hardenberg Berlin.** This historic old-style hotel in the heart of the western downtown is not a quiet place, and the rooms have surely seen better days. Yet the excellent service and the extraordinary breakfast buffet also make this a reliable choice. ⊠ *Joachimstaler Str. 39–40, D–10623,* ☎ *030/882–3071,* FAX *030/881–5170,* WEB *www.hotel-hardenberg.com. 41 rooms. Minibars, in-room data ports, in-room safes, no-smoking rooms, meeting room, parking (fee). AE, DC, MC, V.*

$$ ⊞ **Hotel-Pension Augusta.** A longtime favorite among repeat tourists, the intimate Hotel Augusta is one of the last small hotels on Fasanenstrasse, the Ku'damm's chicest side street. Rooms are decorated in pastel colors, with an odd mixture of frilly and practical elements. You'll especially like the canopy-style bed with curtains and the practical white furniture. All rooms have a private bathroom, and the breakfast buffet is outstanding. ⊠ *Fasanenstr. 22, D–10719,* ☎ *030/883–5028 or (toll-free) 0800/883–5028,* FAX *030/882–4779,* WEB *www.hotel-augusta.de. 33 rooms. Breakfast room, minibars, in-room data ports, in-room safes, no-smoking rooms, dry cleaning, laundry service, parking (fee). AE, MC, V.*

$$ ⊞ **Hotel-Pension Dittberner.** If you've ever wanted to stay in a real Berlin
★ pension, this is the place. The Dittberner, close to Olivaer Platz and next to the Ku'damm, is a typical family-run small hotel in a turn-of-the-20th-century house. The service may sometimes be a bit disorganized, and some of the furniture in the large rooms a little worn, but the warm atmosphere, breakfast buffet, and good rates more than make up for it. ⊠ *Wielandstr. 26, D–10707,* ☎ *030/884–6950,* FAX *030/885–4046. 22 rooms. Breakfast room, dry cleaning, laundry service, concierge, meeting room. No credit cards.*

$$ ⊞ **Hotel Schöneberg.** This three-star hotel behind a beautiful art nouveau facade is a bit out of the way in southern Schöneberg. For a hotel this small, service is very reliable. Although the hodgepodge of styles and decorations in the guest rooms is not the most tasteful, the soft and fairly large beds make up it. ⊠ *Hauptstr. 135, D–10827,* ☎ *030/780–9660,* FAX *030/7809–6620,* WEB *www.hotel-schoeneberg.de. 29 rooms, 2 suites. Breakfast room, bar, minibars, in-room data ports, in-room safes, no-smoking rooms, baby-sitting, dry cleaning, laundry service, business services, meeting rooms, parking (fee). AE, MC, V.*

$$ ⊞ **Quality Hotel Imperial.** As a member of the American Quality Inn hotel chain, this midsize hotel off Ku'damm is your average middle-range hotel with a distinctively American flavor. The relatively small

rooms are somewhat worn out, but the restaurant, Brasserie Vintage (which serves standard German and international fare), and the heated, outdoor rooftop pool, still guarantee a pleasant stay. Be advised, though, that this part of Lietzenburger Strasse is home to some rather seedy nightclubs (although the area is completely safe). ✉ *Lietzenburger Str. 79-81, D–10719,* ☎ *030/880–050,* FAX *030/882–4579,* WEB *www.city-conact-hotels.de. 69 rooms, 12 suites. Brasserie, bar, café, minibars, in-room data ports, no-smoking floor, pool, sauna, exercise room, baby-sitting, dry cleaning, laundry service, concierge, business services, meeting rooms, parking (fee). AE, DC, MC, V.*

$–$$ ★ ⊞ **Hotel-Pension Funk.** Once the huge apartment of international silent film star Asta Nielsen, the Hotel-Pension Funk is a small, pleasant hotel with nice guest rooms. All in all, it exudes an old-style Berlin atmosphere, with heavy dark furniture, thick carpets on parquet floors, and long curtains (just ignore its somewhat dusty appearance). ✉ *Fasanenstr. 69, D–10719,* ☎ *030/882–7193,* FAX *030/883–3329. 15 rooms. Breakfast room. AE, DC, MC, V.*

$–$$ ⊞ **Hotel-Pension Korfu II.** This small pension on a quiet side street off Ku'damm is modern, inexpensive, and comfortable. The Korfu II lacks the atmosphere that so many other small Berlin hotels still have, but the rooms, with their high ceilings and simple furniture, are clean and well kept. Some of the double rooms are more modern and definitely more appealing, decorated with elegant black-and-white furniture. All rooms have a phone and television. ✉ *Rankestr. 35, D–10789,* ☎ *030/ 212–4790,* FAX *030/211–8432,* WEB *www.hp-korfu.de. 19 rooms. Breakfast room, parking (fee). AE, MC, V.*

$–$$ ★ ⊞ **Pension Elite.** A small but upscale pension typical of the side streets off Ku'damm, the Pension Elite caters to adult travelers who enjoy the warm and personal service and the classic-style large rooms. It's also one of the few pensions to welcome pets. ✉ *Rankestr. 9, D–10789,* ☎ *030/881– 5308,* FAX *030/882–5422. 14 rooms. Breakfast room, no-smoking rooms, dry cleaning, laundry service, meeting room, parking (fee). MC, V.*

$–$$ ⊞ **Pension Niebuhr.** This privately run small hotel offers smooth service and a quiet stay on Niebuhrstrasse off Ku'damm. Rooms are simply but tastefully appointed, and the owner will personally serve you breakfast in your room. Taken altogether, this is one of the better pensions in Charlottenburg. ✉ *Niebuhrstr. 74, D–10629,* ☎ *030/324–9595,* FAX *030/324–8021,* WEB *www.pension-niebuhr.de. 12 rooms. Parking (fee). AE, MC, V.*

$ ⊞ **Hotel Börse.** This is not one of the most beautiful or even best-kept small hotels along Kurfürstendamm, but it is definitely the most inexpensive. Above a McDonald's in the heart of the western downtown area, the small Hotel Börse nevertheless provides personal, friendly service and clean (although seemingly worn-out) rooms, which are surprisingly large, given the location. All rooms have a private bathroom, cable TV, and a phone. Be forewarned that breakfast is not the hotel's strength. ✉ *Kurfürstendamm 34, D–10719,* ☎ *030/881–3021,* FAX *030/883–2034. 45 rooms. Breakfast room. V.*

$ ★ ⊞ **Propeller Island City Lodge.** One of Berlin's most eccentric accommodations, this lodging is the creation of multitalented artist Lars Stroschen. Within his home are wildly conceived rooms, such as the dizzying Symbol Room and the monastic Orange Room. Only children traveling with parents get to escape to the Gnome Room, with a low-ceiling keeping those over 4′ 8″ out. There's use of a shared kitchen. Mr. Stroschen will also be happy to prepare dinner for you if you book it in advance. The rooms have neither phones nor TV sets. ✉ *Paulsbornerstr. 10, D–10709,* ☎ *030/893–2533or 030/891–9016,* FAX *030/ 891–8720,* WEB *www.propeller-island.net4.com. 27 rooms. Breakfast room. No credit cards.*

Charlottenburg

$$$-$$$$ ⚏ **Hotel Seehof am Lietzensee.** The prices are way too high for the service and the rooms you get at this traditional Berlin mid-range hotel, but you are paying for proximity to the fairgrounds (just a short walk away) and for the lovely setting of the Lietzensee, just behind the hotel. A nice café terrace overlooks the lake. If there are no fairs or conventions for the time you reserve, you might be able to negotiate a much better deal. ⊠ *Lietzenseeufer 11, D–14057,* ☎ *030/320–020,* FAX *030/3200–2251,* WEB *www.hotel-seehof-berlin.de. 76 rooms, 1 suite. Restaurant, bar, minibars, in-room data ports, no-smoking rooms, room service, massage, indoor pool, sauna, exercise room, baby-sitting, dry cleaning, laundry service, concierge, business services, meeting rooms, free parking. AE, DC, MC, V.*

$$$ ⚏ **Berlin Excelsior Hotel.** As the proud flagship of the local chain Blue-Band-Hotels, the Excelsior likes to call consider itself first-class. This may be an accurate description for some of the larger rooms, which have special features (the top-floor guest rooms have a great view), and for the facilities and the Peacock restaurant—but it's certainly not true for the the hotel personnel. Staff at any of Berlin's rather traditional Blue-Band-Hotels generally lack the warmth you might expect from a four-star property. The rates, however, are unbeatable. It's also a great starting point for exploring the quaint side streets of Charlottenburg. ⊠ *Hardenbergstr. 14, D–10623,* ☎ *030/31550,* FAX *030/ 3155–1002,* WEB *www.hotel-excelsior.de. 317 rooms. Restaurant, bar, minibars, in-room data ports, in-room safes, no-smoking rooms, room service, baby-sitting, dry cleaning, laundry service, concierge, business services, meeting rooms, parking (fee). AE, DC, MC, V.*

$$-$$$ ⚏ **Schlossparkhotel.** The Schlossparkhotel is part of a premier private clinic, and some of the senior citizens treated there take on an extended stay at the hotel. Convalescence is undoubtedly quick, as the hotel has attentive service, modern and spacious rooms, and a truly romantic setting just a stone's throw from the park and palace of Charlottenburg. If you tire of seeing aged guests, just walk down quaint Heubnerweg to the impressive mansion and campus of the EAP, one of Europe's leading private business schools. ⊠ *Heubnerweg 2a, D– 14059,* ☎ *030/326–9030,* FAX *030/3269–03600,* WEB *www.schlossparkhotel.de. 40 rooms. Restaurant, bar, café, minibars, in-room data ports, in-room safes, no-smoking rooms, room service, massage, indoor pool, baby-sitting, dry cleaning, laundry service, concierge, business services, meeting rooms, free parking. DC, MC, V.*

$$ ⚏ **Artemisia.** This small 17th-century townhouse in Wilmersdorf is Berlin's only hotel exclusively for women, and the two floors of rooms are often booked solid. You'll find nice little touches in the bright, airy rooms—from the bed linen and towels to the love seats and nightstand. The owners, Renata Bühler and Manuela Polidori, offer personable and warm service. Not to be missed is a sundeck on the building's rooftop. ⊠ *Brandenburgische Str. 18, D–10707,* ☎ *030/873–8905,* FAX *030/861– 8653. 8 rooms, 1 suite. Breakfast room. No credit cards.*

$$ ⚏ **Econtel.** This family-oriented hotel is within walking distance of Charlottenburg Palace. The spotless rooms have a homey feel and provide closet safes and cable TV; some have minibars. Family rooms have four beds and are decorated especially for kids. A crib, bottle warmer, and potty-chair are available on request free of charge. The breakfast buffet provides a dazzling array of choices to fill you up for a day of sightseeing. ⊠ *Sömmeringstr. 24–26, D–10589,* ☎ *030/346–810,* FAX *030/ 3468–1163,* WEB *www.econtel.de. 205 rooms. Restaurant, bar, in-room safes, no-smoking rooms, baby-sitting, dry cleaning, laundry service, meeting room, parking (fee). AE, MC, V.*

$$ 🖭 **Hotel-Pension Wittelsbach.** The 1970s seem to have been good years here—the prevalence of pink and brown, the furniture covered with soft plastic fabrics, and the appliances are reflections of a far-out time. The Wittelsbach has a friendly atmosphere, welcoming both children and pets, and offers a superb breakfast buffet and a great location on a quiet side street off Ku'damm. If you're traveling alone, spend about €20 more for a double room with a large French bed; the single rooms are tiny and less extravagant. ⊠ *Wittelsbacherstr. 22, D–10707,* ☎ *030/864–9840,* FAX *030/862–1532. 28 rooms, 3 suites. Breakfast room, minibars, in-room safes, no-smoking floor, baby-sitting, meeting room, parking (fee). AE, DC, MC.*

$–$$ 🖭 **Charlottenburger Hof.** A convenient location across from the
★ Charlottenburg S-Bahn station makes this low-key hotel a great value for no-fuss travelers. Kandinsky, Miró, and Mondrian are the muses here; their prints and primary color schemes inspire the rooms and common spaces. Rooms are individually designed and crafted by the staff, and their variety can suit travel groups from friends to couples to families. Whether facing the street or the courtyard, all rooms receive good light; room amenities include TVs and hair dryers. The 24-hour café serves healthy dishes and draws locals too. The Ku'damm is a 10-minute walk away, taxis are easy to catch at the S-Bahn station, and the bus to and from Tegel Airport stops a block away. ⊠ *Stuttgarter Pl. 14, D–10627,* ☎ *030/329–070,* FAX *030/ 323–3723,* WEB *www.charlottenburger-hof.de. 46 rooms. Restaurant, lounge, in-room safes, no-smoking rooms, coin laundry, laundry service, parking (fee). MC, V.*

$–$$ 🖭 **Hotel Charlot am Kurfürstendamm.** Not quite on Ku'damm, the Charlot is two minutes from the boulevard and is on one of Charlottenburg's most upscale and quaintest squares. Because of the low rates, it attracts students and other young groups (so be prepared to have some noise at night), even though it looks like it would be frequented by an older clientele. The rooms are pleasantly decorated and nicely furnished, the staff is quite friendly, and the UFA Arthouse die Kurbel movie theater, just across the street, shows American movies in the original versions. After a flick you might want to sample some wine at one of the various wine bars in the neighborhood, or head to the New Orleans–style restaurant Julep's. ⊠ *Giesebrechtstr. 17, D–10629,* ☎ *030/323–4051,* FAX *030/327–9666. 42 rooms. Breakfast room, minibars, in-room data ports, no-smoking rooms. AE, MC, V.*

$–$$ 🖭 **Pension am Lietzensee.** A good alternative to the small pensions near Kurfürstendamm, the Pension am Lietzensee is a charming little hotel run by owner Carmen Frank. Some of the rooms might be considered somewhat kitschy (one is painted all pink and white), but the beautiful location around the corner from quiet Lietzensee lake is unquestionably superb. ⊠ *Neue Kantstr. 14, D–14057,* ☎ *030/325–4539,* FAX *030/3210–2054. 9 rooms. Breakfast room, minibars, in-room data ports, no-smoking rooms, dry cleaning, laundry service, concierge, business services, meeting room, parking (fee). AE, DC, MC, V.*

$ 🖭 **Hotel-Pension Berolina.** Catering to a mostly young and international crowd, the Berolina offers simple and clean rooms furnished with light pine beds, tables, and cabinets. The plentiful breakfast buffet and a TV in your room are available for an extra charge, and for an additional €9 per day you can get a room with a full kitchen. The pension is near Stuttgarter Platz, not far from the Ku'damm. Unfortunately, the rooms don't have bathrooms. ⊠ *Stuttgarter Pl. 7, D–10627,* ☎ *030/3270–9072,* FAX *030/3270–9073,* WEB *www.hotel-berolina.de. 73 rooms with shared bath. Breakfast room, parking (fee). AE, MC, V.*

Spandau

$$ 🏨 **Hotel Christopherus-Haus.** You don't have to be religious to stay at the Christopherus, a hotel run by the German Protestant church—everyone is welcome. But the hotel, set in the greenery of Spandau, can't deny its church heritage, as rooms, design, and service at the hotel all fluctuate between youth hostel or Boy Scout charm and upscale convention center: an odd but successful mixture. The price is fairly reasonable, and large families or groups will enjoy the relaxed attitude of the staff. ✉ *Evangelisches Johannisstift Berlin, Schönwalder Allee 26, D–13587,* ☎ *030/336–060,* FAX *030/3360–6114,* WEB *www.vch.de/ christopherus.berlin. 98 rooms. Restaurant, in-room data ports, nosmoking rooms, room service, indoor pool, sauna, gym, baby-sitting, bicycles, dry cleaning, laundry service, concierge, business services, meeting rooms, free parking. AE, DC, MC, V.*

$–$$ 🏨 **Hotel Altstadt Spandau.** You don't have to forgo Old Town atmosphere when visiting a European metropolis. The hotel's ideal location in the heart of historic Spandau makes it special. The small and plain hotel is extremely clean, even by German standards, and has a rustic German interior design (with heavy furniture and a lot brown tones). The breakfast buffet is more than filling, and after a day of exploring downtown Berlin you might easily decide to spend the evening unwinding in this homey hotel. U-Bahn Lines 7 and 2 take you to Ku'damm in just about 25 minutes. ✉ *Wasserstr. 4–8, D–13597,* ☎ *030/353–9320,* FAX *030/3539–3213. 25 rooms. Breakfast room, café, no-smoking rooms, bicycles, dry cleaning, laundry service, parking (fee). AE, MC, V.*

Northern Berlin

$$–$$$ 🏨 **Hotel am Borsigturm.** One of the new gems outside the downtown
★   areas is the surprisingly fashionable Hotel am Borsigturm, which opened in 1999 in the heart of Berlin's old industrial district turned high-tech valley. You'll see many sharp IT pros, laptops in hand, enjoying the chic bar, restaurant, and the elegantly designed rooms filled with cherrywood furniture and extremely comfortable beds. It's a 25-minute ride by public transportation to the Ku'damm and only eight minutes to Tegel Airport. Tegel Lake is a ten minute walk away. ✉ *Am Borsigturm 1, D–13507,* ☎ *030/4303–6000,* FAX *030/4303–6001,* WEB *www.hotel-am-borsigturm.de. 102 rooms, 3 suites. Restaurant, bar, minibars, in-room data ports, in-room safes, no-smoking floor, baby-sitting, bicycles, dry cleaning, laundry service, concierge, business services, convention center, meeting rooms, free parking. AE, DC, MC, V.*

$$ 🏨 **Dorint Budget Hotel Berlin Airport Tegel.** The best choice among the few Berlin Tegel Airport hotels, the new Dorint features elegant Italian-style rooms with soundproof windows, two very charming restaurants, and many extra amenities and services that you wouldn't expect from a hotel at this price. ✉ *Gotthardstr. 96, D–13403,* ☎ *030/498–840,* FAX *030/4988–4555,* WEB *www.dorint.de/berlin-budget. 303 rooms. Restaurant, bar, minibars, in-room data ports, in-room safes, no-smoking floor, baby-sitting, dry cleaning, laundry service, concierge, meeting rooms, parking (fee). AE, DC, MC, V.*

Tiergarten

$$$–$$$$ 🏨 **Grand Hotel Esplanade.** This winning establishment exudes luxury in its uncompromisingly modern design, its stylish rooms, and its artworks by some of Berlin's most acclaimed artists. Many rooms on the upper floors have panoramic views of the city, though the furnishings, an homage to the cool Bauhaus style, may not be to everyone's taste. Superb facilities and impeccable service are at your disposal. The enormous grand suite comes complete with sauna, whirlpool, and a grand piano—for €1,948 per night. ⊠ *Lützowufer 15, D–10785,* ☎ *030/ 254–780,* FAX *030/2547–88222,* WEB *www.esplanade.de. 347 rooms, 39 suites. 3 restaurants, bar, lobby lounge, in-room data ports, minibars, no-smoking rooms, room service, pool, hot tub, sauna, steam room, health club, bicycles, shops, piano, baby-sitting, dry cleaning, laundry service, concierge, business services, convention center, meeting room, parking (fee). AE, DC, MC, V.*

$$$ 🔟 **Hotel Berlin.** This is a favorite among tour groups from around the world, so expect a constant and international buzz. Behind the sleek glass facade you'll find rooms with new and modern furnishings with bright blue and red accents, comfortable chairs, and lots of light pine. An added plus is the hotel's location between Ku'damm and the Tiergarten, which will give you some flexibility when planning your sightseeing tours. ⊠ *Lützowpl. 17, D–10785,* ☎ *030/26050,* FAX *030/2605– 2716,* WEB *www.hotel-berlin.de. 671 rooms, 30 suites. Restaurant, bar, minibars, in-room data ports, no-smoking rooms, room service, massage, sauna, gym, baby-sitting, dry cleaning, laundry service, concierge, business services, meeting room, parking (fee). AE, DC, MC, V.*

$ 🔟 **Timmy's Bed and Breakfast.** One of the city's better-known gay pensions, Timmy's is also one of Berlin's few real bed-&-breakfasts. Although most guests are gay men, heterosexuals are also welcome. The owner is very friendly and generous in sharing his knowledge about Berlin's cultural and gay scenes. Rooms are quiet and furnished with dark furniture standing on parquet floors. The only drawback is location; although central, it is in an unpleasant, seedier part of Tiergarten. But the Birkenstrasse U-Bahn is just a few steps away. ⊠ *Perlebergerstr., D–10559,* ☎ *030/8185–1988,* FAX *030/8185–1989,* WEB *www.gaybed. de. 4 rooms. Breakfast room. AE, DC, MC, V.*

Mitte

$$$$ 🔟 **Four Seasons Hotel Berlin.** One of Berlin's best hotels, the Four Sea-
★   sons combines turn-of-the-20th-century luxury (reminiscent of the *Grand Hotel* of Vicki Baum's novel) with modern conveniences like portable phones and fax machines for the business traveler. The large guest rooms have first-class amenities, including free newspapers, overnight dry cleaning, and valet parking. Behind the modern facade, thick red carpets, heavy crystal chandeliers, and a romantic restaurant complete with an open fireplace create a sophisticated and serene atmosphere. ⊠ *Charlottenstr. 49, D–10117,* ☎ *030/20338,* FAX *030/2033– 6119,* WEB *www.fourseasons.com. 162 rooms, 42 suites. Restaurant, bar, minibars, in-room data ports, no-smoking rooms, room service, massage, sauna, health club, baby-sitting, dry cleaning, laundry service, concierge, business services, meeting room, parking (fee). AE, DC, MC, V.*

$$$$ 🔟 **Hotel Adlon Berlin.** Berlin's premier hotel lives up to the reputation
★   of its almost-mythical predecessor, the old Hotel Adlon, which, until its destruction during the war, was considered Europe's ultimate luxury resort. These days the Adlon has become the unofficial guest house of the German government. The lobby is large and light, thanks to its creamy marble and limestone and a stained-glass cupola, and is done in dark blue, garnet, and ocher, a color scheme that continues in the guest rooms. All are identically furnished in 1920s style, with cherrywood trim, myrtle-wood furnishings, and elegant bathrooms in black marble. The more expensive rooms overlook the Brandenburger Tor. ⊠ *Unter den Linden 77, D–10117,* ☎ *030/22610,* FAX *030/2261– 2222,* WEB *www.hotel-adlon.de. 337 rooms, 82 suites. 3 restaurants, 2 bars, café, in-room data ports, in-room safes, minibars, no-smoking floor, room service, pool, hair salon, massage, sauna, health club,*

Eastern Berlin Lodging

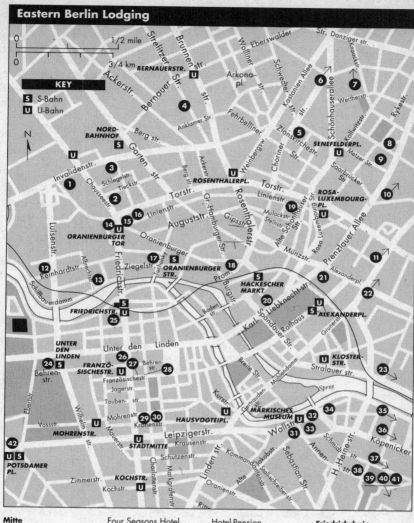

shops, baby-sitting, dry cleaning, laundry service, concierge, business services, meeting room, parking (fee). AE, DC, MC, V.

$$$-$$$$ ⊞ **Grand Hyatt Berlin.** Europe's first Grand Hyatt is probably also the
★ most starkly modern first-class hotel on the Continent. The hotel's minimalist style is a mix of Japanese and Bauhaus design. The large guest rooms (they start at 406 square ft) feature dark cherry-wood furniture and marble bathrooms with heated floors (accessed through sliding doors). The health club and swimming pool, on the top floor, have a wonderful view of Berlin's skyline from the heart of Potsdamer Platz. The Regency Club floor provides special services geared toward businesspeople. The hotel's Vox restaurant serves international and Asian cuisine; it whets the appetite with a "show kitchen," where you can watch the chef prepare your dinner. ⊠ *Marlene-Dietrich-Pl. 2, D–10785,* ☎ *030/2553–1234,* FAX *030/2553–1235,* WEB *www.berlin.hyatt.com. 327 rooms, 16 suites. Restaurant, café, bar, in-room data ports, in-room safes, minibars, no-smoking floor, room service, pool, massage, sauna, spa, health club, baby-sitting, dry cleaning, laundry service, concierge, business services, meeting room, parking (fee). AE, DC, MC, V.*

$$$-$$$$ ⊞ **Dorint am Gendarmenmarkt.** Of the two hotels that overlook the mag-
★ nificent Gendarmenmarkt with its two cathedrals and concert hall, the Dorint is the better choice. A modern designer hotel whose look was created by acclaimed interior architects Klein and Haller, it is a model of understated elegance. Along with the luxurious guest rooms (most with a wonderful view of the historic square), the breakfast room is so impressive with its soaring atrium that you might you might forget to eat. ⊠ *Charlottenstr. 50–52, D–10117* ☎ *030/203–750,* FAX *030/2037–5100,* WEB *www.dorint.de. 70 rooms, 21 suites. Restaurant, bar, café, minibars, in-room data ports, no-smoking floor, room service, massage, sauna, health club, solarium, baby-sitting, dry cleaning, laundry service, concierge, business services, meeting room, parking (fee). AE, DC, MC, V.*

$$$-$$$$ ⊞ **Maritim ProArte.** One of Berlin's last remaining GDR-era hotels has been transformed into a sleek business hotel. With a rather large number of rooms, the Maritim ProArte lacks atmosphere, but provides very good service and has many amenities. Its guest rooms, although spacious, are done in turquoise and purple shades that were more popular in the 1980s. The location, however, is great: Friedrichstrasse and Unter den Linden are right at your doorstep. ⊠ *Friedrichstr., D–10117,* ☎ *030/20335,* FAX *030/2033–4209,* WEB *www.maritim.de. 374 rooms, 29 suites. 3 restaurants, bar, minibars, in-room data ports, no-smoking floors, room service, indoor pool, barbershop, steam room, massage, indoor pool, sauna, health club, solarium, baby-sitting, dry cleaning, laundry service, concierge, business services, meeting rooms, parking (fee). AE, DC, MC, V.*

$$$-$$$$ ⊞ **Westin Grand Hotel.** The service here may not always be first class, but the setting and architecture of this grand hotel make it a preferred choice among American travelers. The neoclassical pink-marble lobby, with a six-story atrium, has polished brass accents, stuccowork, and rich wallpaper. Standard rooms are tastefully decorated in muted tones; bathrooms have large tubs. ⊠ *Friedrichstr. 158–164, D–10117,* ☎ *030/20270,* FAX *030/2027–3362,* WEB *www.westin-grand.com. 358 rooms, 35 suites. 2 restaurants, bar, lobby lounge, in-room data ports, minibars, no-smoking floor, room service, pool, barbershop, hair salon, hot tub, sauna, shops, solarium, baby-sitting, children's programs, laundry service, concierge, business services, convention center, meeting room, parking (fee). AE, DC, MC, V.*

$$-$$$$ ⊞ **Hilton Berlin.** All the right touches are here, from heated bathtubs to special rooms for businesswomen and travelers with disabilities. An executive floor offers a private lounge, free breakfast, late check-in, and larger rooms. The Hilton is also one of the few first-class German

hotels offering discounts to parents traveling with children. When making a reservation, ask for one of the second-floor rooms, which have classic Italianate furnishings. The Hilton overlooks the Gendarmenmarkt and the German and French cathedrals, as well as the classic Schauspielhaus. ✉ *Mohrenstr. 30, D–10117,* ☎ *030/20230,* ⒡ *030/2023–4269,* Ⓦ *www.hilton.com. 543 rooms, 46 suites. 2 restaurants, bar, cafeteria, 2 pubs, in-room data ports, minibars, no-smoking rooms, room service, pool, massage, sauna, health club, dance club, baby-sitting, dry cleaning, laundry service, concierge, business services, meeting room, parking (fee). AE, DC, MC, V.*

$$$ ★ 🏨 **Derag Hotel Grosser Kurfürst.** South of the historic Fischerinsel neighborhood, this modern hotel is a good choice for business travelers or tourists looking for large apartments with immaculate service. All guest rooms have a nice warmth thanks to the heavy use of wood furnishings. An unusual feature of the atrium-style lobby is a statue of the Great Elector Friedrich Wilhelm on horseback jumping out of a wall. A complimentary ticket for public transportation is included with the room rate. ✉ *Neue Rossstr. 11–12, D–10179,* ☎ *030/246–000,* ⒡ *030/2460–0300,* Ⓦ *www.deraghotels.de. 117 rooms, 6 suites, 21 apartments. Restaurant, bar, minibars, in-room data ports, no-smoking floor, room service, massage, sauna, health club, solarium, baby-sitting, dry cleaning, laundry service, concierge, business services, meeting room, parking (fee). AE, DC, MC, V.*

$$$ ★ 🏨 **DeragResidenzhotel Henriette.** The classic and elegant interior—dark oak-paneled walls, heavy carpets, fine linens, and porcelain chandeliers from Dresden—looks historic but is, in fact, new. The Henriette Hotel opened in June 2000 and still exudes the freshness of a brand-new hotel. A special attraction is the four-story atrium-courtyard with sandstone walls. As in all Derag Hotels, service is outstanding, and the fresh seafood served in La Mer restaurant is a real treat. ✉ *Neue Rossstr. 13, D–10179,* ☎ *030/2460–0900,* ⒡ *030/2460–0940,* Ⓦ *www.deraghotels.de. 54 rooms, 11 apartments. Restaurant, bar, minibars, in-room data ports, no-smoking floor, room service, massage, sauna, steam room, gym, baby-sitting, dry cleaning, laundry service, concierge, business services, meeting rooms. AE, DC, MC, V.*

$$$ 🏨 **Heinrich-Heine City-Suites.** Named after the rebellious German poet, this new apartment-hotel close to the historic Nikolai Quarter caters primarily to business travelers on an extended stay. But even if you only want to spend a couple of days, the junior suites are a great deal. All rooms are tastefully decorated with timeless furniture and have a full kitchen as well a minioffice. The wide variety of extra services includes a newspaper and fresh German rolls every morning. ✉ *Heinrich-Heine-Pl. 11, D–10179,* ☎ *030/278–040,* ⒡ *030/2780–4780,* Ⓦ *www.astronhotels.com, 38 apartments. Breakfast room, kitchenettes, no-smoking rooms, room service, concierge, parking (fee). AE, DC, MC, V.*

$$$ 🏨 **Hotel Hackescher Markt.** Not far from the nightlife around the Hackescher Markt and Rosenthaler Platz, this hotel provides discreet and inexpensive first-class services. The hotel doesn't have its own exercise room or pool, but guests can use the facilities of the Hotel Alexander Plaza nearby. Unlike those of many older hotels in eastern Berlin, guest rooms here are spacious and light and furnished with bright pine furniture in the rustic but charming English cottage style. In winter you'll appreciate the under-floor heating in your room, and in summer you can enjoy a coffee in the small courtyard. The staff is quite friendly and attentive. ✉ *Grosse Präsidentenstr. 8, D–10178,* ☎ *030/280–030,* ⒡ *030/2800–3111,* Ⓦ *www.hackescher-markt.com. 28 rooms, 3 suites. Bar, in-room data ports, in-room safes, minibars, no-smoking rooms, room service, baby-sitting, dry cleaning, laundry service, parking (fee). AE, DC, MC, V.*

$$$ 🖾 **La Vie Hotel Joachimshof.** The new La Vie caters to managers and state employees, as the federal government center is not far away. The hotel doesn't have a special atmosphere, just solid service and standard rooms. But the location is great (the Scheunenviertel is just around the corner), and prices are lower than in most other comparable upscale hotels. When making a reservation, ask for a room with a kitchenette, for which there's no extra charge. 🖾 *Invalidenstr. 98, D–10115,* ☎ *030/2039–56100,* FAX *030/2039–56199,* WEB *www.la-vie-hotels.com. 39 rooms, 1 suite, 2 apartments. Restaurant, bar, café, minibars, in-room data ports, kitchenettes, no-smoking rooms, room service, sauna, gym, solarium, dry cleaning, laundry service, meeting rooms, parking (fee). AE, DC, MC, V.*

$$–$$$ 🖾 **Alexander Plaza.** In the heart of the Scheunenviertel, the Alexan-
★ der Plaza is an ingenious combination of a 19th-century hotel and ul-tramodern, highly functional design. All rooms are done in bright earthy colors, using only natural materials for the wooden parquet floors and fine curtains. The contrast between the stucco ceiling and the old mosaic floor elsewhere in the hotel, along with the steel and glass, is striking. The hotel has evolved as a prime destination for a mostly Eu-ropean, trendy jet-set clientele. For €280 you can get one of the Ex-ecutive Suites, which are large and especially cozy corner rooms in the four turrets of the building. 🖾 *Rosenstr. 1, D–10178,* ☎ *030/240–010,* FAX *030/2400–1777,* WEB *www.alexander-plaza.com. 84 rooms, 9 suites. Restaurant, bar, minibars, in-room data ports, no-smoking floor, room service, barbershop, sauna, health club, solarium, baby-sitting, dry clean-ing, laundry service, concierge, business services, meeting rooms, park-ing (fee). AE, DC, MC, V.*

$$–$$$ 🖾 **art'otel berlin-mitte.** This city mansion's philosophy is reflected in
★ its artsy approach to every little detail of life—linen, soaps, bottles, pil-lows, and towels. The walls are decorated with paintings by Georg Baselitz, whose trademark is portraying people upside-down. Though the hotel features Baselitz's works, there's nothing topsy-turvy in the way the hotel is run. The modern elements set within this rococo building make for a stunning composition of old and new. 🖾 *Wallstr. 70–73, D–10719,* ☎ *030/240–620,* FAX *030/2406–2222,* WEB *www.artotel.de. 95 rooms, 4 suites, 10 apartments. 2 restaurants, bar, mini-bars, in-room data ports, no-smoking floor, room service, baby-sitting, dry cleaning, laundry service, concierge, business services, meeting rooms, parking (fee). AE, DC, MC, V.*

$$–$$$ 🖾 **Forum Hotel Berlin.** With its 40 stories above Alexanderplatz, this hotel (owned by Inter-Continental) competes with the nearby TV tower for the title of tallest downtown landmark. As one of the city's largest hotels, it is understandably less personal, at times even unfriendly. The Swiss birch-wood furniture, which decorates all the rooms, has erased any reminders that this was once Socialist East Berlin's show-case hotel. The casino is the highest in Europe and is open until 3 AM. 🖾 *Alexanderpl. 8, D–10178,* ☎ *030/23890,* FAX *030/2389–4305,* WEB *www.interconti.de. 994 rooms, 12 suites. 3 restaurants, bar, in-room data ports, minibars, no-smoking floor, room service, massage, sauna, gym, casino, baby-sitting, dry cleaning, laundry service, concierge, meeting rooms, business services, parking (fee). AE, DC, MC, V.*

$$–$$$ 🖾 **Hotel Allegra.** The Allegra might be considered typical of hotels geared toward female travelers, not only because its name is also the title of Germany's most popular women's magazine, but also because of play-ful and bright colors, the cozy wood atmosphere, and personal service. Add to that its location in the Mitte district, and you are guaranteed a pleasant and easygoing stay, even if you take your husband or boyfriend along. 🖾 *Albrechtstr. 17, D–10117,* ☎ *030/308–860,* FAX *030/3088–6579,* WEB *www.hotel-allegra.de. 100 rooms. Breakfast room, bar,*

minibars, in-room data ports, no-smoking floor, room service, bicycles, meeting room, free parking. AE, DC, MC, V.

$$–$$$ ★ ⌂ **Hotel Gendarm.** A classic Old World–style hotel within a cozy little mansion, the Gendarm is immensely popular both with businesspeople and leisure travelers. The secrets to its success are a prime location off historic Gendarmenmarkt; elegant, late-19th century-looking rooms; impeccable service; and a great breakfast. ✉ *Charlottenstr. 60–61, D–10117,* ☎ *030/206–0660,* FAX *030/2060–6666,* WEB *www.hotel-gendarm-berlin.de. 23 rooms, 4 suites. Breakfast room, bar, café, minibars, in-room data ports, no-smoking floor, room service, hair salon, sauna, solarium, baby-sitting, dry cleaning, laundry service, concierge, business services, meeting rooms, free parking. AE, DC, MC, V.*

$$–$$$ ★ ⌂ **Hotel Luisenhof Berlin.** Tucked away in one of Mitte's oldest houses (built in 1822), the small, intimate Luisenhof has very bright and fairly large rooms, all tastefully appointed in timeless, classic Prussian fashion. Service is good, and the location between Alexanderplatz and the Nikolaiviertel makes the hotel a perfect choice when exploring historic eastern Berlin. ✉ *Köpenicker Str. 92, D–10179,* ☎ *030/241–5906,* FAX *030/279–2983,* WEB *www.luisenhof.de. 26 rooms, 1 suite. Restaurant, bar, minibars, in-room data ports, no-smoking floor, room service, baby-sitting, dry cleaning, laundry service, concierge, business services, meeting room, parking (fee). AE, DC, MC, V.*

$$ ⌂ **ABC Hotel.** On a quiet side street of the Scheunenviertel, this hotel consists primarily of apartments that have special weekend and long-term rates. All rooms are very spacious, and some apartments have a modern kitchen and an open fireplace. The only drawback is the occasional wild mixture of furniture. ✉ *Rheinsberger Str. 78, D–10115,* ☎ *030/443–7670,* FAX *030/4437–6749,* WEB *www.abc-world.de. 9 rooms, 20 apartments. Restaurant, bar, minibars, in-room data ports, in-room safes, no-smoking floor, dry cleaning, laundry service, concierge, business services, meeting rooms, parking (fee). AE, DC, MC, V.*

$$ ⌂ **alameda berlin.** If you've ever wondered what life is like in the many converted lofts of Berlin, the Alameda is the place to find out. The 17 rooms are hidden under the roof of an upgraded tenement house. The rooms, all with modern appointments, have round windows and a small balcony overlooking a typical Berlin courtyard. ✉ *Michaelkirchstr. 15, D–10179,* ☎ *030/3086–8330,* FAX *030/3086–8359. 17 rooms. Breakfast room, café, minibars, in-room data ports, no-smoking rooms. MC, V.*

$$ ⌂ **Artist Riverside Hotel Berlin-Mitte.** This stylish hotel, which opened in 2000, tries to capitalize on Berlin's new international appeal. Service is lagging behind the times, but the late-19th-century-style rooms and location are without a doubt fantastic. ✉ *Friedrichstr. 106, D–10117,* ☎ *030/284–900,* FAX *030/284–9049,* WEB *www.tolles-hotel.de. 17 rooms, 1 suite. Restaurant, bar, in-room data ports, in-room safes, minibars, no-smoking rooms, room service, hair salon, massage, sauna, solarium, business services, meeting rooms. MC, V.*

$$ ★ ⌂ **Honigmond Garden Hotel.** Terra-cotta floor tiles, brown wicker furniture in the small breakfast room, and an intimate green courtyard give this hotel a Mediterranean country-house feel—a rare find in Berlin. The building dates back to 1845 and the purposefully spartan rooms have white walls, polished wood floors, iron-work bedframes, and bright blue bedding. A few rooms open onto the garden. A sister establishment, Honigmond Restaurant-Hotel, is nearby and has rooms for half the price. Service is friendly and personal, and you'll be within walking distance of the Wall memorial on Bernauer Strasse and the modern art museum, Hamburger Bahnhof. ✉ *Invalidenstr. 112, D–10115,* ☎ *030/281–0077,* FAX *030/281–0078,* WEB *www.honigmond-berlin.de. 24 rooms. Breakfast room, minibars, in-room data ports, no-smoking rooms. MC, V.*

$$ ▦ **Hotel-Pension Kastanienhof.** This small hotel in a 19th-century ten-
★ ement house represents the working-class counterpart to the more
luxurious pensions in western Berlin. The rooms are simply furnished
but are spacious and equipped with amenities usually found only in
first-class hotels, such as hair dryers, a minibar, and minisafe. The Kas-
tanienhof is an excellent deal for those bent on exploring the new east-
ern Berlin and nightlife in Prenzlauer Berg and Mitte. ⊠ *Kastanienallee
65, D–10119,* ☎ *030/443–050,* FAX *030/4430–5111,* WEB *www.hotel-
kastanienhof-berlin.de. 34 rooms, 2 apartments. Breakfast room, bar,
in-room safes, no-smoking rooms, bicycles, dry cleaning, laundry ser-
vice, meeting room, parking (fee). MC, V.*

$$ ▦ **Märkischer Hof.** Even though rooms have been completely upgraded in a plush late-19th-century style, a tangible Socialist air per-
vades this old-style East Berlin pension. The location is a big advantage:
Linienstrasse is in northern Mitte district, not far away from the heart
of the hip nightlife scene. ⊠ *Linienstr. 133, D–10115,* ☎ *030/282–
7155,* FAX *030/282–4331. 20 rooms. Breakfast room, café, minibars,
meeting room, free parking. MC, V.*

$–$$ ▦ **Boardinghouse Mitte.** A special long-term apartment-hotel, the the
often-booked-up Boardinghouse is a great place to stay if you want to
indulge in the city's life for more than just the average 2.3 days. The ser-
viced apartments are surprisingly sleek, modern, and airy, and come complete with all the amenities you would expect from a real condo. ⊠
Mulackstr. 1, D–10119, ☎ *030/2838–8488,* FAX *030/2838–8489,* WEB
*www.boarding-house-berlin.de. 21 apartments. Restaurant, bar, in-room
data ports, kitchenettes, no-smoking rooms, bicycles, baby-sitting, dry
cleaning, laundry service, business services, parking (fee). AE, MC, V.*

$–$$ ▦ **Hotel am Scheunenviertel.** This simply furnished but well-kept hotel
offers personal service, a wonderful breakfast buffet, and three restaurants (Mexican, Russian, and German) under one roof. The biggest advantage is its location in the Scheunenviertel, the old Jewish neighborhood
around the New Synagogue. If you want to spend late nights out, you'll
be near the major cultural and entertainment hot spots. Rooms have
decent shower cabins instead of bathtubs. ⊠ *Oranienburgerstr. 38, D–
10117,* ☎ *030/282–2125,* FAX *030/282–1115. 18 rooms. 3 restaurants,
dry cleaning, laundry service. AE, DC, MC, V.*

$–$$ ▦ **Hotel Künstlerheim Luise.** This hotel's name, which means "home
★ for artists," suggests little more than a run-down bohemian commune,
but nothing could be farther from the truth. The Künstlerheim is one
of Berlin's most original small hotels, with 30 rooms each designed and
furnished by a different German artist. The fantastically creative room
designs range from pop to sober classicism to modern minimalism. A
small French breakfast is included in the price, and the location of the
1825 house makes it perfect for exploring the Scheunenviertel. ⊠
Luisenstr. 19, D–10117, ☎ *030/284–480,* FAX *030/2844–8448,* WEB
*www.kuenstlerheim-luise.de. 32 rooms, 1 suite. Brasserie, in-room
data ports, in-room safes. MC, V.*

$–$$ ▦ **mitArt Pension.** This small hotel-pension, typical of the hip Neuer
★ Osten (new east), as Germans still like to call the Mitte district, is steps
away from the Tacheles art center, in the heart of the Scheunenviertel
neighborhood. Guest rooms are nice and clean, with contemporary art
decorating the walls. A special treat is a good night's sleep in the *Mäd-
chenzimmer,* the servant's bedroom, which is upstairs and can only be
reached via a squeaky wooden staircase. It's very small and very romantic. ⊠ *Friedrichstr. 127, D–10117,* ☎ *030/2839–0430,* FAX *030/
2839–0432. 9 rooms. Breakfast room. No credit cards.*

$ ▦ **A & O Backpackers Hostel Berlin.** Covering several floors in an old
redbrick industrial building, the A & O naturally attracts the young
backpacker crowd, which clearly appreciates the luxury of clean white

sheets on Scandinavian pine-wood double bunks and the barbecue restaurant in the courtyard. A real bargain is the room with 10 beds, where you can stay for just €12 a night. ⊠ *Boxhagener Str. 73, D–10245,* ☎ *0800/222–5722,* FAX *030/2900–7366,* WEB *www.aobackpackers.de. 100 rooms. Beer garden, breakfast room, no-smoking rooms, free parking. MC, V.*

$ ⌬ **Artist Hotelpension Die Loge.** This small and central hotel-pension caters to an artsy crowd, even though it's mostly frequented by American and other English-speaking tourists. A self-service breakfast for only €2.50 and a full-blown buffet for €5 are available. When making a reservation, be sure to ask for one of their basic rooms with a private bathroom; they're just €10 extra a night. ⊠ *Friedrichstr. 115, D–10117,* ☎ *030/280–7513,* FAX *030/280–7513,* WEB *www.artist-hotels.de. 8 rooms, 2 apartments. Breakfast room, no-smoking rooms. MC, V.*

Prenzlauer Berg

$$–$$$ ⌬ **Park Plaza Hotel.** This new mid-range hotel under American management is medium-size and comfortable, and the only hotel of its kind in Prenzlauer Berg. It's perfect for exploring the eastern and northeastern districts. Rooms have a European look with very stylish blue, gray, and bright pine-wood furnishings. The food is typical American chain fare. ⊠ *Storkower Str. 160–162, D–10407,* ☎ *030/421–810,* FAX *030/4218–1111,* WEB *www.parkhtls.com. 148 rooms, 7 suites. Restaurant, bar, minibars, in-room data ports, no-smoking floor, room service, health club, baby-sitting, dry cleaning, laundry service, concierge, business services, meeting rooms, parking (fee). AE, DC, MC, V.*

$$ ⌬ **Hotel Jurine.** The small yet exquisitely decorated guest rooms, with cherrywood furniture, dark blue carpets, appealing art on the walls, and many other modern amenities, are the trademark of this family-run hotel. As is often the case in the eastern districts, this hotel is a bit too expensive for the amenities it offers, particularly because breakfast is not included in the price (it's an extra €10). However, the friendly, pet-welcoming attitude of the Jurine family makes up for it. ⊠ *Schwedter Str. 15, D–10119,* ☎ *030/443–2990,* FAX *030/4432–9999,* WEB *www.hotel-jurine.de. 53 rooms. Restaurant, breakfast room, in-room data ports, minibars, no-smoking rooms, dry cleaning, laundry service, concierge, business services, meeting room, parking (fee). AE, DC, MC, V.*

$$ ⌬ **Myer's Hotel.** Representative of sceney Prenzlauer Berg, this small, privately owned family hotel attracts a mostly young, professional crowd. The Myers Hotel is in an old tenement house with simple rooms exuding a distinctive atmosphere of days of yore, but you'll still receive efficient service as well as modern telecommunications amenities. ⊠ *Metzer Str. 26, D–10405,* ☎ *030/440–140,* FAX *030/4401–4104. 41 rooms. Restaurant, bar, minibars, in-room data ports, no-smoking rooms, room service, massage, sauna, gym, baby-sitting, dry cleaning, laundry service, concierge, business services, meeting room, parking (fee). AE, DC, MC, V.*

$–$$ ⌬ **Bornholmer Hof.** Simple and charming, this intimate pension in an old building is inexpensive, but still service-oriented. While family- and teenager-friendly (the four-bed room for €102 is ideal for families), it manages to keep things tidy. Special rooms are designed for travelers with disabilities. The breakfast room welcomes late-rises until until noon. ⊠ *Bornholmer Str. 50, D–10493,* ☎ *030/444–0573,* FAX *030/4473–4402,* WEB *www.bornholmer-hof.de. 31 rooms. Breakfast room, sauna, solarium. No credit cards.*

$ ⌬ **Acksel Haus.** This small hotel in the heart of the hip Kollwitzplatz neighborhood offers apartments only, which are simply furnished with heavy beds and tables on a bare wooden floor. The restored 125-year-old tenement house is typical for Prenzlauer Berg. ✉ *Belforter Str. 21, D–10405,* ☎ *030/4433–7633,* FAX *030/441–6116. 7 apartments. In-room data ports, dry cleaning, laundry service, parking (fee). No credit cards.*

$ ⚏ **Hotel Greifswald.** One of the Prenzlauer Berg's nicest small hotels, the Hotel Greifwald occupies a tenement house with a lovely garden courtyard—where you might enjoy a sunny afternoon writing postcards at a table. Guest rooms are nothing special but are clean and comfortable, and the breakfast buffet (€7.50 extra) is a healthy start. ✉ *Greifswalder Str. 211, D–10405,* ☎ *030/442–7888,* FAX *030/442–7898,* WEB *www.hotel-greifswald.de. 25 rooms. Breakfast room. No credit cards.*

Friedrichshain

$$–$$$ ⚏ **Astron Hotel Berlin-Alexanderplatz.** An amicable and very efficient member of the German Astron chain, this hotel lacks charm but guarantees a comfortable stay in a four-star hotel for a budget rate. The only misleading feature of this otherwise straightforward hotel is its name: in fact, the hotel is in the district of Friedrichshain (just off the public park), quite a distance from Alexanderplatz. Nevertheless, it's a good starting point for exploring eastern and northeastern Berlin. ✉ *Landsberger Allee 26–32, D–10249,* ☎ *030/422–6130,* FAX *030/4226–13300,* WEB *www.astron-hotels.de. 162 rooms, 42 suites. Restaurant, bar, minibars, in-room data ports, no-smoking floor, room service, massage, sauna, exercise room, dry cleaning, laundry service, concierge, business services, meeting rooms, parking (fee). AE, DC, MC, V.*

$$ ⚏ **Gold Hotel Garni am Wismarplatz.** This midsize, three-star, chain hotel is off the beaten track near Friedrichshain's nicer squares, but near an U-Bahn stop. The simple rooms are a good deal for families or groups, particularly those with three bedrooms, which at €105 (including breakfast) are a steal. ✉ *Weserstr. 24, D–10247,* ☎ *030/293–3410,* FAX *030/2933–4110,* WEB *www.gold-hotel-berlin.de. 39 rooms. Breakfast room, bar, in-room safes, no-smoking floor, meeting room. V.*

Köpenick

$$$–$$$$ ⚏ **Dorint Hotel Berlin Müggelsee.** In the southeastern outskirts of the city, Berlin's largest and some say most beautiful lake is just beyond your balcony here. The first-class rooms are comfortable and fairly spacious, and each floor is decorated in a very different style. Rooms on the ground floor are furnished with heavy, dark German woods; the second floor, which many guests prefer for its airy environment, has an Italian accent and elegant cherry-wood furniture; the third floor is reminiscent of a Japanese house with dark woods and Asian prints. Unter den Linden is a 20-minute drive away. ✉ *Am Grossen Müggelsee, D–12559,* ☎ *030/658–820,* FAX *030/6588–2263,* WEB *www.dorint-berlin.de. 172 rooms, 4 suites. 2 restaurants, bar, in-room data ports, in-room safes, minibars, no-smoking rooms, room service, hair salon, massage, sauna, steam room, tennis court, bowling, health club, boating, bicycles, billiards, solarium, dry cleaning, laundry service, convention center, meeting rooms, free parking. AE, DC, MC, V.*

$$ ⚏ **Courtyard by Marriott Berlin-Köpenick.** As an American chain hotel, it looks identical to the many other efficient yet not very charming Courtyard hotels throughout the world. But you know what you get for your money—reliable service, quality food, and the facilities of a first-class hotel—along with a bit more, including a beautiful view of the Dahme River and the Köpenick Schloss. Although Olt Town Köpenick and the Müggelsee are within walking distance, the eastern and western downtown areas are 20–40 minutes away by public transport. The hotel is a good choice if you prefer greenery or if you need to leave the city via

the Schönefeld Airport, which is only 10 minutes away. ✉ *Grünauer-str. 1, D–12557,* ☎ *030/654–790,* FAX *030/6547–9555,* WEB *www.courtyard.com. 190 rooms. Restaurant, bar, minibars, in-room safes, no-smoking floor, room service, massage, sauna, gym, solarium, baby-sitting, dry cleaning, laundry service, concierge, business services, meeting room, parking (fee). AE, DC, MC, V.*

$$ ⊞ **Holiday Inn Berlin Schönefeld Airport.** With its warm and comfortable atmosphere, this hotel will far exceed your expectation of any airport accommodation. The hotel mostly serves airline crews, businesspeople, and stopover passengers, and is a good choice for its tasteful, Scandinavian-style pinewood rooms, extensive wellness services, and good restaurant. ✉ *Hans-Grade-Allee 5, D–12529,* ☎ *030/634–010,* FAX *030/6340–1600,* WEB *www.berlinschoenefeld.holiday-inn.com. 192 rooms, 3 suites. Restaurant, bar, minibars, in-room data ports, in-room safes, no-smoking floor, sauna, gym, solarium, baby-sitting, bicycles, dry cleaning, laundry service, concierge, business services, meeting rooms, parking (fee). AE, DC, MC, V.*

Neukölln

$$–$$$ ⊞ **Estrel Residence Congress Hotel.** Germany's biggest hotel may seem huge and anonymous, but it's the best deal in town for upscale rooms and service. The hotel is in the unappealing working-class district of Neukölln, some 20 minutes from the downtown areas. But the modern hotel offers all the amenities you could think of and guarantees quiet efficiency and smooth comfort at incredibly low prices. Rooms are decorated with Russian art. The lobby hall is a breathtakingly bright atrium with water basins, plants, and huge trees. The festival center adjoining the hotel features musicals. ✉ *Sonnenallee 225, D–12057,* ☎ *030/68310,* FAX *030/6831–2345,* WEB *www.estrel.com. 1,045 rooms, 80 suites. 6 restaurants, bar, lobby lounge, in-room data ports, minibars, no-smoking floor, hair salon, sauna, health club, theater, baby-sitting, children's programs, dry cleaning, laundry service, concierge, business services, convention center, parking (fee). AE, DC, MC, V.*

Kreuzberg

$$$ ⊞ **Riehmers Hofgarten.** The small rooms may be too spartan for many
★ travelers, but they are modern, quiet, and functional. The Riehmers's true appeal comes from its location in an impressive late-19th-century tenement house with a special courtyard. The architecture and richly decorated facade hint that 100 years ago the aristocratic officers of Germany's imperial army lived here. ✉ *Yorckstr. 83, D–10965,* ☎ *030/7809–8800,* FAX *030/7809–8808,* WEB *www.hotel-riehmers-hofgarten.de. 20 rooms. Restaurant, bar, no-smoking rooms, room service, laundry service, parking (fee). AE, MC, V.*

$$–$$$ ⊞ **Hotel Antares.** The high-rise Antares is a good choice if you want to explore Kreuzberg and Potsdamer Platz, as the hotel is between these two very different areas. Despite its claim of being a four-star hotel, it lacks both atmosphere and service. However, the views from the basic yet unusually large rooms (400 square ft) more than make up for it. The hotel is popular among businesspeople. ✉ *Stresemannstr. 97, D–10963,* ☎ *030/254–160,* FAX *030/261–5027,* WEB *www.hotel-antares.com. 81 rooms, 4 suites. Restaurant, bar, minibars, in-room data ports, no-smoking rooms, room service, massage, sauna, gym, solarium, baby-sitting, dry cleaning, laundry service, concierge, business services, meeting room, parking (fee). AE, DC, MC, V.*

$–$$ ⊞ **Hotel Anhalter Bahnhof.** If you don't mind the rather unappealing '70s-style fake-wood paneling on every wall of this hotel, then the small pension is actually quite likable for its quiet and comfortable setting and pleasant staff. Just a few steps away are the sad ruins of the Anhalter Bahnhof, and all Kreuzberg sights are within walking distance. The hotel rates are unbeatable, especially if you take a room without a bathroom. All prices include breakfast. ⊠ *Stresemannstr. 36, D–10963,* ☎ *030/251–0342,* 𝖥𝖠𝖷 *030/251–4897,* 𝖶𝖤𝖡 *www.hotel-anhalter-bahnhof.de. 36 rooms. Breakfast room, in-room safes, parking (fee). AE, DC, MC, V.*

$ 🏠 **die fabrik.** The fabrik is a huge but still friendly youth hostel–style accommodation, mostly welcoming backpackers from overseas. Rooms are airy, rather spacious, and basically clean, and the staff is very helpful and knowledgeable about the district's nightlife in the western part of the city. Part of a residential building, the fabrik is a very social place—you might meet locals like former squatters, hopeful artists, Turkish neighbors, or get the chance to flirt with that gorgeous young blonde Swede. ⊠ *Schlesische Str. 18, D–10997,* ☎ *030/611–7116,* 𝖥𝖠𝖷 *030/618–2974,* 𝖶𝖤𝖡 *www.diefabrik.com. 40 rooms. Café. No credit cards.*

$ 🏠 **Hotel Transit.** Calling itself an international youth hostel, the Transit attracts a younger clientele (although not the typical backpacker crowd), creating an easygoing and friendly atmosphere. The hotel is on two floors of a 19th-century industrial building and has simply furnished, clean rooms that have up to six beds each (the six-bed room for €150 is the best deal in town). The special "sleep in" rate for only €18 is unbeatable, though you have to share a room with six beds. All guest rooms have their own showers, but the bathrooms are communal. ⊠ *Hagelberger Str. 53–54, D–10965,* ☎ *030/789–0470,* 𝖥𝖠𝖷 *030/7890–4777,* 𝖶𝖤𝖡 *www.hotel-transit.de. 49 rooms. Breakfast room, bar, bicycles, meeting room, parking (fee). AE, MC, V.*

$ 🏠 **Pension Kreuzberg.** Angelika Dehner's small pension is a modern interpretation of the good old Berlin *Hotelpension*. The rooms are simple but very clean, and the breakfast buffet is more than satisfying. Bathrooms on each floor are shared by guests. The rooms with multiple beds (3–5) are a fair deal for just €22 a night per person. Service is very warm and Mrs. Dehner is happy to share personal advice on sightseeing, primarily around Kreuzberg. ⊠ *Grossbeerenstr. 64, D–10963,* ☎ *030/251–1362,* 𝖥𝖠𝖷 *030/251–0638. 12 rooms. Breakfast room, parking (fee). No credit cards.*

Zehlendorf

$$$$ 🏠 **Ritz-Carlton Schlosshotel.** The small but extremely luxe Schlosshotel sits in the verdant setting of the Grunewald. The palacelike hotel is full of classic style and is lavishly decorated—it might remind you of a late-19th-century château. It was designed by Chanel's Karl Lagerfeld, who also completed a special suite for himself, which is made available to guests if the master himself is not staying in Berlin. The service is amazingly personal but never intruding. ⊠ *Brahmsstr. 10, D–14193,* ☎ *030/895–840,* 𝖥𝖠𝖷 *030/8958–4800,* 𝖶𝖤𝖡 *www.ritzcarlton.com. 54 rooms. Restaurant, bar, lobby lounge, in-room data ports, minibars, no-smoking rooms, room service, pool, beauty salon, massage, sauna, exercise room, baby-sitting, dry cleaning, laundry service, concierge, business services, meeting room, parking (fee). AE, DC, MC, V.*

$$ 🏠 **Concorde Hotel Forsthaus.** Golfing is still fairly new to most Berliners, and the Hotel Forsthaus ("house in the forest") has been a pioneer in the golf-hotel business. The hotel looks more like your typical German suburban middle-class home, despite its romantic name. The lure of the hotel is the golf course right next to it, and just around the corner, the lovely Wannsee, with its beaches, and the dense Grunewald. ⊠ *Stölpchenweg 45, D–14109,* ☎ *030/805–8680,* 𝖥𝖠𝖷 *030/8058–68100. 20 rooms. Restaurant, bar, minibars, in-room data ports, in-*

room safes no-smoking rooms, room service, 18-hole golf course, putting green, baby-sitting, dry cleaning, laundry service, business services, meeting rooms, parking (fee). AE, DC, MC, V.

$$ 🏨 **Landhaus Schlachtensee.** This villa bed-and-breakfast offers personal and efficient service, well-equipped rooms, and a quiet setting in the Zehlendorf district. The nearby Schlachtensee and Krumme Lanke lakes beckon you to swim, boat, or walk along their shores. ✉ *Bogotastr. 9, D–14163,* ☎ *030/809–9470,* 𝖥𝖠𝖷 *030/8099–4747. 20 rooms. Breakfast room, free parking. AE, MC, V.*

$–$$ 🏨 **Haus La Garde Berlin.** This small pension in the green Schlachtensee area in the far southwest is a top choice if you like heavy German oak furniture, colorful old carpets, and heavy, soft down comforters. The owner, Mrs. Rathgeb, is a perfect hostess in her fairy tale–like old villa and beautiful garden and is eager to help with anything you might need or want to know during your stay in Berlin. ✉ *Bergengruenstr. 16, D–14129,* ☎ *030/801–3009,* 𝖥𝖠𝖷 *030/802–4008. 4 rooms. Breakfast room, in-room safes, no-smoking rooms, bicycles, free parking. AE, DC, MC, V.*

$–$$ 🏨 **Rasthaus und Hotel Grunewald.** This large business-oriented hotel is a no-nonsense, straightforward establishment catering mostly to groups and conventioneers. The sober-looking lobby and rooms are standard quality. It's recommendable primarily if you plan to visit Berlin with a larger group, since group rates and specially arranged events are the hotel's strengths. The prime location in peaceful Grunewald is also respite from the daily hustle and bustle of a business trip. ✉ *Kronprinzessinnenweg 120, D–14129,* ☎ *030/803–040,* 𝖥𝖠𝖷 *030/8030–4100. 44 rooms. Restaurant, bar, minibars, in-room data ports, in-room safes, no-smoking rooms, baby-sitting, dry cleaning, laundry service, concierge, business services, meeting rooms, free parking. AE, DC, MC, V.*

5 NIGHTLIFE AND THE ARTS

Paris may be the City of Light, but Berlin is unquestionably Europe's City of the Night, pulsing with young talent and energy. From the classical performing arts to the archly decadent avant-garde, Berlin has it all, and more. The chemistry explodes in the streets and in the backrooms of the city's infamous bars and clubs. An ultimate chameleon, the city bestows its beguiling gift on its revelers. Here, it really is possible to be anything you desire, even if that means reinventing yourself night after night.

By Jody K.
Biehl

BERLIN IS AN EXTREME PLACE. Its nightlife is no different. Most bartenders don't know the meaning of a last call, and for many Berliners sunrise is the first sign a party is over. What you find largely depends on how and where you look. Berlin's best bars don't work to attract a wide crowd; instead, they cultivate a personality.

Music, too, is a dizzying patchwork. For some, techno is still the ultimate Berlin sound, while other young electronic musicians have moved on to drum 'n' bass, electro, jungle, and mixes of all three. A lively reggae and hip-hop scene also flourishes, and Latin music and dancing are increasingly popular.

Almost all bars offer table service, and usually you can just walk in and find a table without waiting to be seated. Keep in mind that in Berlin appearances can be deceiving. Beat-up exteriors often contain hidden posh salons. This is a city where the unexpected can—and often does—happen.

FIND OUT WHAT'S GOING ON

The best way to find out what's happening in the city is to do what Berliners do: pick up a copy of *Zitty, Tip,* or *Prinz.* Each appears every two weeks and has a detailed listing of arts and entertainment events. Another helpful guide is the *Berlin Programm,* a monthly guide to art, museum, and theater attractions. The guides are in German, but they are fairly easy to decipher. For the latest on the house, techno, and hip-hop club scene, look for *(030),* a free weekly flyer available in bars, cafés, and clubs around town. The only English-language magazine available is *Berlin–the magazine,* published four times a year by the city's tourist information center.

NIGHTLIFE

Trying to categorize Berlin watering holes is a maddening exercise. Even before you've started drinking, the lines between cafés, bars, lounges, and Kneipen tend to blur. In Berlin it is entirely possible to eat breakfast, lunch, afternoon cakes, and dinner in the same establishment that will further ply you with copious amounts of late-night cocktails. In general, however, the terms *bar* and *lounge* connote a place where tall drinks and cocktails are served in an upscale setting. If you're lucky, you might be able to hustle a tiny bowl of olives or a handful of peanuts from a friendly waiter, but forget trying to get any real food. The only exception is around midnight, when vendors start to peddle high-priced sandwiches to starved bar clientele. (The most popular sandwich is garlic, which is far from romantic, but is also a sure-fire way to hide the smell of alcohol during a random police auto stop.) Most Berliners hit bars after dinner, and many don't open until 9 PM. The hottest times are between 1 AM and 3 AM.

Kneipen, by contrast, are down-to-earth hangouts, somewhat comparable to English pubs. They are good spots for a quick beer, or a coffee or a hot chocolate in the middle of the day. You might also opt for a Berlin specialty—Berliner Weisse (low-alcohol beer) with a *Schuss* (shot of sweet syrup). You can choose from red (raspberry) or green (woodruff). The concoction comes in a bowl-shape glass and can be sipped through a curved straw. Wine in Kneipen is usually expensive and almost universally awful. Kneipe food tends to be simple but hearty. Bartenders and servers in all establishments expect a 2%–5% tip, and most places don't take credit cards. Unless they are very busy, most servers will let you run up a tab until you are ready to leave.

If you want to bar-hop, hit the bustling (and increasingly yuppie) area in Mitte around Hackescher Höfe, and Oranienburgerstrasse. If you're looking for a younger, grungier scene, try Prenzlauer Berg between Lychenerstrasse, Schönhauer Allee, and Danzigerstrasse. Berliners refer to this triangle as "LSD." If you prefer serenity and old-style class, head for well-established spots in Schöneberg, Tiergarten, and Charlottenberg.

Bars

Akba Lounge. In the front it is vintage East: a quiet, terribly smoky bar in an unrenovated building not far from the gentrified Kollwitzplatz. Inside, blood-red lamps cast eerie shadows across the faces of hip twentysomethings hoping to score. The music jumps from reggae to Latin to drum 'n' bass, but the ambience is always erotically charged. ⊠ *Sredzkistr. 64, Prenzlauer Berg,* ☎ *030/441–1463. Metro: Eberswalder Strasse.*

Ankerklause. This small, usually packed bar sits on the bank of the Landwehrkanal and is a place of legend. It attracts a young, somewhat ratty crowd and serves famously cheap drinks. When the sun shines, the café scene spills onto the sidewalks overlooking the canal and transforms the scene into a garden of chatter and casual flirting. The lively Turkish Market runs along the canal on Tuesday and Friday. Alternative music and a dance floor animate the nights. ⊠ *Maybachufer 1, Neukölln,* ☎ *030 /693–5649. Metro: Kottbusser Tor; Schoenleinstrasse.*

Bar am Lützowplatz. The cocktail menu here is the size of a small guidebook and the blond-wood bar is the longest counter in town. Well-dressed patrons sample the pricey drinks, and each other, from either the sidewalk tables, the bar, or the few black-leather seats in the back. The sleek establishment has been around for years. Its busiest nights are Thursday through Sunday. ⊠ *Am Lützowpl. 7, Tiergarten,* ☎ *030/262–6807. Metro: Nollendorfplatz.*

Blue Note Bar. This West Berlin bar had its heyday in the 1980s and it's still a prime spot for young movers and shakers. Freshly renovated in 2000, it has a cosmopolitan look and a happy hour that starts at 10 PM. Live bands and club nights with DJs loosen up the somewhat snobbish scene. ⊠ *Courbierestr. 13, Schöneberg,* ☎ *030/218–7248. Metro: Nollendorfplatz.*

Bierhimmel. From the outside this looks like just another one of Berlin's mediocre bars. But if you go inside and through a set of swinging doors, everything is bathed in red light, including the radiant drag queens who frequent this hidden gem. The bar is 1950s kitsch, and the cocktails are killer. ⊠ *Oranienstr. 183, Kreuzberg,* ☎ *030/615–3112. Metro: Kottbusser Tor.*

Cocktailbar Baal. A favorite among local actors and actresses (some with work, many without), this snug underground bar mixes luscious drinks that have Hollywood names and a showy touch. ⊠ *Mulackstr. 13, Mitte,* ☎ *030/285–7091. Metro: Weinmeisterstrasse.*

Greenwich. Two 15-ft-long aquariums line the interior of this chic little hot spot popular with both gays and straights. Upstairs, low tables and soft beige chairs provide comfortable corners in which to converse, but the noise level is usually so high that good conversation is impossible. On a busy night you'll probably find yourself elbow to elbow with an attractive stranger, so just smile and nod. ⊠ *Gipsstr. 5, Mitte,* ☎ *no phone. Metro: Weinmeisterstrasse.*

Harry's New York Bar. The Grand Hotel Esplanade's pricey institution is the sister of the famous Paris hangout of the 1920s. It is by far the best lobby bar in town and one of the few in the city with live piano music. Businesspeople try their best to relax under the melange of portraits of American presidents and modern paintings. ⊠ *Am Lützowufer 15, Tiergarten,* ☏ *030/2547–8821. Metro: Nollendorfplatz.*

Kumpelnest 3000. This kitschy den's reputation is as wild as its carpeted walls. Gays and heteros mingle and groove together on the tiny dance floor, and no one pays attention to who goes home with whom. The best time to go is late on Friday or Saturday night. Caipirinhas are among the better mixed drinks. There's no tap beer—just bottled Becks. ⊠ *Lützowstr. 23, Tiergarten,* ☏ *030/261–6918. Metro: Kurfürstenstrasse.*

Newton. A sleek example of new Berlin chic, this bar exalts Helmut Newton's larger-than-life photos of nude women across its 12-ft-high walls. The photos exude a calm elegance that perfectly matches the scenic location on Berlin's baroque Gendarmenmarkt. This is definitely one of the most stylish settings in Mitte. ⊠ *Charlottenstr. 57, Mitte,* ☏ *030/ 2061–2999. Metro: Stadt Mitte.*

Oxymoron. If you are longing for a taste of the famous Berlin salons of the 1920s and 1930s, this exquisite bar tucked into the equally stunning Hackesche Höfe is for you. The violet-color seats are plush, the chandeliers glorious, and the servers remarkably friendly. Some even speak English. As it's a combination restaurant, club, and bar, you can both begin and end an evening here. ⊠ *Rosenthalerstr. 40/41, Mitte,* ☏ *030/2839–1885. Metro: Hackescher Markt.*

Reingold. Although it's not far from the buzzing hub at Oranienburgerstrasse, this fancy lounge can be tricky to find. It's on a quiet backstreet and has only a small golden sign to mark the entry. A large, forbidding door provides another barrier, as does the requirement that all guests must ring a small bell to be admitted. Once inside, the soft golden lighting, long bar, and maroon 1930s-style easy chairs are intoxicating. The drink list is astonishingly complex and the clientele casually well-dressed. You won't find many tourists here. ⊠ *Novalisstr. 11, Mitte,* ☏ *030/2838–7676. Metro: Oranienburger Tor.*

Shark-Club. Forget scenic aquariums stocked with puny goldfish. This place is the big leagues. Real sharks swim in a 4,224-gallon (6 ft by 24 ft) saltwater aquarium. The mood is dark and edgy, with huge black-leather booths and fluorescent blue lighting. The dance floor is usually packed, and DJs play the kind of music that doesn't leave you in your seat for long. Don't be intimidated by the three doormen hulking about the entrance. Just smile and walk right in. Jackets are required for men, and women in jeans will be turned away. ⊠ *Rosmarinstr. 8–9, Mitte,* ☏ *030/2063–5063. Metro: Französische Strasse.*

Wiener Blut. This groovy bar attracts a mellow thirtysomething crowd that likes to lounge on its dark orange sofas and drink colorful cocktails. On Wednesday and Saturday DJs play soul, funk, and big beat tunes, while Sunday is reserved for live music, including jazz trios. ⊠ *Wienerstr. 14, Kreuzberg,* ☏ *030/618–9023. Metro: Görlitzer Bahnhof.*

Wine Bars

It's taken years, but the notion of drinking wine with a meal is finally catching on in this beer-swilling city. Good wine is still hard to come by in cafés and bars, but specialty stores have started to carry fine vintages. Wine bars, too, are working hard to entice an upscale clientele.

As for homegrown vintages, keep in mind that Germany has 13 wine regions and, despite the unforgiving climate, produces more than 20 wine varieties. Riesling, Silvaner, and Müeller-Thurgau top the list, both in quality and quantity.

Bacco. Wine maker Helmut Hane serves more than 300 organic wines, champagnes, cognacs, whiskeys, schnapps, and grappas in his shop, which sits adjacent to the bustling Bergmannstrasse market hall. Soft cheese and tapas help wash down the tasty libations. Bacco is open until 10 PM, and nearby are pricey antiques and secondhand clothes shops and stylish cafés that cater to a funky, bohemian-bourgeois crowd. ⊠ *Marheinekepl. 15, Kreuzberg,* ☎ *030/692–9813. Metro: Gneisenaustrasse.*

Gerstensack. A perfect ambience for wine tasting is found in this wine cellar that seems to have come straight out of a postcard from Heidelberg. The furniture is all wood, and there is an old-fashioned charred fireplace. When it is sunny, you can sit outside. ⊠ Fichtestr. 31, Kreuzberg, ☎ 030/694–8703. Metro: Südstern.

Nö! Weingalerie and Café. The low-key atmosphere here is the perfect setting for amateur wine tasters not out to spend big money. Most customers opt for the five-wine special, which lets them test five wines for for less than €12. The wine comes with a small plate of cheese and bits of baguette. The servers are friendly and never snobby. Since it's not far from eastern Berlin's major shopping district, it makes a nice early-evening place to relax. ⊠ *Glinkastr. 24, Mitte,* ☎ *030/201–0871. Metro: Stadt Mitte.*

Weinstein. In the spunky heart of Berlin's most happening district, this nonchalant wine bar has acquired a remarkably loyal clientele. Its cozy interior is lined with old wine barrels, and the food is exquisitely matched to the offbeat list of wines. You can order a regular glass (0,2 l) or a half a glass (0,1 l) for tasting. The location makes for a perfect beginning to a night out on the town or for pairing drinks with theater or music in Mitte. Reservations are advised. ⊠ *Lychenerstr. 33, Prenzlauer Berg,* ☎ *030/441–1842. Metro: U-Bahnhof Eberswalder Strasse.*

Biergartens

The German passion for beer is legendary, as is their love of nature. So, it comes as no surprise that the Biergarten—a place to drink beer under a canopy of trees—is so popular. When it comes to beer appreciation, Prussian Berlin can't keep up with jovial, Bavarian Munich, but Berliners don't mind trying. The outdoor beer hall can be a saving grace for nonsmokers tired of the semipermanent haze that clings to the air and walls of most bars. In summer, cafés and Kneipen with any green nearby often try to create makeshift Biergartens.

Although beer is the main draw, most Biergartens also serve bratwurst (a long, white pork sausage served curling out of a round roll), Jagdwurst, or Bockwurst (red pork sausage eaten with a smear of mustard). Vegetarians are almost always out of luck, although sometimes big salted pretzels and potato salad are offered.

Café am Neuen See. Take a break from the big city in this lovely spot in the Tiergarten. Tables and benches extend into the woods under a shady covering of some of the city's oldest trees. Nearby, you can rent row- and paddleboats on the lake. ⊠ *Lichtensteinallee 1, Tiergarten,* ☎ *030/254–4930. Metro: Tiergarten.*

Gartenhaus Tacheles. This ultra-East cult center is a must-see for any first-time Berlin tourist. The crumbling outer building (once a shopping center) became a squatter's paradise after the Wall fell and eventually transformed into the hippest art space in town. The backyard sculpture garden is more urban decay than pastoral paradise. Still, the beer is good, and when the sun is setting on a warm evening, this quirky space perfectly captures the restlessness of the city. ✉ *Oranienburgerst. 54–56, Mitte,* ☎ *030/281–6119. Metro: Oranienburger Tor.*

Golgatha. On a summer night you'll find half of Kreuzberg drinking, dancing, and grilling in this festive, family-friendly spot in the middle of Viktoriapark. As you squeeze into picnic tables and listen to folksy bands, you might feel like you're attending a giant family reunion. At night the place becomes an animated (if somewhat youthful) disco. ✉ *Kreuzbergstr. 48–64, in Viktoriapark, Kreuzberg,* ☎ *030/785–2453. Metro: Yorckstrasse; Platz der Luftbrücke.*

Haus Zenner/Eierschale. This big, semitouristy spot is on the Spree River in the middle of Treptower Park. The park, which also features the stunning Soviet memorial to fallen soldiers of the Soviet army, is the hub for city boat tours. The crowd ranges from robust teenagers to cane-carrying grandparents, and in summer bands perform daily. A nearby stand rents bikes. ✉ *Alt-Treptow 12–17, in Treptower Park, Treptow,* ☎ *030/533–7370. Metro: Treptower Park.*

Prater. A real melting pot, this beer garden is tucked behind one of the busiest and most compact of Prenzlauer Berg's bustling streets. Here you'll find everything from horn-rimmed intellectuals to 80-year-old former Communist workers. Actors from the nearby left-wing Volksbühne theater frequent it, as do Green Party politicians. In addition to the usual fare, a rustic restaurant serves hearty bowls of potato and lentil soup. At night, it turns into a frisky disco scene, with live bands and large dance floors. ✉ *Kastanienallee 7–9, Prenzlauer Berg,* ☎ *030/448–5688 for beer garden or 030/247–6772 for events. Metro: Eberswalder Strasse.*

Cabaret/Varieté

Bar Jeder Vernunft. It looks like a large billowing circus tent in the middle of a parking lot. Inside, it's all mirrors, glass, and old-time charm. If it's modern cabaret you desire, you can't beat this jazzy setting featuring some of Berlin's best-loved acts, including American singer and comedian Gayle Tufts. For much of the year, a late show is added at midnight on Friday and Saturday. ✉ *Schaperstr. 24, Wilmersdorf,* ☎ *030/883–1582. Metro: Spichernstrasse.*

BKA–Berliner Kabarett Anstalt. Known for its wicked humor and guest entertainers, this is an old favorite of the alternative crowd from Kreuzberg, the city's most ethnically diverse neighborhood. There are also performances in the BKA Luftschloss, a tent that stands year-round across from the Lustgarten on Unter den Linden. ✉ *Mehringdamm 34, Kreuzberg,* ☎ *030/251–0112. Metro: Potsdamer Platz; Hackescher Markt for the tent.*

Cafe Theater Schalotte. This comfy café and theater features a wide variety of shows, the majority of which are top quality. Few are in English, though. If you are in town in November, look for the European Acapella Festival here. ✉ *Behaimstr. 22, Charlottenburg,* ☎ *030/341–1485. Metro: Richard-Wagner-Platz.*

Chamäleon Varieté. Let yourself pretend you are back in Berlin of the 1920s in this beautiful old theater. The casts are talented but a far cry from the days of Marlene Dietrich. Still, the shows are usually funny and fairly easy for non–German speakers to understand. The late show

---

Close-Up

COME TO THE CABARET

CABARET—EVEN SAYING IT ALOUD evokes a smile. For non-Berliners, it conjures images of a bowler-top Liza Minnelli, a swooning Marlene Dietrich, and scantily clad dancers singing punchy numbers. For Berliners the images are twofold. There are the golden years of the 1920s and early 1930s, when the scandalous Anita Berber performed her sinuous stripteases, satirists Bertolt Brecht and Kurt Tucholsky were the toasts of the town, and the unflappable Werner Finck asked Nazi soldiers if he should speak more slowly so their small brains could understand his jokes.

There are also the black years, from 1933 to 1945, when Hitler's propaganda minister Joseph Goebbels shut down well-loved cabarets and chased out or killed talented artists, replacing them with hand-selected national "stars." Today cabaret is a staggering mix of satire, sentimentality, and silliness. Some truly talented performers are all but reinventing the genre, creating startling new work. Other promoters try to relive the glory days by sinking big money into showy revues filled with acrobats and clowns. These types of shows are usually billed as *Varieté* rather than cabaret.

Good German acts to look for include: Martina Brandl (a sweetly melancholy singer who mixes stories with original songs), Evi Niessner und Mr. Leu (an erotically charged act between two first-class musician/singers), Teufelsberg Productions (a hysterical drag cabaret), Tanya Ries (who sounds like a young Kate Bush), and the Stepinskis (tap-dancing comediennes). Entertaining acts in English include: Gayle Tufts (pop tunes and comedy), Rick Maverick (satiric poetry), and Priscilla Be (biting monologues).

---

is usually the most adventurous, a time when new Berlin talents take the stage hoping to prove themselves. ⊠ *Rosenthalerstr. 40–41, Mitte,* ☎ *030/282–7118. Metro: Hackescher Markt.*

Chez Nous. If you're looking for glamour, glitz, feathers, and falsies, this 92-seat house will surely be a favorite. Drag queens and celebrity look-alikes tease the crowd with lip-synching and light antics understandable even to non–German speakers. Credit cards are not accepted. ⊠ *Margurgerstr. 14, Tiergarten,* ☎ *030/213–1810. Metro: Zoologischer Garten.*

Friedrichstadtpalast. Big musical variety shows and long-legged, scantily clad women wow the more than 900 spectators (usually working-class German tourists) that can pack this Las Vegas–style show palace. Though the sheer dimensions of the Friedrichstadtpalast are breathtaking—the three stages can be transformed into a water basin, a circus arena, or an ice-skating rink—this modern version lacks the style of its predecessor of the Roaring '20s. ⊠ *Friedrichstr. 107, Mitte,* ☎ *030/2326–2474. Metro: Friedrichstrasse.*

Kalkscheune. The building is vintage 1840s and has the slightly decadent feel of an old-time cabaret. All the seats are good because the stage is set up as theater-in-the-round. Some performers sing in English. Every Sunday Berlin's popular cabarettist and performance artist Dr. Seltsam (Dr. Strange) takes the stage. ⊠ *Johannisstr. 2, Mitte,* ☎ *030/ 2839–0065. Metro: Oranienburgerstrasse.*

Kleine Nachtrevue. Opened by talented cabarettist Sylvia Schmidt, this little gem sparkles with authenticity. The setting is sexy, with small tables arranged close together. There are 40-minute shows in the early evening that provide a taste of cabaret without dragging on endlessly. ⊠ *Kurfürstenstr. 116, Schöneberg, ☎ 030/218–8950. Metro: Wittenbergplatz.*

Roter and Grüner Salons. These two separate performance spaces in the Volksbühne offer a huge variety of programs. Variety doesn't have to mean mainstream—some shows are very racy and keep up the saucy spirit of the 1920s. Others are somewhat folksy and seem like they are geared for German Omas. The spaces look like their names: one has pomegranate red walls and plush easy chairs; the other is all iguana green. Wednesday is tango night at the Red Salon. ⊠ *Volksbühne, Rosa-Luxemburg-Pl., Mitte, ☎ 030/2406–5807 or 030/3087–4806. Metro: Rosa-Luxemburg-Platz.*

Wintergarten Varieté. Come on in for a virtual paradise of clowns, acrobats, magicians, and dancing girls. The professionally run shows are slick, light, and entertaining. Look for Dennis Lacombe, Berlin's most famous clown. Tickets can be more expensive than at other cabarets, but the sets are also more elaborate. The theater is an homage to the magnificent Wintergarten variety theater that stood on Friedrichstrasse and was destroyed in World War II. ⊠ *Potsdamerstr. 96, Tiergarten, ☎ 030/250–0880. Metro: Kurfürstenstrasse.*

Casinos

Casino Berlin. Not so fashionable or international, the casino is worth a visit for its breathtaking location on top of the Forum Hotel at Alexanderplatz. ⊠ *Alexanderpl., Mitte, ☎ 030/2389–4113. Metro: Alexanderplatz.*

Spielbank Berlin. Berlin's newest and leading casino on Potsdamer Platz, with roulette tables, three blackjack tables, and slot machines, stays open from 2 PM to 3 AM. ⊠ *Marlene-Dietrich-Pl. 1, Mitte, ☎ 030/255–990. Metro: Potsdamer Platz.*

Dance Clubs

Clubbing is practically an art form in Berlin. On most Friday and Saturday nights the city streets are awash with tiny cars packed full of twenty-, thirty-, even fortysomethings headed for a night on the town. And even on weekdays the early commute is a bizarre mix of ambitious professionals and bleary-eyed club goers heading home to crash.

With the rise of the techno scene and the fall of the Berlin Wall in 1991, the city gained legendary status on the club circuit. Impromptu clubs opened in abandoned buildings and along the "death strip" that used to separate East and West. The thumping insistence of techno became the voice of a generation of Germans who were again forced to confront both the end and the beginning of their history. Now, the scene is largely splintered, and most clubs mix up the styles and sounds. Big-name DJs pass through town often, and Berlin has a surprising number of local stars. A few names to look for include: Paul van Dyk (trance), Clé (house), and Tanith (big beats).

The biggest club event of the year is the Love Parade, on a mid-July weekend. It's a citywide outdoor rave party, complete with floats, wild costumes, and lots of pounding techno beats. Millions of people descend on the city to dance in front of the Brandenburg Gate, at the Victory Column, and in streets all across town. The police and Green Party members consider it a nightmare, but city officials love all the cash it brings in.

Cox Orange. Underground and usually smoky, clubby Cox Orange has a dark sort of charm. The music is as mixed and international as the crowd, and for those who don't like to dance there are plenty of corners for chatting. ⊠ *Dirkenstr. 40, Mitte,* ☏ *030/281–0508. Metro: Alexanderplatz.*

Delicious Doughnuts. It looks like a Mafia stronghold. Surly men in too-tight black T-shirts guard the entrance of what seems to be a seedy bar. Truth is, this is one of Berlin's most classic clubs, somewhere you can hear good DJs spin music every day of the week and where the dance floor is big enough to strut your stuff on. The music hovers around jazzy groove, trip-hop, and drum 'n' bass. The bar up front is snug and inviting, and if you get hungry, they really do serve doughnuts. ⊠ *Rosenthaler Str. 9, Mitte,* ☏ *030/283–3021. Metro: Rosenthaler Strasse.*

Icon. This well-loved former brewery basement has an underground atmosphere and is popular among young artists and writers in Prenzlauer Berg. To get in (the entrance is in the courtyard, just north of Milastrasse), walk down several staircases into a long stone cellar. The lighting is magical, and the acoustics are excellent. Music ranges from techno to drum 'n' bass. ⊠ *Cantianstr. 15, Prenzlauer Berg,* ☏ *no phone. Metro: Eberswalder Strasse.*

Metropol. Berlin's largest disco also stages concerts and is a magnet for twentysomething tourists. The darkened dance floor upstairs is the scene of a magnificent laser light show. Regular appearances by the Kit-Kat-Club and other special gay events, which are nothing short of sex parties, attract hundreds of dancers. The disco is open Friday and Saturday only. ⊠ *Nollendorfpl. 5,* ☏ *030/217–3680. Metro: Nollendorfplatz.*

90 Grad. This jam-packed disco plays hip-hop, soul, and some techno and really gets going around 2 AM. Women come fashionably dressed and go right in, but men usually have to wait outside until they get picked by the doorman. There is a backroom bar where conversation is possible. ⊠ *Dennewitzstr. 37, Tiergarten,* ☏ *030/262–8984. Metro: Kurfürstenstrasse.*

WMF. Now in its fifth location, this legendary club got its name from a silverware manufacturer whose warehouse it once used. The space is huge, well ventilated, and bedecked with video screens. The crowd is casual and often has an anything-goes attitude. Once frequented by those fleeing the monotony of techno, the club has now changed its tune and added thumping booms to its repertoire. The outdoor deck has a breathtaking view of the New Synagogue on Oranienburgerstrasse. ⊠ *Ziegelstr. 22–23, Mitte,* ☏ *030/2887–8890. Metro: Oranienburgerstrasse.*

Gay and Lesbian Bars and Clubs

Gay and lesbian pride erupted in Berlin in the 1960s and hasn't stopped since. The gay community is one of the biggest—and by far the most infamous—in Europe. From leather and chains to ABBA, this town covers the whole range of gay culture. In the 1920s Berlin was the first city in the world with an openly gay population. Most of the current action is concentrated in Schöneberg (around Nollendorfplatz and Motzstrasse). This is the same area where, in the 1930s, the young Marlene Dietrich sang erotically charged songs at the Eldorado (now a supermarket). It's also where Christopher Isherwood penned stories that became the basis for the film *Cabaret.*

Despite Schöneberg's dominance, Kreuzberg, Mitte, and Prenzlauer Berg also see their share of gay fun. Although there are some men-only and women-only clubs, mixed gay and lesbian bars are on the rise. Two seasonal highlights are the Motzstrasse gay parade, in early June, and the Christopher Street Day parade (the Saturday closest to June 27.)

Check out the magazines *Siegessäule, (030),* and *Sergej* (free and available at many bars) for the latest nightlife events.

Anderes Ufer. Berlin's oldest gay bar, this hip Kneipe attracts a mixed gay and lesbian crowd. It's a good place to collect information on upcoming gay and lesbian events. The space doubles as a gallery and features art and photography by local artists. The atmosphere is mellow, and the music is usually from the 1950s and 1960s. ⊠ *Hauptstr. 157, Schöneberg,* ☎ *030/784–1578. Metro: Kleistpark.*

Die Busche. One of East Berlin's oldest and flashiest discos for lesbians and gays, this kitschy club moved to a new locale along the Spree River in the 1990s. If no night is a good night until you hear ABBA, this is the place to be. ⊠ *Mühlenstr. 11–12, Friedrichshain,* ☎ *030/296–0800. Metro: Warshauerstrasse.*

Hafenbar. The decor and the energetic crowd make this bar endlessly popular and a favorite singles mixer. Once a month a wild and wacky theme party takes place. At 4 AM people move next door to Tom's Bar, open until 6 AM. ⊠ *Motzstr. 18, Schöneberg,* ☎ *030/211–4118. Metro: Nollendorfplatz.*

Knast. Its name means "jail," and it takes its prisoners seriously. Packed with leather, chains, and riot gear galore, this fetish joint is not for amateurs. It's men-only here. Porno videos abound, and the dark room is well used. The cruise hits full swing on weekends. ⊠ *Fuggerstr. 34, Schöneberg,* ☎ *030/218–1026. Metro: Wittenbergplatz.*

Mann-O-Meter. From the stacks of magazines and newspapers and the friendly waiters, you can get extensive information about gay life, groups, and upcoming events. Talks are held in a cozy backroom café. Safe-sex materials are for sale, and the staff speak English. It's open weekdays 3 PM–11 PM, Saturday 3 PM–10 PM. ⊠ *Motzstr. 5, Schöneberg,* ☎ *030/216–8008. Metro: Nollendorfplatz*

MS TitaniCa. If you like high energy and wild women, don't miss this party. Once the music starts, the only thing standing still is the dance floor. The women-only party is put on by MegaDyke Productions and takes place on board the MS *Sanssouci,* a double-decker boat docked permanently near the Oberbaumbrücke in Kreuzberg. Downstairs, dancers gyrate to serious house beats. Upstairs, it's all 1970s and 1980s classics. The party takes place the first Friday of every month from March to November. ⊠ *MS Sanssouci, Gröbenufer 8, Kreuzberg,* ☎ *030/611–1255. Metro: Schlesisches Tor.*

Roses. A true melting pot, this sparkling den of kitsch is a perfect place to flirt and flounce. It's a favorite of drag queens and kings and is in the middle Kreuzberg, not far from the dance club SO36. The drinks are good, the bartenders ready to relate their personal stories, and the surprises many. ⊠ *Oranienstr. 187, Kreuzberg,* ☎ *030/615–6570. Metro: Görlitzer Bahnhof.*

Schall und Rauch. Named after one of Berlin's earliest cabarets, this very low-key bar has become one of the most popular meeting points in eastern Berlin. The food is simple but good, and the cocktails are fabulous. This is a good place to end a long afternoon or start an evening. ⊠ *Gleimstr. 23, Prenzlauer Berg,* ☎ *030/448–0770. Metro: Schönhauser Allee.*

SO36. An old punk hangout turned legendary Kreuzberg club, SO36 is popular among gays, lesbians, and heteros. The program has remained the same for years: Monday, Electric Ballroom–Techno; Wednesday, Hungry Man, a mostly male party with house music; Sunday, pair dancing with lessons. Look out for the monthly Jane Bond parties, with house and soul music, and the bimonthly Gay Oriental Dance parties, featuring belly-dancing transvestites, drag kings, and every other manifestation of man- and womanhood. ⊠ *Oranienstr. 190, Kreuzberg,* ☎ *030/6140–1306. Metro: Kottbusser Tor.*

Jazz Clubs

Berlin's lively music scene is dominated by jazz, rock, and folk. The jazz scene is good although not staggering. Among the best local performers is Peter Broetzmann, founder of the Berlin Free Music Production and a mean sax player. For jazz enthusiasts *the* events of the year are the summer Jazz in the Garden festival and the autumn international Jazzfest Berlin, which takes place at the Haus der Kulturen der Welt and at Podewil. For jazz festival information call the Haus der Kulturen der Welt (⊠ John-Foster-Dulles-Allee 10, ☎ 030/397–870). For great listening in your hotel room, flip the dial to 101.9 FM, known as Jazz Radio.

A-Trane. Stylish A-Trane is very posh and attracts a largely yuppie clientele. It's often used for radio recordings. Monday and Tuesday are usually free, and on Saturday there is a late-night jam session that lasts until 5 AM. ⊠ *Pestalozzistr. 105, Charlottenberg,* ☎ *030/313–2550. Metro: Savignyplatz.*

B-Flat. Young German artists are featured almost every night in the large and cavernous club. The jam sessions focus on free and experimental jazz. Once a week dancers cut a rug on swing night. ⊠ *Rosenthaler Str. 13, Mitte,* ☎ *030/280–6349. Metro: Rosenthaler Platz.*

Flöz. The sizzling jazz at this cellar club sometimes accompanies theater presentations. This is a good spot to see young hopefuls testing out their sound. ⊠ *Nassauische Str. 37, Wilmersdorf,* ☎ *030/861–1000. Metro: Berlinerstrasse.*

Junction Bar. A taste of New York in the 1940s is dished out here. The stage is up front, the lounge in the back. Jazz and all its offshoots— swing, Latin, contemporary, and even jazz poetry and blues hold sway. The walls are decorated with news articles about the American civil rights movement in the 1960s. ⊠ *Gneisenaustr. 18, Kreuzberg,* ☎ *030/ 694–6602. Metro: Mehringdamm.*

Podewil. This unadorned space used to be the headquarters of East Berlin's Communist youth organization. Now, it's an avant-garde musical catchall. Jazz is about as conservative as the repertoire gets, and when a good group plays the mood can be magical. ⊠ *Klosterstr. 68– 70, Mitte,* ☎ *030/247–496. Metro: Klosterstrasse.*

Schlot. This cozy basement club has the perfect atmosphere for an intimate evening. Unpretentious and edgy, it hosts good bands that have not yet made a name for themselves. Check the calendar. Sometimes comedians and cabaret-style singers headline. ⊠ *Kastanienallee 29, Prenzlauer Berg,* ☎ *030/448–2160. Metro: Eberswalder Strasse.*

Quasimodo. The most established and popular jazz venue in the city has a frenetic basement atmosphere and a know-it-all attitude. The best bands usually play here, and it's often standing room only. Touring American and Brazilian bands attract huge, hip-swaying crowds. The room is large, dimly lighted, and often terribly smoky. ⊠ *Kantstr. 12a, Charlottenburg,* ☎ *030/312–8086. Metro: Zoologischer Garten.*

Kneipen

The city's roughly 6,000 pubs all come under the heading of *Kneipen*— the place around the corner where you stop in for a beer, a snack, and conversation—and sometimes to dance. Other than along Ku'damm and its side streets, the happening places in western Berlin are around Savignyplatz, in Charlottenburg; Nollendorfplatz and Winterfeldplatz, in Schöneberg; Ludwigkirchplatz, in Wilmersdorf; and along Oranienstrasse and Wienerstrasse in Kreuzberg. In eastern Berlin (Mitte) most of the action is north of and along Oranienburger Strasse and around Rosenthaler Platz and the Hackesche Höfe. Kollwitzplatz is the hub in Prenzlauer Berg, but the twenty- to thirtysomething crowd often prefers Helmholzplatz, Kastanienallee, and the streets around the Eberswalder·Strasse U-Bahn.

Broker's Bier Börse. In this frenzied little place the cost of beer depends on "market prices." Large screens on the wall tell you the "worth" of each of the 15 beers at any given minute. The place starts to hop around 5 PM and can be quite a wild ride. ⊠ *Schiffbauerdamm 8, Mitte,* ☎ *030/3087–2293. Metro: Friedrichstrasse.*

E. & M. Leydicke. This historic spot is a must for out-of-towners. The atmosphere is pure Old World, the service grand, and the prices legendarily cheap. The proprietors operate their own distillery and have a superb selection of more than 20 sweet wines and liqueurs. ⊠ *Mansteinstr. 4, Schöneberg,* ☎ *030/216–2973. Metro: Yorckstrasse.*

Gorki Park. If you can't decide between drinking in Prenzlauer Berg or dancing in Mitte, this tiny Russian-owned bar-café makes a perfect middle ground. It's right between the two districts and caters to everyone from Russian immigrants to German lawyers. The little Russian treats (pirogis, *wareniki,* and blini) are pricey but delicious. In summer, tables hit the street, and this becomes a charmingly sunny locale to pass part of a day. ⊠ *Weinbergsweg 25, Mitte,* ☎ *030/448–7286. Metro: Rosenthaler Platz.*

Green Door. This Schöneberg classic used to be Berlin's well-loved Havanna Bar. Despite the name change, the city's hip and wildly dressed crowd still huddle around the long curvy bar to share outstanding cocktails. There really is a green door. ⊠ *Winterfeldstr. 50, Schöneberg,* ☎ *030/215–2515. Metro: Winterfeld Platz.*

Hackbarths. This is only one of many similar alternative coffee shop–cum–bars frequented by students and the young art crowd in the Oranienburger Strasse neighborhood. The food is microwaved and mediocre, but at night the bar becomes a hothouse for young lonely hearts hoping to get lucky. ⊠ *Auguststr. 49a, Mitte,* ☎ *030/282–7706. Metro: Weinmeisterstrasse.*

Ici. As if it were a private literary salon, this cozy café is strewn with copies of Proust, Camus, and Goethe, and the work of local artists adorns the walls. It's quiet and romantic (if you can get a table), and there's a good selection of wine by the glass. ⊠ *Auguststr. 61, Mitte,* ☎ *030/281–4064. Metro: Oranienburger Tor.*

Keyser Soze. One of Berlin's trendiest pubs keeps an understated and cool setting. The service may be sluggish, but the drinks and the atmosphere are as sleek and polished as the huge glass windows that look out onto the bustle. Almost everyone wears black. If you're hungry and a fan of Bavarian cuisine, try the Nürnberger *Bratwürstl.* ⊠ *Tucholskystr. 31, Mitte,* ☎ *030/2859–9489. Metro: Oranienburger Tor.*

Obst und Gemüse. Among the first Mitte bars to open after the Berlin Wall fell, this Kneipe (whose name means "fruit and vegetables") has a casual charm and authenticity that keeps crowds coming back. Take a window seat, order a bagel and a beer, and enjoy the activity along lively Oranienburgerstrasse and in front of Tacheles. At night entertainers, including fire jugglers, perform outside. Prostitutes dressed in leather and plastic getups also stroll Oranienburgerstrasse, adding a

SHOULD I *STEH* OR SHOULD I GO?

I F YOU STRAY INTO LESS-THAN-TOURISTY NEIGHBORHOODS, you may encounter two typically Berlin watering holes—the *Eck-Kneipe* (corner pub) and the *Steh-Cafe* (stand-up café). Be forewarned. Both are locals-only joints, and newcomers (especially ones who don't speak German) will not be well received. You may be greeted with a glare or ignored entirely.

The Steh-Cafe is just what it says it is—a place to stand and drink. They often pop up outside family-owned grocery shops and consist of little more than a tall, white plastic table. Around the table, men—often in the colorful overalls laborers and blue-collar workers wear—drink their morning, afternoon, and evening beers. You see them more in the east, where for years this was where gossip passed and lifelong bonds slowly formed. Generally speaking, these groups are impenetrable. Don't even try to start a conversation.

The Eck-Kneipe is usually a dark little bar that looks as intriguing as it does menacing. Inside, it's probably filled with smoke and horrid German pop music. The clientele is almost exclusively male, and almost everyone knows each other. Most are usually well past sober and speak a slurred version of the already incomprehensible Berlin dialect. As in the Steh-Cafe, strangers are regarded with suspicion and generally not welcomed. Try your luck if you must and order a round of drinks among friends, but consider yourself warned.

sinful edge to any evening. ⊠ *Oranienburgerstr. 48–49, Mitte,* ☎ *030/ 282–9647. Metro: Oranienburger Tor; Oranienburgerstrasse.*

Coffeehouses

Barcomis. American owner Cynthia Barcomi effectively brought the American coffee craze to Berlin. She not only roasts her own beans but serves them with bagels, muffins, and super brownies. She also has a huge assortment of Celestial Seasonings teas. The servers (like almost everyone in the place) speak English. It's on bustling Bergmannstrasse, a fun place for shopping, eating, and poking about antiques stores; there are two other branches in Mitte. ⊠ *Bergmannstr. 21, Kreuzberg,* ☎ *030/694–8163. Metro: Gneisenaustrasse.*

Einstein. This beautiful Viennese-style coffeehouse is housed in an old mansion and has a pretty backyard patio where tuxedo-clad waiters hustle to serve steaming bowls of coffee and delicious apple strudel (beware: the waiters are known for their surliness and their no-nonsense manners). A branch opened on Unter der Linden, but it has none of the classy air of this Berlin classic. ⊠ *Kurfürstenstr. 58, Tiergarten,* ☎ *030/261–5096. Metro: Nollendorfplatz.*

Café Savigny. Newspaper-reading intellectuals sip little cups of black coffee at this old-style café on one of western Berlin's finest squares. The streets are lined with designer boutiques, and the service and desserts are just as exquisite. ⊠ *Grolmanstr. 53–54, Charlottenburg,* ☎ *030/312–8195. Metro: Savignyplatz.*

Live Music

The rock scene, enmeshed in its postpunk and posttechno phase, is still trying to find itself, but because living in Berlin is still fairly cheap, there are many talented young bands. The folk scene includes a full array of Eastern influences and can be enchanting.

Arena. This scrappy-looking space used to be a maintenance lot for city buses, but now it hosts big concerts and large theater productions. Most bands fall into two categories: so alternative they are grateful to have a venue or bordering on mainstream and anxious to preserve their edgy image. Smashing Pumpkins and Prodigy have played here. ⊠ *Eichenstr. 4, Treptow,* ☎ *030/533–7333. Metro: Treptower Park.*

Hackesches Hof Theater. This intimate little concert space nestled in the Hackesche Höfe is a perfect spot to catch Klezmer, Yiddish, and Eastern European folk concerts. ⊠ *Rosenthalerstr. 40–41, Mitte,* ☎ *030/283–2587. Metro: Hackescher Markt.*

Insel. This miniature castlelike venue is secluded on a tiny island in the Spree River. It used to be a Communist youth club but now offers an exotic backdrop for local and international bands. It's great in summer, when the roof terrace opens and offers smashing views of the Spree. ⊠ *Alt Treptow 6, Treptow,* ☎ *030/534–8851. Metro: Planterwald or Treptower Park.*

Knaack Club. If you're looking for fringe or are interested in how Berlin's youth spend their evenings, this three-level dilapidated disco is it. The club has a rather flexible booking policy, and the range runs from alternative rock to very alternative rock. ⊠ *Greifswalderstr. 224, Prenzlauer Berg,* ☎ *030/442–7060. Metro: Greifswalderstrasse.*

Pfefferberg. This dilapidated arena became a cult hangout in the early 1990s. It's lost some of its original flair, but the colonnaded terrace still emanates shabby chic, and the crowd is refreshingly mixed. In the summer a large beer garden surrounds the performance space. Reggae and world music are the staples, but an occasional punk band will still slip in. ⊠ *Schönhauser Allee 176, Prenzlauer Berg,* ☎ *030/4438– 3112. Metro: Senefelder Platz.*

Tempodrom. As of December 2001, this nomadic multicultural music venue has settled in Kreuzberg. Each summer it hosts the Heimatklänge, a seven-week music festival devoted to a particular theme, from Brazilian music to "Soul-to-Soul" to traditional wedding tunes. ⊠ *Askanischer Platz 6-7, Kreuzberg,* ☎ *030/318–6140. Metro: Anhalter Bahnhof*

Tränenpalast. Gloomy blue on the outside and laden with disco balls and kitschy chandeliers on the inside, this venue is a stunning example of Berliners' ability to reappropriate and laugh about their history. For decades, the cavernous building—whose name means "Palace of Tears"—served as a border transfer between East and West. It was here, at the Friedrichstrasse station, that Westerners who had been allowed to visit Eastern family and friends had to say their tearful goodbyes. Today, it's been transformed into a trendy nightclub with space for 2,000 and an ever-changing list of events including cabaret, jazz, salsa, celebrity parties, and fashion shows. Most of the GDR flavor is gone, but a few touches remain. ⊠ *Reichstagsufer 17, Mitte,* ☎ *030/2062– 0011. Metro: Friedrichstrasse*

Velodrom. This huge sports arena books big mainstream stars. It was built in 1997 as part of Berlin's failed attempt to win the 2000 Olympics bid. ⊠ *Paul-Heiser-Str. 29, Mauerpark, Prenzlauer Berg,* ☎ *030/4430– 4714. Metro: Landsberger Allee.*

THE ARTS

For the 30 years it was divided into East and West, arts in Berlin flourished. Each side furiously tried to outdo the other and prove its artistic superiority. Funds flowed into theaters, dance companies, and opera houses. When the Wall fell in 1989 and the city unified, much of that support fell, too. Artists, directors, and ensembles struggle between two routes of survival: pushing the envelope of creativity or dishing out easy, crowd-pleasing shows sure to sell. As a result, programming is usually a kooky mix of old classics and edgy premieres.

One constant debate circles around Berlin's three opera houses and the three ballet companies based in them. In an attempt to save money in the late 1990s, the Senate voted to merge the three dance companies into one: Berlin Ballet. The merger, which would have cost about 60 dancers their jobs and severely limited the dance repertoire in the city, was highly unpopular and as yet has not occurred. Rumors of a similar fate swirl around the three opera houses and their companies, but for the moment all remain securely separate. Theaters, too, have faced a constant array of change, as ensembles have been cut and then rebuilt and directors have flip-flopped from house to house.

One highlight of all this flux is that directors without a permanent house or company often use the city itself as a backdrop for their work. Construction sites, abandoned buildings, and former East German rallying halls have all served as impromptu stages. Almost nothing is impossible in this spicy, vibrant scene.

The Berliner Festwochen (Berlin Festival Weeks), held annually from August through September, include concerts, operas, ballet, theater, and art exhibitions. Every September some of the world's best theater companies come to town. For information and reservations contact **Festspiele GmbH** (Kartenbüro, ✉ Budapester Str. 50, D–10787, ☎ 030/254–890, FAX 030/2548–9111). You can also try to book on-line at www.ticketonline.de. The site is not easy to navigate and if you want specific seats, it is easier to talk directly to an agent.

BUYING TICKETS

Many hotels will book seats for you, and there are several ticket agencies in town. Most of the big stores (Hertie, Wertheim, and Karstadt, for example) also have ticket agencies. Many larger theaters accept ticket orders over Web sites, but the sites aren't glitch-free, and often it is still easier to order from an agency. One good site to try is www.berlin.de/home/Marktplatz/tickets/.

The **Hekticket offices** (✉ Karl-Liebknecht-Str. 12, off Alexanderplatz, ☎ 030/2431–2431; ✉ Zoo-Palast movie theater, off Hardenbergpl., ☎ 030/2309–930) offer discounted and last-minute tickets. **Showtime Konzert- und Theaterkassen** (✉ KaDeWe, Tauentzienstr. 21, ☎ 030/217–7754; Wertheim, ✉ Kurfürstendamm 181, ☎ 030/882–2500) is a reliable but often busy place to get information. Someone always speaks English. **Theater- und Konzertkasse City Center** (✉ Kurfürstendamm 16, ☎ 030/882–6563) has very friendly tellers who will usually hustle to get you just what you want. Since they take time with customers, the lines can sometimes get very long.

Classical Music

Classical music in Berlin is as glorious as it is diverse, especially in spring and summer when the city hums with outdoor concerts. Music has always been integral to German culture, and even the average German has a basic knowledge of the major works of Beethoven, Bach, and Brahms.

The city's economic woes have led to huge slashes in the city's arts budget in recent years. Ticket prices have therefore shot up, and conductors have started to choose ever-more traditional, crowd-pleasing fare.

For 19th-century traditionalists, there is the superb Berlin Philharmonic, home to a world-class orchestra led by the expert hands of conductor Claudio Abbado. Abbado follows a long line of star conductors at the Phil, including Willhelm Furtwängler and Herbert von Karajan, for whom the building was built. Simon Rattle is scheduled to take over from Abbado during the 2002 season. The Deutsches Sinfonie-Orchester has less of a reputation but can be equally magical. For those seeking out contemporary music, Danish director Michael Schonwandt has done wonders with the Berliner Sinfonie-Orchester. Germany's premier modern group, the Ensemble Modern, makes regular stops in Berlin, and if it happen to be playing while you are in town, don't miss it.

As far as opera goes, Berlin rarely attracts superstars, but the local voices are solid and tickets to the three houses fairly easy to come by. Alternative performances can also be seen at the small but surprisingly good Neuköllner Oper and the Berliner Kammeroper. The opera houses are also home to the city's ballet troupes. If you plan to just stop by and get tickets for whatever is playing, be careful you don't end up with seats for the ballets *Swan Lake* or *Cinderella* instead of an opera.

Philharmonie mit Kammermusiksaal. This is not only Berlin's premier classical music center, it is also one of the city's most daring buildings architecturally. It's golden lines are bold, organic, and utterly modern. Some Berliners despise it, but over the years it has become an accepted architectural landmark. Designed in 1963 by Hans Scharoun, the center is famous for its fabulous acoustics. Inside, the audience of up to 2,400 people does not face the performing orchestra but actually surrounds it on three different levels within a pentagon-shape hall (actually, the acoustics directly behind the orchestra are lousy). The Berlin Philharmonic dates back to 1882, but it became most famous under the renowned conductor Herbert von Karajan. The adjacent Kammermusiksaal is dedicated to chamber music. ⊠ *Matthäikircherstr. 1,* ☎ *030/254–880 or 030/2548–8132. Metro: Kurfürstenstrasse.*

Hochschule der Künste. This horribly ugly building is the place where Berlin's future maestros strive for greatness. The concert hall is among the largest in the city and is often a good place to see rising talent and lesser-known orchestras and soloists who can't afford to book big concert facilities. Tickets for student concerts are free. ⊠ *Hardenbergstr. 33,* ☎ *030/3185–2374. Metro: Ernst-Rueter-Platz.*

Konzerthaus Berlin. This three-in-one hall is both an architectural gem in the center of historic Berlin and a prime venue for classical music concerts. Designed by Karl Friedrich Schinkel in 1821, the building was destroyed during the war and then restored in 1984. It has two main spaces for concerts: the Grosser Konzertsaal, which hosts orchestras, and the Kleiner Konzertsaal, which provides an enchanting setting for chamber music. Both the excellent Berliner Sinfonie-Orchestra and the imaginative Deutsches Sinfonie-Orchester are based here. Downstairs, the small Musik Club hosts occasional concerts. ⊠ *Schauspielhaus, Gendarmenmarkt 2,* ☎ *030/2030–92101. Metro: Französische Strasse*

Meistersaal. The little Meistersaal salon is one of the loveliest venues in the city for intimate concerts. Its design is classic and the acoustics wonderful. The performers are probably not as well known as those performing in the Kammermusiksaale at the Berlin Phil, but the quality may be just as good. ⊠ *Kötjemerstr. 38, Kreuzberg,* ☎ *030/264–9530. Metro: Anhalter Bahnhof.*

Waldbühne. Modeled after an ancient open-air Roman theater, the Wald-bühne accommodates nearly 20,000 people at opera, classical, or rock concerts. ⊠ *Am Glockenturm, close to Olympiastadion,* ☎ *030/305–5079. Metro: Olympia Stadium.*

Church, Museum, and Small Concert Halls

Most Germans are not religious, but they do take their church music seriously. Dozens of churches offer afternoon concerts, especially in sum-mer and in the month before Christmas. Museums, likewise, often take advantage of their setting and are a wonderful place to hear small trios or soloists. A few select spots offer regular musical offerings. For a com-plete listing of what is playing, check the magazines *Tip* or *Zitty*.

Akademie der Künste. This multipurpose hall offers everything from music to films to literary readings to small expositions. It has two rooms that hold 200–500 people, and most of the performances are con-temporary in nature. ⊠ *Hanseatenweg 10, Tiergarten,* ☎ *030/3900–0764. Metro: Hansaplatz.*

Ballhaus Naunynstrasse. Catch offbeat and exciting new music at this Kreuzberg cultural center. The repertoire ranges from classical to Asian, and the crowd is usually a mixed group. The rectangular room seats 150. The Berliner Kammeroper (Berlin Chamber Opera) sometimes plays here and is well worth seeing. ⊠ *Naunynstr. 27, Kreuzberg,* ☎ *030/2588–6644. Metro: Moritzplatz.*

Berliner Dom. Damaged during the war, this classic late-19th-century church on the eastern edge of the Museum Island was left largely abandoned during the 30 years of Communist rule. The restored church hosts frequent organ and choral recitals. ⊠ *Lustgarten, Mitte,* ☎ *030/2026–9136. Metro: Hackescher Markt.*

Schloss Friedrichsfelde. The GDR's former state guest house is used oc-casionally as a concert hall for classical performances, mostly cham-ber music. ⊠ *Am Tierpark 125, Friedrichshain,* ☎ *030/513–8142. Metro: Tierpark.*

Staatsbibliothek-Otto Braun Saal. Afternoon and early-evening concerts and recitals take place in this book-filled chamber in the state library. ⊠ *Potsdamerstr. 33, Tiergarten,* ☎ *030/2661. Metro: Potsdamer Platz.*

St. Matthäuskirche. This little brick beauty is next to the Berlin Phil-harmonic and is a good alternative if you can't get into the Phil or if you prefer something smaller. The acoustics are great and the music programming top-notch. ⊠ *Matthäikirchpl., Tiergarten,* ☎ *030/262–1202. Metro: Potsdamer Platz.*

Zionskirche. The redbrick church with a feisty political history dates from 1866. It features a wide variety of classical music, with an em-phasis on *Alte Musik* (Bach and pre-Bach) and modern religious music (Fauré, for instance). A specialty are classical a cappella pieces for one or more singers. At times it also stages ultramodern classical music by contemporary composers. Fees vary, depending on who is performing, and concerts usually start at 8 PM. ⊠ *Zionskirchpl., Prenzlauer Berg,* ☎ *030/449–2191. Metro: Senefelderplatz.*

Dance

As with opera and classical music, dance companies have seen their share of budget cuts in recent years. Still, city officials are determined to refit the new Berlin in the mold of the old and to once again turn it into a capital of contemporary dance. Choreographer and dancer Sascha Waltz (now at the Schaubühne) has certainly made a name for herself.

The two ballet companies have different styles. The Deutsche Oper has shifted ballet directors numerous times but maintains a reputation for young, fresh, contemporary work. Frequent guest choreographers and dancers give the program an international flavor. Udo Zimmermann is scheduled to take the helm in the 2002 season. The repertoire of the Staatsoper Unter den Linden is heavy on crowd-pleasing classics. In an attempt to gain more status since the Wall fell, the former East Berlin company has tried to pull in big-name guest performers such as Ronald Petit and Patrice Bart. The world-renowned German choreographer, Pina Bausch, is based in Wuppertal and makes an occasional appearance in Berlin. In 2001 she came for the festival weeks and performed at the Volksbühne.

Hebbel Theater. Largely dedicated to dance, the Hebbel offers some of the most intelligent and thought-provoking shows in the city. Long-legged theatergoers sometimes find the tightly packed rows cramped. ⊠ *Stresemannstr. 29, Kreuzberg,* ☎ *030/2590–0427. Metro: Hallesches Tor.*

Podewil. A former East Berlin cultural center, this little gem has developed quite a reputation for experimental performance pieces. You can find almost everything here. Tanzwerkstatt, a group that books modern ensembles, is based here. ⊠ *Klosterstr. 68–70, Mitte,* ☎ *030/2474–9777. Metro: Klosterstrasse.*

Tanzfabrik. This 100-seat house has a tiny stage and a small company that performs innovative but not always polished pieces. The main function of the Tanzfabrik is as a contemporary dance school, and it offers more than 50 classes a week. ⊠ *Möckernstr. 68, Kreuzberg,* ☎ *030/786–5861. Metro: Yorckstrasse.*

Theater am Halleschen Ufer. Founded in 1962, this theater overlooks the Landwehr Canal and is one of the best places in Europe to see independent contemporary dance. Dance makes up more than half the programming, and dance festivals in April and October feature new dance trends in Berlin. ⊠ *Hallesches Ufer 32, Kreuzberg,* ☎ *030/251–0941. Metro: Möchernbrücke.*

Film

Germans go to the movies more often than other Europeans, and in Berlin the choices are overwhelming. The city has more than 200 screens, and an increasing number of mainstream cinemas are showing films in English. Art-house cinemas also sometimes show indie films in their original language. In summer the city parks are aglow with open-air cinemas (*Freiluftkinos*).

In the past few years multiplexes with huge popcorn counters, snazzy cafés, and air-conditioning have opened. Many have at least one theater screening Hollywood films in English. One thing to beware of is that Germans much prefer dubbing to subtitles. Unless a film is marked *OF* or *OV* (*Originalfassung,* or original version) or *OmU* (original, with subtitles), it is probably dubbed. (Also, Germans tend to like their popcorn with caramelized sugar rather than salt. If you are a traditionalist, make sure you ask for salty, or you could be in for a sticky surprise.)

Ticket costs vary tremendously, depending on the day of the week and the time of day. Tickets are cheapest weekdays—usually Tuesday, Wednesday, and/or Thursday—before 6 PM and can cost as little as €3. Weekend evenings are most expensive, and tickets range from €6 to €9.

In February Berlin hosts the **Internationale Filmfestspiele Berlin (Berlinale)** (☎ 030/2548–9254), the second-largest film festival in the world, at which the Golden Bear award is bestowed. Tickets can be bought up to three days in advance at either the Europa-Center (⊠ Breitscheidpl. 5, Tiergarten, ☎ 030/348–0088, Metro: Zoologischer Garten) or Kino Internationale (⊠ Karl-Marx-Allee 33, Mitte, ☎ 030/242–5826, Metro: Alexanderplatz). For a program listing or a full festival pass, go to the **Berlinale Shop** (⊠ Budapesterstr. 48, Tiergarten, ☎ 030/2548–9254, Metro: Zoologischer Garten).

Films in English

Babylon. This small, twin-screen theater is a bit run-down but shows almost exclusively British and indie films in English. The tellers are usually friendly and well versed in film history. Don't confuse it with the art house of the same name in Mitte. ⊠ *Dresdnerstr. 126, Kreuzberg,* ☎ *030/614–6316. Metro: Kotbusser Tor.*

CinemaxX Potsdamer Platz. The American-style cinema palace with 19 screens shows big Hollywood films in English and German. Small cafés and bars abound, as does an American-style mall. CinemaxX is one of the few places in the city that takes credit-card reservations by phone. ⊠ *Potsdamerstr. 5, Tiergarten,* ☎ *030/4431–6316. Metro: Potsdamer Platz.*

CineStar im Sony Center, CineStar IMAX im Sony Center. If you don't like the choices at CinemaxX, around the corner is this eight-screen complex plus an IMAX theater. This real Berlin novelty can get crowded. A second IMAX, with films in 3-D, is also across the street. ⊠ *Potsdamerstr. 4, Tiergarten,* ☎ *030/2606–6400. Metro: Potsdamer Platz.*

Odeon. This quirky shoebox theater is in the heart of Schöneberg and is a favorite among English-speaking expats. Come ahead of time because the comfy seats can sell out. ⊠ *Hauptstr. 116, Schöneberg,* ☎ *030/781–5667. Metro: Innsbrucker Platz.*

UCI Kinowelt Zoo Palast. Berlin's most famous cinema is a registered landmark. It stands on the site where the glitzy Ufa-Palast-Zoo premiered Germany's hottest films from 1923 until 1943. The theater was rebuilt for the 1957 Berlin film festival and quickly became West Berlin's most glamorous movie house. Today the theater is a bit run-down, but it is still one of the city's only old-style houses with a stage-like screen. The theater has nine screens, and on two they can run both the soundtrack of the original film and a dubbed German version. ⊠ *Hardenbergstr. 29a, Charlottenburg,* ☎ *030/2541–4777. Metro: Zoologischer Garten.*

UFA Arthouse die Kurbel. The three-screener has all of the comforts of a multiplex without actually being one. The service is efficient, the seats comfortable and well cared for, and usually at least two of the films are in English. There is handicapped access. ⊠ *Giesebrechtstr. 4, Charlottenburg,* ☎ *030/883–5325. Metro: Adenauer Platz; Savignyplatz.*

Open-Air Cinemas

For an updated program for any *Freiluki* (open-air cinema), surf to www.independents.de then click "Kinos," then "Freiluftkinos." The summer movies usually start around 9:30 PM, once it gets dark.

Freiluftkino Friedrichshain. Hidden among the trees in Volkspark Friedrichshain, this is a wonderful place to take in a film. ⊠ *Im Volkspark Friedrichshain, Kreuzberg,* ☎ *030/2936–1629. Trams 5, 6, 8, or 15 to Platz der Vereinten Nationen.*

Freiluftkino Kreuzberg. This outdoor venue is behind the Bethanien Arts Center—just follow the signs tied to the lampposts. ⊠ *Mariannenplatz 2, Kreuzberg. Metro: 8 Kotbusser Tor.*

Freiluftkino Museuminsel. Not strictly in a park and having probably the most unusual setting is this cinema on Museum Island. ⊠ *Bode-*

str., in front of the Alte Nationalgalerie ☎ *030/2472–7801. Metro: Hackescher Markt.*

Musicals

Estrel Festival Center. For musicals such as *West Side Story, Shakespeare & Rock 'n' Roll, A Chorus Line,* and *Cabaret* (all translated into German), head to the Estrel. ⊠ *Sonnenallee 225/Ziegrastr. 21–29, Neukölln,* ☎ *030/6831–6831. Metro: Sonnenallee.*

Grips Theater. The classic Berlin musical *Linie 1* tells the story of a young girl who comes to Berlin hoping to meet a rock star she has a crush on. As she searches for her love, she rides subway Line 1 and meets a variety of characters. Written by Volker Ludwig in 1986, the play with its 18 songs has been seen by more than 2 million people and has achieved cult status. ⊠ *Altonaer Str. 22, Charlottenburg,* ☎ *030/391–4004. Metro: Hansaplatz.*

Theater des Westens. Germany's leading musical theater usually features popular American musicals and mediocre German copies. The shows are guaranteed to be light, the sets elaborate, and almost every ending happy. In-house productions have included hits like Cabaret and Porgy and Bess. The interior frescoes are terribly gauche, but luckily the lights go out quickly. ⊠ *Kantstr. 12, Charlottenburg,* ☎ *030/882–2888. Metro: Zoologischer Garten.*

Stella Musical Theater. Stella has staged the *Hunchback of Notre-Dame* for years, and there seems to be no end date in sight. ⊠ *Marlene-Dietrich-Pl. 1, Tiergarten,* ☎ *030/01805–4444. Metro: Potsdamer Platz.*

Opera

Deutsche Oper Berlin. This ghastly 1961 granite building is so prison-like that Berliners have dubbed it "Sing-Sing." Inside, the decor is pleasant, but it is certainly not grand like its sister on Unter den Linden. Still, the company is solid and the staging grand. ⊠ *Bismarckstr. 34–37, Charlottenburg,* ☎ *030/3410–249 or 030/343–8401. Metro: Charlottenburg.*

Komische Oper. The reputation of this light-opera house has soared under the expert guidance of artistic director Harry Kupfer and his talented Russian-American musical director, Yakov Kreizberg. Kupfer is one of the few East Germans to really make it in the post-Wall theatrical world. Both men are scheduled to leave at the start of the 2002 season and will be replaced by the team of Andreas Homoki and Kirill Petrenko. Like Kupfer and Kreizberg, they are known for their bold and often radical interpretations of comic operas. Most operas are sung in German. Half-price tickets are available at the box office after 11 AM on the day of the performance. ⊠ *Behrenstr. 55–57, Mitte,* ☎ *030/ 4799–7400 or 01805/304–168. Metro: Französische Str.*

Neuköllner Oper. This is no place for grand arias, breathtaking scenery, or grand emotions. This is opera for the proletariat—bubbly, fresh, and often very funny. You might happen on a long-forgotten opera, a favorite musical, or a slapstick comedy. Tickets are much cheaper (€15–€31) than at the three major houses, and the crowd is much more casual. ⊠ *Karl-Marx-Str. 131–133, Neukölln,* ☎ *030/6889–0777. Metro: Karl-Marx-Strasse.*

Staatsoper Unter den Linden. This is classic opera, complete with chandeliers and champagne. Built as the Prussian Royal Opera under Frederick the Great in 1742, the building was designed to look like a Greek temple, with Corinthian columns and a classical pediment. Bombs destroyed it during World War II, but the East German government considered it a showpiece and rebuilt it with elaborate wall paintings and glittering chandeliers in 1955. For years musical director Daniel Barenboim has been pushing to reinvigorate what was sometimes a staid program. Stars like Pavarotti and Domingo occasionally perform. In the small but lavish Apollo Saal you can also hear chamber music. Tickets can be hard to come by, so book early. The box office is open weekdays 10–6, weekends 2–6; you can make phone reservations weekdays 10–8, weekends 2–8. ⊠ *Unter den Linden 7, Mitte,* ☎ *030/2035–4555. Metro: Französische Strasse.*

Theater

Theater in Berlin is outstanding, and performances are almost always in German. The exceptions are operettas and the (nonliterary) cabarets. Of the city's impressive theaters, the most renowned for both their modern and classical productions are the Schaubühne am Lehniner Platz, Deutsches Theater, and Kammerspiele. For English-language theater try the Friends of Italian Opera.

Berliner Ensemble. The house built by East German playwright Bertolt Brecht is really called the Theater am Schiffbauerdamm. Under Brecht in the 1950s this was the most cutting-edge stage in Europe. It has lost much of its luster, but artistic director Claus Peymann still manages to stage innovative performances with the Berliner Ensemble. The company is solid, albeit not standout. The theater is cozy and has a little garden outside for wandering during intermission. ⊠ *Bertolt-Brecht-Pl. 1, Mitte,* ☎ *030/282–3160. Metro: Friedrichstrasse.*

Deutsches Theater. In a picturesque courtyard in Mitte, this classic house performs bourgeois favorites with aplomb. The interior is elegant, with large chandeliers and a roomy stage. Long regarded as among the best companies in Berlin, the theater is losing its longtime director, Thomas Langhoff. Next door there is the equally good, but much smaller and low-key Kammerspiele. ⊠ *Schumannstr. 13, Mitte,* ☎ *030/2844–1222 or 030/2844–1225. Metro: Friedrichstrasse.*

Friends of Italian Opera. This dungeon of a theater is in a Kreuzberg alley and can get cold in the winter and blistering hot in the summer. Still, it is one of the only places to see classic and modern shows in English. It gets its name from the Marilyn Monroe film *Some Like It Hot,* in which mafiosi disguised themselves as "friends of Italian opera." The quality varies from performance to performance, but the ambience is always oddball and the crowd intriguing. Look for the Out to Lunch Theater Company, Berlin's most reliable English-language ensemble. ⊠ *Fidicinstr. 40, Kreuzberg,* ☎ *030/691–1211. Metro: Platz der Luftbrücke.*

Komödie/Theater am Kurfürstendamm. These two large theaters produce light comedies and satires that cater largely to German tourists. Busloads arrive for matinee performances. Although the theaters operate separately, the offerings are much the same. ⊠ *Kurfürstendamm 206 and 209, Charlottenburg,* ☎ *030/4702–1010, 030/4799–7440. Metro: Uhlandstrasse.*

Kulturbrauerei. Opened in 1999, this former brewery resembles a little brick-and-stone village and has rapidly become a hot nightspot. It not only houses an assortment of theaters, dance, and performance spaces but also cafés and a multiplex cinema. Occasionally an opera is performed, and in the summer you can tango outdoors on selected evenings. Even if you don't catch a show, it's worth a walk-through—especially on a balmy summer night. ⊠ *Knaackstr. 97, Prenzlauer Berg,* ☎ *030/441–9269. Metro: Eberswalder Strasse.*

Maxim Gorki Theater. The studio theater itself is superb, the company, sadly, is not. Still, director Bernd Wilms has made sustained efforts to keep the program solid and sometimes produces truly remarkable work. Wilms will most likely leave by 2002 to take the helm at the Deutsches Theater. The repertoire consists of modern classics, with an emphasis on German and Russian playwrights. Don't go unless your German is flawless. ⊠ *Am Festungsgraben 2, Mitte,* ☎ *030/2022–1115. Metro: Friedrichstrasse.*

Renaissance-Theater. Opened in 1927, this magnificent house looks every bit what an old-fashioned theater should. It has comfortable, red-upholstered seats; a low, wide chandelier; and a large stage. The repertoire, too, is a bit old-fashioned and generally consists of international hit dramas that are reworked in German. ⊠ *Hardenbergstr. 6, Charlottenburg,* ☎ *030/312–4202. Metro: Ernst-Reuter-Platz.*

Schaubühne am Lehniner Platz. This three-pronged theater built by Bauhaus architect Erich Mendelsohn has a reputation for all-around excellence. Adjoining theaters can be used separately or open up to form one huge auditorium. Peter Stein served as director in the 1960s and 1970s, and such contemporary luminaries as Robert Wilson and Luc Bondy have directed here. In 1999 Berlin's hottest team of young directors—dancer/choreographer Sasha Waltz and actor/director Thomas Ostermeier—took reign and have given the somewhat stuffy theater a new buzz, with community outreach programs, dance workshops, and international and German premiers. Most performances are in German, but those directed by Waltz include a large amount of dance. ⊠ *Kurfürstendamm 153, Charlottenburg,* ☎ *030/890–023. Metro: Adenauerplatz.*

Theater am Halleschen Ufer. In addition to its dance programming, this stage also caters to fringe theater and solo performances (some in English). ⊠ *Hallesches Ufer 32, Kreuzberg,* ☎ *030/251–0941. Metro: Möchernbrücke.*

Theater Zerbrochene Fenster. Large and airy, this converted factory provides a natural setting for offbeat theater. The choices tend to be heavy, dark, and contemporary, and there are sometimes performances in English. ⊠ *Fidicinstr. 3, Kreuzberg,* ☎ *030/691–2932. Metro: Platz der Luftbrücke.*

Volksbühne am Rosa-Luxemburg-Platz. The hugely popular "People's Stage" is headed by Frank Castorf, an East German who has a cultish following for his ultramodern and aggressively experimental style. The program changes daily, and the name of the day's play is posted on a large banner that waves on top of the theater's monolithic, columned exterior. Inside, the seats are shabby, and the wood-paneled walls and bar evoke the feeling of cold-war James Bond scenes from the 1960s. The staff is young and amiable. The adjacent Roter and Grüner salons have programs of their own. ⊠ *Rosa-Luxemburg-Pl., Mitte,* ☎ *030/247–6772 or 030/2406–5661. Metro: Rosa-Luxemburg-Platz.*

Children's Theater

Grips Theater. The Grips Theater puts on a huge assortment of programs for children of all ages, as well as the Berlin classic *Linie 1,* which concerns itself with a young woman's ride on the subway and the various characters she meets. ⊠ *Altonaer Str. 22, Charlottenburg,* ☎ *030/391–4004. Metro: Hansaplatz.*

Berliner Figuren Theater. For very small children, try Berlin's oldest puppet theater, where intricate dolls dance, carry on, and bring fairy tales to life. ⊠ *Yorckstr. 59, Kreuzberg,* ☎ *030/786–9815. Metro: Yorckstrasse.*

Klecks. If your kids speak no German but like to participate, head for Klecks. The marionette and puppet house hires animated young actors who just love to get young kids riled up. It's a little out of the way, but your kids are sure to have fun. ⊠ *Schinkestr. 8–9, Neukölln,* ☎ *030/693–7731. Metro: Schöleinstrasse.*

6 OUTDOOR ACTIVITIES AND SPORTS

If all that art, culture, and history is beginning to wear you down, a spot of activity in the fresh air may breathe some new life into your vacation.

By Tim Reid

ALTHOUGH EXERCISE ISN'T THE FIRST THING that crosses Berliners' minds as they awake from a beer-induced slumber, the outdoors is something they revel in. No longer polluted by the large-scale industry that coughed out plumes of smoke in the first part of the 20th century, Berlin's air now benefits from an economy based on table service and Internet connections. As coal heating has disappeared through residential renovation, so too has the faint yellow haze that once hung in winter skies.

With a remarkably rich array of parks, lakes, and woodland oxygenating the air, it's no wonder Berliners spend so much time outdoors. The sun needs only to wink from behind a cloud and the parks are full of barbecuers, sunbathers, and hastily organized games of soccer and Frisbee. The only problem faced by the avid jogger is how to negotiate his or her way round the pavement obstacles dropped off by Berlin's community of dogs. The bicycle continues to be an extremely popular and conscientious mode of transport. Bicycle lanes and quiet streets offer relative safety, and the vast size of Berlin means that cycling can be an effective form of exercise while commuting. Outside the city center, the waterways of the Havel and nearby lakes are perfect half-day getaways. And whoever prefers to pump iron indoors won't be disappointed with the number of fitness studios from which to choose.

Soccer continues to be Germany's main passion and Berlin's main participant team sport. The city has some of the most impressive and up-to-date facilities and arenas in Germany. Venues such as the Olympic Stadium and the Velodrom can also double up to host international sporting events. Thanks in part to a rise in the Berlin teams' fortunes, spectator sport has never enjoyed so much attention.

GREEN SPACES AND BEACHES

Two-thirds of Berlin is made up of water, woods, and meadows, and the benefits of this are not lost on your average local. Although nothing has been scientifically proven, the smile on a Berliner's face always seems wider when his or her rear end is parked on grass. In summer, open-air cinemas (*Freiluftkinos*) in selected parks are all the rage.

Grosser Müggelsee

Tucked far away in Berlin's southeast corner, Grosser Müggelsee is an ideal destination on a summer's day. When you're done lounging at the lake's Strandbad Müggelsee/Rahnsdorf, where there is also a nudist section, your €3 also entitles you to the use of the sauna, basketball, and volleyball facilities. For an extra charge you can rent a canoe or paddleboat, and when all that activity starts to take its toll, you can replace those expended calories in the Braustubl restaurant, next to the Berliner Burgerbräu brewery. ⊠ *S-Bahn 3 Friedrichshagen, then Tram 61 to Strandbad Müggelsee.*

Grunewald

Berlin's largest forest lies in the southwest and is easily accessed by the S-Bahn. Popular with the horsey set, dog walkers, cyclists, and joggers, Grunewald is the city's most-visited green retreat. In the north of the forest a mix of mostly young and gay bathers dips into the small **Teufelssee.** The nearby Teufelsberg, an artificial hill made from World War II rubble and once topped by U.S. army intelligence listening devices, attracts sledders in hordes after a snowfall. The **Jagdschloss Grunewald** (Grunewald Hunting Palace), on the southern edge of the forest, is open daily to the public. Not to be missed is the **Grunewald-**

turm (Grunewald Tower), on the western edge of the forest. From the 344-ft-high platform of this memorial to Wilhelm I you can see as far as Potsdam. Those with vertigo can wait in the comfort of the restaurants below.

The southeast periphery of Grunewald offers three nearly contiguous lakes. At **Grunewaldsee** you'll find an extremely pleasant stretch of sand and some naked swimmers on the signposted "Bullenwinkel" (*Freikörperkultur [FKK]*) beach. Toilets are on hand, but the concession stand is on the other side of the water near the Jagdschloss. On the southern edge of **Krumme Lanke** there are portable toilets, a food stall, and two small sunbathing areas with access to the water. Get there early, as it can get rather crowded on sunny days. Nonswimmers should take special care or not take the plunge at all, as after the initial shelf the lake is fairly deep in parts. Although people do swim in the **Schlachtensee,** there are not many suitable areas to lay out a beach towel between the trees. More advisable is to buy a couple of beers, rent a rowboat at the southeastern corner, and enjoy the peace and quiet without getting wet. ⊠ *S-Bahn 7 Grunewald is the easiest route, but it is also possible to arrive by U-Bahn 1 Krumme Lanke or S-Bahn 1 Schlachtensee.*

Tiergarten

Right in the middle of Berlin, the Tiergarten was originally hunting territory for the Prussian princes in the 16th century and was opened around the same time as the Brandenburg Gate, immediately to the east of it. Various monuments of animals were added in the 18th century when the grounds became a park. An exquisite combination of trees, grassy areas, watery spots, and winding pebbly paths, Tiergarten offers everything that can be expected from a day in the country. Popular with strollers, joggers, cyclists, and tree huggers, the park is also a favorite cruising point for gay men—the Löwenbrücke (Lion Bridge), in particular, is a hot spot at night. In summer the Turkish "national sport" of barbecuing takes place in earnest, particularly in Grosser Tiergarten, and kids and sun soakers descend on the area in equal numbers. At **Café am Neuen See** (⊠ Lichtensteinallee), in the park's southwest, you can enjoy drinks and light meals at tables next to the water and, perhaps afterward, hire one of the nearby rowboats. ⊠ *S-Bahn station Unter den Linden for eastern edge, or S-Bahn station Tiergarten near middle of park. Bus 100 goes through park past some of the landmarks. Café am Neuen See can be reached by Bus x9, 100, 187, or 341.*

Volkspark Friedrichshain

Volkspark Friedrichshain is only one of many public parks in Berlin. In the eastern district of Friedrichshain, its peripheries are marked by Landsberger Allee, Am Friedrichshain, and Danziger Strasse. Popular with young and old, the park includes such attractions as an open-air stage, a summer pool, a beach volleyball pitch, a skateboarding area, and a café. Particularly interesting are the numerous memorials. As well as those to the revolutionary Red Sailors of Kiel, the dead of the 1848 March Revolution, and the German members of the International Brigade who fought in the Spanish Civil War, there is the beautiful fairy-tale fountain (Märchenbrunnen) dedicated to the victims of rickets. A leisurely walk up the path to the top of the tree-covered hill will reward you with a nice view. ⊠ *From Alexanderplatz station take Tram 5, 6, 8, or 15 to Platz der Vereinten Nationen or, alternatively, Bus 100 to edge of park.*

Wannsee

Wannsee is known by the most imaginative as Berlin's Riviera. Part of the Havel River in southwest Berlin, the 642-acre lake attracts sailors, waterskiers, windsurfers, bathers, grannies, and families. When the sun shines, the average Berliner pulls on the sandals and jumps onto S-Bahn 1. **Strandbad Wannsee** is the most popular destination, with all its clean water for swimming, sand, and facilities, but well-off locals head to the yachting clubs along the banks. The surrounding woodland and the island Pfaueninsel, where smoking is strictly forbidden, are perfect for a stroll or a picnic. ⊠ *S-Bahn 1, S-Bahn 7 Wannsee; for Strandbad Wannsee, S-Bahn 1, S-Bahn 7 Nikolassee, then Bus 513.*

PARTICIPANT SPORTS AND FITNESS

If you like keeping active while traveling, you're in the right place. A plethora of outdoor public facilities including basketball courts, soccer fields, and table-tennis tables are scattered all over town. It's not uncommon to find pickup games of soccer in parks on weekends. You turn up and take part—no connections required. Fitness studios are plentiful, but if you splurge on an expensive hotel, it should guarantee decent sporting facilities, with weights and exercise bikes in-house.

If it's more serious competition you require, then one of the various sports federations (*Verbände*) in Berlin will be able to help. For information on any of the less mainstream sports or for further information on any sport, contact the **Landessportbund Berlin** (Berlin Regional Sports Federation, ⊠ Jesse-Owens-Allee 2, ☎ 030/300–020).

Beach Volleyball

The game that captured the world's imagination at the 2000 Olympics has finally caught on in Berlin. Although it hasn't quite emptied the soccer stadiums, beach volleyball could now be described as an up-and-coming pastime. Because of a lack of sufficient coastline in Berlin, someone came up with idea of **City Beach Berlin** (⊠ Michelangelostr., at corner of Hanns-Eisler-Str., ☎ 0177/247–6907, Metro: S-Bahn Greifswalder), a complex of both indoor and outdoor beach-volleyball courts. Prices vary between €11 and €21 per hour, depending on the time of day and whether you are outdoors or inside.

Bicycling

Bike enthusiasts often start their tours at the peripheral U- and S-Bahn stations like Potsdam, Grunewald, and Bernau. For specific cycling routes, get in touch with Fahrradstation, which will provide a free booklet on the best places to take your wheels. Those looking for a way to combine exercise and sightseeing can't go wrong with a trip between Alexanderplatz and Spandau. As well as passing many of Berlin's tourist attractions on the way (Unter den Linden, Tiergarten, the Victory Column, and Schloss Charlottenburg), the route is easy to follow. For the recreational cyclist, the numerous inner-city parks and green spaces like **Grunewald, Tiergarten,** and **Volkspark Friedrichshain** offer a safer alternative.

Call the **Allgemeiner Deutscher Fahrrad-Club** (ADFC; ⊠ Brunnenstr. 28, ☎ 030/448–4724, Metro: U-Bahn 8 Rosenthaler Platz) for information and rental locations, or rent your bikes at some of the major hotels for approximately €16 for 24 hours. The ADFC also has a workshop where you can carry out your own repairs.

Fahrradstation (⊠ Friedrichstr. 141–142, within the station, ☎ 030/2045–4500, Metro: Friedrichstrasse; ⊠ Bergmannstr. 9, ☎ 030/215–1566, Metro: U-Bahn 7 Sudstern, Gneisenaustrasse; ⊠ Rosenthaler Str. 40–41, ☎ 030/2859–9895, Metro: S-Bahn Hackescher Markt) rents green bikes by the day for between €11 and €20.50 (insurance is extra) or by the week. You must leave your passport as a security deposit. For €11 you can take part in a two- to three-hour bike tour of the city. Call for other locations but, if possible, head for the Friedrichstrasse branch, as it is the most central and is open 365 days a year.

Insider tours (⊠ S-Bahn platform of Bahnhof Friedrichstrasse, ☎ 030/ 692–3149, WEB www.insidertour.de. Metro: Friedrichstrasse) will take you on a four-hour bike tour (€18, starting at 10:30 AM), which incorporates everything that is in its walking tour. Groups are limited to ensure an intimate and personal experience, and a bike rental can be arranged for around €8. A credit card or passport is necessary to leave as a deposit.

Fahrrad Vermietung Berlin (⊠ Kurfürstdendamm, ☎ 030/261–2094) rents black bikes with baskets, which it keeps in front of the Marmorhaus movie theater, opposite the Kaiser-Wilhelm-Gedächtniskirche. Bikes are rented by the day (not 24 hours), and you must leave either €103 or your passport as security. If no one is there, just wait. The attendant is probably signing up a bus tour nearby and will return shortly.

Golf

Berlin's flat landscape, low winds, and relatively dry summers allow for pleasant golfing conditions. Although it's quite popular with the locals, golf remains mostly a members-only sport, but listed here are places that accept visitors. The **Golf-Verband Berlin-Brandenburg e.V.** (⊠ Haderslebener Str. 26,, ☎ 030/823–6609, Metro: U-Bahn 1 Breitenbachplatz) answers general golf queries. Berlin's leading club is the **Golf- und Land Club Berlin-Wannsee e.V.** (⊠ Am Golfweg 2, Zehlendorf, ☎ 030/806–7060, FAX 030/806–70610, Metro: S-Bahn Wannsee, then Bus 118 or 318). Set in Berlin's woodsy southwest, it offers the choice of a par-72, 18-hole course, a smaller 9-hole course, and a driving range. Among the services on offer are golf lessons from the pro. This, as with most other things at the club, doesn't come cheap.

At **Golfclub Schloss Wilkendorf e.V.** (⊠ Am Weiher 1, OT Wilkendorf, Gielsdorf, ☎ 03341/330–960, Metro: S-Bahn 5 Strausberg Nord) there is both an 18-hole course, designed with the help of former Open and U.S. Masters champion Sandy Lyle, and a 6-hole course. A *Platzreife* (German Golfing Certificate) is required for the 18-holer on the weekend, when prices are higher. There are also golf clubs available to rent. After reaching the S-Bahn station Strausberg Nord, a short taxi ride is recommended to get here.

At **Öffentliches Golf-Zentrum** (⊠ Chauseestr 94-98, ☎ 030/285–7001, Metro: U-Bahn Zinnowitzer Strasse) you'll find over 50 practice mats (5 sheltered) from which you can fire balls onto a 100,000-square-m piece of land. Three PGA teachers on site give lessons. The facilities are open all year regardless of the weather. Not the classiest driving range in the world, it is nevertheless a welcome green retreat in Mitte. Clubs and information can be obtained at Golf Shop Midway just down the street at Habersaathstrasse 34.

If you're a beginner or simply want to stop your swing from becoming rusty, then head for the **Öffentliche Golf-Übungsanlage Berlin-Adlershof** (⊠ Rudower Chaussee 4, Adlershof, ☎ 030/6701–2421, Metro: S-Bahn Adlershof). As well as a driving range there are four par-3 holes on which to determine if that new improved back swing has made the difference. Clubs are available for hire.

Health Clubs

A number of fitness clubs in Berlin require a year's contract, registration fees, and monthly dues. However, this is not always necessary. The listings below are representative of what you will find in the Yellow Pages under "Sportschulen und Studios." Although no day pass is available at **Arena Sport & Freizeitcenter** (✉ Obertrautstr. 1–21, ☎ 030/251–2078, Metro: U-Bahn 6, U-Bahn 7 Mehringdamm), it has monthly and 10-visit passes. This will give you full access to all exercise classes.

Fit Sportstudio (✉ Richard-Wagner-Pl. 5, ☎ 030/342–6502, Metro: U-Bahn 7 Richard-Wagner-Platz) has friendly staff members who speak both English and German and will be more than willing to instruct you in how to use their well-maintained equipment. Your membership card will be accepted in three other locations in the city. This is an added bonus because the prices are a good value.

Gold's Gym (✉ Immanuelkirchstr. 3, ☎ 030/442–8294, Metro: U-Bahn 2 Senefelderplatz, Tram 1 Knaackstrasse) is part of the American fitness chain, which has a large list of facilities. The day-use fees are pricey, but if you are a member in the United States and present your membership card, it's possible to work out for two weeks without charge.

The chain **Jopp Frauen-Fitness** (✉ Tauentzienstr. 13, ☎ 030/210–111, Metro: Zoologischer Garten, Kurfürstendamm) is just for the ladies. Choose between a three-month or 10-visit package, but you must specify whether it's exercise classes or weights that you want. Your card entitles you to visit any one of the five branches in Berlin.

Kreuzberg's small, friendly, and gay-friendly **Jump!** (✉ Stresemanstr. 74, ☎ 030/262–666, Metro: S-Bahn Anhalter Bahnhof) has day passes for weightlifting and aerobics.

At least a month's pass is necessary at **Oasis** (✉ Stresemannstr. 74, ☎ 030/262–6661, Metro: S-Bahn 1, S-Bahn 2 Anhalter Bahnhof) to use the wide array of equipment. Good facilities and a fine swimming pool await you.

Ice-Skating

The **Berliner Eissport-Verband** (Berlin Ice Sport Federation, ✉ Fritz-Wildung-Str. 9, ☎ 030/823–4020, Metro: S-Bahn 4 Hohenzollerndamm), in Wilmersdorf, should be able to give you the lowdown on all clubs, ice rinks, and events. The federation has nothing to do with the skating that takes place on frozen lakes and rivers.

Mid-October through mid-March beginners and veterans alike can take something from the **Horst-Dohm-Eisstadion** (✉ Fritz-Wildung-Str. 9, ☎ 030/824-1012, Metro: S-Bahn 4 Hohenzollerndamm) in Wilmersdorf. As well as having an outer ring for speed freaks, there's a nice inner circle where the ice dancers and those with wobbly ankles can enjoy the atmosphere of a baby pool on ice.

The **Erika-Hess-Eisstadion, Wedding** (✉ Müllerstr. 185, ☎ 030/4575–5555, Metro: U-Bahn 6 Wedding) is one of very few reasons to come to Wedding, but with the cheapest skating in town, you can't complain. It's open October through March.

Jogging

The **Tiergarten** is the best place for jogging in the downtown area. Run its length and back, and you'll have covered 8 km (5 mi). Joggers can also take advantage of the grounds of **Charlottenburg Palace,** 3 km (2 mi) around. For longer runs (anything up to 32 km/20 mi), make for the **Grunewald.** In general, all these wooded parks are safe. You should, however, avoid Grunewald and Tiergarten on dark winter evenings. Those who find pounding the streets a rather lonely experience can join the gang at **Lauftreff Grunewald,** who meet on Wednesday evening at 6 at the Mommsenstadion (⊠ Waldschulallee 34, Metro: S-Bahn Eichkamp). Jogging and jollity are the order of the day when this group heads off en masse through Grunewald. Newcomers will be heartily welcomed, but it's best to e-mail the organizers beforehand to let them know you're coming.

Krumme Lanke and **Schachtensee** are also favorite jogging haunts because of their idyllic settings. Particularly suitable for exercising is the **Laufstrecke Schlachtensee** (⊠ Am Schlachtensee, Metro: S-Bahn 1 Schlachtensee), in Zehlendorf, where the wide woodland paths and lakeside scenery lend themselves well to an hour or two of running. A number of refreshment stalls and shops will allow you to take a breather when needed.

Sailing

For a capital city Berlin provides the visitor with quite a number of places to sail. As well as punting around on Müggelsee, the keen sailor can carve a path through the waves from the ample shores of Wannsee, either north to Spandau and Tegel or south toward Potsdam. Boating is also a possibility farther north on the lakes of Brandenburg and Mecklenburg.

To take personal responsibility for a rented vessel, you'll need a sailing certificate (*Amtlicher Sportbootführerschein-Binnen*) issued by the **Berliner Segler-Verband** (⊠ Bismarckallee 2, Charlottenburg, ☎ 030/893–8490, ℻ 030/8938–4219, Metro: S-Bahn Halensee, Bus 119), which also has information on sailing clubs and events. Those with sailing experience can take a six-day theory course that covers the rules for the Berlin waters.

Inexpensive boat tours around the city's rivers, lakes, and canals are very popular. You will find pickup spots at several points of interest along the banks of the Spree River and the Landwehrkanal. If, however, you want to be sure of having a quality experience, get in touch directly with **Stern und Kreisschiffahrt GmbH** (⊠ Puschkinallee 15, ☎ 030/536–3600). In doing so you can hire a boat and be served hand and foot while experiencing the joys of Berlin's waterways at a serene pace, or simply find out more about where and when normal tours stop and start.

Reederei Heinz Riedel (⊠ Planufer 78, ☎ 030/691–3782) runs customized personal tours but tends to concentrate on the Spree and the canals and does not travel to the suburbs.

As well as giving lessons, the **Segelschule Hering** (⊠ Bielefelder Str. 15, ☎ 030/861–0701, ℻ 030/861–6261, Metro: U-Bahn 7 Konstanzer Strasse) rents out boats on Grosse Steinlanke—a patch of water on the Havel See near Wannsee. Between April and October you can rent lakefairing craft at **Am Grossen Fenster** (⊠ Grosses Fenster 1, Zehlendorf, ☎ 030/803–7137. Metro: S-Bahn 1, S-Bahn 7 Nikolassee).

If you can't be bothered with pursuing a Berlin license, you can always tag along with a club like the **Deutsch-Britischer Yacht Club** (⊠ Kladower Damm 217a, ☎ 030/365–4010, S-Bahn 7 to Spandau, then Bus 134 to Klinik Berlin). There you can delight in a variety of different watery activities in all sorts of waterbound craft and afterwards join the club members for some socializing.

SAUNA ETIQUETTE

GERMANS ARE VERY COMFORTABLE WITH THEIR BODIES— this is the land of the *Frei Körper* ("free body," meaning clothes-free) after all. Here are a few tips for your first trip to the sauna. Number one, nudity is healthy. You can keep your underwear on, but people will just wonder what you're hiding. Women who can't get into that free-body frame of mind can visit places that have hours reserved for women only. Bring two towels, because whatever you do, don't sweat on the furniture—that's why you've got the second towel: to lie on. Shower before your sauna and before you hit the plunge pool, but make sure your body is dry before entering the sauna to avoid boiling yourself. Fifteen minutes in the heat should be enough. A typical sauna sequence consists of a warm shower, 15 minutes of sauna, a cold shower and optional dip in the plunge pool, and a 10- to 30-minute rest. Don't overdo it. Three sequences is usually plenty for one evening. Dehydration can be a problem, so drink plenty of water or fruit juice. A mature and discreet attitude toward the situation and other patrons is always preferable, so don't stare or giggle at unusual or unusually placed birthmarks or tattoos. Most public swimming pools have sauna facilities, but to avoid the curious gazes of guileless children, it's best to pay a little more money and go to a private establishment.

Saunas, Spas, and Bath Houses

Hamam (Turkish Bath, ⊠ Mariannenstr. 6, ☎ 030/615–1464, Metro: U-Bahn 8 Kottbusser Tor, U-Bahn 1 Görlitzer Bahnhof) is a Turkish bath for women only and is where to cleanse one's body and relax one's soul, and vice versa. Unwinding in the Turkish bath and Finnish sauna is the perfect way to get away from the stresses and strains of everyday life—or even travel.

If you can brave your way past the seedy-looking exterior of **Kaminsauna** (⊠ Hubnerstr. 4, ☎ 030/4201–6476, Metro: U-Bahn 5 Frankfurter Tor), you'll discover inside a sauna with a family atmosphere. Soft light, relaxing music, and a "snoring room" indicate the pace. Every hour the attendant will pour water and essential oils onto the brazier in the Finnish sauna. If you catch her in the right mood, she may also explain why.

Enter **Russisch-Römisches Dampfbad** (Stadtbad Mitte, ⊠ Gartenstr. 5, ☎ 030/281–0666, Metro: S-Bahn Nordbahnhof) via the elevator in the Stadtbad Mitte public pool complex and proceed to the third floor. The friendly staff will be more than happy to show you how it's done, but don't talk too loud—people are here to relax after all. Tuesday and Thursday are for women only.

Thermen (⊠ Europa-Center, Nürnberger Str. 7, ☎ 030/261–6031, Metro: Wittenbergplatz) in the Europa-Center is quite good. It incorporates pools (indoor and out), a summer garden, steam baths, Finnish saunas, a café, table tennis, and billiards facilities and someone to massage your weary body.

Racquetball, Squash, and Tennis

Because of the nature of private tennis clubs (of which there are many in the area), it can be a task getting past the front gates. The **Tennis-Verband Berlin-Brandenburg** (Berlin-Brandenburg Tennis Federation, ✉ Auerbacher Str. 19, Charlottenburg, ☎ 030/825–5311, Metro: U-Bahn 7 Grunewald) should be able to assist you with your inquiries. More often than not, tennis courts are part of larger sport centers, and renting a court in winter will set you back more than in the sunny months—prepare yourself for an hourly rate of as much as €25 when it's cold outside.

The **Tennisplätze am Ku'damm** (✉ Cicerostr. 55A, ☎ 030/891–6630, Metro: U-Bahn 7 Adenauerplatz) courts are convenient if you want to try out the new racquet you've just bought in the Kurfürstendamm area.

Tennis & Squash City (✉ Brandenburgische Str. 53, Wilmersdorf, ☎ 030/873–9097, Metro: U-Bahn 7 Konstanzer Strasse) has seven tennis courts, four badminton courts, and 11 squash courts. There are also an in-house sauna and solarium, and you can take advantage of coaching and aerobics and dance classes.

The **tsf** (✉ Richard-Tauber-Damm 36, ☎ 030/742–1091, Metro: U-Bahn 6 Alt-Mariendorf; ✉ Galenstr. 33–45, Spandau, ☎ 030/333–4083, Metro: U-Bahn 7 Rathaus Spandau) has nine indoor courts and a sister facility in Spandau.

The eight indoor tennis and 12 badminton courts at the **TCW tennis center Weissensee** (✉ Roelckestr. 106, ☎ 030/927–4594, Metro: S-Bahn Greifswalder Strasse) are popular with racquet sports enthusiasts, but its list of other amenities, including restaurants, saunas, and a summer terrace, means just about anyone could spend a half a day there.

Spok (Sport- und Kulturzentrum Pankow (✉ Nordendstr. 56, ☎ 030/ 447–1034, S-Bahn 4, 8, 85 or U-Bahn 2 to Pankow, then Tram 53 to Nordendstrasse) proves that racquet sports and beer drinking can go hand in hand.

Rollerblading

Although it is still officially illegal to rollerblade in the street, Berlin's skating fraternity occasionally gathers on Wednesday evening at S-Bahnhof Tiergarten for a communal mid-city sweep. Check with the tourist information office to find out exactly where the activity is least frowned upon. It's perfectly permissible to skate in most parks, but you'll feel particularly welcome at certain places. At **Volkspark Wilmersdorf** (✉ Hans-Rosenthal-Pl., Metro: U-Bahn 4 Rathaus Schöneberg; S-Bahn 4, U-Bahn 4 Innsbrucker Platz) you will find asphalt areas for BMXs, rollerblades, and skateboards. **Böcklerpark** (✉ Prinzenstr., Kreuzberg U–1 Prinzenstrasse) has a half-pipe for rollerbladers and skateboarders and a track and ramps for cyclists. From the fellow extreme sports fans you meet here, you can find out where the hip kids are currently grazing their knees.

Skates are rented at **Boarderline** (✉ Köpenicker Str. 9, ☎ 030/611–6484, Metro: Schlesisches Tor) for €8 per day. **Roadworx** (✉ Motzstr.9, ☎ 030/2175–2005, Metro: Nollendorfplatz) rents skates for €11 (€16 for the whole weekend). In Grunewald, **Skatecity** (✉ Hohenzollerndamm 143, ☎ 030/8972–2394, Metro: S-Bahn Hohenzollerndamm) rents blades for €6 (€13 for the weekend).

Swimming

Lakes

Berliners don't have to look very far to find all the trappings of a holiday resort—six rivers, more than 150 watery spots including 50 lakes, 35 islands, and more than 30 beaches are all within the city limits. When summer arrives, usually preceded by a fairly cold winter, city residents just want to get outside and absorb some nature. Sometimes they like to share it. *Freikörperkultur* (FKK) is the German version of naturism, or nudism. This is a tradition that was kept alive in the former East Germany and the custom seems to have rubbed—and, er, stripped—off on everyone else. Serious naturists join special FKK clubs. A call to the **Landesverband Freikörperkultur Berlin-Brandenburg e. V.** (LFK; ⊠ Ostpreussendamm 85 B, ☎ 030/7138–9310, Metro: S-Bahn 25 Osdorfer Strasse) will let you know where to find specially signposted areas for nude bathing at lakes or beaches. Wherever you plant yourself, don't be surprised if the chap next to you suddenly gives in to the call for bodily freedom, sign or not. It's only natural, after all.

In general, between mid-May and September, outdoor pools and lakeside beaches are transformed into mini-Majorcas, where tourists and locals sunbathe, play on water slides, and swim. Try to stick to the official swimming areas unless you want to take away some microscopic mushroom-shape friends that you didn't arrive with. Lakes like **Schlachtensee** and **Krumme Lanke** are rumored to be clean, but that very much depends on who was there just before you. Try not to stand on the bottom if you can help it, as even in these enlightened times, a body of water can easily be mistaken for a garbage can. **Strandbad Wannsee** (⊠ Wannseebadweg 25, Zehlendorf, ☎ 030/803–5612, Metro: S-Bahn 1, S-Bahn 7 Nikolassee, then Bus 513) is Europe's largest lakeside swimming area. With the list of activities available on this 3,300-ft-long sandy beach, including exercise classes, boat rentals, and eating, swimming needn't be the only thing on your mind. Although it's usually packed, it's really the only safe place to swim on Wannsee and has the added bonuses of water slides and a nudist section.

At **Strandbad Müggelsee** (⊠ Fürstenwader Damm 838, Köpenick, ☎ 030/648–7777, Metro: S-Bahn 3 Friedrichshagen, then Tram 61), on the northern shore of Berlin's biggest lake, you'll find beach bathing and a nudist section.

Near Strandbad Müggelsee you can swim off the beach at **Seebad Friedrichshagen** (⊠ Müggelseedamm 216, ☎ 030/645–5756, Metro: S-Bahn 3 Friedrichshagen).

Pools

A couple of tips before you dive in: *Normale Bäder* are pools at a temperature of 26°C (79°F) or just below. *Warmbäder* are 27°C (80°F) or above.

Blub Badeparadies Lido (⊠ Buschkrugallee 64, ☎ 030/3060–9060, Metro: U-Bahn Grenzallee) has indoor and outdoor pools, a sauna garden, hot whirlpools, and a solarium.

The **SEZ** (⊠ Sport- und Erholungszentrum Landsberger Allee 77, ☎ 030/421–820, Metro: S-Bahn Landsberger Allee) is an ideal one-stop activity shop where, as well as swimming pools and a diving board, there are saunas, a solarium, bowling facilities, and a café.

Probably Berlin's most popular facility, the **Sommerbad Kreuzberg** (⊠ Prinzenstr. 113–119, ☎ 030/616–1080, Metro: Prinzenstrasse) is usually referred to as Prinzenbad. As it's in the heart of Kreuzberg, its patrons are typically multicultural. Nudity and courting go hand in hand with swimming and sunbathing, but with only a thin wire fence separating paradise and the canal-side path, you're better off staying at home if you want privacy.

Sommerbad Olympiastadion (⊠ Olympischer Pl., ☎ 030/3006–3440, Metro: U-Bahn Olympiastadion) is Berlin's most impressive pool. Overlooked by sculptures of athletes, this outdoor pool made in Nazi Germany for the 1936 games may instill you more with fear than Olympic spirit.

Actually a protected monument, **Stadtbad Charlottenburg** (⊠ Krumme Str. 9–10, ☎ 030/3438–3860 Old Hall, 030/3438–3865 New Hall, Metro: U-Bahn 2 Deutsche Oper) boasts an art nouveau ceiling from 1898. If you're not there to look at pretty tiles, the new hall is a better place in which to thrash out a few laps.

Stadtbad Mitte (⊠ Gartenstr. 5, ☎ 030/3088–0910, Metro: U-Bahn 8 Rosenthaler Platz; S-Bahn 1 Nordbahnhof) has recently enjoyed a touch of renovation. There's even a 165-ft-long pool for the more serious swimmer.

SPECTATOR SPORTS

A new breed of spectator is developing in Berlin. No longer are the Saturday-afternoon faithful looked down on with a sneer. Spectator sports have almost become fashionable, as more and more of the thinking types creep out of the woodwork and into the stands. During the last European soccer championships, televisions were even set up on the pavement in Oranienburger Strasse. Some of this change can be credited to the vast commercialization that is taking place in European sports. Romantics may wish to point out that since the fall of the Wall, leagues from the former East and West have amalgamated, a community spirit has grown, allegiances have been formed, and healthy rivalries are now free to form as at no time during the cold war. Skeptics would retort, however, that apart from a meager handful of exceptions, most former Eastern teams have shriveled into prunes. All but a few Dynamos have disappeared (it was the word *Dynamo* in a team's name that associated it with the GDR's secret service) and have been conveniently replaced by more rousingly neutral titles.

Although it still remains to be seen whether the capital city can produce a soccer team that can challenge the rest of the country, the alternative sports seem to be placing Berlin firmly on the sporting map. It's just a pity that not one of them is intrinsic to Germany. Ice hockey, the next biggest sport after soccer, is big business in Germany at the moment, and especially in Berlin. Tickets for most sporting events are available at the stadiums, over the phone, on Web sites, or through ticket agencies in the city.

Basketball

While all the other Berlin sports teams are trying to prove their worth, only **Alba Berlin e.V.** basketball team (⊠ Max-Schmelling-Halle, am Falkpl., ☎ 030/5343–8000 for tickets or 030/5343-8000 for information, WEB www.albaberlin.de, Metro: U-Bahn 2 Eberswalder Strasse) has something to show for its efforts. League and cup winners in 1997, Alba is considered one of the big forces in European basketball as it continues to dominate the German League. Between September and May, fans flock to the new 10,000-seater stadium, the Max-Schmelling-Halle, in Mauerpark, which is in the former no-man's-land between Prenzlauer Berg and Wedding. Although tickets for normal games reach €21, you'll have to dig quite a lot deeper if you want to see a big European encounter.

Football

Formed in 1999, Germany's representative in the NFL Europe is **Berlin Thunder** (✉ Friedrich-Jahn-Sportpark, Cantianstr. 24, ☎ 030/3110–2222, WEB www.berlin-thunder.de, Metro: U-Bahn 2 Eberswalder Strasse). In a move that could prove to be an American sport gone too far, Berliners are being asked not only to support a team that has never before existed, but also to take to their hearts a completely alien sporting culture. Aside from this, the title being played for (the World Bowl) is merely a focal point of a league set up to be harvested for the NFL in the United States. Because of this, the season is played during the summer, when, luckily for the organizers, the soccer league is on its summer vacation. If anything at all can be learned from this circus, it is that under no circumstances does Berlin need a baseball team. To witness such an event the spectator should be prepared to part with anything up to €36—popcorn and hamburgers not included.

Horse Racing

The most beautiful racetrack east of Paris, **Galopprennbahn Hoppegarten** (Racetrack at Hoppegarten) has a proud heritage, yet struggles to compete with other large racetracks in Germany. The Galopprennbahn was built in 1868 and was inspired by the more luxurious tracks at Paris-Longchamps and Chantilly. It nevertheless quickly emerged as one of Europe's top centers for equestrian sports, and drew the high society of the German Empire. After World War II the track was still fully operational but lacked the glamour of its heyday. In 1992 the original owner, the Union-Klub, repurchased the property and has since struggled to reestablish it as the capital's premier sports venue (tennis, boxing, and golf still attract more of the upper crust than the racetrack does). The setting is utterly perfect, as the historic grandstands, including the old *Kaisertribüne*, built for the royal court, still stand on the charming grounds. The audience, more down-to-earth than sophisticated, doesn't quite bring in the top dollars the owners had hoped for. Berliners bet while chewing Currywurst and drinking beer instead of indulging in oysters and champagne. To get to Hoppegarten, take the S-Bahn train S-5 in the direction of Strausberg-Nord. Hoppegarten has its own S-Bahn station. ✉ *Goetheallee 1, Dahlwitz-Hoppegarten*, ☎ *03342/38930*, WEB *www.galopprennbahn-hoppegarten.de*. ☻ *Races Apr.–Nov., Sat. or Sun. at 1.*

Ice Hockey

Since the forming of the breakaway DEL (Deutsche Eishockey Liga) in 1994, which brought together the elite of German ice hockey (including, admittedly, the odd American), the sport has hardly looked back. And what's more, Berlin has two teams to be proud of. After failing to make an impact on the new league in the first few years, the **Berlin Capitals** (✉ Eissporthalle, Jaffestr., ☎ 0180/523–7454 for tickets, WEB www.berlin-capitals.com, Metro: S-Bahn Westkreuz, S-Bahn Eichkamp) have finally started to fill those big shirts of theirs. Having assembled a team to challenge their city rivals at the end of the 1990s, the Caps are now considered by some the superior team in Berlin. Ticket prices range from €10 to €39.

The **EHC Eisbären Berlin** (✉ Sportforum, Steffenstr., ☎ 030/971–8400 for tickets; 030/9718-4040 for information; WEB www.eisbaeren.de, Metro: S-Bahn 10 Landsberger Allee, then Tram 5 or 15) are finding out what it's like to be a big fish in a big pond. Having been GDR ice hockey champions 15 times (in the smallest league in the world), the former SC Dynamo are battling hard to be noticed in the German league but have made a good impression in the first few years. Prices for tickets are between €15 and €36.

Soccer

Soccer, or *Fussball* (football), is Germany's main sport. Success at both the club and international levels in the last century has ensured that Germany has a great soccer tradition. Unfortunately, there has been little to cheer about in Berlin until now, but things seem to be changing. **Hertha BSC** (✉ Olympischer Platz 3, ☎ 030/300–9280, WEB www.herthabsc.de, Metro: Olympiastadion) is Berlin's biggest soccer club. After years of mediocrity and a couple of bribery and match-fixing scandals, Hertha is getting its act together. Investment from the Bertelsmann empire when the club was close to bankruptcy was used to import better players and has elevated it to its present level in the Erste Bundesliga, the top division in the country. Fans come by the thousands (between 50,000 and 80,000, to be precise) to their home ground, the Olympic Stadium, which will be totally renovated in time for the World Cup Finals in 2006. Hertha's Web site, which is also in English, is the best place to find out about games, tickets, and everything else.

West Berlin's second-biggest soccer team, **Tennis Borussia** (✉ Mommsenstadion, Waldschulallee 34–42, ☎ 030/306–9610, Metro: S-Bahn 75 Grunewald, S-Bahn 5 Eichkamp), appears to be going to the dogs. It is seemingly destined for a lengthy stay in the regional leagues, as the minuscule size of the crowd it draws reflects the standard of the soccer on the field. Recent premonitions of its rise to soccer fame were sadly seen upside-down in a mirror and TeBe (its affectionate nickname) would now be seen as ambitious if they even dreamed of being mediocre. The number that do turn up to home games is reported to be swollen by a movement of people who don't like Hertha's faction of slightly right-wing supporters.

1. FC Union Berlin (✉ Stadion An der Alten Försterei, Köpenick, ☎ 030/657–2585. Metro: S-Bahn 3 Köpenick) is one of the two old East Berlin teams. "Iron Union" is known for its diehard supporters and is given credit for not giving in to political pressures in the GDR. Their atmospheric 24,000-capacity stadium at the Alte Försterei benefits from its beautiful green surroundings, but don't be fooled—these guys are not out for a Saturday-afternoon walk in the park. Their undying loyalty was rewarded at the end of the 2001 season with promotion into the 2. Bundesliga (the second top league in the country) and an appearance in the DFB Pokal (German Cup) final. Sadly, they didn't manage to keep the cup in the capital, but their efforts were rewarded by a place in the 2001–2002 UEFA Cup competition, as their opponents had already claimed a place in a European competition thanks to their Bundesliga position.

Berliner Fussball Club Dynamo (✉ Sportforum, Steffenstr., Hohenschönhausen, ☎ 030/975–1178, Metro: S-Bahn Frankfurter Allee, then Tram 23 or S-Bahn Landsberger Allee, then Tram 5 or 15) don't seem to be doing themselves any favors. Having been unable to decide exactly what to call themselves, they have reverted back to using "Dynamo," the name that marked them as the Stasi's club. Ten-time winners of the GDR league, they became known as the *Schiebemeister* (cheating champions). These days the quality of soccer they play in the lower reaches of the regional leagues would be enough of a deterrent on its own, but when you have to share a run-down terrace with skinhead fans like theirs . . .

Special Events

Because Berlin is becoming the focal point of a new Europe, international sporting events take place all the time. The **Velodrom** (✉ Paul-Heyse-Str. 29, ☎ 030/443–045, WEB www.velodrom.de, Metro: S-Bahn Landsberger Allee) hosts sporting events from cycling to all year-round. Visit its Web site to find out what's on when you're in town.

The last weekend in September heralds the arrival of the **Berlin Marathon** (✉ Berlin Marathon, Alt-Moabit 92, ☎ 030/302–5370), the world's third largest. To take part you'll need to pay between €36 and €62, depending on when and where you apply. As many as 30,000 people have participated in past runs.

Said to be one of the biggest women's international tour events, the **German Tennis Open** (✉ LTTC Rot-Weiss, Gottfried-von-Cramm-Weg 47–55, ☎ 030/8957–5510 for information, 030/8957–5520 for tickets, WEB www.german-open-berlin.de, Metro: S-Bahn 7 Grunewald) attracts a host of tennis stars to play on the red clay of the Rot-Weiss Tennis Club as part of the WTA Tour. Held every May for a week, these powerful women will always bring in a crowd in good weather.

Berlin once used to host the final meet of the prestigious track-and-field "Golden Four." The **ISTAF Athletics Meeting** (✉ Olympiastadion, Olympischer Pl. 3, ☎ 030/243–1990 for tickets, 030/4430-4430 for information, WEB www.istaf.de/en, Metro: S-Bahn 5 Olympiastadion) was the finale of a series of four meetings where the atheletes who won their event at all four meetings could take a share in 20 kilograms (44 pounds) of gold. As with most things these days, the competition has been expanded into a "Golden League," with Berlin being the seventh of seven venues. The meeting, however, remains one of the top international athletic events on the calendar.

Having been one of the original venues of the **DFB Pokal Endspiel** (German Soccer Cup Final; ✉ Olympiastadion, Olympischer Pl. 3, ☎ 030/3006–3430, WEB www.dfb.de, Metro: U-Bahn 2 Olympiastadion [Ost], S-Bahn 5 Olympiastadion), when World War II was in its infancy, the Olympic Stadium is once again the proud host of the event. Because all the teams in Germany take part, the DFB Pokal often sets up David-versus-Goliath clashes, when some of the lower lights in German soccer get the chance to shine on the big stage—sometimes even in the final.

7 SHOPPING

Berlin's history has never allowed any one
part of the city to proclaim itself the center
of commerce. For more than 40 years the
tree-lined Kurfürstendamm, with its glass
display boxes and designer stores, was
West Berlin's unrivaled mile of shopping.
Yet since reunification, development
has burgeoned, bringing a host of new
stores and variety to the capital's far-flung
districts. The former East Berlin has rapidly
caught on to entrepreneurship and entices
shoppers with glitzy new malls and quirky
boutiques between its Prussian landmarks.
The constant state of flux means there will
always be delightful discoveries to be
made—a crumbling facade might suddenly
reveal a neon-lighted sneaker shop.

By Nicola
Varns

S HOPPING IN BERLIN REQUIRES PLANNING—a weekend spree may
be a fruitless venture, as most stores close at 4 PM on Saturday
and don't open at all on Sunday. For one-stop spending head to
Charlottenburg (essentially western downtown Berlin) which caters to
mainstream and exclusive tastes and has by far the greatest concentration of stores in the city. It also has a reputation as being a fairly
conservative district, where ladies in fur coats walk their poodles. The
fur coat brigade can be spotted in Mitte around Friedrichstrasse and
the Nikolaiviertel—most credit cards are welcomed by stores in these
areas.

Mitte's Hackescher Markt is the place for younger, fashion-conscious
shoppers, with a buzzing atmosphere and building sites to pick your
way through. For more alternative gifts and clothing, Prenzlauer Berg
and Kreuzberg abound with record and secondhand clothing stores.
The multicultural scene here is lively. Schöneberg is an established district brimming with antiques, gift shops, and bookstores. For the all-
under-one-roof experience, department stores can be found in
Charlottenburg and Mitte, but each district also has its own small individual stores to discover.

Typical Berlin souvenirs depict its sights—the Brandenburg Gate, the
Reichstag, and the television tower are popular motifs. The bear is a
Berlin symbol, rearing up quite often on T-shirts, ashtrays, beer mugs,
and in cuddly teddy-bear form. Memorabilia from the German Democratic Republic is popular—from allegedly genuine pieces of the Berlin
Wall to models of Trabant cars. Sweet treats include chocolate *Katzen-
zungen* (cats' tongues), *Baumkuchen* ("tree cake" with chocolate layers), and *Lebkuchen,* a Christmas specialty.

Duty-Free Shopping
Most larger stores display the tax-free shopping sign, which entitles
you to save up to 12% on value-added tax (VAT). Ask in the store for
a Global Refund Cheque—the staff will help to fill out the details. Smaller
stores that are not members of Global Refund will issue you a German form. Declare your purchases and have the form stamped at customs at the last European airport you leave. You may cash in your checks
either at the Global Refund office at the airport or have the refund credited to a credit card or bank account.

Sales and Shipping
At the moment, sales are only legally allowed twice a year. The winter sales (Winterschlussverkäufe, or WSV for short) usually take place
at the end of January and the summer sales (Sommerschlussverkäufe—
SSV) in August. Most stores participate in these sales, as do most
Berliners, so be prepared for crowds. Throughout the year a few items
may be reduced, which will be labeled either as *reduziert* (reduced) or
Sonderangebot (special offer). Only a few stores will ship goods; it is
expensive, and the customer pays. Shipping a package yourself from
the post office is reliable and cheaper than most courier services.

Charlottenburg

Charlottenburg retailers reminisce fondly about the days when they
had the monopoly on exclusive shopping in the city. Yet in terms of
choice, number, and proximity of stores, Charlottenburg is still unrivaled. The Kurfürstendamm has a proud and established commercial
history, whereas Friedrichstrasse, in Mitte, is still more tentative in tout-
ing its wares. The Ku'damm, as locals call it, is one of Berlin's main
traffic arteries. Prices here are often heftier than in other parts of the

city, but the tree-lined sidewalks are gorgeous and most shop owners speak English. The best shopping section runs east from Adenauerplatz down into Tauentzienstrasse, including the side streets. If you're looking for labels such as Chanel, Gucci, Louis Vuitton, Yves Saint Laurent, and Cartier, their stores can be found on this stretch of the Ku'damm and south of it on Fasanenstrasse. Cutting north on Knesebeckstrasse or Grolmanstrasse leads directly to Savignyplatz. The streets around this square are packed with upscale fashion and design boutiques, and small antique shops are scattered around backstreets such as Pestalozzistrasse and Grolmanstrasse. Tauentzienstrasse is home to more affordable stores such as Benetton, the Gap, Esprit, and Hennes & Mauritz, and culminates in Kaufhaus des Westens (KaDeWe), Berlin's shopping pièce de résistance, on Wittenbergplatz.

Department Stores, and Shopping Centers

Karstadt Sport. Karstadt Sport's four floors of sportswear and equipment cover everything from ice-skates to golf clubs. Souvenirs of Berlin teams, for example, Hertha BSC soccer shirts or Berlin Thunder (American football) baseball caps, can be purchased on the ground floor. The top floor has a special Adidas department and an American bar with Internet access. ⊠ *Joachimstalerstr. 5–6,* ☎ *030/880–240. Metro: Zoologischer Garten.*

Kaufhaus des Westens (KaDeWe). Classy KaDeWe is Europe's largest department store. Glass art deco elevators rise and fall noiselessly between seven floors of luxury items. The greatest treat is the gourmet food emporium on the sixth floor. Flare your nostrils to take in the aromas of roasting coffee beans, sizzling sausages, and freshly baked bread. Berliners dress up to sip champagne and gossip on the barstools. The self-service restaurant on the seventh floor is an airy oasis of palms and mosaics, where two bars, buffets of traditional German fare, vegetarian food, and salads (you pay for your food by weight) offer welcome respite from the sheer exhaustion of choice. Any item bearing the gold KaDeWe label, from tubs of goose liver and truffles to bear-shape jars of ketchup and mustard, makes a perfect gift. ⊠ *Tauentzienstr. 21,* ☎ *030/21210. Metro: Wittenbergplatz.*

Stilwerk. This mall is dedicated to innovative interior design and sexy home furnishings. Enter with credit cards at your peril. Viewed as an exhibition space, it is an aesthetic delight, but will you be able to stop at buying a pink Conran broom? Get a glimpse of how the perfect home could look, from glamorous Hollywood-style bathrooms to wall-to-wall cherry-red leather sofas. Four floors of individual stores tout tempting gadgets from Alessi toothpaste caps to Poccino espresso machines. Kartell offers candy-color plastic furniture, Grüne Erde has a series of natural cotton and wicker, and Bulthaup is the Rolls-Royce of kitchens. ⊠ *Kantstr. 17,* ☎ *030/315–150. Metro: Zoologischer Garten/Savignyplatz.*

Wertheim. A large but not too overwhelming store with a good selection of gifts, cosmetics, clothing, and stationery, Wertheim carries a broad price range of goods. The food department in the basement is delightful and less expensive than KaDeWe, with juice, champagne, and coffee bars at which to drop your bags and rest your weary feet. ⊠ *Kurfürstendamm 231,* ☎ *030/883–8152. Metro: Kurfürstendamm.*

Markets

Strasse des 17. Juni. Every weekend from as early as 7 AM to as late as 7 PM, the stalls of this market stretch for almost a mile from Tiergarten station. One part is dedicated to antiques of all sizes and qualities, and the other has arts and crafts stalls. There are some fascinating

Western Downtown Berlin Shopping: Charlottenburg, Schöneberg,

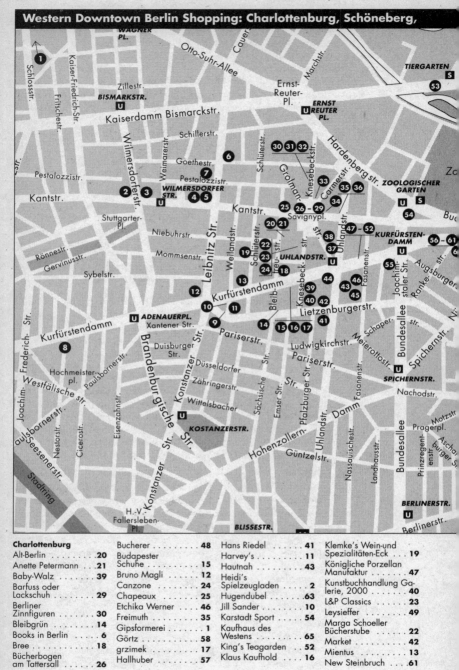

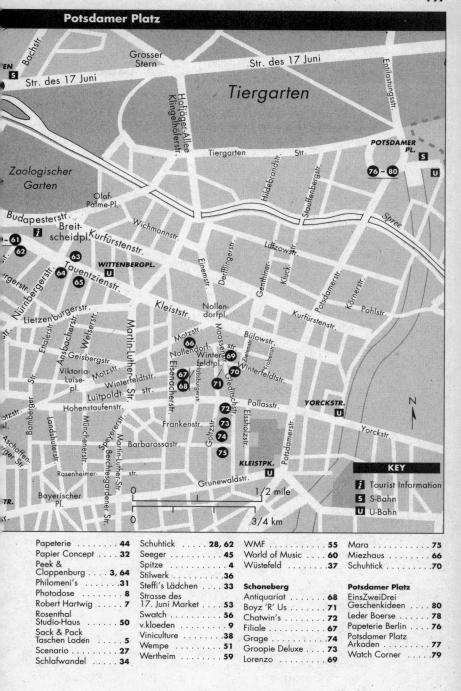

KEY

🛈 Tourist Information
Ⓢ S-Bahn
Ⓤ U-Bahn

finds in both sections, as well as decent secondhand clothing. ⊠ *Strasse des 17. Juni. Metro: Tiergarten.*

Specialty Stores

ANTIQUES

Alt-Berlin. This shop specializes in 17th- and 18th-century antiques. Among a wide selection of Prussian furniture, musical instruments, and vintage hardware, you can browse for anything from pocket-size souvenirs to grandfather clocks. Shipping poses no problem. It is open weekdays 11–6 and Saturday 11–2. ⊠ *Bleibtreustr. 48,* ☎ *030/881–6756. Metro: Savignyplatz.*

BOOKS

Books in Berlin. The whole cozy store is dedicated to English-language fiction and specialist books. The friendly owner will trade books in the secondhand section, and information on cultural and literary events in Berlin is posted. ⊠ *Goethestr. 69,* ☎ *030/313–1233. Metro: Savignyplatz.*

Bücherbogen am Tattersall. A fine assortment of showbiz books— from biographies to stage production manuals—is stocked here. There are sections specializing in comedy and costume design, Berlin stars past and present, international film, and the performing arts. ⊠ *S-Bahnbogen 585,* ☎ *030/3150–3750. Metro: Savignyplatz.*

Hugendubel. Here's a delight for bookworms. A decent selection of English-language contemporary fiction, novels, classics, and crime capers is on the first floor (that's second floor to Americans) alongside a free gift-wrapping service. Secluded alcoves and chairs are strewn around the store to encourage leisurely browsing, and the quiet intellectual buzz of newspaper reading and laptop tapping prevails in the café. The travel guides on the third floor include a range of well-known publishers in English, and children's books in English can be found on the second floor along with dictionaries. ⊠ *Tauentzienstr. 13,* ☎ *030/214–060. Metro: Zoologischer Garten.*

Kunstbuchhandlung Galerie 2000. For more than 30 years this has been Berlin's top address for books on art, architecture, photography, and design. The largest sections are on photography and non-European art, and you can find some out-of-print works as well. Half the 33,000 titles are in English. The staff is only too pleased to help and advise. ⊠ *Knesebeckstr. 56–58,* ☎ *030/883–8467. Metro: Uhlandstrasse.*

Marga Schoeller Bücherstube. Lovers of literature will feel at home in this old-fashioned and quaint store. In addition to English-language classics and fiction there are excellent sections on women's writing, New Age inspirations, academic books, and African and black authors. Translations of German writing are in good supply, and the store organizes literary events with the British Council. ⊠ *Knesebeckstr. 33,* ☎ *030/881–1112. Metro: Savignyplatz.*

CAMERAS AND ELECTRONICS

Photodose. Enthusiasts willing to venture off the main drag will find Berlin's largest selection of secondhand cameras, and a staff willing to give expert advice. Photodose also specializes in equipment for the likes of Nikon, Leica, and Canon and develops film. ⊠ *Kurfürstendamm 150,* ☎ *030/8954–0677. Metro: Adenauerplatz.*

Wüstefeld. A favorite among locals, Wüstefeld has all manner of cameras, photographic equipment, and accoutrements from household names as well as from professional brands such as Hasselblad. It also does repairs and overnight film developing. ⊠ *Grolmanstr. 36,* ☎ *030/ 881–9696. Metro: Savignyplatz.*

CLOTHING AND ACCESSORIES

Anette Petermann. This local designer believes in perfect workmanship, and her clothes are a delight of Berlin haute couture. Roses are her trademark, ruched into pinstripe jackets or taffeta stoles. Crushed organza evening wear or functional wool and fur are popular with local celebrities. In-house tailors are happy to oblige with alterations, and Anette herself will offer advice and her own philosophy. ✉ *Bleibtreustr. 49,* ☎ *030/323–2556. Metro: Savignyplatz.*

Barfuss oder Lackschuh. This trendy shoe store for men and women seduces with its display of footwear as "objets d'art." Shiny sneakers, comfy Campers, and casual Clarks for pounding the dance floor and the sidewalk adorn the shelves in vibrant colors. ✉ *Knesebeckstr. 86,* ☎ *030/3150–7261. Metro: Savignyplatz;* ✉ *Oranienburgerstr. 89,* ☎ *030/2389–1991. Metro: Hackescher Markt.*

Bleibgrün. Women's catwalk fashion is for sale at haute-couture prices in these adjacent shoe and clothing boutiques. Gowns, bustiers, and generally outrageous garments by Gaultier, Paul Smith, and Susanne Bommer can be conveniently paired with wedge-heel shoes that defy the laws of physics, silver pumps with diamond-encrusted heels, kinky boots with lime fur trims, and beach bags decorated with a shoreful of seashells. ✉ *Bleibtreustr. 29–30,* ☎ *030/821–689. Metro: Uhland-strasse.*

Bruno Magli. A high-end shoe store for men and women, Bruno Magli is where to hunt down that elusive pair of Versace red-silk pumps. Magli mostly stocks Italian labels and all manner of impractical but lavish strappy shoes sporting bows, beads, and beautiful buckles. Cerrutti hosiery and bijou Louis Vuitton handbags complete the picture, but the first-class goods don't come cheap! ✉ *Kurfürstendamm 62,* ☎ *030/ 883–7760. Metro: Adenauerplatz.*

Budapester Schuhe. The original store at Kurfürstendamm 199 stocks handmade and timeless men's dress shoes and brogues, mostly from top English, Austrian, and Hungarian shoemakers. The new store across the street also does a snazzy selection of men's Prada beachwear and sneakers. Women can drool over Dolce and Gabbana kitten heels and Stephane Kélian's fruity sandals, whereas kids have little more than Prada sneakers from which to choose. ✉ *Kurfürstendamm 199,* ☎ *030/ 881–1707. Metro: Adenauerplatz;* ✉ *Kurfürstendamm 43,* ☎ *030/881– 1701. Metro: Adenauerplatz;* ✉ *Friedrichstr. 81,* ☎ *030/2038–8110. Metro: Friedrichstrasse.*

Chapeaux. Milliner Andrea Curti designs hats for pop stars, first ladies, and mothers-in-law. Her creations range from wacky and wonderful to understated and practical, but she prides herself on her frank opinion—if it doesn't suit you, she won't make it for you. You can select her designs in a variety of colors and fabrics. The shop is open weekdays noon–7, Saturday noon–4. ✉ *Bleibtreustr. 51,* ☎ *030/312–0913. Metro: Savignyplatz.*

Freimuth. Since 1814 Freimuth has supplied gentlemen with top hats, trilbies, rakish berets, and walking canes. Ladies, too, can choose from a classic range of hats for all occasions. The sofas and antique furniture provide a taste of Old Berlin, and the hatboxes are particularly delightful. ✉ *Kurfürstendamm 33,* ☎ *030/881–6865. Metro: Uh-landstrasse.*

Görtz. Berlin's largest shoe store has styles, prices, labels, and sizes to suit everyone. Current fashions take up much of the show space, but classics, Wellington boots, bridal footwear, and comfy seats in which to try on the wares on are in no way overlooked. ⊠ *Kurfürstendamm 13–14,* ☏ *030/881–1707. Metro: Kurfürstendamm.*

Hallhuber. "Nothing but clothes" is Hallhuber's motto, offering both men and women three floors of spangly party gear, slick office wear, and trendy casual clothes. Hallhuber's own eye-catching collections are complemented by casual designer labels such as Calvin Klein and Guess, making it a store to suit most pockets. When shopping weariness sets in, a small lounge with sparkling wine, free water, and magazines awaits on the ground floor. ⊠ *Kurfürstendamm 13,* ☏ *030/881–2078. Metro: Kurfürstendamm.*

Harveys. Harveys specializes in Japanese and Belgian labels and offers enthusiastic advice when you're choosing between cool menswear for all occasions. The loose-fitting Issey Miyake suits, inventive and classic Comme des Garçons shirts, chunky boots, and accessories are aimed at the avant-garde professional. ⊠ *Kurfürstendamm 186–7,* ☏ *030/883–3803. Metro: Adenauerplatz*

Hautnah. Yes, Berlin does have a reputation for leather, rubber, and shiny latex, and this is where to come and get that breathtaking red cat suit! Tight, sky-blue hot pants, full-length spike-heel boots, feather boas, and spray-on dresses start at the tamer end of the range and ascend to eyelid-batting "fantasy outfits" for Berlin's more eccentric nightclubs. ⊠ *Uhlandstr. 170,* ☏ *030/882–3434. Metro: Uhlandstrasse.*

Jil Sander. The flagship store of German fashion legend Sander is the place to find the ultimate little black dress—for around €513. Her designs are simple and understated, in gorgeously soft fabrics that demand to be caressed. A favorite with serious but sexy German businesswomen, wearing Sander is an expression of confidence. Her menswear is adventurous, with colors and cuts to suit clubland as well as the creative office. ⊠ *Kurfürstendamm 185,* ☏ *030/886–7020. Metro: Adenauerplatz.*

Market. Teenage techno fans come to Market to buy their tent-size flares, fat orange sneakers, silver disco boots, and the ultimate in urban armor—T-shirts adorned with neon rubber spikes. Check out the great accessories, such as panda handbags and glittering dog collars. ⊠ *Uhlandstr. 29,* ☏ *030/883–6255. Metro: Uhlandstrasse.*

Mientus. A true gentleman's outfitter, Mientus stocks labels such as Armani, Jean Paul Gaultier, and Boss. Row upon row of blazers, sports jackets, and suits cater to every business and formal occasion. The staff exudes the quiet hush of serious service, and an in-house tailor is available for alterations. Classic polo shirts in more than 20 colors, dress shirts up to €308, designer underwear, and a rainbow of silk ties effortlessly make up for any suitcase omissions on your business trip. ⊠ *Wilmersdorferstr. 73,* ☏ *030/323–9077. Metro: Wilmersdorferstrasse;* ⊠ *Kurfürstendamm 52,* ☏ *030/323–9077. Metro: Adenauerplatz.*

New Steinbruch. The younger crowd just follows the music downstairs to find a skimpy Love Parade outfit, favorites being spangly bikinis, 6-inch platforms, and baby-pink fake-fur wraps. The store has a good selection of jeans, street surf wear, and those lethal Buffalo boots—a hit among Berlin teenagers. ⊠ *Kurfürstendamm 237,* ☏ *030/8855–2126. Metro: Zoologischer Garten.*

Peek und Cloppenburg. P and C's five floors hold a mind-boggling variety of women's, men's, and children's clothing. The style tends more toward the conservative, but garish bad-taste items can be found with minimal effort. The choice of labels guarantees something within everyone's budget, and there is a reasonably priced selection of leather jackets and coats. Berlin designer Joop's store, on the top floor, and the international designer department, in the basement, should not be missed. ⊠ *Tauenzienstr. 19,* ☎ *030/212–900. Metro: Kurfürstendamm;* ⊠ *Wilmersdorferstr. 109,* ☎ *030/315–9100. Metro: Wilmersdorferstrasse.*

Spitze. The name means both "lace" and "great," but the great antique lace tablecloths are nothing compared to the wonderful vintage clothes. Tailored suits, sequin frocks, and satin ball gowns are hung chronologically from the turn of the 20th century to the 1960s. A fabulous collection from the 1920s and 1930s evokes the cabaret feel of Berlin, and accessories include antique hatboxes and tapestry bags. Spitze's aficionados include Donna Karan. ⊠ *Weimarerstr. 19,* ☎ *030/313–1068. Metro: Wilmersdorferstrasse.*

FOOD AND DRINK

King's Teagarden. Werner Schmitt, owner of one of the country's best tea specialty shops, holds several patents for tea products. Among the more than 200 teas, you can also choose from his own unique blends. ⊠ *Kurfürstendamm 217,* ☎ *030/883–7059. Metro: Uhlandstrasse.*

Klemke's Wein-und Spezialitäten-Eck. You can purchase a whole magnum of Moët et Chandon for under €51 and vintages to quaff or collect from this specialist in German, Italian, and French wines. A good selection of cognac is also available, as is traditional German hot food during the day. Knowledgeable staff will guide you through the gloriously dusty wine racks. ⊠ *Mommsenstr.9,* ☎ *030/881–1909. Metro: Savignyplatz.*

Leysieffer. Chocolate heaven! Your loved ones will agree should you give them some gorgeously gift-wrapped champagne truffles, novelty minipralines, tea-time cookies, or luxurious boxes of seasonal delights such as Baumkuchen and peppermint Lebkuchen. Oh, just be naughty and indulge yourself. ⊠ *Kurfürstendamm 218,* ☎ *030/885–7480. Metro: Uhlandstrasse.*

Philomeni's. Nuts about nuts? Philomeni is! The bubbly Greek nutritionist is on a successful mission to make healthy sweets such as pralines from dried fruits and fine ginger-roasted almonds instead of the usual sugary variety. Just one slice of her top-selling "bachelor cake" nourishes those poor souls with ever-bare refrigerators. Her delicious quiches, fresh pasta, and bright displays and service are an inspiration. ⊠ *Knesebeckstr. 97,* ☎ *030/3180–2507. Metro: Savignyplatz.*

Viniculture. Classed by gourmets as one of Germany's best wine stores, Viniculture stocks a selection of affordable to top-bracket European and New World wines. Wine coolers, English-language copies of *Wine Spectator,* and single-malt whiskeys are also on sale, as are sandwiches from a mouth-watering deli counter. ⊠ *Grolmanstr. 44–45,* ☎ *030/ 883–8174. Metro: Zoologischer Garten.*

GIFTS AND GADGETS

Berliner Zinnfiguren. Selling entire battalions of tin soldiers from the Viking era and Napoleonic wars to the present day, this 65-year-old store is aimed more at military enthusiasts than children. It has a large collection of books and videos on military history, most of which are in English. Also in the store are decorative tin figures and special paints to touch up scratches. ⊠ *Knesebeckstr. 88,* ☎ *030/315–7000. Metro: Savignyplatz.*

Gipsformerei der Staatlichen Museen Preussischer Kulturbesitz. If you long to have the Egyptian Museum's Queen Nefertiti bust on your mantelpiece at home, check out the state museum's shop, open weekdays 9–4, which sells plaster casts of treasures from the city's museums. ⊠ *Sophie-Charlotten-Str. 17,* ☎ *030/326–7690. Metro: Westend.*

Scenario. Tucked under the elevated tram tracks, Scenario has gorgeous stationery, silver snuffboxes, costume jewelry, designer key rings, neat photo frames, and irresistible knickknacks. ⊠ *Savignypassage Else-Ury-Bogen 602,* ☎ *030/312–9199. Metro: Savignyplatz.*

Schlafwandel. Making bedtime a joy, this store sells night wear, from velvet dressing gowns to silk pajamas, as well as fleecy nightshirts and vibrant towels. Its range of bedding includes sunny satin sheets, patterned pillowcases, and fluffy blankets. ⊠ *Kantstr. 21,* ☎ *030/312–6523. Metro: Savignyplatz.*

HOUSEWARES

Etchika Werner. One of the world's leading interior designers, Etchika Werner will totally redesign, upholster, and furnish your home should you so desire. With hundreds of vibrant fabrics for wall coverings, curtains, and upholstery, she will create for you an individual look. Her style is elegant and antique, and imitation Biedermeier and Empire pieces, chunky knickknacks, and modern ornaments can all be bought in her store. ⊠ *Fasanenstr. 68,* ☎ *030/881–4600. Metro: Zoologischer Garten.*

Königliche Porzellan Manufaktur. The former Royal Prussian Porcelain Factory, also called KPM, produces fine porcelain. The delicate, hand-painted china can be bought full-price at KPM's two stores or more cheaply at the factory salesroom on Wegelystrasse, which sells seconds at reduced prices. ⊠ *Kurfürstendamm 27,* ☎ *030/886–7210. Metro: Adenauerplatz;* ⊠ *Unter den Linden 35,* ☎ *030/206–4150. Metro: Friedrichstrasse;* ⊠ *Wegelystr. 1,* ☎ *030/390–090. Metro: Tiergarten.*

Rosenthal Studio-Haus. For designer crockery and glassware, look no farther. Bauhaus tea services, Versace champagne flutes, and hand-painted espresso cups adorn the spiral staircase leading to a heavenly selection of champagne accessories and Bulgari soft furnishings. Understated Riedel grappa glasses cost €41 a shot, with packing and delivery service included. ⊠ *Kurfürstendamm 226,* ☎ *030/885–6340. Metro: Zoologischer Garten.*

WMF. Germany's most popular cutlery is renowned for for its quality and durability. The solid, functional stainless-steel kitchen gadgets have won numerous design prizes, and most households aspire to at least a vegetable knife or weapon-size whisk. The giant pepper mills, tabletop corkscrews, and chunky cheese graters are for serious chefs. ⊠ *Kurfürstendamm 229,* ☎ *030/882–3941. Metro: Zoologischer Garten.*

JEWELRY AND WATCHES

Bucherer. One of Berlin's new and upscale jewelers, Bucherer carries fine handcrafted jewelry, watches, and other stylish designer accessories. ⊠ *Kurfürstendamm 26A,* ☎ *030/880–4030. Metro: Uhlandstrasse.*

grzimek. With antique jewelry from the early 18th century on to choose from, you can take a seat on the couch before deciding whether you really need that €20,512 Cartier necklace. The tiny store's chunky coral-and-gold chokers or classic emerald brooches are for wearers as well as collectors. The friendly shopkeeper speaks English. ⊠ *Kurfürstendamm 200,* ☎ *030/881–4113. Metro: Uhlandstrasse.*

Klaus Kaufhold. Cologne jewelry designer Kaufhold shares his exhibition space and a philosophy of sleek minimalism with fellow German designers such as Niessing and Henrich + Denzel. Ribeiro's rubber and diamond rings and Niessing's matt platinum and diamond pieces

are conscious understatements of pure taste. ⊠ *Kurfürstendamm 197,*
☎ *030/8847–1790. Metro: Uhlandstrasse.*

Swatch. Swatch sells colorful Swiss watches and accoutrements for everyone's pocket. Jelly–bean or chunky aluminum straps can be bought to
mix and match, along with cute kids' watches, and huge clock versions
of the wristwatch. ⊠ *Kurfürstendamm 17,* ☎ *030/8860–775. Metro:*
Kurfürstendamm.

LUGGAGE AND LEATHER GOODS

Bree. The smell of natural leather wafts at you on entering the shop.
Bree has won design awards for its brightly colored, tough "Punch"
pieces, including unusual rollover sailor bags. These are a trendy urban
accessory, but a classic range of handbags and satchels is also available in black or beige, coveted by both men and women. ⊠ *Kurfürs-*
tendamm 44, ☎ *030/883–7462. Metro: Uhlandstrasse.*

Sack & Pack Taschen Laden. This store has its own saddler hand-make
its practical satchels in natural leather, using no artificial products to
treat or dye the leather. Rucksacks and serviceable luggage are the focus,
rather than beaded clutch bags. The store's own products are eminently
more affordable than the designers it also stocks. Schoolchildren make
good use of the cylindrical leather pencil cases. ⊠ *Kantstr. 48,* ☎ *030/*
312–1513. Metro: Wilmersdorferstrasse.

Seeger. A top luxury brand, Seeger describes itself as the "cashmere
of leather." The service is wonderful—no wonder Whoopi Goldberg
came here to stock up on her luggage collection. Doctors' bags, sleek
briefcases, soft leather travel slippers, women's handbags and purses
in the classic Seeger colors—beige, cognac, ocean blue, and raspberry—all look fantastic on the minimalist shelves. ⊠ *Fasanenstr. 27,*
☎ *030/8855–4490. Metro: Kurfürstendamm.*

MUSIC

Canzone. This CD and record store is dedicated to world music. Tucked
behind the S-Bahn in Savignypassage, their catalog is diverse and comprehensive, with the likes of Asian dance music, Arabian drumming,
Hungarian gypsy music, and Turkish tango. ⊠ *S-Bahn Bogen 583,* ☎
030/312–4027. Metro: Savignyplatz.

Robert Hartwig. Hartwig has a wonderful collection of vinyl, shellac,
old 78s, and a broad range of classical and cabaret music as well as a
good selection of German composers recorded by local and world orchestras and conductors. Many 1930s German pop and ballad singers
nestle among the collections, and the adjoining antique shop is also a
delight—by appointment only. ⊠ *Pestalozzistr. 23,* ☎ *030/312–1211.*
Metro: Wilmersdorferstrasse.

L & P Classics. This store stocks a large range of classical CDs. Major
composers are listed alphabetically, with sections on opera, chansons,
early music, and jazz. Friendly service, copies of *Gramophone* magazine, as well as numerous leaflets and posters advertising classical
music events make the trip worthwhile. ⊠ *Knesebeckstr. 33–34,* ☎ *030/*
8804-3043. Metro: Savignyplatz.

Hans Riedel. The present Mr. Riedel's grandfather founded this music
store in 1910. It is one of Europe's largest stockers of international sheet
music, dating from original handwritten volumes from the 17th century to books of current pop songs. Mr. Riedel takes his clientele seriously and has a steady flow of satisfied customers. The store is full
of browsing music lovers and has a bookish feel, with some instruments
and a host of English-language publications also on sale. ⊠ *Uhland-*
str. 38, ☎ *030/882–7395. Metro: Uhlandstrasse.*

World Of Music. This all-encompassing mainstream store focuses on pop, rock, and chart music. A large dance music section divides into techno for the fast beats and club culture for mellower tunes. There are separate sections for hip-hop, heavy metal, and punk, with listening points all over the store. Film soundtracks, international artists (including a section on German musicians of all genres), world music, jazz, and classical music are in no way underrepresented. ⊠ *Augsburgerstr. 36–42,* ☎ *030/885–7240. Metro: Kurfürstendamm.*

STATIONERY

Papeterie. Papeterie has an array of executive desktop items such as designer scissors, pens by Parker and Waterman, luxury lighters and ashtrays, personal organizers, stationery, and gift paper. Although the store has an upmarket feel, greeting cards start at around €1.50. ⊠ *Uhlandstr. 28,* ☎ *030/881–6363. Metro: Uhlandstrasse.*

Papier Concept. Step inside for beautiful handmade paper, from rolls of silky violet to sheets of textured moonscape silver. Smart Italian, wholesome Nepalese, or diaphanous Japanese designs offer the ultimate gift wrap. Select a sheet and have a diary, notebook, or photo album bound in it. Writing paper from lime to terra-cotta, matching pens, and regular office stationery are also available. ⊠ *Knesebeckstr. 6–7,* ☎ *030/313–0875. Metro: Savignyplatz.*

TOYS AND CHILDREN'S CLOTHING

Baby-Walz. Stocking a wide range of maternity wear and everything imaginable for the new baby from off-roader push chairs and soft blankets to Swedish baby carriers. The clothes and accessories are for kids up to six years, and baby's clothing is measured in centimeters, not age. ⊠ *Knesebeckstr. 56–58,* ☎ *030/887–1680. Metro: Uhlandstrasse.*

Heidi's Spielzeugladen. Heidi Mallmann has been selling handmade wooden toys for more than 25 years. Brands like Selecta and Nic only use natural products such as beeswax to treat their wood. Delightful dollhouses, rocking horses, animal figures, puppets, and decorations for kids' bedrooms are just a few of her irresistible wares. ⊠ *Kantstr. 61,* ☎ *030/323–7556. Metro: Wilmersdorferstrasse.*

Steffi's Lädchen. Steffi has a nice range of traditional wooden toys, such as Brio model railways and bright rolling caterpillars. Wooden jewelry and kids' accessories, and numerous Janosch items (such as the cute stripey tiger-duck) are very popular with German children. ⊠ *Knesebeckstr. 18–19,* ☎ *030/312–3339. Metro: Uhlandstrasse.*

v. kloeden. Traditional German toys here include Steiff teddy bears (with the trademark ear button), expensive Käthe Kruse dolls, handcrafted angel figurines from the Erzgebirge, Anker building blocks, wooden chess sets, and Berlin monopoly. Enthusiastic staff will show you around and explain to adults and children alike how to play. ⊠ *Wielandstr. 24,* ☎ *030/8871–2512. Metro: Adenauerplatz.*

Schöneberg

Schöneberg is a fairly sedate area for shopping, with some gems of stores around the attractive Winterfeldtplatz. There is a fantastic market there on Saturday morning, mostly good for fresh produce but with lots of crafts and gifts stalls in the weeks before Christmas. A popular gay neighborhood, Schöneberg has a number of gay-owned shops on Nollendorfstrasse—just look for the large rainbow flags snapping in the wind. Antiques and secondhand bookstores abound. From Wittenbergplatz a tour around Keithstrasse, Eisenacher Strasse, Fuggerstrasse, Kalckreuthstrasse, and Motzstrasse takes in antiques shops of varying size and quality. Goltzstrasse is not only great for antiques, but trendy shops, bars, and cafés, too.

Specialty Stores

ANTIQUES

Grage. One of several good antiques shops on Goltzstrasse, Grage has larger pieces of furniture, most of which come from the Berlin area. Enormous couches, pianos, silver cutlery, and ornate desks are suitable for collectors and spontaneous buyers alike—but sending it home is your problem! Grage's shop at No. 15, across the street, sells smaller knickknacks. ⊠ *Goltzstr. 38,* ☎ *030/216–7313. Metro: Eisenacherstrasse.*

BOOKS

Antiquariat. Here you'll find a huge selection of secondhand German literature and academic books, many of which are antique. Some beautifully gold-bound art nouveau volumes nestle among the shelves, as does a reasonable selection of English hard- and paperback fiction. Some classical records are at the back of the store. This is just one of several good antique bookstores on Winterfeldstrasse. ⊠ *Winterfeldstr. 54–56,* ☎ *030/215–4819. Metro: Nollendorfplatz.*

Chatwin's. Named in honor of author Bruce Chatwin, this store is dedicated to travel writing. A large number of the guidebooks are in English, and there's also a section on contemporary and classic Anglo-American literature, as well as good stationery. ⊠ *Goltzstr. 40,* ☎ *030/2175–6904. Metro: Eisenacher Strasse.*

CLOTHING AND ACCESSORIES

Boyz 'R' Us. If you guys have ever enviously wondered why girls get to choose from so many more styles, colors, and fabrics, here is your chance to grab that pink-gingham shirt or spangly turquoise top you've always dreamed of. Patterned jeans, skirts designed for men, and loud tartan pants make this store a magnet for gay and straight clubbers. A small number of each item keeps the store exclusive—labels include Coration, the Berlin designers collective. ⊠ *Maassenstr. 8,* ☎ *030/2363–0640. Metro: Nollendorfplatz.*

Groopie Deluxe. The emphasis in this delightful store featuring mostly Berlin women's-wear designers is on street fashion, but this is in no way proscriptive—anything goes in Berlin. Anja Lafin sews her pretty and feminine garments herself; Nix and Overdose make casual, low-maintenance clothing; and for serious contenders there's science-fiction costume club wear from Spoast. Great bags, purses, and jewelry add the final touch of glamour. ⊠ *Goltzstr. 39,* ☎ *030/217–2038. Metro: Nollendorfplatz.*

Schuhtick. The four branches of this Berlin shoe store have a quirky range of chunky, angular footwear for men and women as well as party stilettos and demure work wear. Schuhtick's wares are considerably less expensive than similar designer styles. ⊠ *Maassenstr. 5,* ☎ *030/217–0886. Metro: Nollendorfplatz;* ⊠ *Savignypl. 11,* ☎ *030/315–9380. Metro: Savignyplatz;* ⊠ *Tauenzienstr. 5,* ☎ *030/2140–9817. Metro: Wittenbergplatz;* ⊠ *Karl-Liebknecht-Str. 9,* ☎ *030/242–4012. Metro: Alexanderplatz.*

GIFTS AND GADGETS

Lorenzo. Gorgeous candles, stationery, coffee mugs, silk scarves, and furry personal organizers are just some gifts ideas at Lorenzo's. The unusual silver jewelry comes from as far afield as India and Mexico, with huge amber stones or fine filigree to choose from. ⊠ *Maassenstr. 11,* ☎ *030/216–1537. Metro: Nollendorfplatz.*

Mara. Selling handcrafted jewelry from the Schliff workshop around the corner, this shop's artists have been making sparkly necklaces from materials as diverse as colored plastic to Swarovski crystal for 21 years. With a large line of hair accessories (plain or with gems), futuristic earring holders for their bold brass and silver designs, and decorative pens, everything in this boutique is certainly original. ✉ *Goltzstr. 52,* ☎ *030/215–2582. Metro: Eisenacherstrasse.*

Miezhaus. A fat toy cat purrs in the window of this store that has everything for cat lovers. An array of kitchen items, games, stationery, and ornaments featuring felines fill the store. ✉ *Nollendorfstr. 31–32,* ☎ *030/2363–0980. Metro: Nollendorfplatz.*

HOUSEWARES

Filiale. This store features domestic delights from gleaming '50s-style food mixers to understated glassware, from bright ice crushers to fish-bedecked shower curtains. An aesthetically pleasing range of home and office organization and storage systems has the solutions to unclutter your environment. Luggage and bags from Calvin Klein and trendy shopping trolleys are also for sale. ✉ *Winterfeldtstr. 42,* ☎ *030/215–7475. Metro: Nollendorfplatz.*

Potsdamer Platz

Department Stores and Shopping Centers

Potsdamer Platz Arkaden. When they opened in October 1998, the Arkaden were touted as Berlin's most exciting mall. Locals turn up in droves to check out what is still a relatively new concept for Berlin. It has around 120 stores and a good food hall on the first floor, but compared to other cities it's nothing special. Fine for weekly family shopping with its supermarket and thrift stores, or for regular clothes shopping at stores such as Benetton, Esprit, and Eddie Bauer, the attraction of Potsdamer Platz lies more in its fascinating new architecture, its IMAX cinema complex, and its very existence in an area that was a dustbowl just a decade ago. ✉ *Potsdamer Pl.,* ☎ *030/2559–270. Metro: Potsdamer Platz.*

Specialty Stores

GIFTS AND STATIONERY

EinsZweiDrei Geschenkideen. This is one of the few stores in Berlin with greetings cards and gift paper for all possible occasions. Should you be looking for novelty trinkets like eggcups with legs, chattering dolphin clocks, or cuddly animal heads to mount on the wall, you will adore it. Ornate photo frames and paperweights, inflatable waste bins, and starfish toilet seats are just a few of the playful wares on offer. ✉ *Potsdamer Pl. Arkaden, Alte Potsdamer Str. 7,* ☎ *030/2529–7629. Metro: Potsdamer Platz;* ✉ *Friedrichstadtpassagen, Friedrichstr. 67,* ☎ *030/2094–5925. Metro: Französischerstrasse.*

Papeterie Berlin. In addition to a host of typical Berlin souvenirs—ashtrays, pencils, postcards, mini–Berlin bears—the store stocks a wide variety of gift and office stationery, including handmade wrapping paper, wax seals, calendars, and executive pens and organizers. ✉ *Potsdamer Pl. Arkaden, Alte Potsdamer Str. 7,* ☎ *030/2529–7668. Metro: Potsdamer Platz.*

LUGGAGE AND LEATHER

Leder Börse. This is the place if you're looking for designer luggage, leather ware, and Goldpfeil, the classic quality German label recognizable by the sleek little arrow on its fastenings. Porsche Design's briefcases and wallets are only marginally less desirable than the cars! A good collection of squidgy, tough-weave Mandarin Duck rucksacks and casual shoulder bags complete the wide selection. ⊠ *Potsdamer Pl. Arkaden, Alte Potsdamer Str 7,* ☎ *030/2529–7545. Metro: Potsdamer Platz.*

Mitte

Mitte is in the process of rapid change. Derelict backyards are being turned into showcase squares with fancy fountains and numerous exclusive workshops and boutiques. Street fashion struts its stuff around Oranienburgerstrasse and the sleekly renovated Hackesche Höfe, so the streets leading off from both (especially Neue Schönhauser Strasse) are good for highbrow, trendy clothes and shoe shops. Friedrichstrasse was envisaged as the eastern challenger to the Ku'damm, but with only a quarter of the Ku'damm's retail space it is struggling to compete. Even so, its well-designed malls deserve a visit. Alexanderplatz, glorious in its 1920s heyday, is now a soulless slab of socialist-realist-style concrete, but locals love to shop there despite only one noteworthy department store. A better bet is to cross past the splendid Rotes Rathaus (Red Town Hall) to the Nikolaiviertel, known as the "cradle of Berlin"—the oldest and arguably quaintest district. Here are heaps of touristy shops, and places to eat and drink abound. The elegant promenade Unter den Linden leads to the Brandenburg Gate and is still establishing itself as a shopping mile.

Department Stores and Shopping Centers

The Friedrichstadtpassagen stretches several blocks alongFriedrichstrasse, encompassing the chic malls Quartier 206, Quartier 207, and their upscale department stores. Quartier 205 is a food court with goodies like a smoothies bar, hot German fare, and bagels.

Quartier 206 Departmentstore. The Quartier 206 is itself a chic mall with exclusive designer boutiques such as Gucci, DKNY, and Strenesse Gabriele Strehle. One highlight is Etro, with its gorgeous Italian paisleys, vibrant patterns, embroidered scarves, and luxury home collection. A stylish café in the center has a live pianist. The Quartier 206 Departmentstore is a labyrinth of plush boutiques with men's and women's designer wear. Ball gowns and luxury accessories, women's wear from Berlin's Claudia Skoda, Helmut Lang menswear, the posh coffee shop, cigar counters, and pricey French cosmetics all exude elegance and charm. ⊠ *Friedrichstr. 71,* ☎ *030/2094–6240. Metro: Französischer Strasse.*

Galeries Lafayette. This French department store within Quartier 207 was lucky enough to be designed by architect Jean Nouvel, the man who gave Lyon its opera house and Paris its Institute du Monde Arabe and Cartier Institute. The ground floor beckons with its glorious range of luxury items from Joop snakeskin cell-phone holders to Clinique products to various designer and low-key clothing collections. Walk toward the center to peer into the huge and dizzying steel-and-glass funnel that is circled by six floors of merchandise. The gourmet food hall is the gateway to the realm of the senses. Caviar, sushi, great coffee, and pastries from the store's homeland can be enjoyed in a little oasis of French culture. The *épicerie* sells an aromatic selection of French cheeses, sinfully large boxes of chocolates, and mouthwatering antipasti. To prepare haute cuisine at home, treat yourself to industrial-strength Le Creuset pots and bright and breezy tableware. ⊠ *Französische Str. 23,* ☎ *030/209–480. Metro: Französische Strasse.*

Galeria Kaufhof. Galeria Kaufhof stocks a wide range of luggage, jewelry, clothing, sports equipment, and the usual department store goods. The food hall overambitiously describes itself as a "gourmet's paradise," but does provide everything a decent supermarket should, yet rarely

208

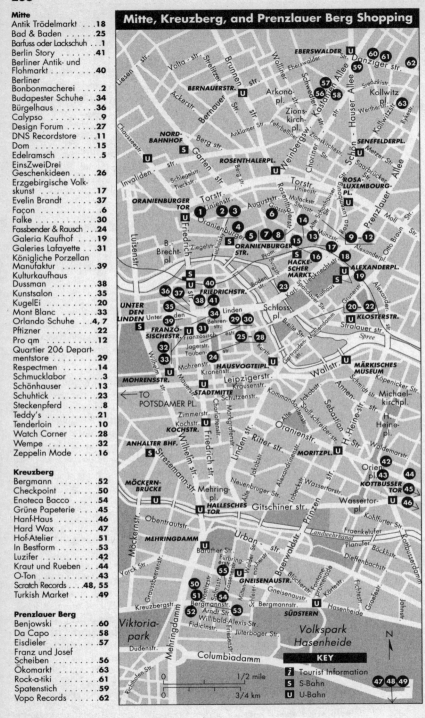

Mitte, Kreuzberg, and Prenzlauer Berg Shopping

KEY

ℹ️ Tourist Information
S S-Bahn
U U-Bahn

does, in Berlin. Great German sausage and cold meats, a nice salad bar, and a good confectionery warrant a walk-through. ⊠ *Alexanderpl.,* ☎ *030/247–430. Metro: Alexanderplatz.*

Specialty Stores

ANTIQUES

Antik Trödelmarkt. Tucked under the S-Bahn line, this market has a motley collection of valuable antiques and flea-market trash. The array of leather doctor's bags, pinball machines, Louis Philippe tables for around €257, silver spoons, sailor's chests, and GDR memorabilia makes browsing good fun. ⊠ *Dircksenstr S-Bahnbogen 128,* ☎ *030/0179/ 593–3878. Metro: Alexanderplatz.*

Berliner Antik- und Flohmarkt. Running under the Friedrichstrasse station S-Bahn tracks (*S-Bahnbogen*) is one of the largest and more established areas dealing in antique art. More than 30 individual stalls offer everything imaginable, from expensive lamps and art deco jewelry to bargain books. The market is closed Tuesday. ⊠ *Georgenstr.,* ☎ *030/208–2645. Metro: Friedrichstrasse.*

BOOKS AND MUSIC

Berlin Story. From specialty guide books to historic maps and posters of the city, this book store carries all things Berlin. Of the thousands of titles, many are available in several languages. ⊠ *Unter den Linden 10,* ☎ *030/2045–3842. Metro: Friedrichstrasse.*

DNS Recordstore. Electronic dance music is a more serious affair than you might think. DJs and *Trainspotter* fans come here to stock up on their vinyl, whether their groove be minimalist techno, U.K. two-step, or French house. Essential slip mats, record bags, and T-shirts complete the image, as do the turntables and lack of girls. ⊠ *Alte Schön-hauser Str. 39–40,* ☎ *030/247–9835. Metro: Rosa-Luxemburg-Platz.*

Kulturkaufhaus Dussmann. With four civilized floors on which to peruse and consume culture, Dussmann's is inspiring. Rent a free Disc-man and sit in the basement theater seats envisioning musicians to accompany your classical music or opera selection. Or flick through CDs expertly categorized from independent to Dixieland, Latin jazz to gospel, all near ample listening stations. German artists are upstairss should you want to check out pop by Rosenstolz or Ute Lemper's chansons, and there is a great world-music section. English speakers can delight in DVDs, videos, books about Berlin, and translated German works. The airy gallery encourages you to read or surf the Web. Musical souvenirs include Mozart busts and Janis Joplin dolls. The store closes unusually late—10 PM, Monday through Saturday. ⊠ *Friedrich-str. 90,* ☎ *030/20250. Metro: Friedrichstrasse.*

Pro qm. "Per square meter" is a self-consciously stylish bookstore offering the glossy volumes you never realized you always wanted on your coffee table. With a large section on architecture and urban philosophy, the selection also encompasses pop culture, fashion, design, mass- and multimedia, and biographies. Around half the seductive tomes are in English. ⊠ *Alte Schönhauser Str. 48,* ☎ *030/238–4680. Metro: Rosa-Luxemburg-Platz.*

CLOTHING AND ACCESSORIES

Evelin Brandt. Berlin designer Brandt enjoys dressing her female clientele in strikingly chunky cuts. Her no-nonsense casual and classic garments and elegant evening wear reflect a pragmatic yet slick German attitude to fashion. There are five branches in Berlin. ⊠ *Friedrichstr. 153A,* ☎ *030/204–4444. Metro: Friedrichstrasse;* ⊠ *Savignypl. 6,* ☎ *030/313 8080. Metro: Savignyplatz*

Calypso. With the motto "High Heels Forever," this secondhand shoe shop does not disappoint (whether one can really wear the things is another matter). With footwear from the sublime to the ridiculous, boots for hiking and biking, gold sandals, and many original '60s and '70s pairs, you'll find lots of choices and bargains. The shoes can be ogled weekdays noon–8, Saturday noon–4. ⊠ *Münzstr. 16,* ☎ *030/281–6165. Metro: Weinmeisterstrasse*

Façon. Designer wares hang like exotic blossoms from the ceiling, and a sewing machine hums from the workshop at the back. Simple shifts and textured knitwear by local designer Hannoh, rustic felt accessories, and absurd hats set the tone. The number of local designers represented here is increasing, and the philosophy of all of them is functional fashion. ⊠ *Gipsstr. 5,* ☎ *030/2839–0966. Metro: Hackescher Markt.*

Falke. Falke socks and underwear are household staples in Germany and are indeed a mark of quality. Men's business and casual wear is set apart from the rest by unusual details, with adventurous garments such as male sarongs and quirky cufflinks. ⊠ *Quartier 206, Friedrichstr. 71,* ☎ *030/2094–6110. Metro: Französische Strasse.*

Orlando Schuhe. For shoes to die for, check out this exhibition of beautiful footwear that runs from comfortable, high-fashion sneakers to sex-kitten heels. Women's and men's shoes are in two stores, both very cool and typical of Mitte. *Women's shoes:* ⊠ *Rosenthalerstr. 48,* ☎ *030/2840–7858. Metro: Hackescher Markt; men's shoes:* ⊠ *Oranienburgerstr. 86,* ☎ *030/281–9838. Metro: Hackescher Markt.*

Respectmen. This store features designer menswear, including shiny disco pants, paint-bespattered fake fur, and cool Paul Smith suits. Women can find equally irreverent designs and amusing accessories down the street in the new Respectless store at No. 19. ⊠ *Neue Schönhauser Str. 14,* ☎ *030/283–5010. Metro: Hackescher Markt.*

Tenderloin. For ironic evening wear this is the place to dress yourself. Garish frilly frocks and original '60s floral fashions come secondhand, as do '70s leather coats and sportswear. New clothes are on sale, too, in the form of tough urban fabrics and unusual knitwear. Wigs, comedy handbags, false eyelashes, and sunglasses will complete your outfit. Even retro furniture such as '50s salon hairdryers is here for the taking. ⊠ *Alte Schönhauser Str. 30,* ☎ *030/4201–5785. Metro: Weinmeisterstrasse.*

Zeppelin Mode. Zeppelin is synonymous with slick, understated midprice clothing for men and women about town. With unusual fabrics and tailored suits, these garments and shoes are suitable for the office and after-work events. An interesting selection of Vivienne Westwood accessories is also stocked. ⊠ *An der Spandauer Brücke 7,* ☎ *030/2408–7830. Metro: Hackescher Markt.*

FOOD

Berliner Bonbonmacherei. Traditional Berliner sweets are made in the store using original recipes and methods. Watch the confectioner at work rolling fat lime candy blankets into Berliner *Maiblätter* (leaf-shape pastilles with a distinctive woodruff flavor). Choose from a colorful variety such as golden nougat, strawberry and plum, or sage cough sweets. The store is closed on Monday and Tuesday. ⊠ *Heckmannhöfe, Oranienburgerstr. 32,* ☎ *030/612–7337. Metro: Hackescher Markt.*

Fassbender & Rausch. Fassbender & Rausch were the proud Berlin chocolatiers who founded the family business in 1863. They once supplied the Prussian royal court, and fantastic souvenirs range from chocolate Berlin bears to Brandenburg Gates, boxes of "thank you" pralines, and marzipan figures. The giant chocolate renditions of Berlin sights are worth a visit alone, and liqueurs and squares of chocolate with varying cocoa content can be bought by weight. There is even a special line for diabetics. ⊠ *Charlottenburg 60,* ☎ *030/2045–8440. Metro: Stadtmitte.*

GIFTS AND GADGETS

Bad & Baden. This store has everything to make bath time fun and luxurious, such as huge soft towels in every color imaginable, including cute gift packs with cuddly animal bath toys. Pastel scrubbing brushes, bath toys, essential oils, and sauna accessories will have you longing for a hot tub. Slip into a fluffy bathrobe—in classic white toweling, blazing gold velvet, or leopard-skin print silk. ⊠ *Friedrichstadt Passage, Friedrichstr. 67,* ☎ *030/2838–8010. Metro: Französischer Strasse.*

Bürgelhaus. The store is a specialist in traditional blue-and-white-spotted pottery from the Bürgel area in the state of Thuringia. Local potters have been making these pretty handcrafted ceramics for centuries. You can buy a whole dinner service or just a natty utensil, with soft table furnishings to match. ⊠ *Friedrichstr. 154,* ☎ *030/2045–2695. Metro: Friedrichstrasse.*

Edelramsch. Translating as something like "classy trash," the name of the store denotes a popular Berlin style. Fake tiger-fur handcuffs, plastic carrying bags decorated with roses, great stationery, fun trinkets, and superb costume jewelry are typical "trashy" items. Joke-shop wares and cheerful staff make it a joy to browse and play here. ⊠ *Krausnickstr. 1,* ☎ *030/2759–6388. Metro: Hackescher Markt.*

Erzgebirgische Volkskunst. Everything sold here comes from the Erzgebirge mountain area in deepest Thuringia, where craftsfolk became famous for their nutcracker figures. Their traditional hand-carved wooden ornaments like Christmas pyramids or little incense burners in the guise of baker, hunter, chess player or other quaint figures, are very popular among Germans and tourists alike. ⊠ *Dircksenstr. 50,* ☎ *030/2838– 8010. Metro: Hackescher Markt.*

KugelEi. Tucked behind the Nikolaikirche is the only store of its kind in Europe. An authorized dealer of Fabergé eggs, it sells quaint decorative eggs and baubles hand-painted by local artists. The owners are proud of the individual craftsmanship and stock designs from glitzy glass to scenes depicting countryside or Berlin motifs such as the bear or Reichstag. For prices ranging from €2.5 to €2,564, you can pick out a unique and traditional German gift for seasonal or permanent home decoration. ⊠ *Spandauer Str. 25,* ☎ *030/2472–7575. Metro: Alexanderplatz.*

Kunstsalon. Intoxicating for those with a penchant for drama are the props, costumes, and imitation antiques from the Berlin opera houses on sale here. Plenty of kitsch and fun items of the furry heart cushion variety make up the other wares. Berlin souvenirs include the game Memory, with GDR images, and paraphernalia related to the Ampelmann— the cute little red and green pedestrian-traffic-light man. ⊠ *Unter den Linden 41,* ☎ *030/2045–0203. Metro: Friedrichstrasse.*

HOUSEWARES

Design Forum. The brightly colored tableware and gleaming stainless-steel gadgets are eye-catching and will liven up any kitchen. Also stocked are Ritzenhoff glasses for wheat beer, champagne, and schnapps, which are shaped and hand-painted accordingly and beautifully presented in a gift box. ⊠ *Friedrichstadtpassagen, Quartier 205, Friedrichstr. 68,* ☎ *030/2094–5062. Metro: Französischer Strasse.*

Dom. This is an inexpensive store for crazy household odds and ends and furniture, from disco balls to Chinese lanterns, plastic candelabras to mock-baroque mirrors, and fake sheepskin rugs to orange-plastic storage boxes. ✉ *Hackescher Markt,* ☎ *030/2809–8367. Metro: Hackescher Markt.*

Schönhauser. Here are some more of those retro items that typify Berlin and urge you to turn your home into a '70s disco. Giant sofas in an excellent range of colors, bulbous lamps, plastic wall sculptures, fantastic stationery, platform-boot key rings, and designer revivalist crockery all vie for attention. ✉ *Neue Schönhauser Str. 18,* ☎ *030/ 281–1704. Metro: Weinmeisterstrasse.*

JEWELRY AND WATCHES

Schmucklabor. Young gold- and silversmiths have their workshop on site, making individually handcrafted and unique collections using materials from finely layered platinum to chunky matte silver. Jewelry designer Matthias Frank mostly works with silver and sells his rings that resemble minispaceships for €144 and up. ✉ *Heckmannhöfe, Oranienburgerstr. 32,* ☎ *030/445–5196. Metro: Hackescher Markt.*

Watch Corner. This store sells trendy designer timepieces by the likes of Fossil, Diesel, Baby-G, and DKNY at the more affordable end of the market. ✉ *Friedrichstadtpassagen, Friedrichstr. 71,* ☎ *030/2045– 0100. Metro: Französischer Strasse;* ✉ *Potsdamer Pl. Arkaden, Alte Potsdamer Str.,* ☎ *030/2529–2595. Metro: Potsdamer Platz.*

Wempe. If you are looking for exclusive jewelry and watches in the top price bracket, then Wempe stocks its own classic watches, clocks, and jewelry as well as pieces by Rolex, Cartier, Tag Heuer, IWC, and other chronometer icons. They have fine diamond and pearl jewelry for all occasions and tastes, but unfortunately not for all pockets. ✉ *Friedrichstr. 82,* ☎ *030/2039–9920. Metro: Französischer Strasse;* ✉ *Kurfürstendamm 215,* ☎ *030/882–6878. Metro: Uhlandstrasse.*

LEATHER AND LUGGAGE

Mont Blanc. The finest luxury leather ware, from executive briefcases, penholders, wallets, and belts to beauty cases, handbags, and purses, is available here alongside a top selection of pens, blotter pads, jewelry, and other items. ✉ *Friedrichstr. 80,* ☎ *030/2038–8350. Metro: Französischer Strasse.*

Pfitzner. The workshop in the Nikolaiviertel began more than 100 years ago in Prenzlauer Berg making handcrafted leather, suede, lambskin, and some fur garments. Styles are generally conservative and expensive, such as the bright dyed leather and fox-fur coats. ✉ *Poststr. 7,* ☎ *030/242–3280. Metro: Alexanderplatz.*

TOYS

Steckenpferd. Treat a child to this funhouse filled with popular wooden toys, dolls, board games, puppets, kites, plastic swords, joke items, magic sets, fancy dress costumes, and children's musical instruments. The large shiny cones (*Einschulungstüte*) for sale are filled with stationery, sweets, and treats and are given to kids on their first day of school. ✉ *Rosenthalerstr. 49,* ☎ *030/3087–2097. Metro: Hackescher Markt.*

Teddy's. As the name suggests, this Nikolaiviertel shop is teddy-beartastic. The bear is a symbol of the city of Berlin, making it a popular souvenir as well as a cuddly toy. Lots of old-fashioned Teddys are for sale, German favorites being Steiff and Hermann. Familiar bear characters like Paddington and Pooh are represented, along with a range of clothing and supplies for one of the all-time best companions. ✉ *Propststr. 4,* ☎ *030/247–8244. Metro: Alexanderplatz.*

Prenzlauer Berg

A fantastic spot for breakfast cafés, buzzing bars, and restaurants, Prenzlauer Berg does not offer stunning shopping opportunities. If you like offbeat clothes and record shops, however, you'll be in your element. Discovering that few tourists venture here during daylight hours may make your foray all the more stimulating. The heart and soul of former East Berlin, many of the streets off Danziger Strasse and Schönhauser Allee retain much of the brown coal–smelling charm of GDR days, though Western investments have spruced up many buildings.

Markets

Ökomarkt. Every Thursday noon–7 pm, local environmentlists organize a green market. All produce sold is locally grown or made—from Werder apples to sheepskin waistcoats. The market has a lively atmosphere, with stalls selling hot herbal tea and vegetarian snacks, and the square itself is a delight. ⊠ *Kollwitzpl.,* ☎ *030/4433–9137. Metro: Senefelderplatz.*

Specialty Stores

CLOTHING AND ACCESSORIES

Eisdieler. This name is a play on the German word for ice-cream parlor, which is where these five local designers first set up shop in Mitte. They met while studying fashion in Berlin and began selling Eisdieler T-shirts over the counter while sewing in the backroom. Each has a separate label and line of street fashion, collectively covering jeans, high-tech sportswear, and retro club wear worn by young, hip, arty types. ⊠ *Kastanienallee 12,* ☎ *030/285–7351. Metro: Eberswalder Strasse;* ⊠ *Auguststr. 74,* ☎ *030/285–7351. Metro: Hackescher Markt.*

Rock-a-Tiki. This is a fabulous rockabilly store with great new '50s-style clothing including blue jeans, baseball jackets, and a winsome line of cocktail-style shirts. This is the right place to find Hawaiian prints, martini-glass buttons, cocktail swizzles, and fun fridge magnets. There is also a pin board with information on local rock-and-roll events. ⊠ *Danzigerstr. 3,* ☎ *030/4373–9760. Metro: Eberswalder Strasse.*

Spatenstich. Rummage through the color-coordinated racks of fashion from the 1930s to the 1980s, which are heavy on knitted tank tops and bad-taste shirts. Play with the crocheted scarves, leather shorts, and great hats to find an undeniably original party outfit. ⊠ *Danzigerstr 10,* ☎ *030/6284–3009. Metro: Eberswalder Strasse.*

FOOD AND DRINK

Benjowski. Herr Benjowski has the largest selection of Chinese, Japanese, and Taiwanese teas in Berlin. He has a beautiful range of Asian teapots and bowls, some of which are antique, and stocks many herbal, fruit, and rare teas. Berlin Sawade pralines are also sold here, in boxes or by weight. ⊠ *Danzigerstr. 3,* ☎ *030/442–7939. Metro: Eberswalder Strasse.*

MUSIC

Da Capo. No one will rush you or stop you from smoking in this relaxingly retrospective store. Everything is secondhand, and the storekeeper insists on vinyl only, with a specialist range of '60s and '70s music to peruse at your leisure. Original Beatles 7-inch records cost around €7.50, and rarities are available at higher prices. Jazz, blues, and world music all have large sections, as do East German works, which are now collectors' and true enthusiasts' items. ⊠ *Kastanienallee 96,* ☎ *030/448–1771. Metro: Eberswalder Strasse.*

Franz und Josef Scheiben. This store is run by vinyl enthusiasts for like-minded customers, with an emphasis on jazz, soul, funk, and disco.

Stacks of 7-inch records and '70s progressive rock albums, an extensive range of German new wave (Neue Deutsche Welle), and that unforgettable national invention "Krautrock" make the store a true collector's find. ⊠ *Kastanienallee 48,* ☎ *030/4171–4682. Metro: Eberswalder Strasse.*

Vopo Records. This is just how a record store should be—staff and customers oozing enthusiasm; great posters, stickers, and T-shirts; gig info, and ticket sales. Rock and pop are the main thrusts, with special sections on heavy metal, German punk and hip-hop, and obsolete East German bands. The vinyls are appealingly cheap, and the staff is only too pleased to help you find what you are looking for. ⊠ *Danzigerstr. 31,* ☎ *030/4404–4925. Metro: Eberswalder Strasse.*

Kreuzberg

Kreuzberg was always an "alternative" district of West Berlin, with a large Turkish population and a fair share of artists, students, draft dodgers, and squatters. It has two main shopping drags. The area around Oranienstrasse has a bohemian and grungy feel. Surrounding Mehringdamm is slightly more upmarket Kreuzberg. Bergmannstrasse, which begins at Mehringdamm, abounds in specialty stores, and there are some great cafés in which to rest your feet.

Markets

Turkish Market. Every Tuesday and Friday you can find heaps of local color at Turkish stalls on the Maybachufer. Exotic fruits and vegetables; Turkish breads, sweets, delicatessen offerings, and *halal* meats; flowers, and fresh fish make grocery shopping an absolute delight. Local farmers from Brandenburg also come to sell their produce. The market is also a great spot to buy cheap clothing and fabrics. The stalls are open 11–6. ⊠ *Maybachufer. Metro: Schöleinstrasse.*

Specialty Stores

CDS AND RECORDS

Hard Wax. For those who are superserious about their wheels of steel, this dance music store has techno, drum 'n' bass, and down tempo all subdividing into worlds of their own. The format is mostly vinyl, which is filed according to label. DJs experiment with the tunes on the turntables while acting very cool indeed. ⊠ *Paul-Linke-Ufer 44A, (2nd yard, 3rd floor),* ☎ *030/6113–0111. Metro: Kottbusser Tor.*

Scratch Records. A large collection of jazz, blues, reggae, and dub vinyl awaits discovery in the backroom, and the main collection hones in on rock, pop, indie, and dance. There is a mixture of secondhand and new vinyl and CDs—the store buys as well as sells. The Zossenerstrasse location carries similar stock. Its sister store Soultrade across the street in Sanderstrasse specializes in soul, funk, and dance and is a favorite DJ haunt. ⊠ *Kottbusser Damm 15,* ☎ *030/691–3867, Metro: Schöleinstrasse;* ⊠ *Zossenerstr. 31,* ☎ *030/6981–7591. Metro: Gneisenaustrasse.*

CLOTHING AND ACCESSORIES

Bergmann. Mellow Bergmann does casual and club wear for men and women, with clean-cut, laid-back labels such as Diesel and Carhartt setting the tone. The Spanish label Custo and Miss Sixty create quirkier garb. ⊠ *Bergmannstr. 2,* ☎ *030/694–0390. Metro: Mehringdamm.*

Checkpoint. For alternative chic try Checkpoint, which sells mostly secondhand shoes and clothing. The racks hold cheap leather trousers, jackets, winter coats, army gear, tailored suits, and shirts from €3.5. New clothing includes chunky wool pants, fitted Swiss army coats, satin trousers, and T-shirts sporting unusual Berlin motifs. A bin holds

Lederhosen for kids or skinny women. ⊠ *Mehringdamm 57,* ☎ *030/ 694–4344. Metro: Mehringdamm.*

Luzifer. This collective of local fashion designers started selling tie-dye clothing for Berlin's alternative scene in 1972. Their style is still alternative, with an emphasis on unusual baggy pastoral and tailored military cuts in vibrant colors. Classic linen suits and woolen dresses also have their place, as do hooded waistcoats and dungarees. The designers insist on natural fibers, mostly wool, linen, and hemp. ⊠ *Oranienstr. 38,* ☎ *030/615–2239. Metro: Kottbusser Tor.*

FOOD AND DRINK

Enoteca Bacco. This store and wine bar carries a wonderful selection of organically grown wines. Reds are mostly from France, Spain, and Italy, and the German wines are mostly whites. Relax and order tapas while sampling specialty grappas, vintage spirits, and fruit liqueurs, or even cooking or salad oils, all of which can be bought by the liter from the attractive glass vats on the shelves. ⊠ *Marheineke Pl. 15,* ☎ *030/ 692–9813. Metro: Gneisenaustrasse.*

Kraut und Rüben. Health food such as whole-grain breads, organic fruit and vegetables, and free-range dairy and meat products are the specialty of this women's collective. They stock a good selection of vegetarian products, nuts, lentils, and other nutritious foodstuffs. ⊠ *Oranienstr. 15,* ☎ *030/614–1075. Metro: Kottbusser Tor.*

GIFTS AND GADGETS

Grüne Papeterie. Most stationery in this store is recycled and environmentally friendly. Nepalese gift-wrap, lovely cards and postcards, notepads and writing paper, pretty photo albums, and the usual range of office supplies make browsing and buying irresistible. ⊠ *Oranienstr. 196,* ☎ *030/618–5355. Metro: Kottbusser Tor.*

Hanf-Haus. Everything in the Hanf-Haus is made from the versatile hemp plant: tea, chocolate, hard-wearing clothes, and bags. Posters of marijuana leaves and the history of cannabis adorn the walls. There are soap and rope—but no dope—and all goods are THC-free, so you can enjoy fully legal herbal remedies. ⊠ *Oranienstr. 129,* ☎ *030/614– 8102. Metro: Kottbusser Tor.*

Hof-Atelier. Big bold hammocks and oriental lamps, Zen ornaments, Mexican sculptures, and jewelry featuring emeralds and moonstones are some typical artisan wares on offer here. The workshop on site makes leather bags with unusual shapes and mix-and-match trims. ⊠ *Bergmannstr. 105,* ☎ *030/6940–1396. Metro: Mehringdamm.*

HOUSEWARES

In Bestform. This is the place for matching glass sundae dishes, vases, and fruit bowls in bottle green, fuchsia, or violet. Other shelves are packed with fluffy daisy cushions, Keith Haring coffee cups, and bold gadgets. Pretty napkins round off the tableware collection. ⊠ *Bergmannstr. 8,* ☎ *030/694–0399. Metro: Mehringdamm.*

O-Ton. Handcrafted ceramics in subtle matte tones are made and sold on site. The tea cups, saucers, and pots have a slightly Asian influence, but they also have the practical German addition of a tea-light warmer to place underneath. The team members have been making their individual pottery for 10 years and are happy to produce to order. ⊠ *Oranienstr. 165A,* ☎ *030/615–3866. Metro: Kottbusser Tor.*

8   SIDE TRIPS

Enveloping Berlin is the dreamy green
countryside of Brandenburg. Sandy pine
barrens and forests of birch and linden trees
make up the tranquil landscape, inviting you
to slow down and match the pace of towns
where time seems to have stood still.

T HE ENERGETIC CORE OF BERLIN QUICKLY SUBSIDES into the quaint but poor and sparsely populated state of Brandenburg. The pristine countryside southeast of the metropolis is a pastoral retreat into the lush marshes and canals of the Spreewald (Spree Forest). Potsdam, the state capital southwest of Berlin, draws day-trippers to its magnificent palace grounds and baroque town setting. Historically, Berlin and Brandenburg have always belonged together as part of the state of Prussia, but World War II and the ensuing division of Germany and Berlin took their toll on the relations between town and country. Even more than a decade after reunification, many Berliners have still never explored their hinterland. A popular vote in both states to unite the two failed miserably, and right-wing attacks against immigrants in the small towns of Brandenburg further cultivates the dislike many Berliners feel toward their neighbors—a dislike that is often mutual. However, a growing number of Berliners have been moving to Brandenburg, and the state, which has been plagued by unemployment and an unsatisfactory infrastructure for quite some time, is attracting high-tech companies to cities like Frankfurt an der Oder and Potsdam.

By Jürgen Scheunemann

POTSDAM AND SANSSOUCI

Potsdam retains the imperial character lent it by its many years as a royal residence and garrison quarters. Founded around 993, the city has many fine and stately baroque buildings downtown, as well as inviting neighborhoods with cobblestone alleys from ages past—their survival is indeed a miracle as Potsdam was heavily damaged in 1945 and only slowly reconstructed. But even the war could not harm the splendor of Potsdam's world-famous landmark, the Prussian palace and gardens of Frederick the Great's Sanssouci. The city of 144,000 is becoming increasingly proud of its own heritage and hence more independent of "big brother" Berlin. The many show-business celebrities who choose Potsdam—especially the villas on the shore of the Heilige See—as their main residence gives Potsdam an additional boost of prestige.

Potsdam

20 km (12 mi) southwest of Berlin.

The Alter Markt (Old Market Square) is Potsdam's city center and a showcase of stately Prussian architecture. The old Rathaus (city hall), built in 1755, has an officious facade and a gilded figure of Atlas atop the tower. Wander around some of the streets of the square, particularly Wilhelm-Külz-Strasse, to admire the handsome restored burghers' houses. The domed **Nikolaikirche** (St. Nicolas Church) dates from 1830 and is one of the region's most beautiful churches. The square neoclassical structure with columns was designed by Karl Friedrich Schinkel. In front of it is the **Ägyptischer Obelisk** (Egyptian Obelisk), erected by Schloss Sanssouci architect von Knobelsdorff in 1753–55, which shows the portraits of famous Prussian architects. ⊠ *Am Alten Markt*, ☒ *Free.* ☉ *Mon. 2–5, Tues.–Sat. 10–5, Sun. 11:30–5.*

One of Germany's best film museums, the **Filmmuseum Potsdam** focuses on the development of the Babelsberg studios and film production in the GDR—mostly the early, famous DEFA works. These first movies revealed a more critical, and artistically more sophisticated attitude toward Germany's Nazi past than those produced in the West. Some of these early films from the late 1940s and early 1950s—when Communist censorship was not yet in place—count among the high points of German film culture. The museum lies within the Marstall

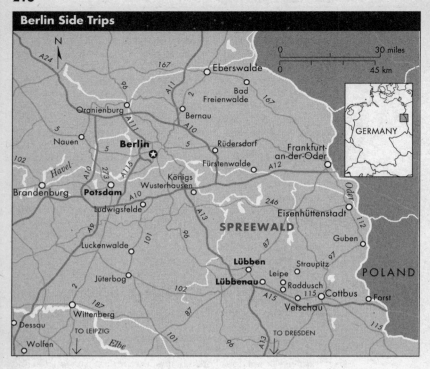

Berlin Side Trips

of Potsdam's old palace, the only part of the palace to survive World War II. Built in 1685 by Johann Arnold Nering, it once served as a winter garden for Mediterranean plants. Exhibits are not in English. ⊠ *Breite Str. and Schlossstr.,* ☎ *0331/271–810,* WEB *www.filmmuseum-potsdam.de.* ⊠ *€5.* ⊙ *Tues.–Sun. 10–6.*

The **Haus der Brandenburgisch-Preussischen Geschichte** (House of Brandenburg-Prussian History) hosts changing exhibits within the baroque royal carriage house, the restoration of which was completed in August 2001. ⊠ *Am Neuen Markt 9,* ☎ *0331/201–3944.* ⊠ *€3.* ⊙ *Daily 10–6.*

One of the extravagant-looking buildings in Potsdam serves a simple purpose—to pump up ground water for the fountains in Sanssouci. This **Dampfmaschinenhaus** (steam engine plant), or "Die Moschee" (the mosque) was built in an Arabian-Moorish style in 1842 with a striped facade, cupola, and minaretlike tower. Inside, you can still inspect the steam engine whose power once produced fresh water for Sanssouci. ⊠ *Breite Str.,* ☎ *0331/969–4248.* ⊠ *Free.* ⊙ *Mid-May–mid-Oct., weekends 10–5.*

The two-street **Holländisches Viertel** (Dutch Quarter) lies three blocks north of the Alter Markt. "Soldier king" Friedrich Wilhelm I built the settlement in 1732 to entice Dutch artisans to help build up the city, which shared a watery landscape with their homeland. Few Dutch came and only 20 families settled permanently in the gabled and mansard brick houses. Today cafés, pubs, and small shops are nestled in the little houses, and the area is Potsdam's most visited neighborhood. The **Jan-Bouman-Haus** dates to 1735 and allows a glimpse into everyday life in the Dutch colony at Potsdam. ⊠ *Mittelstr. 8,* ☎ *0331/280–3773.* ⊠ *€1.50.* ⊙ *Mon. and Fri. 1–6, weekends 12–7.*

At the north end of Potsdam, the log-cabin houses of the **Russische Kolonie Alexandrowka** (Russian Colony Alexandrowka; ✉ Puschkinallee) were built in 1826 for 12 Russian members of a choir, who had once fought side by side with Prussian troops against Napoléon. Prussian king Friedrich Wilhelm III had the homes outfitted completely, from tea cups to cows, and named the small enclave after his ally, Czar Alexander I. The buildings are still inhabited by descendants of the Russians (who were forced to marry and produce sons in order to keep the homes). Above the settlement is the small Russian Orthodox church **Alexander Newski** (✉ Kapellenberg), with impressive icons from Russia.

The **Belvedere auf dem Pfingstberg** is an over-the-top lookout point built by the "Romantic king" Friedrich Wilhelm IV in 1850. Above layers of archways and arcades, a long winding stairwell brings you to the roof, where points of interest in view are engraved on the railing. ✉ *Pfingstberg, off Puschkinallee.* 🎫 *Donation.*

Prewar Germany ranked among the world's best and biggest movie markets. That glorious past comes to life at **Filmpark Babelsberg.** The studios and stages in Potsdam-Babelsberg, once run by the firm UFA, were Europe's largest film production sites. It was here that milestones of film history, such as *Die Nibelungen, Metropolis,* and *The Blue Angel,* were produced. Directors Fritz Lang, Erich von Strohheim, and Josef von Sternberg, as well as actors Greta Garbo, Marlene Dietrich, and Peter Lorre began their careers here. The Nazis, however, transformed the studios into their main propaganda tool, producing mostly comedies and war movies of the worst kind. After the war East Germany's DEFA tried to revive the proud UFA tradition. Since the dissolution of DEFA in the 1990s, mostly television productions are filmed here, along with Hollywood movies like *Enemy at the Gates.* A tour of the 115-acre area includes trained animal shows, stuntman presentations, special effects exhibits—like the submarine from the set of *The Boat*—as well as a guided tour through the studios and a chance to see historic film costumes. ✉ *Grossbeerenstr., S-Bahn stop Babelsberg, then Bus 690 or 698,* ☎ *01805/ 345–672.* 🎫 *€15.* ☉ *Mid-Mar.–Nov., daily 10–6; Jul.–Aug., daily 10–8.*

Dining and Lodging

$ ✕ **Preussischer Hof.** For genuine Berlin and Brandenburg cooking, try this restaurant in the heart of Potsdam. Among the favorite dishes is *Gepökeltes Eisbein auf Weinsauerkraut mit Erbsenpüree und Salzkartoffeln* (pickled pork hocks on wine sauerkraut with mashed peas and boiled potatoes). Weekly specials add to the relatively small menu. ✉ *Charlottenstr. 11,* ☎ *0331/270–0762. No credit cards.*

$$–$$$ 🏨 **Hotel am Luisenplatz.** This intimate hotel hides a warm, upscale elegance and friendly, personal service behind a somber-looking facade.
★ The large rooms are decorated in typical Prussian colors—dark blue and yellow—and all have a bathtub. The biggest draw, however, is the hotel's location, offering a spectacular view of historic Luisenplatz and its restored Prussian city mansions. ✉ *Luisenpl. 5, D–14471,* ☎ *0331/ 971–900,* FAX *0331/971–9019,* WEB *www.hotel-luisenplatz.de. 22 rooms, 3 suites. In-room safes, minibars, dry cleaning, laundry service, meeting room, parking (fee). AE, DC, MC, V.*

$$ 🏨 **Das kleine Apartmenthotel.** Tucked away in a redbrick 18th-century house built in traditional Dutch style, this small and charming hotel offers apartments only. Surprisingly large, they are furnished in a modern, timeless style and equipped with a home office. The hotel is centrally located in downtown Potsdam. ✉ *Kurfürstenstr. 15, D–14467,* ☎ *0331/279–110,* FAX *0331/279–111,* WEB *www.hollaenderhaus.pots-*

dam.de. 22 rooms. Bar, minibars, sauna, dry cleaning, laundry service, business services, meeting rooms, parking (fee). AE, MC, V.

Sanssouci

2 km (1.25 mi) west of Potsdam.

★ Prussia's most famous king, Friedrich II—Frederick the Great—spent more time at his summer residence, **Sanssouci** in Potsdam, than in the capital Berlin. Its name means "without a care" in French, the language Frederick tried to cultivate in his own private circle and within the court. Some experts believe Frederick actually named the palace "Sans, Souci," which they translate as "with and without a care," a more apt name; its construction caused him much trouble and expense and sparked furious rows with his master builder, Georg Wenzeslaus von Knobelsdorff. His creation nevertheless became one of Germany's greatest tourist attractions. To reach the palace from downtown, you can walk westward down Gutenbergstrasse or Brandenburger Strasse. Executed according to Frederick's impeccable French-influenced taste, the palace, built between 1745 and 1747, is extravagantly rococo, with scarcely a patch of wall left unadorned. To the west of the palace are the **New Chambers** (☎ 0331/969–4206; 🎫 guided tour €2.50; ☉ Apr.–mid-May, weekends 10–5; mid-May–mid-Oct., Tues.–Sun. 10–5), which housed guests of the king's family; originally it functioned as a greenhouse, until it was remodeled in 1771–74.

Just east of Sanssouci is the **Bildergalerie** (Picture Gallery; ☎ 0331/969–4181; 🎫 €2; ☉ mid-May–mid-Oct., Tues.–Sun. 10–5), with expensive marble from Siena in the main cupola. The gallery displays Frederick's collection of 17th-century Italian and Dutch paintings, including works by Caravaggio, Rubens, and Van Dyck. ⊠ *Sanssouci Central Visitor Information, Besucherzentrum an der Historischen Mühle,* ☎ *0331/969–4200; 0331/969–4201; 0331/969–4202 for recorded information,* 🌐 *www.spsg.de.* 🎫 *€11 for 1-day pass valid for all bldgs. and museums in Sanssouci and Potsdam; guided tour €5.* ☉ *Apr.–Oct., daily 9–5; Nov.–Mar., Tues.–Sun. 9–4.*

★ The **Neues Palais** (New Palace), a much larger and grander palace than Sanssouci, stands at the end of the long, straight avenue that runs through Sanssouci Park. It was built after the Seven Years' War (1756–63), when Frederick loosened the purse strings while fighting against Austria, Russia, France, and Sweden. It's said he wanted to demonstrate that the state coffers hadn't been depleted too severely by the long conflict. The Neues Palais has much of interest, including an indoor grotto hall with walls and columns set with shells, coral, and other aquatic decor. The upper gallery contains paintings by 17th-century Italian masters and a bijou court theater in which drama and opera performances are still given. ⊠ *Strasse am Neuen Palais,* ☎ *0331/969–4255,* 🌐 *www.spsg.de.* 🎫 *€4, including guided tour.* ☉ *Apr.–Oct., daily 9–5; Nov.–Mar., weekends 9–4.*

Schloss Charlottenhof stands on its own grounds in the southern part of Sanssouci Park. After Frederick died in 1786, the ambitious Sanssouci building program ground to a halt, and the park fell into neglect. It was 50 years before another Prussian king, Frederick William IV, restored Sanssouci's glory. He engaged the great Berlin architect Karl Friedrich Schinkel to build this small palace for the crown prince. Schinkel gave it a classical, almost Roman appearance, and he let his imagination loose in the interior, too—decorating one of the rooms as a Roman tent, with its walls and ceiling draped in striped canvas. ☎ *0331/969–4228.* 🎫 *Tour €3.* ☉ *Mid-May–mid-Oct., Tues.–Sat. 10–5.*

Just north of Schloss Charlottenhof on the path back to Sanssouci are later additions to the park. In 1836 Friedrich Wilhelm IV built the **Römische Bäder** (Roman Baths; ☎ 0331/969–4224; 🖾 €1.50, additional charge for special exhibitions). The **Orangerie** (☎ 0331/969–4280; 🖾 guided tour €2.50) was completed in 1860; its two massive towers linked by a colonnade evoke an Italian Renaissance palace. Today it houses 47 copies of paintings by Raphael. The lovely **Chinesisches Teehaus** (Chinese Teahouse; ☎ 0331/969–4222; 🖾 €1) was erected in 1757 in the Chinese style, which was then the rage. The **Italianate Peace Church** (1845–48) houses a 12th-century Byzantine mosaic taken from an island near Venice.

NEED A BREAK? Halfway up the park's Drachenberg Hill, above the Orangerie, stands the curious **Drachenhaus** (Dragon House), modeled in 1770 after the Pagoda at London's Kew Gardens and named for the gargoyles ornamenting the roof corners. It now houses a popular café.

Resembling a rambling half-timber country manor house, **Schloss Cecilienhof** (Cecilienhof Palace), the final addition to Sanssouci Park, was built for Crown Prince Wilhelm in 1913 in a newly laid-out stretch of the park bordering the Heiliger See, called the New Garden, on the northeastern side of the city. It was here that Allied leaders Truman, Attlee, and Stalin hammered out the fate of postwar Germany at the 1945 Potsdam Conference. From Sanssouci you can reach the New Garden with any tram or bus going toward the Neuer Garten station. ☎ 0331/969–4244, 🕸 www.spsg.de. 🖾 €4, including guided tour. ⊗ Apr.–Oct., Tues.–Sun. 9–5; Nov.–Mar., Tues.–Sun. 9–4.

Atop the **Klausberg** in the park's western section is the palacelike **Belvedere**. Built in 1770–72 as an observation platform for the royals, the building was Frederick the Great's last project in Sanssouci before his death. You too can enjoy the spectacular view from the platform.

Potsdam and Sanssouci A to Z

To research prices, get advice from other travelers, and book travel arrangements, visit www.fodors.com.

Potsdam is virtually a suburb of Berlin, a half-hour trip by car, bus, or S-Bahn. Traffic is heavy, however, and traveling by S-Bahn is recommended. The most effortless way to visit Potsdam and its attractions is to book a tour.

BOAT TRAVEL

Boats leave the Wannsee S-Bahn station harbor for Potsdam four times a day, between April and September. A roundtrip ticket costs €8.50. ➤ CONTACT: **Stern- und Kreisschifffahrt** (✉ Puschkinallee 15, Berlin, ☎ 030/5363–600, 🕸 www.sternundkreis.de).

CAR TRAVEL

From central Berlin take Potsdamer Strasse south until it becomes Route 1 and then follow the signs to Potsdam. A faster way is taking the highway, the *Avus* (A–115) from Messedamm through Zehlendorf to Potsdam.

PUBLIC TRANSPORTATION

There is regular service from the bus station at the Funkturm on Messedamm 8 (U-Bahn 1 Kaiserdamm) to Potsdam. You can also take Bus 118 from the S-Bahn and railway station Wannsee to Jagdhausstrasse in Potsdam, and then continue with Bus 106 to Potsdam's Bassinplatz, Hauptbahnhof, and other stations. To tour Potsdam' historic district, leave the bus at Bassinplatz. An alternative is Bus 638, which departs from Spandau (take U-Bahn 7 to Rathaus Spandau) to Potsdam.

The S-Bahn 7 line to Potsdam is really the best way to go. Change at Potsdam for the short S-Bahn trip (RE line 1·) to the Potsdam-Charlottenhof (for Schloss Charlottenhof) and Wildpark (for Neues Palais) stations. Two regional trains, RE 1 and RE 3 also connect Berlin and Potsdam. From the Potsdam train station, take trams 90, 92, or 95 into the city.

TOURS

All major sightseeing companies based in Berlin have three- to four-hour tours of Potsdam and Sanssouci for about €25. The best guide, however, is the Potsdam tourist office, which runs two tours from April through October. Its three-hour tour, including Sanssouci, costs €20; the 1½-hour tour of the city alone is €14. Both tours are offered in English and German. The regular tours offered within the Sanssouci palace buildings are in German only.

➤ FEES AND SCHEDULES: **Berliner Bären Stadtrundfahrten** (BBS; ✉ Seeburgerstr. 19b, Berlin, ☎ 030/3519–5270, WEB www.sightseeing.de). **Berolina Berlin-Service** (✉ Kurfürstendamm 220, corner Meinekestr., Berlin, ☎ 030/8856–8030, WEB www.berolina-berlin.com). **Bus Verkehr Berlin** (BVB; ✉ Kurfürstendamm 225, Berlin, ☎ 030/885–9880, WEB www.bvb.net). **Severin & Kühn** (✉ Kurfürstendamm 216, Berlin, ☎ 030/880–4190, WEB www.severin-kuehn-berlin.de).

VISITOR INFORMATION

Postdam's tourist offices are open weekdays 10–6 and weekends 10–2.
➤ TOURIST INFORMATION: **Potsdam tourist office** (✉ Touristenzentrum am Alten Markt, Friedrich-Ebert-Str. 5, Postfach 601220, D–14467 Potsdam, ☎ 0331/275–580, FAX 0331/2755–899; ✉ Brandenburger Str. 18, ☎ 0331/275–5888, WEB www.potsdam.de).

SPREEWALD

The Spreewald is a unique natural conservation area southeast of Berlin. This almost pristine landscape of wetlands, dark forests, canals, and uncharted waterways, rivers, and lakes covers nearly 1,300 square km (500 square mi) and is one of the most popular getaways for Berliners. The Spreewald is also known for its people, a blend of Germans and the Slavic Sorben, and for specialties such as freshwater fish and *Spreewald-Gurken* (pickles), and for the many fairy tales that have come from this rugged and mysterious area.

From one of the region's major towns, Lübben, or Lübbenau, explore the narrow, shallow rivers by boarding one of the flat-bottom wooden boats called *Kähne*, which are punted along with long poles. Boats dock at restaurants on hidden forest islands.

Lübben

64 km (40 mi) southeast of Berlin via A–13 and north on B–87

Lübben, the region's old residence of the Saxon prince electors, sits on the banks of the Spree River. The peaceful little town of 15,000 was hit hard in World War II. Despite reconstruction, only a few historic buildings, such as parts of the city wall, the Ständehaus, and the Paul-Gerhardt-Kirche, have survived. The main tower of the castle **Schloss Lübben** is the only accessible historic building. ✉ *Ernst-von-Houwald-Damm.* ☾ *Tues.–Sun. 10–5.*

The small but fascinating **Spreewald-Museum** features a local art exhibit and many historic items of local craft work. ✉ *Torhaus, Am Topf-*

*markt 12, ☎ 03542/2472. ⌨ €1.50. ☉ Apr.–Oct., daily 10–6; Nov.–
Mar., by appointment only.*

Lübbenau

74 km (46 mi) southeast of Berlin via A–13 and north on B–115

The town of Lübbenau has the largest harbor in the Spreewald region,
and is proud to be its unofficial "capital." The Old City district is around
the **Marktplatz** and **Ehm-Welk-Strasse,** which are lined by simple mansions dating back to the early 19th century. On the market, near the
city church, you can see a *Postmeilensäule* (distance marker) dating
back to 1740 that serves as a reminder that Lübbenau was once was
part of Saxony. Northwest of the market is another square, the Topf-
markt, on which stands the peculiar **Torhaus** (gate house). Dating from
1784, it has a whale's cheekbones hanging in the gate. The bones were
the eccentric gift of a thankful merchant to the city council.

Follow the nature trail from the Lübbenau canal harbor to the **Frei-
landmuseum Lehde** (Lehde Open-Air Museum), which features three
old farmhouses typical of the Spreewald, historic handicrafts, traditional costumes, and one of the area's oldest barge-building shops. ⌨
*Lehde, An der Gliglitza, ☎ 03542/2472. ⌨ €3. ☉ Apr.–Oct., daily
10–6; Nov.–Mar., by appointment only.*

Dining and Lodging

$$–$$$ ✕🏨 **Romantikhotel zur Bleiche.** One of the largest and most beauti-
★ fully set hotels in the Spreewald region, the extensive Hotel zur Ble-
iche not only features open-air restaurants on the river banks but also
a wonderful wellness and swimming-pool area. Guest rooms have a
sophisticated country style and include all the amenities you would expect from a big-city, first-class resort. Room rates include breakfast and
a five-course gourmet meal. You can explore the river with the hotel's
paddle boats. ⌨ *Bleichestr. 16, Burg D–03096, Exit 3 (Vetschau) off
A–15, 2 km in direction Burg-Kolonie; ☎ 035603/620, ℻ 035603/
60292, 🌐 www.hotel-zur-bleiche.de. 83 rooms, 7 suites. 7 restaurants,
bar, in-room data ports, minibars, no-smoking floor, room service, indoor pool, barbershop, hot tub, massage, sauna, steam room, health
club, baby-sitting, dry cleaning, laundry service, concierge, business services, meeting rooms. No credit cards.*

$ ✕🏨 **Kolonieschänke.** Within a historic wooden-beam town mansion,
the small *Gaststätte*—named for the first Slavic Sorb colonists who arrived here some 250 years ago—is a quaint and romantic choice both
for dining and lodging. The restaurant ($) serves traditional Spreewald
fare, including freshly baked bread from an original Wendish oven. The
few guest rooms in the adjoining "Heuhotel" are simply but tastefully
furnished. A big plus is the hotel's private boat pier. Bikes and paddleboats are for rent. ⌨ *Ringchaussee 136, Burg D–03096, ☎ 035603/
6850, ℻ 035603/68544, 🌐 www.kolonieschaenke.de. 16 rooms.
Restaurant, minibars, bicycles. No credit cards.*

$ ✕🏨 **Hotel-Pension Dubkow-Mühle.** This family-owned pension in the
small village of Leipe, north of Raddusch, is one of the oldest pubs (established 1737) in the Spreewald. The building is an old mill in a lovely
garden surrounded by canals and wetlands. Guest rooms are quiet and
spacious; most come with a shower; only two have bathtubs. The
hotel's restaurant ($$$–$$$$) serves solid local fare. The hotel also of-
fers individual boat trips. Leipe can be reached via the B–320 north
(from exit 3 at Vetschau on A–15) to Burg; turn left in Burg onto the
country road that leads northwest to Leipe. ⌨ *Leipe/Spreewald D–
03226, ☎ 03542/2297, ℻ 03542/41722, 🌐 www.dubkow-muehle.de.
19 rooms. Restaurant, boating, bicycles. No credit cards.*

Spreewald A to Z

To research prices, get advice from other travelers, and book travel arrangements, visit www.fodors.com.

CAR TRAVEL

The Spreewald is 60 km (37 mi) southeast of Berlin and easily accessible with a 45-minute ride on the A–13 toward Cottbus. To reach Lübben, take the B–87 north (from Exit 8, Duben).

TOURS

Several boat tours depart from the Grosser Hafen in Lübbenau. Tours usually cost €2.50 for one hour and can last as long as eight hours. You can rent your own paddleboat at Bootsverleih Ingrid Hannemann or Bootsverleih Petrick, April–October, daily 8–7 for about €4.50 for one hour (or €16 for a whole day). In Lübben, several companies and ferrymen's associations operate from the harbor.

➤ FEES AND SCHEDULES: **Bootsverleih Ingrid Hannemann** (⊠ Am Wasser 1, Lübbenau, ☎ 03542/3647). **Bootsverleih Petrick** (⊠ Am Schlosspark, Lübbenau, ☎ 03542/3620). **Fährmannsverein Flottes Rudel** (⊠ Eisenbahnstr. 3, Lübben, ☎ 03546/2626). **Kahnabfahrtsstelle Am Holzgraben** (⊠ Dammstr. 72, Lübbenau, ☎ 03542/2221).

TRAIN TRAVEL

Trains to Lübbenau depart from Berlin's Alexanderplatz station and the Ostbahnhof (train Lines RB 41 and RE 2).

VISITOR INFORMATION

➤ TOURIST INFORMATION: **Fremdenverkehrsverein Lübben** (⊠ Ernst-von-Houwald-Damm 15, D–15907, ☎ 03546/3090, FAX 03546/2543, WEB www.luebben.com). **Fremdenverkehrsverein Lübbenau** (⊠ Ehm-Welk-Str. 15, D–03222 Lübbenau, ☎ 03542/3668, FAX 03542/46770, WEB www.spreewald-online.de). **Tourismusverband Spreewald e.V.** (⊠ Lindenstr. 1, D–03226 Raddusch, ☎ 035433/72299, FAX 035433/7228, WEB www.spreewald-tourist.de).

SACHSENHAUSEN MEMORIAL

The only Nazi concentration camp near the Third Reich capital of Berlin is today called the Sachsenhausen Gedenkstätte (Sachsenhausen Memorial). Established in 1936, it was the first concentration camp on German soil and was mainly used for political prisoners; three years before its official opening, it had already served as a hastily established makeshift camp, used for Berlin opponents of the Nazis. Most of its 200,000 inmates had to work in weapons production facilities in and around Berlin. Sachsenhausen also served as a training camp for SS officiers who would be sent to other camps throughout Europe. In 1961 the camp was made into a memorial to its victims. The area has a few preserved facilities and barracks, as well as a museum.

After World War II the Soviet Army made the camp *Speziallager Nr. 7* (special camp No. 7), where Germans were held as labor prisoners. In the past years, the memorial has been attacked several times by right-wing teenagers. To reach Sachsenhausen, take S-Bahn 1 from Friedrichstrasse to Oranienburg, the last stop. The ride will take 45–50 minutes. From the station it's a 25-minute walk, or you can take a taxi. Oranienburg is 35 km (22 mi) north of Berlin via A–111. ⊠ *Str. der Nationen 22, Oranienburg,* ☎ *03301/2000.* ◱ *Free.* ☉ *Apr.–Sept., daily 8:30–6; Oct.–Mar., daily 9–4:30 (last admission 30 mins before closing).*

9 PORTRAIT OF BERLIN

A Tale of Two Cities

A TALE OF TWO CITIES

EAVING THE NEWSPAPER OFFICES, I'm buttonholed by a stranger who shows me a photo. "Excuse me," he says, "Is this here?" I study a Polaroid, not all that old, showing a deserted street flanked by bomb sites and blocked off by a wall of concrete slabs topped by barbed wire. Not just a wall, then—THE WALL, once Berlin's claim to fame. And some distance behind it, the ugly silhouette of one of the assembly-line apartment blocks the Communists put up in the 1970s. We're standing in the center of Berlin on a street lined with spanking new postmodernist office buildings in garish colors. Next to us, a cement mixer is churning out material for more. Young businesspeople are swarming purposefully in all directions or having a quick coffee and sandwich at one of the sidewalk cafés. In the distance, past the newly renovated apartment blocks on Leipziger Strasse, the graceful form of the Schauspielhaus on Gendarmenmarkt is just visible. It's somewhere else, a totally different world. "Yes," I tell the stranger, "This was here."

The amazing thing about the Wall is how completely it's disappeared. When Axel Springer, West Germany's most powerful newspaper publisher and an ardent anti-Communist, set up his headquarters here, in a dust-blown wasteland directly bordering on East Berlin, it was a political demonstration of defiance. John F. Kennedy visited the offices and looked down on the Wall he had been unable to prevent, while just two blocks down the street, at Checkpoint Charlie, American and Russian tanks faced off at one of the flash points of the cold war. Now, on the bustling corner of Friedrichstrasse and Kochstrasse, Gypsies from Romania sell Red Army memorabilia—fur hats, binoculars, assorted medals—to Japanese tourists who forlornly wander, map in hand, along streets that must remind them of Tokyo and ask passersby: "Where is the Wall?"

It went up overnight, on August 13, 1961. After the regime that had built it collapsed, there was a short, strange interlude when it became a quarry for souvenir hunters chipping away with hammer and chisel. You can still buy flakes of the Wall, cellophane-wrapped and certified as original by make-believe ministries, but the unedifying edifice has dissolved, it seems, into thin air.

For most Berliners, however, there remains "the Wall in the mind." Anyone who grew up in the long shadow the Wall cast is still an "Ossi" or a "Wessi" at heart: an "Eastie" or a "Westie." On the surface, it's hard to tell the difference: Ossies often sport jeans, once a status article, whereas, so as not to be mistaken for Ossies, most Wessies prefer other types of casual clothing. Ossies tend to talk with a broader Berlin accent, an asset in a society that idealized the proletariat, whereas Wessies have done their best to drop what was viewed as a vulgar jargon, a liability in a society that dearly wanted to be refined and cosmopolitan. Despite their denim and accents, Ossies are still more formal. Ten years after the Wall came down, the members of the East German blues band I sat in with still shook hands all around every time we met to rehearse. Among West German bluesmen, shaking hands would have been considered terribly petit bourgeois. But these are just the surface manifestations of a divide that goes deeper than that. Going to and from work, the movies, the doctor, Berliners crisscross a city that has grown together so fast the joints are no longer visible. But East and West Berlin are still two distinct cities of the mind.

The history books tell us the West won the cold war. In Berlin the outcome is more complicated. The grim postwar look of East Berlin has disappeared—no doubt about that. The automobiles and buildings and stores have changed almost beyond recognition. But for East Berliners their city remains what it was: the capital. West Berlin, on the other hand, though superficially intact, has all but vanished from the face of the earth.

West Berlin was a capitalist island in the Communist sea. And like a kind of political Galapagos, West Berlin developed its own specific ecology. In the first decades of the cold war, West Berliners adopted an outpost mentality. They were defending the bastion of the Free World against the Red Menace. Berlin was an open wound, a constant reminder that the "German question" was still unresolved: that the German people were still denied the unity and self-determination promised them by the victors of World War II. Holding out was West Berlin's mission, and there was little time and less inclination to reflect on the Nazi past, the burden of shame and guilt for the destruction of European Jewry that was planned here, even for sorrow over the loss of the Jewish element that had made Berlin the most vibrant city of prewar Europe. Hadn't Kennedy said that all free men were proud to say, "Ich bin ein Berliner"?

THE WALL CHANGED EVERYTHING, though it took West Berliners some time to realize it. The United States and West Germany still pumped money into the "Showcase of Capitalism" but it was little more than that—a shop-window prop. Financial power resided in Frankfurt, political clout in Bonn, the media in Munich, trade in Hamburg, industry on the Ruhr. Meanwhile, the malcontents and outcasts of West Germany's economic miracle found themselves washed up as castaways on the sands of West Berlin: students fleeing the draft; intellectuals, poets, and artists lured by the surreal situation of the city between two worlds, cheap rents in apartments whose previous tenants had gone where the money was, and the prospects of a job in the overblown academic and cultural sector financed by a never-ending stream of subsidies from the West. From 1968, when the student revolt exploded here, West Berlin's "scene" was the self-conscious avant-garde of intellectual Germany. Any new fashion or fad, from anarchist communes to Zen Buddhism, was proclaimed here first—only to be abandoned the moment "West Germany," as the uncool rest of the republic was derisively called, adopted it.

The real symbol of West Berlin was neither the Kurfürstendamm, the upmarket shopping boulevard (now fighting a losing battle against fast-food joints and factory outlets), nor the temples of high culture ranged around the Kulturforum (now dwarfed by the neighboring entertainment palaces of Potsdamer Platz); neither the ruined Kaiser-Wilhelm Gedächt-

niskirche, a stark reminder of the ravages of war among the carefree shoppers and skateboarders on Breitscheidplatz, nor the Hansa Viertel near Zoo station, constructed as a vision of the city of the future (today a monument to yesterday's architectural blunders)—no, it was the Wall itself. It shielded the island biotope from the winds of change raging in the rest of the world. When the Wall fell, West Berlin was blown away.

East Berlin is a different case. For one thing, the Soviet sector comprised the old political, administrative, and cultural heart of the city around the Royal Palace. And then the Communist state made East Berlin its capital, pouring resources and manpower into this Showcase of Socialism much as the United States and West Germany funneled money into West Berlin. The competition between the two halves of the city took on absurd dimensions: East Berlin had a university, West Berlin had to have two; West Berlin had an opera house, East Berlin had to have two; West Berlin had a zoo, East Berlin had to have one as well. Now the city has three opera houses, three universities, and two zoos, none of which it can afford (not to mention a plethora of libraries, art galleries, museums, institutes, and diverse administrative buildings).

Within East Germany, East Berliners were the envied denizens of a city that was unequivocally the center of political and economic power and of cultural and intellectual life. Indeed, since many of them were employed by the myriad institutions serving the state, from the Stasi headquarters on Normannenstrasse to Bertolt Brecht's Berliner Ensemble theater near Friedrichstrasse, they are to this day prone to lament the passing of socialism. While new government and office buildings are being built, decrepit apartment blocks and rundown inner-city neighborhoods are renovated, and modern shopping malls and multiplex movie houses cater to the new consumerism, East Berliners nevertheless regularly cast their vote for the PDS, the revamped successor to the defunct Communist Party. Even the artists and literati who used to meet surreptitiously in private apartments or churches in Prenzlauer Berg to listen to illicit recordings of singer-songwriter Wolf Biermann, or to exchange manifestos denouncing Stalinist repression, seem to regret the demise of their enemy. Who to protest against now? How to define their dignity in a society that sees them not as dangerous enemies of the state but as quaint relics of a bygone era?

Two monuments to that Socialist era dominate the geographical center of Berlin. One is the soaring TV tower on Alexanderplatz, visible from the farthest corners of the city. Designed as a symbol of Communism's heaven-storming belief in human progress emancipated from the constraints of religious superstition, the silver globe at its top reflects the sun—much to the consternation of the constructors—in the form of a giant golden cross. A five-minute walk from the base of the tower leads you to Schlossplatz, once the site of the Royal Palace: residence of the Hohenzollerns, kings of Prussia and—from 1871 till 1918—emperors of Germany.

Damaged but not destroyed in World War II, the palace, an architectural treasure famous throughout Europe, was blown up by the Communists as a symbolic renunciation of German feudalism, militarism, and imperialism. Before dynamiting the building, however, they carefully removed the main portal stone by stone—and reassembled it some 50 yards to the south, where it adorns the facade of the exquisitely banal box that housed East Germany's supreme organ of government, the Staatsrat. This was done because Karl Liebknecht—cofounder of the Communist Party with Rosa Luxemburg—had proclaimed the short-lived Soviet Republic of Germany from that very portal in 1918. On the site of the palace, the new masters erected a tribune from which they could review the many parades held in their honor. Later, Erich Honecker built the Palace of the Republic here, a steel, glass, and marble monstrosity nicknamed "Ballast of the Republic," housing the "People's Chamber," which rubber-stamped Communist edicts. In a fine touch of historic irony, it was here that the first and last freely elected parliament of East Germany voted to dissolve the state and opt for reunification in 1990. Shortly afterward, the Palace of the Republic was found to be full of poisonous asbestos and closed to the public.

As of this writing, Berlin is discussing the future of this historically saturated ground. Situated at the end of Unter den Linden, in the very heart of the city's cultural center, flanked by the neobaroque bulk of the Berliner Dom and by the wonders of Museum Island, it is arguably the most architecturally challenging and rewarding site in the world today. Should the old Royal Palace be reconstructed to complement the Prussian cityscape that Berliners are rediscovering as their heritage? Should the Palace of the Republic be restored, a monument to the second German dictatorship and to the peaceful revolution that did away with it? Or should something completely new be erected here, to embody the aspirations of the new Germany? Berliners love this kind of debate—it fits their self-image as citizens of an ongoing work in progress rather than a finished entity. The argument has been going on since reunification, and given the sorry state of the city's finances, it will probably continue for some time. But sometime around 2010 I'm pretty sure some stranger is going to corner me on bustling, beautiful Schlossplatz, pull out a crumpled Polaroid showing today's derelict wasteland and ask in disbelief: "Tell me, is this here?"

— Alan Posener

INDEX

Icons and Symbols

★   Our special recommen-
    dations
✕   Restaurant
🏠   Lodging establishment
✕🏠 Lodging establishment
    whose restaurant war-
    rants a special trip
😊   Good for kids (rubber
    duck)
☞   Sends you to another
    section of the guide for
    more information
✉   Address
☎   Telephone number
🕐   Opening and closing
    times
💳   Admission prices

Numbers in white and black
circles ③ ❸ that appear on
the maps, in the margins, and
within the tours correspond
to one another.